My God and Me

Listening, Learning and Growing on My Journey

An Autobiographical Devotional

LaShawnda Jones

Jazzy Media LLC
New York, New York
August 2009

Other books by LaShawnda Jones

Poetry
Clichés: A Life in Verse
(Jazzy Media LLC)

Contributor
Go, Tell Michelle: African American Women Write to the New First Lady
(Excelsior Editions)

Compiled and Edited by
Barbara A. Seals Nevergold and Peggy Brooks-Bertram

Available at:
www.mygodandme.info
www.amazon.com
www.bn.com

Please note: Names in this book have been changed to protect the privacy of people I have interacted with over the years. Unless otherwise cited and noted, all events are written from my perspective and understanding. This book is only meant to be an accounting of the life experiences that have impacted and matured me spiritually.

God bless you, LaShawnda

My God and Me: Listening, Learning and Growing on My Journey. Copyright ©2009, 2010 by LaShawnda Jones. All rights reserved. Jazzy Media LLC Printed In the United States of America. No part of this book may be used or reproduced in any manner whatsoever without written permission except in the case of brief quotations embodied in critical articles and reviews. For more information, please visit www.mygodandme.info or write to lashawnda.jones@mygodandme.info.

Unless otherwise indicated, all *Old Testament* and *New Testament* scripture quotations are taken from the New King James version on www.Bible.com, © 1995 Bible.com Ministries, Dewey, Arizona.

All word definitions are taken from www.Dictionary.com*Unabridged (v 1.1)*, Based on the Random House Unabridged Dictionary, © Random House, Inc. 2006.

Category: Mind, Body, Spirit – Inspiration & Personal Growth

Second edition. ISBN: 978-0-9776179-7-5

Dedication

My God and Me is dedicated to three of my dearly departed...

Terry Ann Stuart
(née Jones)
1960-1996
Mother

Nicolette Stuart
1982-1983
Baby Sister

Antoine Jones
1976-2007
Younger Brother

I trust my mother, sister and brother are resting in the love and comfort of God's embrace. Their time with me was brief, but I remember them always. We know neither the day nor the time we will be called home. Use your time and your life wisely in the service of your God and His people.

...and to my beloved who still breathes but is not living

Kim Jones
Younger Sister

*God is with you, as are my prayers.
I believe it, therefore through my faith, I know you are covered by my love.
1 Peter 4:8*

Contents

A Blessing for My Daughters — 9
Preface: Life West of the Grand Canyon — 11
Introduction — 13

Episodes of Clarity

Life Cycle — 17
30 Random Things About Me — 18
No More Complaints — 19
Better Than You Should Be — 21
Who Am I in Christ? — 26
Practicing What I Preach — 28
Self-Image is Everything — 32
Reflections on Weight Conversations — 36
Smoke and Mirrors: The Confusion of Fantasy — 40
Chunky Dunkin' — 43
Out of the Mouths of Babes: My Body, Your Image — 45
This is Why I'm Hot — 48
Speak Power and Prosperity Into Your Life — 50
They Say I'm Lucky... — 53
Forged in Adversity — 58
Every Day is a Big Deal — 59
Next of Kin — 62
One Second — 64
Who U Wit? — 65
Some Things About Funerals — 68
Best Things in Life — 72
Can I Love You? — 73

Family and Friend Relationships

- Words, Part One — 77
- Defining Family and Friend — 78
- Covenant of Friendship — 80
- Levels of Teaching — 84
- God of Good and Evil — 87
- Emotional Side Effects of Friendship — 90
- Importance of Words — 95
- Hindsight: Seeing Friends as Something Else — 97
- And Me? — 100
- Don't Grow Weary of Doing Good — 102
- Things Women Do and Say — 104
- Dichotomy of Jemini — 108
- Healing Graces — 113
- Eulogizing Antoine — 115

Cultivating My Spirit

- Journal: Friday, January 13, 2006 — 119
- Priscilla on the 5 — 121
- Speak Your Feelings — 123
- A Road I Must Travel Alone — 125
- 8 Wrong Places to Find Yourself — 129
- Growing Through Vulnerability — 130
- Speaking Rock — 133
- Becoming Whole and Holy — 134
- Rebounding — 136
- Big Girl, Little Closet — 138
- How Are You Living? — 142
- Boss Lady: A Brief Illusion of the Triumph of Evil — 145
- Pop Culture Messiah — 148
- Take Me — 151

Practicing Patience Through Dating

- Build it...   155
- Reconciling My Sexiness with My Celibacy   156
- Ladies, You're the Prize!   161
- Men   163
- Set Apart   164
- Dating Anxiety   169
- Good Touch, Bad Touch   173
- And it Don't Stop!   175
- Sugar Daddy M.O.   179
- Technology Upgrade, Personal Downgrade   183
- Call Me Naïve...   185
- I Never Asked You Out...   188
- REVELATIONS   189

Preparation for the Marriage Relationship

- If I were the Author of my life   195
- 25 Things to Think Twice About Before You Marry   197
- Foolish of Me   203
- Life Isn't Fair, Dream Anyway   206
- Fascinating Womanhood: What does he see in her?   209
- So, what are you really saying?   210
- Prepare for Marriage?   211
- Seeking Satisfaction   216
- Man Friend Lessons   217
- Preparing for Marriage: Learning from Bad Examples   224
- Scandalous   231
- Marriage: Work It!   237
- Tell Me You Love Me   240
- #1 Predictor of Divorce   242
- You're Being Prepared Anyway, Why Not Focus?   245
- Girl v. Woman   248
- girl vs. WOMAN   249

☯ where r u?   254
Imagining Life   255
☯ Gratitude   259
Family Man   260
☯ Galaxy Quest   263
A Happy Marriage is No Accident   264
Beautifully Imperfect   267
Our Nakedness   269
☯ Lover & Lovee   273

 Appendix

Things I Don't Like About Myself   277
Things I Absolutely Love About Myself   278
If I Could Kiss It....   279
Evaluating My Life Balance   280
Self-Image Survey   281
How Much Do You Know About Marriage?   283
Building A Firm Foundation   285
Family Mission Statement   287

📖 Scripture Index   289
📖 Resource List   293

☯ = Poem

A Blessing for My Daughters

Young daughter, as you grow into an inquisitive little girl, a precocious teen and a delightful young woman you may have moments of self-doubt. We all do. But, never forget, life is a never ending journey that began in love. Keep that knowledge – build on it, grow from it, use it to gather strength as you mature on your walk.

Days may come when you question your purpose. Know that your purpose is for greatness and you were born with everything you need to fulfill it. Every step of your journey is preparation for everything to come. You'll climb mountains and tumble into valleys; you'll rest in fragrant pastures and be refreshed with cleansing waters. You may feel like you're completely alone, but your Big Brother is walking with you. You may feel as if there's no reason for all the walking and falling, or the long rests and waits, but your Father has a plan. You'll rejoice with laughter and rant in tears. Give equal thanks for your troubles and your blessings, for even your pain will benefit you.

Don't be fooled when you view others from the distance of your height or depth or through the lens of your grief and solitude. Their route may look smooth and uneventful. You may be tempted to pray for their ease, swiftness and surefootedness. Don't. Pray instead for wisdom, guidance, and strength or other characteristics of Grace that will help you through your whole journey, not just a portion of it. Pray that the obstacles you encounter, the enemies you face and the many disappointments that weigh you down become opportunities to fellowship deeper with God. Stay focused, remain faithful, keep moving and your life will be a blessing to others.

Preface
Life West of the Grand Canyon

Arizona is beautiful, breathtaking, majestic, and serene. My family moved there from the Midwest when I was ten years old. For three years, I literally lived in a valley and didn't mind. In every direction there was an endless mountain range. I wasn't intimidated by mountains then. Mountains were surreal from a distance and a simple extension of the earth up close. Indeed, traversing mountains was no different than walking on level ground – the earth was beneath me and the sky was above.

During my time in Arizona, I lived as a child of the dessert – running across plateaus and dancing in monsoons. Resting during siesta and glorying in sunsets. I lived in a great land that spoke God's name with every breeze and each ray of dawning and setting light. I was one with the land but felt as if I was missing the most wondrous experience – the Grand Canyon.

The summer I turned fourteen I was sent to Milwaukee, Wisconsin to babysit for an aunt. I didn't think it would be a permanent arrangement. At the time I wasn't too concerned that I hadn't yet journeyed to the Grand Canyon to see it with my own eyes. I knew I would return to my beloved desert. However, it was seven years before I set foot in Arizona again. I stayed for several months but left yet again without seeing that portion of God's great work.

Three years later a friend and I decided to take a road trip across the southwest. We flew into Las Vegas, meandered into Arizona and coasted to California. The only thing I insisted on was spending time at the Grand Canyon. We drove many endless hours through hot dry desert just so I could finally lay my eyes on one of God's amazing carvings and sculptures. When we finally got to the Grand Canyon, my joy turned to slight disgruntlement. We were west of the West Rim, outside the western wall of the canyon. Meaning, we couldn't see into the canyon at all! My view was blocked by a rock wall towering into the sky. It was an amazing area with beautiful scenery, but it was not what I was looking for.

That's the story of my life. From that day on, I claimed my first book about my life would be titled *Life West of the Grand Canyon*. This title represented how wrong my life was to me. How I always get so close to my goals, yet somehow fall short of actually achieving them. Fortunately, through the years, I've learned God has always given me exactly what I've needed, when I've needed it. He has always been present and actively orchestrating my exposure and lessons. So, upon reflection, *My God and Me* became a more fitting title to illustrate how the life experiences I had perceived as errors have actually been the right lessons for me to grow on.

During my last visit to the Arizona desert, nearly nine years after I had reached the western wall of the West Rim, I finally got to look down into the canyon from various vantage points. It was breathtaking. Awe-inspiring. I was giddy and speechless. It was on this trip, over twenty-two years after I had first stepped foot in Arizona, that I looked up and saw a heart-shaped cloud moving over a mountain. My God always speaks amazingly awesome words of love to me. I placed my hand over my heart and replied, "I love you back!"

Introduction

Do you know the day and time you first believed? Perhaps you know people who claim they've been walking with Christ for eight years, nine months and ten days or some detailed variation? I am not one of those people. I cannot pinpoint the moment I first believed. Nor do I recall a time of non-belief. However, most of my life, I resisted practicing my beliefs. I resisted obeying God. I resisted His call. Though I have always felt God's presence in my life, I used to hope He would let me roam wild and carefree before taming me with His Word. I never quite got wild, nor was I ever free of cares, but I did get a lot of bumps on my head and many bruises to my ego. All have been lessons to grow on.

Prior to my move to New York City in the fall of 2005, God was someone I had great ideals about but not someone I knew personally. I had heard of His wonderful works and had actually experienced His works in my own life, but I didn't think He was really paying attention to me. There were so many other people for Him to be concerned with. During those years, God was like a wardrobe accessory I put on most days then promptly forgot I was wearing.

The Book of Ecclesiastes tells us repeatedly there is nothing new under the sun. As I have studied the Bible, grown more confident in God's Word and more knowledgeable of his methods, I've come to see that even the way He deals with His people today is similar to the model of Biblical relationships we have been given. I've been able to identify parallels between my life and Biblical stories. The parallel that most influences *My God and Me* is God's instruction to Abram to leave his country and his kindred. Abram did as instructed and had terrible difficulties from the outset. However, those difficulties did not deter him in his faith or his belief that God would do as He said He would do.

 Meditation Verse: Genesis 12:1-3

Now the LORD had said to Abram: "Get out of your country, from your family and from your father's house, to a land that I will show you. I will make you a great nation; I will bless you and make your name great; and you shall be a blessing. I will bless those who bless you, and I will curse him who curses you; and in you, all the families of the earth shall be blessed."

I believe I have been called away from my family and the community of my youth in order for God to better prepare me for His work. I have gone through many difficulties that have strengthened my faith and deepened my fellowship with my God. I know I will have many more tests and trials before my journey is complete, but I am so much better prepared now than I was a few years ago.

I used to tell people I grew up in the church; I knew about God and Jesus. My declaration has changed. Now, I know God, Jesus and the Holy Spirit! I live in them as they live in me. Awesome! What wondrous power the Trinity gives me from day to day! Yes, I am in love; a deep, abiding love that has nothing to do with this world. I am awed and humbled by the way my God takes care of me, I am amazed by the examples my Savior provided me and I am continually enlightened by the awareness and revelations the Holy Spirit allows me. I desire nothing more than to be obedient to the instructions God speaks to me. I sincerely seek to be in His presence and to please Him. I didn't experience any of this until my isolation triggered my personal evolution. Or rather, my isolation allowed me time and space to focus on my evolution, as well as my relationship with God.

This collection of previously posted blogs is a record of the transformation my spirituality and life focus have undergone over the last four years. In the beginning, I railed against being set apart from everyone and everything familiar to me; I didn't like being by myself. However, I am grateful for the process He put me through, for I have learned to depend on and commune with my Father God. The time I've spent talking to Him exclusively has taught me to hear Him better. Even as I weaned myself off the false dependency of family and friends, I had to also wean myself off of my "self" dependency. I learned quickly that nothing outside the will of God is going to take place in my life. He is my protector, guide and provider. When I began to recognize, accept and trust His care and provisions, I was able to let go of my issues bit by bit and rely more and more on Him.

When I began blogging, my only intent was to entertain and promote. However, as I have reread and edited this collection, I am truly humbled by the message God is giving you through me. I am blessed by the amount of cleansing and lifting He has done within me. This book is a synopsis of my life. Some stories may seem very un-Christian – in fact maybe the whole collection will cause you to question my "Christianity." That's fine – I'm not concerned with being judged by anyone. This is a record of my honest thoughts, opinions and experiences at the time I chronicled them. I don't want anyone to think for a moment that aspiring to a Christ-like character and existence is easy or without lapses and outward desires. Some words are mine, but most, I believe, are simply delivered through me. I pray you find some words within these pages to help you and contribute to your continued growth.

May God continue to bless and keep you.

LaShawnda

Episodes of Clarity

Life Cycle

Out of the night of winter
Into the light of spring
Blossoming with so much greater
Life in summer
Even autumn offers hope
Cycling, cycling
Growing, growing
Through it all
Becoming

30 Random Things About Me

1. I am happiest when I have people around to love and give to
2. I expect that my life partner will be claiming me any day now
3. I don't like walking into a dark, empty apartment at the end of the day
4. I have a deep distaste for being taken advantage of and taken for granted
5. I was never as "man crazy" as I acted at times
6. New York City is exhausting me
7. I self-published two books of poetry and still don't consider myself a poet
8. Losing my mother devastated me; losing my brother numbed me; my sister keeps me in limbo
9. I feel as if I have a well of love just bubbling over to give to someone or everyone, and no one is interested in receiving it
10. I've grown from every situation in my life
11. I used to resent my problems – now I actively look for the lessons in them
12. I don't like traveling alone, but prefer it to unpleasant company
13. I've visited 46 states and performed in most of them as a model
14. I can't abide liars
15. Honesty is the best policy with me
16. I love music
17. I have tried to take my heart back from some people, but they wouldn't let go
18. I am spiritual, not religious
19. I'm suspicious of "hard and fast" rules and people who don't think for themselves
20. I've only recently realized most people don't know what or who Love is
21. My favorite gift from my mother was a dictionary; my favorite gift from a friend was a study Bible
22. *The Color Purple* is my favorite movie; "Celie" feels like my other name
23. I value loyalty above most things
24. Forgiveness is a process you can't do on someone else's terms
25. As much as technology keeps us in touch, it keeps us disconnected
26. Out of many millions of profiles, eHarmony has never found one match for me
27. I hate dating, love children and haven't figured out how to get one without going through the other
28. I'm not a networker, I'm a relationship builder
29. I believe God has always held me in the palm of His hand
30. I feel blessed no matter my sorrows

No More Complaints

Life has a way of winding its own path. Before accepting this truth, I stayed *in the process* of planning great things. Whenever my life veered away from my plans I believed myself in crisis, shut down and went into self-evaluation mode.

Drastic changes began to reshape my life in 2004. The first of two life-altering situations was the decision to start a publishing business, Jazzy Media. The second was my decision to move to New York City from Milwaukee, Wisconsin in 2005. My employment situation was not ideal at the beginning of 2004 and by mid-year it worsened to unemployment. For months, I waited for inspiration for the next big thing. *New York City* lit up in my mind and energized me. My only source of income at the time was unemployment insurance. I had no savings and no wealthy relatives. My accessibility to cash, or lack thereof, was not a determining factor, nor a detriment to the developments taking place in my life.

Numerous people have since asked me how I was able to do these two things over the span of two years, during which I was unemployed for eighteen months. How were my actions and expenditures possible with such limited income? The only answer I could give was, "It's all by the grace of God." I then offered an offhand shrug to further illustrate how little control I had over the outcome of anything my hands touched. There was no need to examine my situation any deeper. No need to attempt to explain such favor in any other terms. I knew I was being guided, protected and provided for. Yet even with that knowledge, I found cause for complaint. Even while benefiting from my God's wonderful benevolence, I chose to be dissatisfied with my lot. The road ahead of me was unfamiliar, and I was made to travel without companions. That was not what I wanted. Not what I asked for. Certainly, my difficulties were not part of my plans.

For a few years surrounding my move to New York City, I focused primarily on my difficulties. Those years were debilitating to my spirit and my hope. Focusing on the negative crippled me. When I came out of that depressed state I endeavored to go a year without complaining – at least not to other people. My goal was to keep any whining between me and my God.

Even during that time, when I wasn't feeling great about my life, people shouted my blessings to me. They replied to each of my complaints with a positive they saw exhibited in my life. After a while they simply asked, "What the heck are you complaining for?" I had to sit back and ask myself the same question.

That is why God has given us relationships. We are able to interact with many different people who reflect aspects of ourselves back to us. From this process, we can view our lives from different perspectives.

My friends make me look very good when they itemize the good things manifested in my life. It's intrinsically human to look at others and see things you wish you had. No matter how we attempt to satisfy ourselves, there will always be a desire for a little more of something else. Even as I sit and gush over my friends and their children, they're trying to pry juicy single life tidbits from me. It's amazing how the grass always appears greener in your neighbor's garden – the flowers more lush and vibrant. A year after my cross-country move, I stopped complaining about my dry patches. Instead, I began turning dirt and planted more seed for the positive things I want to bear fruit from. This is an unending process. Continuously, I churn, feed and water my trouble spots until they are as vibrant and lush as the rest of my garden.

Consider this: *My God and Me: Listening, Learning and Growing on My Journey* is a selection of the best flowers from my garden. I have pruned them and set them in a beautiful vase to share their beauty and fragrance with you. They beautify our space as we sit down to talk. It's storming outside but you are relaxed in the comfort of my home as we recline in overstuffed chairs before a roaring fire. Between us are a tea service and the vase of flowers – long-living, death resistant, Word – reinforced flowers. Each bloom represents a well-learned lesson or a lesson in progress. It is my hope you are able to take from my bouquet and plant buds of value into your life.

Meus ortus est vestri ortus.

Meditation Verse: 1 Corinthians 10:1-13

Moreover, brethren, I do not want you to be unaware that all our fathers were under the cloud, all passed through the sea, all were baptized into Moses in the cloud and in the sea, all ate the same spiritual food, and all drank the same spiritual drink. For they drank of that spiritual Rock that followed them, and that Rock was Christ. But with most of them God was not well pleased, for *their bodies* were scattered in the wilderness.

Now these things became our examples, to the intent that we should not lust after evil things as they also lusted. And do not become idolaters as *were* some of them. As it is written, *"The people sat down to eat and drink, and rose up to play."* Nor let us commit sexual immorality, as some of them did, and in one day twenty-three thousand fell; nor let us tempt Christ, as some of them also tempted, and were destroyed by serpents; nor complain, as some of them also complained, and were destroyed by the destroyer. Now all these things happened to them as examples, and they were written for our admonition, upon whom the ends of the ages have come.

Therefore let him who thinks he stands take heed lest he fall. No temptation has overtaken you except such as is common to man; but God *is* faithful, who will not allow you to be tempted beyond what you are able, but with the temptation will also make the way of escape, that you may be able to bear *it*.

Better Than You Should Be

Be better than people think you should be.

Some people feel cursed when family and friends have high expectations. Others are depressed when they can't seem to achieve their own expectations. I don't suffer from either case. I suffer from friends and family who think I am doing better than I should be.

The most shocking words my dad, Peewee, ever spoke to me were words of criticism about my non-ghetto personality. I was born in Gary, Indiana and lived there until age five. He and mother were both raised there and didn't leave until their early twenties. Since then, I have lived on my share of south sides, projects and dilapidated housing. I've also known my share of drug dealers and code words to travel safely through a neighborhood.

I never had a true father/daughter relationship with Peewee. Even when he was in the home, up until around my twelfth summer, he was not a fatherly-type person. As an adult, I have told him repeatedly that his lack of interest in fatherhood was apparent even when I was a child. I never had any illusions where he was concerned. From ages seven to eleven, I deflected friends' requests to play at my house by telling them my dad was prejudiced. The kids always asked what I meant by that. My matter-of-fact reply was, "My dad doesn't like kids."

Shortly after returning from a college semester abroad in Paris in 1999, I started working on a relationship with Peewee. While in France, I'd had an epiphany during a day trip to Chartres Cathedral. After walking around the cathedral, I went into a restaurant restroom and broke down in uncontrollable sobs and incomprehensible prayer. I prayed in different languages, English and French being among them. I don't remember the words but I remember begging God to allow me another moment with my mother; I wanted to hug her one last time and tell her I love her.

My mother died in August 1996. From the day she died to the day I broke down in that bathroom stall, I remember very little of my life. Those three years are like a black expanse of nothingness. No memories from that period are attached to any timeline. Everything in my life was shaded, dull and grey. Dark, dank and not worth mentioning. Until the day I spent at Chartres Cathedral. That night I had a dream awash in light. Pure, bright, beautiful light. I was in a house that resembled the last house my mom, brother, sister and I had lived in together. Me, my brother, and sister were lounging in the living room when the front door opened to frame my mother. She was standing there smiling in white flowing raiment, glowing and backlit by a brighter light. So ethereal. Her arms were outstretched towards me. I rushed into her arms, hugged her tightly and told her repeatedly how much I loved her. My gut-wrenching sobs woke my roommate up, who then shook me awake.

Perhaps that was the first supernatural communication I willingly accepted from God. I asked, he replied. That visit changed my heart. Allowing me that moment with my mother gave me a better understanding of love, not complete, but better. My mother had professed her love of her husband Peewee pretty much till the day she died. I returned home to Milwaukee thinking an appropriate tribute to her memory would be to mend my relationship with him.

Peewee claimed he knew everything there was to know about me because I was just like him. I recoiled every time such words left his lips. Royally recoiled. See, even with my special power of focusing on the good in people, I am drained of energy trying to focus on the good in Peewee. But I held on for nearly six years, thinking he wasn't all that bad. He was just a sad, broken, middle-aged man who was finally ready to appreciate the love and accept the responsibility of his family. Besides, I told myself repeatedly, if my mom loved him, there must be some redeeming qualities in him. Eventually, I accepted that my mom's special powers were much greater than mine.

One of my last conversations with Peewee took place shortly after Christmas 2005, three months after I had relocated to New York City. The transition was tough on me. I had a lot of time alone to think about every relationship I had and how they have helped to shape who I am. My relationship with Peewee affected how I embraced and moved forward in my womanhood. He molested me for a number of years in my youth. I reported him. He apologized and did his prison time. He has always been repentant and I had no wish to live in unforgiveness, so I stepped towards forgiveness and attempted to heal myself and our relationship in tandem. However, not all good intentions are good ideas.

I was honest enough with my feelings and goals to tell him we may never have a true father/daughter relationship, but I thought we could have a working friendship. That Christmas I went on a date with a man who was rather aggressively trying to touch and grab me. Despite being told explicitly what type of physical touch and interaction I was comfortable with, he insisted on repeatedly grabbing me how and where he wanted to. Towards the end of the night he tried to drape his arm around my shoulders, I deftly sidestepped him. He released an outburst of anger at me, "Don't pull away from me, woman! I'm not a rapist!"

That stunned me like nothing else ever from a relative stranger's lips. The date was effectively over at that point. I couldn't focus. I kept functioning, but I wasn't present. My dating life started playing in my mind in slow motion. I wondered if this man said what many men before him wanted to say. I wondered if I had always been so obviously jumpy and standoffish when interacting with men. Most likely, since I don't trust men until I'm comfortable trusting them.

Peewee happened to call me that night just as I got home. He was the first person I spoke to after a traumatic date, so I did what we all do in such situations – I talked about what was bothering me. After describing the night I realized the other end of the phone was silent. I thought about the last thing I said, *"Don't pull away from me, woman! I'm not a rapist,"* my unguarded moment escalated. "Oh, God, I'm talking to a rapist! You can't understand what I'm feeling. I can't talk to you about this. I have to go." That's when I realized Peewee and I would never have a real friendship either. He was the root and source of the biggest roadblock I had for personal development, spiritual growth and a healthy relationship with a man – he violated my youth, my trust, my sexuality and our relationship. He destroyed my sense of self, trampled my innocence and muted my voice.

Despite years of trying to heal myself and build a healthy rapport with him, it all crumbled like dust when confronted with the reckless words from a random date. Despite my desire to heal and forgive, there was still hurt and uncertainty in me. I was upset with Peewee because he never wanted to talk about this issue that altered not only our lives, but our family and continued to affect the quality of all our relationships. I had asked him numerous times to talk with me through our issues – in person, on the phone, via email, but he wasn't interested in talking. He always claimed to be waiting for the right moment. There are no "right" moments.

He called one more time after that night. He knew I was upset, but he wasn't interested in discussing the underlining issues. Instead, he chose to alternate between needling, pushing and avoidance. On that last call, when his needle didn't get the desired results, he pushed harder. He's not a reader of the Word and at the time I didn't know enough to speak it to him. *"And you, fathers, do not provoke your children to wrath, but bring them up in the training and admonition of the Lord." (Ephesians 6:4)* He missed the mark there.

"I know you're pissed," he said. "I know you're upset. Why won't you just blow up and get it over with?"

"Because I'm not really pissed. I'm just thinking," I replied.

"Bullshit! Pull out the ghetto! I know you have it in you."

I literally pulled the phone away from my ear to look at it, *"Excuse me?"*

"You may act like you're not from the ghetto, but you are and sometimes you just need to let it show."

I calmly told Peewee, "Let me assure you – there's *nothing* ghetto about me. Eighty thousand dollars worth of education pounded it all out."

He is representative of my family; they don't respect education much, they prefer "street smarts." This is probably why I don't think it's much to brag about. So, please allow me to pop my collar for a moment. I studied at the Sorbonne in France. My courses covered literature, civilization, politics and business. I tested into one of the top levels in the program. All my Sorbonne courses were taught in French – a language I first taught myself from library books at age thirteen. For those of you who don't know, the Sorbonne beats out Harvard – in age, snobbery and prestige. The beginning of the institution dates back to 1150 A.D.

To quote Oliver Wendell Holmes, "Man's mind, once stretched by a new idea, never regains its original dimensions." I agree. It makes no sense to value a way of life that does nothing but oppress while making the inferior believe in a false superiority. I left Gary when I was five. I lived in ghettoes and projects for less than three years total. At the time of this conversation with Peewee, I was thirty. Therefore, his comment translated to: the first five years of my life should dictate how I live my life. He was effectively telling me twenty-five years of education, life experience and growth should have less of an impact on how I handle situations than the first five that apparently mark me as a child of the ghetto.

I'm better than that!

My mother dropped out of school in the eighth grade when she had me. Her mother had stopped going to school in the sixth grade to work the Mississippi cotton fields. There is no legacy of educated women in my family. Yet, there was a desire to know, to learn, to improve. My mother did not help me with homework, nor did she attend any of my many school games or activities. She didn't know my friends or their families, even though she gave permission for me to hang out at their homes. None of that was her mothering style. Honestly, it never bothered me.

My mother was responsible for cultivating my character. Her style is rooted in my heart and softens my view of the world. Although I always tell people the first book my mom bought me was a dictionary when I was ten, she actually started my reading much earlier. As far as I know, my first Dr. Seuss reader set, a gift from Mom when I was about three years old, is still in my grandmother's basement.

My mother loathed taking government assistance and maintained up to three jobs to stay off of it. Even though we never had money to spare, she made us set the table to eat dinner, we didn't wear jeans to school, we wore school clothes (dresses, skirts, blouses, and slacks), we had a curfew and a bedtime. Above all, we were made to respect our elders no matter what they did or said. She raised self-respecting individuals who have a great respect for others. Mom did this without a guidebook, without a role model, without an education and without anyone expecting anything from her efforts.

I remember visits from aunts, uncles and cousins when one of them would comment on how well behaved Terry's kids were. "Why, you speak so proper," they would exclaim in surprise, "Terry's kids are always so clean." I always wondered why they were so surprised that Terry had clean, well-behaved, and well-spoken children. It wasn't until I attained adulthood that I understood that those relatives thought my mother was parenting better than she should have been as an unwed teen.

I remember one aunt in particular telling me I was stupid, retarded and that I would amount to nothing. She told me I would be a dropout like my mother. She insisted I was ugly, too skinny, too black, too whatever.... I remember complaining to my mother (sometimes the insults were said in front of her) and she would only be concerned with how I handled myself – "You didn't talk back, did you?" Or she would shush me, if I looked like I was about to say something. Under no circumstances were we allowed to disrespect our elders and my mother never saw a need to confront her peers and demand her children be treated with loving care and respect.

Sadly, I don't remember my mother ever coming to my defense. Then again, neither do I have memory of her defending herself. She did, however, tell me the things people told me about myself were not true. No elaborate speech, simply, "You're not stupid; you know you're not retarded; don't worry about what they said." That's pretty much my attitude about everything. I know what I know. I know who I am. I know my strengths and my weaknesses.

My mother gave me intangible gifts. I don't have many photos of her – the memory of her is in my blood, in my hands, in my heart, in the way I live my life. She lives on in me. She is the foundation of my womanhood. My dad damaged me, but I am a better woman than the bruised shell he would have me continue being. I am a regal, self-possessed and self-aware individual. Whether my mother meant to or not, her examples built up my character. She never thought I was better than I should be. She taught me how to be me. That's a concept a lot of people struggle with – just being themselves.

Everyone has the God-given ability to choose how they conduct their lives. On an individual basis we need to nurture our inner selves. We are all given divine choice on how we conduct our lives.

You need to know that no damage is irreparable. God has an awesomely amazing way of healing us from the tiniest fissure to the widest chasm in our mind, our heart, our spirit and our personality. However, you are responsible for seeking and asking for His help *and* following through on His instructions. Ultimately, you are the one who will answer for the way you spend your life. You will bear both fruit and consequences for all you do. So... do more than what's expected by people; don't fall victim to their low ideas for you. I implore you to be better than people think you should be. Open your heart and mind and grow into all God created you to be!

Meditation Verse: Ephesians 6:1-4, 10

Children, obey your parents in the Lord, for this is right. *"Honor your father and mother,"* which is the first commandment with promise: *"that it may be well with you and you may live long on the earth."* And you, fathers, do not provoke your children to wrath, but bring them up in the training and admonition of the Lord.

Finally, my brethren, be strong in the Lord and in the power of His might.

Who I Am In Christ

The below list of scripture itemizing who we are in Christ was set before me the first year I began focusing on my Biblical studies in New York. Reading it, learning it, believing the words and promises listed was revolutionary to my life. It was a miraculous balm to my soul and spirit. *Who I Am in Christ* is from *Victory Over Darkness* by Dr. Neil Anderson. The listed scriptures are from the Bible. Read it. Believe it. Live it.

I am accepted

I am God's child	John 1:12
As a disciple, I am a friend of Jesus Christ	John 15:15
I have been justified	Romans 5:1
I am united with the Lord and am one with Him in spirit	1 Corinthians 6:17
I have been bought at a price and belong to God	1 Corinthians 6:20
I am a member of the body of Christ	1 Corinthians 12:27
I have been chosen by God and adopted as His child	Ephesians 1:3-8
I have been redeemed and forgiven of all my sins	Colossians 1:13-14
I am complete in Christ	Colossians 2:10
I have direct access to the throne of grace through Jesus Christ	Hebrews 4:4-16

I am secure

I am free from condemnation	Romans 8:1-2
I know God works for my good in all things	Romans 8:28
I cannot be separated from the love of God	Romans 8:37-39
I have been established, anointed and sealed by God	2 Corinthians 1:21-22
I am hidden with Christ in God	Colossians 3:1-4

I am confident God will complete the good work He started in me	Philippians 1:6
I am a citizen of Heaven	Philippians 3:20
I have not been given a spirit of fear, but one of power, love, and self-discipline	2 Timothy 1:7
I am born of God, and the evil one cannot touch me	1 John 5:18

I am significant

I am a branch of Jesus Christ, the true vine	John 15:5
I have been chosen and appointed to bear fruit	John 15:16
I am a temple of the Holy Spirit	1 Corinthians 3:16
I'm a minister of reconciliation for God	2 Corinthians 5:17-21
I am seated with Jesus Christ in the heavenly realm	Ephesians 2:6
I am God's workmanship	Ephesians 2:10
I may approach God with freedom and confidence	Ephesians 3:12
I can do all things through Christ, who strengthens me	Philippians 4:13
I am free	Romans 8:1

Practicing What I Preach

"Our deepest fear is not that we are inadequate. Our deepest fear is that we are powerful beyond measure. It is our light not our darkness that frightens us. We ask ourselves 'who am I to be brilliant, gorgeous, talented and fabulous?' Actually, who are you not to be? You are a child of God. Your playing small doesn't serve the world. There's nothing enlightened about shrinking so that other people won't feel insecure around you. We were born to make manifest the glory of God that is within. It's not just in some of us; it's in everyone. And as we let our own light shine, we unconsciously give other people permission to do the same. As we are liberated from our own fear, our presence automatically liberates others."
– A Return to Love, Marianne Williamson

When I first read the above quote, the words impacted me immediately and deeply. Every word seemed to strike my heart and embed itself.

Our deepest fear is not that we are inadequate. Our deepest fear is that we are powerful beyond measure.

Imagine: the fear of being great. We commonly refer to this as an inferiority complex. I was diagnosed as a young woman of twenty-one. At the time, I was an hourly manager at McDonald's, being trained by one of the best managers I've ever had, Chris. For three years, he personally supervised my management training and development. I learned more about business and management from him than I did in college.

One of our most memorable conversations took place one day when he picked me up for work. I don't remember the exact topic of the conversation, but I know I was talking through an internal debate. I had three great opportunities before me that summer: teaching English as a second language in Japan or France, or pursuing a writing fellowship at a top university I was interested in. I added a fourth option while seeking Chris's advice on which route to take: stay in Milwaukee, working at McDonald's where I felt safe and secure.

Chris looked at me with horrified eyes at the mention of my fourth option and said, "*You are one of the most superior people I know, yet you have the biggest inferiority complex!"* He continued to diagnose me, but I think about that part of his statement very often.

Four months after moving to New York City I had a conversation with my friend Andrea that had a profound effect on me. Andrea and I had forged a bond in college that grew tighter through several jobs, crazy sexual attractions, one broken engagement, a few cross-country moves and many difficulties. Everything had been more difficult than expected after I moved to New York. My unemployment status did not change with the move, as I had hoped. By the time of our conversation, I had been unemployed for nearly a year and a half and was subsisting on short-term promotional work. The three years prior to my unemployment were filled with positions in which I was either bored or miserable. My "career" had turned into a résumé list of job after job that did my education, passion and talents no justice. None of the jobs satisfied me. When I arrived in New York I was only landing interviews for $10-an-hour jobs, competing against high school graduates, people with some college courses and laid-off middle managers. I had reached a new professional low.

The economy and job market were not good. My spirit and enthusiasm had taken a beating. So much so, that Andrea confronted me one night on the phone. "I'm worried about you," she said, "and I have been thinking of how to ask you this question. I know how you feel about yourself inside, but how do you feel about yourself outwardly?"

I asked her to elaborate.

"Well, your height, your size, your complexion, your appearance? I'm wondering if something is coming across in your interviews that conveys a discomfort or uncertainty."

"Ah... Well... I am quite comfortable with my height [5'11], my size, and my complexion. I am okay with me. There have obviously been periods in my life where I had issue with something about myself. But overall, I am not uncomfortable with my outward appearance. However, I am aware that some people find me intimidating. I have a presence that makes some people uncomfortable, so I constantly try to downplay my presence. The longer I go without getting a suitable employment offer, the more my shoulders hunch in interviews. Perhaps, that's my attempt to convince the interviewers I am a good fit for jobs I wouldn't have even considered applying for two years ago."

"I can see that," she replied. "I have such a powerful personality that I downplay it with my size. People aren't intimidated by a petite woman [5'3]. So, I use my appearance to my advantage to not appear threatening. However, I know that the power of my personality can bring a room to a standstill."

Your playing small doesn't serve the world. There's nothing enlightened about shrinking so that other people won't feel insecure around you.

I often repeat this line to myself, when I catch myself playing small. I do it more often than one would suspect and with the people one would least expect – my friends and family.

A couple of weeks prior to my conversation with Andrea, I had gone to Paris. I had just lost another short-term job, had no money and no prospects. How did I cope? I accepted a roundtrip ticket to Paris from my friend, Sasha. She and I had been roommates when we studied in Paris seven years earlier. Days before I was terminated, Sasha called with a sweet offer: four days in Paris, she had a free ticket for me, all I had to pay for was our hotel room and my food. I accepted. I only informed two other friends before leaving the country – Andrea and someone else in New York whom I sent copies of my passport and ID, in case of an emergency.

The trip started off well but turned into a disappointing experience. My emotions were too jumbled to enjoy Paris, but yet again the city brought me light and clarity. I had hoped to have healing talking marathons with my old friend, but Sasha went man-crazy and I spent an inordinate amount of time accompanying her around the city to meet up with some young French guy. When I returned home, I had several messages. A couple of people were asking where the heck I was because no one had heard from me in days.

I honestly didn't think anyone would notice my extended absence, but quite a few people were perturbed with me. However, when they heard where I had been, shock set in: "I can't believe you just took off to Paris!" Another friend, Dianna, hung up on me, when I answered her question, "Where have you been all week, Jones?" I called her back and asked her if her phone had dropped the call.

"No, I hung up! I can't believe you went to Paris without me. Harry *[her ex live-in boyfriend]* is going next week without me too. It's like everyone is going to Paris!"

This is where my ability to diminish myself came in. I said, "Well, Dianna, it's nothing to be upset about. If it makes you feel better *[famous words]* it was a horrible trip! And it's not like I could afford it! Sasha flew for free and had a discount ticket for me." Then I shared the major irritations of my trip. She laughed and enjoyed my exaggerated bad experiences, then promised to share the story with her friends. So, that's the story I stuck to, in order to keep people at ease. Lord forbid I somehow escape from my daily depression of living alone in a large, expensive city with no regular employment!

Luckily, I was able to share with Andrea the *ah-ha moments* that made the trip very worthwhile. I was able to share with her the deeper experiences and lessons from my week abroad. It hit me – again, I was playing small! Not many people can make an impromptu trip to Paris seem insignificant, but I managed just fine. I realized then that the people who are eased by my misery and discomfort are not people I wish to maintain relationships with.

That week, in reflection, I realized I had reduced many significant moments in my life to punch lines. Inadvertently, perhaps arrogantly, because I felt people would feel better about themselves if they believed I didn't think much of myself.

And as we let our own light shine, we unconsciously give other people permission to do the same. As we are liberated from our own fear, our presence automatically liberates others.

It takes a great effort and consciousness to live fully as *your* self. Even those of us who are fully aware of who we are, and are sometimes proud of being that person, wish for acceptance by everyone else. We don't want to appear different. More ambitious, experienced, principled, traveled – more ourselves than facsimiles. In my desire to fit in with others, I have dimmed my light for most and shined it for only a few.

Who am I not *to be brilliant, gorgeous, talented and fabulous? What right do I have to play into the small-mindedness of people?* We create our own environment. We all have jealous friends who are not sincerely happy about the good things in our lives. We may even be that jealous friend. It is how we handle the manifestation of that jealousy that determines how we move forward. We stand upon our own building blocks in life. We grow from our own lessons. The foundation we build on indicates the health of our relationships.

As I learn to practice what I preach, I encourage you to shine your light on your fears. Believe me, they will disappear – fear cannot stand up to confrontation. Give yourself permission to be you. This may be a no-brainer to some, but it's a necessity many live without: permission and freedom to be who you are.

Meditation Verse: Jeremiah 1:4-7

Then the Word of the LORD came to me, saying: "Before I formed you in the womb I knew you; before you were born I sanctified you; I ordained you a prophet to the nations."

Then said I: "Ah, Lord GOD! Behold, I cannot speak, for I *am* a youth."

But the LORD said to me: "Do not say, 'I *am* a youth,' for you shall go to all to whom I send you, and whatever I command you, you shall speak.

Self-image is Everything.

Self-image: The idea, conception, or mental image one has of oneself

You need to know who you are. Everything in your life will derive from how you view yourself because self-image *is* everything.

Even before I realized I am a spirit created in the image of God, housed in a body animated by His breath *(Genesis 1:27)*, I knew I was not what people of the world wanted me to believe I was. If I saw myself as others treat me, I would see nothing. A person of very little importance, worthless and without merit. Someone to ignore, disregard and do nothing for. I would be invisible even to myself, if I saw myself as others treat me.

After I realized I belong to God, once I embraced the fact that my body is a temple of His Holy Spirit and understood that my Father sees me as He created me, I was then able to accept my greatness. He didn't make any mistakes with me, or with you.

Jazzy Media and Me

In 2004 I started Jazzy Media. I had been thinking over small business options for a couple of years before deciding on something involving full-figure fashion and publishing. The first consideration for starting a business was having the ability to operate from home. I wanted the option of expanding and reducing my business operations based on my future family needs. The structure had to be mobile, flexible and functional on a part-time basis. In addition, I had to have a passion for the work. Once I decided on full-figure fashion, my thoughts then fleshed out a product to best portray the inherent beauty which resides in the fullness of a woman's form. *VoLux Full-Figured Calendar* was born. My goal with *VoLux* was to display beauty we don't see often in America. I wanted to portray the full-figured woman as desirable and fashionable. I wanted to provide a representative platform for women of all shapes and sizes. *VoLux* spoke to the physical woman.

My business was conceived and birthed in Milwaukee, Wisconsin. Milwaukee is my hometown – I went to high school and college there and my widest base of friends is there. My network helped my venture receive a great deal of local press. Exposure with *VoLux Full-Figured Calendar* led to speaker requests from local universities to speak on body image and self-esteem. I quickly developed a prototype body image workshop and began presenting in classrooms and conferences throughout the year. At that point, my body image workshops spoke to the emotional woman.

For five years I struggled trying to make Jazzy Media profitable. I never wavered in my belief that my business was developing as a vehicle to achieve the livelihood and lifestyle I envisioned for myself and my future family. What fueled this belief was the fact that I had no practical experience doing anything I did for my business, yet everything fell smoothly into place. I had no prior experience in self-publishing or graphic design or model searches, yet the process was relatively effortless. Don't get me wrong - I sweated, cried and toiled, but everything I needed for my business came to me; all my ducks were lined up for me with neat instructions on how to proceed to the next step.

Shortly, after I moved to New York, I realized I was at war with myself. *VoLux* had taken on a life of its own. People didn't look at the pictures and see the purity of my intent. They saw pure sex. I wasn't trying to sell sex. I was trying to sell the idea of positive body image no matter a woman's shape or size. I became increasingly uncomfortable and disturbed by the feedback people were giving me about my product. Men and women told me my calendar was the sexiest they've seen in my industry category. No one paid attention to my inspirational quotes or fashion tips. I became conflicted. I learned a bitter lesson – people will see what they want to see, not what you want them to see. My internal conflict led to the demise of *VoLux Full-Figured Calendar*. Growing the calendar had become excruciating, but I learned a lot from the entire process.

I learned to accept my sensuality and bask in my femininity. I was also confronted strongly with my spirituality. My spiritual and physical aspects were warring against one another, putting me into an emotional upheaval. Those weren't the lessons I expected to learn from my entrepreneurial pursuit. Maturing in my womanhood was not the expected result either. However, I am a much better person for the experience.

Part of my struggle was my determination to stay true to Jazzy Media's mission statement: *[to] create and perform based on the premise that positive self-image builds self-esteem, which in turn reflects one's inner beauty onto one's surroundings. We are committed to contributing to the positive self-image of all who come in contact with our products and services.* Rather lofty, I know, but I'm either going to go all out or stay home. I wanted to make a positive impact on everyone who came in contact with my work. The feedback for *VoLux* was overwhelmingly... *base*. There was nothing lofty about the effusive praise my beauty and physique garnered. I had no interest in being lifted to fashion or beauty icon status, even if only in the plus-size fashion community. I simply wanted to be an influence for people to enhance their lives.

The Industry and Society

For my purposes, "full-figure" represented a size range between straight-size and plus-size. While developing and operating Jazzy Media, the only pertinent research for my projects was lumped in with plus-size industry statistics. I later learned that body image and self-esteem have become extensions of the plus-size industry in regard to self-love no matter one's size. My body conscious vocabulary has grown considerably over the years. I used to use *body image* and *self-esteem* interchangeably. *Body acceptance* and *size acceptance* are terms I had not heard prior to doing research for my workshops. However, body image, self-esteem, body acceptance and size acceptance are not issues solely experienced by full-figure or plus-size women. Males and females of all ages, shapes and sizes experience concerns about their body image and self-esteem. No one is helped by constantly being inundated with media and film industry ideas of perfect beauty and perfect body types.

Low self-esteem is not the root of all evil. However, unending projections of "perfect" images are one root of low self-esteem. Beauty is not an exclusionary term, but the fashion industry and media outlets work hard to make it appear so. Their projections of what is beautiful exclude the majority of the world's population. Wouldn't you much rather know you are made perfect in Christ Jesus and are complete in Him? When God finished making you He said, "Behold! S/he is very good!" *(Genesis 1:31)*

My outlook on life has changed since I learned how marvelous and wonderful I am to my Creator. How do you receive that knowledge?

God and You

We all have the body God gave us. When we learn to accept that, we are better off as individuals. No two people are created exactly the same. Even identical twins are different by the order of their birth and more notably, their personalities. In Jeremiah 1:5 God tells us, "Before I formed you in the womb I knew you..." Don't insult God by hating yourself. He created a good thing when He created you!

We can't choose the body we are born with. However, we can choose how we maintain it. You need to know who you are. You need to appreciate and believe you are wonderfully and awesomely made. *(Psalms 139:14)* There were no mistakes made with your molding – God did not accidentally breathe his life into your body. It was purposeful. You are here for a reason. You are important. You are loved. You need to see all this in yourself and project it.

When I was thirteen years old I made a conscious decision to build and protect my self-esteem. I didn't grow up with anyone speaking positive words into me or my life, but somehow I knew I had to build myself up with words. Whenever someone criticized me, I said something positive about myself. After a while, people started telling me I was far too defensive. They didn't expect me to object to their negativity. They told me I needed to learn how to take constructive criticism. I considered that. Eventually, I started responding to that reproach with, "I'm fine with *constructive* criticism, but your criticism isn't building me up." Their words were intended to knock me down or "put me in my place." In their opinion, I was far too confident. This process taught me selective hearing.

Since my college days I have come across many older women who have congratulated me on my self-confidence. They claimed to be impressed by my positive self-esteem. One of the older women introduced me to the teachings of Dr. Myles Munroe. During one of our discussions of Dr. Munroe she congratulated my mother for a job well done instilling such strong self-esteem in me.

"Thanks, but my mother didn't do that; I did." She was a bit taken aback. Sure, my mother planted a seed by reminding me I knew who I was, but I made a conscious decision to nurture that seed.

We are the result of our thinking.

Believing that, I thought good thoughts about myself because I wanted to be a good person and live a good life. You may know this philosophy better as: *I think I can* or Proverbs 23:7, as *he thinks in his heart, so is he.*

Meditation Verse: Genesis 1:27-31

So God created man in His *own* image; in the image of God He created him; male and female He created them. Then God blessed them, and God said to them, "Be fruitful and multiply; fill the earth and subdue it; have dominion over the fish of the sea, over the birds of the air, and over every living thing that moves on the earth."

And God said, "See, I have given you every herb *that* yields seed which *is* on the face of all the earth, and every tree whose fruit yields seed; to you it shall be for food. Also, to every beast of the earth, to every bird of the air, and to everything that creeps on the earth, in which *there is* life, *I have given* every green herb for food"; and it was so. Then God saw everything that He had made, and indeed *it was* very good.

Reflections on Weight Conversations

When I lived in Milwaukee, I had a regular exercise schedule and routine. That discipline didn't travel with me to New York. Though I joined a gym within two weeks of relocating, I was not able to get with anybody's program nor was I able to stick to any plan. During my first three years in New York I gained nearly twenty pounds. I didn't sweat the ten-pound weight gain or the fifteen, but twenty was too much. That galvanized me into the gym.

Shortly after recommitting myself to a gym and a goal, my high school friend Tosha engaged me in a workout conversation. She was trying to admonish me about not sticking strictly to my workout goals and diet plans. I told her, "I'm flexible." Then I asked, "Why is everyone in such a hurry to lose weight? Why are women starving themselves, emaciating themselves? Killing themselves for the elusive, high-maintenance skinny body?" She had recently lost forty pounds and wanted to lose more. Her workout schedule was extensive and expensive. Her goal was to be skinnier than she was in high school.

Faye, my neighbor, was a healthy, glowing, beautiful size six at the beginning of last year. She's fifty-one years old and has had seven pregnancies and four successful births. She's perhaps 5'3 and her 6'4 Texas-size husband has called her Big Mama and told her she's "too big" for most of their twenty-year relationship. As a result, during the years I've known her she's done at least three to four starvation "diets" during which she will not put food in her mouth for fourteen to thirty straight days. Each starving period has been triggered by an imminent visit to her doctor who told her what her ideal weight should be. Therefore, she starves to get to the weight for her doctor visit then binges after. The other times are triggered by her annual family vacation to the Caribbean. She doesn't walk around in bikinis, she doesn't even know how to swim, but she wants the society-ideal bikini body before touching down on the island because her husband wants her skinnier than she was thirty years and seven pregnancies ago. In the span of four months last year, Faye starved herself down to a double-zero dress size. She was only about 135 pounds to start with. Because her self-image is wrapped up in what one person said he wants, she's killing herself.

I mention Faye because around that time she made two comments to me about my weight and I had to stop her in her tracks. I understand misery loves company, but friend or not, she can find someone else to belittle in her misery. I don't have the patience for it. She invited me over for a barbeque that spring. I don't hide my love of sugar and carbs, I couldn't if I tried. So, as I sat at her kitchen counter enjoying mini cinnamon rolls, she said, "You shouldn't eat like that. I'm concerned. You've gained a lot of weight since your brother died." My brother had died nearly a year prior. On the surface, her words could be taken as sincere, loving concern. However, my experience with Faye has revealed she does not know what love is. Because she had made a similar comment a few months before, I was more prepared with a response. I was also much more aware of how much she hated her own body. I refuse to see myself through the eyes of someone who does not at least love herself.

"I've only gained about twenty pounds."

"That's a lot of weight."

"I've lost about seven pounds in the last two weeks."

"That's a lot to lose in such a short time! What have you been doing?"

"I've been working out. I started jogging." End of conversation.

Just like I enjoy a comfortable workout, I enjoy enjoying my food. The diehard gym-nuts cringe when I say this, but there is no need for me to deprive myself of whatever I want. That being said, I have nearly mastered the art of *all things in moderation*. I don't starve myself and I don't binge. If I'm craving a chocolate chip cookie or a brownie sundae, I treat myself. I've learned from experience, the alternative is to ignore that craving and end up bull-dozing through a bag of cookies and two brownie sundaes when I can't take the restriction anymore. Afterwards, I feel sick and disappointed in myself. How much better for me to just have that one cookie or sundae when the mood strikes? Surprisingly, the mood doesn't strike as often as it used to, simply because there is no deprivation. I don't feel as if I'm missing out on anything.

Did you notice how Faye had a critique no matter my weight? People can only share what they know. The only voice she listens to is her husband's. He has spent the twenty years of their shared life belittling and hating her. Faye has willingly fed on his spirit-assassinating hatred and has regurgitated it to her children. Since she has only known such sad fruit, that's all she shares with her children and friends. I'm not interested in drinking from her cup, though.

After Tosha tore into me like a terrier for being lax on my exercise routine, my rebuttal was, "I prefer to give myself permission to mess up. Yeah, I can be strict with myself, castigating myself for lapses in control and such, but instead I think of the many people who start each year off with a resolution to lose weight. They join a gym, struggle through a couple of workouts, and then give up. Why do they give up? Because they missed a couple of planned sessions. Or because they enjoyed a big meal over a holiday weekend and felt the diet was shot. Or their lifestyle couldn't really support the drastic changes their diet demanded. There are many reasons why people fall off the good, healthy-living wagon, but if they gave themselves permission to mess up, it would be much easier to get back into their routine after falling off. It's the pursuit of perfection that screws us up. 'I have to adhere to the diet 100%; I can't deviate an inch!' So once there's a deviation, you chuck the whole thing. No. I give myself permission to mess up."

She hadn't thought of it that way. She's hardcore now because she's been out of the gym for several years. I was a regular at the gym for seven years before I moved to New York City. I had a workout schedule of three to five days a week, depending on my goals. Even with that proven discipline, I could not develop a routine for nearly three years after I moved. I haven't stopped trying to create a routine, though. Most of my attempts just haven't worked with the new parameters of my life, like living in upper Manhattan and working in lower Manhattan. Sometimes the last thing I want to do is get off the train and re-route to a gym, thus getting off the straight line of my commute between home and work.

Nearly a decade ago, I traveled for nine months in a fashion show, the Ebony Fashion Fair, as the only full-figured model with a troupe of fifteen straight-size models (i.e. skinny chicks). I modeled size 18/20 clothes as a size 14/16. They had to take in all my outfits, fitting them snuggly to my voluptuous hourglass figure, but they wanted me enough to make the effort. Even knowing that, I allowed the snide, catty comments from the other girls to get to me. Some called me fat, told me my breasts were so big they looked like a butt. A couple of people even told me that if not for the "tits and ass" I wouldn't even be full-figured. So I started working out on the road and stopped eating three meals a day. I went down to maybe one meal and snacks. We had a mandatory weigh-in every Friday. My weight dropped fast and the fitted clothing started sagging on my diminishing curves. Within a couple of weeks, I got a call from the corporate office followed immediately with a "talking to" from the stage manager and model supervisor. "LaShawnda, what are you doing? We didn't hire you to be a straight-size model. We hired you for the full-figured slot. If you keep losing weight, you're out of a job. There are plenty of ladies who would love to be in your shoes. Literally! The next couple of weigh-ins we want to see more weight on you!"

From that point on, I considered a major part of my job to be eating. There has never been a sweeter revenge! Those same girls who had been diligently chipping away at my self-esteem with their acidic comments were forced to watch me eat a full plate of whatever I wanted plus dessert while they picked at low-calorie dry salads and sucked on ice-cubes in order to maintain figures that were zipped and taped into sheer sheath gowns and skin-tight leather jumpsuits. Yet I was the one who brought the crowd to its feet every night; I was the only model that got fawned over after *every* show. So much so, I eventually stopped attending the receptions; the attention to my "figure and beauty" was too much for me. People said things to me they never would have said had they known me personally.

I learned there's something to be said for appreciating our body in its natural state. We're not all meant to be the same size, weight, height or shape.

I was twenty-five when I modeled for the Ebony Fashion Fair show. I thought I had a pretty concrete sense of who I was, but I am still amazed people were able to infiltrate and alter my self-perception. That experience showed me that environment and time can effect change even against the strongest mind and will.

I admonish you to have an unshakable faith in the work God has put into you and your life. Don't allow people to speak against it or to act against His interests for you. I can't say it enough – knowing who you are is paramount.

Meditation Verse: Matthew 6:25-34

"Therefore I say to you, do not worry about your life, what you will eat or what you will drink; nor about your body, what you will put on. Is not life more than food and the body more than clothing? Look at the birds of the air, for they neither sow nor reap nor gather into barns; yet your heavenly Father feeds them. Are you not of more value than they? Which of you, by worrying, can add one cubit to his stature?

"So why do you worry about clothing? Consider the lilies of the field, how they grow: they neither toil nor spin; and yet I say to you that even Solomon in all his glory was not arrayed like one of these. Now if God so clothes the grass of the field, which today is, and tomorrow is thrown into the oven, *will He* not much more *clothe* you, O you of little faith?

"Therefore do not worry, saying, 'What shall we eat?' or 'What shall we drink?' or 'What shall we wear?' For after all these things the Gentiles seek. For your heavenly Father knows that you need all these things. But seek first the kingdom of God and His righteousness, and all these things shall be added to you. Therefore do not worry about tomorrow, for tomorrow will worry about its own things. Sufficient for the day *is* its own trouble."

Smoke and Mirrors: The Confusion of Fantasy

Being real is real important to me. Can't beat truthfulness and honesty. On the surface, that may appear to conflict with the full-figured fashion calendar I produced. Oddly enough, however, producing a calendar showcasing real women styled like fashion models seemed like the realest thing I could do at the time. Initially, I was completely anti-retouching, but quickly learned from my buying audience, retouching was a minimum expectation. I learned fast that neither men nor women wanted to see *real* women in a photo spread – dimples, lines, creases, blemishes or fleshy rolls. They wanted fantasy women. Long hair, colored hair, long nails, high heels, nipped-in waist, flared hips, narrow hips, overflowing cups, empty cups, cups that fit just right, lingerie model, perfect mother, accommodating wife... the endless list of expectations encompassed different elements and developed varied fantasies. What it came down to for my work: whatever you are is not good enough.

My friend Dianna came to visit me for a week two years after I relocated. We modeled together for the Ebony Fashion Fair starting in 2000. She's six feet even with fair skin, hazel eyes, a large natural curly fro and a slim, fit size six. She is always well-groomed – brows, hands, feet, etc. This woman gets "photo ready" to go to the grocery store – make-up, shiny hair, juicy lips, modelesque clothes.... I'm sure you get the picture – I felt a twinge of discomfort anticipating her visit.

My style is comfort before beauty. That preference makes me the bane of all my fashionable friends' social existence. If I am going to the grocery store first thing in the morning, it's a finger fluff to the hair (or plopping on a hat) and sweats. My lips get attention only if they're chapped. And my ever present glasses are firmly perched on my nose. Yes, people, I wear glasses. And I enjoy wearing glasses for various practical and psychological reasons.

Dianna said she would help me sell my calendar and poetry books on 125th Street in Harlem that weekend. We got ready for the street sale after returning from the grocery store early Saturday. Dianna got even more glammed up for 125th Street than she did for the grocery store. I thought I was doing something by switching my conservative brown frames (glasses) for my flashy red and blue ones. I was not in the mood to get dressy and flashy. I pulled on my red VoLux Thick n' Sexy T-shirt, a nice cute olive green skirt with red and gold piping and was seriously looking for white socks and sneakers to finish my outfit. Dianna vetoed that and urged me to look through my assortment of knee-high boots – where I came across a nice dark brown leather pair. In the bathroom, I brushed through my wavy curls from a week-old set. I had just put on a neutral eye shadow and mascara when Dianna called out, "Put on some blush!" Which meant I had to put on a bit of foundation to smooth my tones. Before I did that, I heard, "Gloss!" I was proud to call back, "I'm doing that right now." I put on a sheer gloss and lined my lips with a plum liner. She came in to look, "You need to make your lips *greaz-zy.*" I put on a lip gloss with extra sparkle. Dianna checked my progress. I looked at her from under my lashes and said, "I guess the glasses are going next." She harrumphed, rolled her eyes and left the bathroom to get a brighter blush. Mine was too dull, she said.

I did get one compliment. She told me I looked like I had slimmed down quite a bit since she last saw me. Since I hadn't seen the inside of a gym in at least two months, I just gushed a *thank you.*

It's funny how I fall into this familiar routine with my glamour friends, because to my comfort-before-beauty friends I am the glamour girl. I went out with Zoë, the week prior to Dianna's visit, to a taping of the Def Poetry Jam in Times Square. She's an associate from Milwaukee who had just relocated to New York that month. I got home from work later than I had anticipated the night we were supposed to meet. I called and told her I was running late and would just throw something on. The line went silent. After a few seconds, she said, "When you say 'throw something on' what exactly do you mean?" I laughed, because she was right to be worried if I wasn't in the mood to look good. I described my outfit. She approved.

My last photo shoot with Doug, another model friend from my Ebony Fashion Fair days, was for my collection of poems, *Fantasies: A Metamorphosis of Sexual Attraction.* Doug is perhaps the closest thing I have to a male friend. During the shoot, I made self-conscious comments. I remember my comments vaguely but I remember his responses clearly. As we posed face to face, I asked, "Doug, do I need to cover my pimple more?" As he angled over me, "Can you see my chin hair?" As he leaned in towards me, "Is my roll showing from this position...." After the first comment, he said, "What are you talking about?" After the second, "I don't see anything." The third time, he shut me up, "Will you stop pointing out your flaws. I didn't even notice anything until you said something. You look good."

I think that's the gist of my conflict. No matter how much smoke I fan in front of the mirror I still see myself without any adornment. I know what is beneath the make-up and feel like a con artist selling a tall tale. Others not only see the fantasy, they *want* to believe the fantasy is the real thing. They expect me to embody the fantasy – voluptuous sexpot with men falling at her feet. I didn't mind perpetrating the myth on paper, in my calendar, but, in person, I am not the least bit interested in maintaining any part of the fantasy.

My old friend Leila once tried to set me up with someone. She called to tell me she showed him one of my modeling pictures.

"Why did you show him that picture?"

"So he would know what you look like."

"I'm not showing up looking like my photos."

"I'm sure he doesn't expect that...."

But they do. That's where my disclaimers come in: make-up washes off; figure fluctuates; brain is active.

I was at the end of a year-long internship in Milwaukee when I got selected for the Ebony Fashion Fair tour. Leila was one of two friends I'd met during my internship. Somehow an announcement was made around the office that a model was in everyone's midst. I remember making copies in the copy room one day and a woman who had never spoken to me before came in and said, "You know, you are simply gorgeous. Good luck with the modeling." I was stunned. I was nearly twenty-five and that was the first time anyone had told me I was gorgeous or beautiful or anything – randy men don't count. And I looked the same as I did the day before when no one knew anything about my modeling.

No, I don't take compliments well. Some people think I'm fishing because I brush them off. I think people say what they think I want to hear. Either way I've learned that people want to believe in fantasies. Eventually, I came to understand if I try to represent and exploit full, feminine beauty, I shouldn't be surprised when people want to get up close and personal with the representative.

Dianna reinforced things I knew but wasn't consistent with maintaining. It's okay to glam myself up and fan smoke in front of the mirror everyone is looking at me through. Fantasy, in moderation, isn't necessarily a bad thing.

However, I maintain the following and hope it's true for you as well. There are only a few people to whom I have ever wanted to be beautiful. That beauty has nothing to do with the way I look. It has everything to do with personality, chemistry, connection and relationship. As long as I bring a smile to the faces of my loved ones when they see me or a smile to their voice when they hear from me, I'm all good, because those are the people who really see me, as I am, without any adornment or embellishments through the smoke and mirrors.

Meditation Verse: Song of Solomon 1:5-6

I *am* dark, but lovely, O daughters of Jerusalem, like the tents of Kedar, like the curtains of Solomon. Do not look upon me, because I *am* dark, because the sun has tanned me. My mother's sons were angry with me; they made me the keeper of the vineyards, but my own vineyard I have not kept.

Chunky Dunkin'

Prudence is the mother of a high-school friend, Chloe. Chloe's daughter, Blossom is my goddaughter. I'm a member of their extended family.

Prudence lives part of the year in her cottage in the Upper Peninsula of Michigan. The U.P. is an outcrop of land bordering Wisconsin, sandwiched between Lake Superior to the north and Lake Michigan to the south. A couple of summers ago I accepted Prudence's standing invitation and visited her over the Fourth of July holiday. I flew into Milwaukee, rented a car, swooped up Chloe and Blossom and together we drove the five hours north to the cottage. Prudence's neighbors were hosting the holiday festivities. They are always wonderful hosts. I met Evelyn and her family about ten years ago and have only seen her three to four times total, but I hear about her all the time through Prudence. I know she gets regular updates about me as well. We are updated so expertly, it's always like old buddies getting together to catch up when we are in the same space. Prudence and Evelyn enjoy teasing me about my activities. To this group (age fifty plus, conservative, upper-middle-class Midwesterners) I have a very exciting and adventurous life.

Chloe, Blossom and I arrived later than expected and were instructed to drive straight to Evelyn's house for dinner. After dinner, Evelyn looked at me and offered, "LaShawnda, we're going chunky dunkin' tonight... you can come, but you can't laugh."

I looked at all the laughing faces of her family and friends and cautiously inquired, "What's *chunky dunkin'*?"

"It's skinny dippin' for chunky people!"

Laughing, I told her I would love to join them! "I won't laugh, but you can't look!"

"Deal!"

Evelyn tried to recruit all the women at dinner but it ended up just being me, her, her two daughters – Kate, age ten and Cyndi, age six – and my goddaughter, Blossom, age nine.

Blossom said she didn't want to swim naked. I told her she didn't have to, "Do only what you're comfortable doing, sweetie." So, she kept on her suit.

Cyndi looked at Blossom then at me and said, "Mom, I want to go swimming in my clothes." Mom agreed.

We went out after sunset. The horizon was a vibrant purple, pink and red blend bouncing off a metallic grey-blue lake. It was breathtaking! We walked down to the lake from their back yard. Evelyn was stripped and in the water before I got my shoes off. Cyndi was next, followed by Kate. Blossom stood by waiting, or should I say, daring me to follow-through on the "naked swimming" as she called it.

So, I stripped, all the while trying to cover with my arms and hands what my clothes were uncovering. My arms were crossed over my chest as I stepped into the water. COLD! I adjusted to the chill a foot at a time. Within seconds, Kate yelled out from where she and her mom were waiting for me to join them, about twenty-five feet from shore, "LaShawnda, let your boobies go! They want to be free! They want to be free... let your boobies be free!"

I almost lost my footing.... I didn't expect to hear anything like that from anyone there, least of all one of the girls! But sure enough, when I let them go, they floated quite freely. My girls were extremely happy being fancy free in the water, floating unhindered. They were beautifully buoyant!

I can count the times in my life when I've let go of all my inhibitions and just been free. I had always looked at letting go as something of a free-fall – it sounds good but the strain of holding on somehow feels safer. After all, I know what I'm holding on to, but I have no idea what I could fall into when I let go.

I had to remind myself, I'm not in a season of falling; I'm floating into a season of soaring! That knowledge not only feels good, it's freeing!

We all need someone to anchor us to something from time to time. It's in the company of the familiar that we feel our safest. Then again, safety is an illusion, isn't it? Sometimes we need to let people go and sometimes we just need to let go of our illusions and perceptions about those people. I'm learning to do both.

It has taken a while, but I've come to learn that in letting go, I am trusting God. I don't need to hold on to safety, comfort or the familiar. I can let these things go, pass me by or recede into the background. Anything that is meant for me will stay put, the connection will remain; I don't have to worry about possible loss. I don't have to fear a painful landing. My Father God has me firmly in hand; He is guiding me. Even as I let go of issues and concerns in my life, I am holding on firmly to my faith and belief that He will work all things to my good.

Meditation Verse: Romans 8:28-30

And we know that all things work together for good to those who love God, to those who are the called according to *His* purpose. For whom He foreknew, He also predestined *to be* conformed to the image of His Son, that He might be the firstborn among many brethren. Moreover whom He predestined, these He also called; whom He called, these He also justified; and whom He justified, these He also glorified.

Out of the Mouths of Babes
My Body, Your Image...

Your choice: Accept or Reject

On the way back up from the lake after our chunky dunkin' session, Kate walked over to me and shared, "My dad calls us (Kate, Cyndi and Evelyn) three full moons when we're out dunkin'. LaShawnda, if we're full moons, what are you?"

Evelyn answered with a robust laugh before I could say anything, "The dark side of the moon!"

"No. I have a full moon as well. It's no different from yours." I was a bit surprised they thought there was a difference between our anatomies because of skin color. I didn't think such a basic question would come up as much as Evelyn and her daughters have been exposed to Prudence's multi-cultural extended family.

"No, LaShawnda, you have a harvest moon!" Kate declared triumphantly.

"Okay. I'll take that." Every harvest moon I've seen has been lush, vibrant, excessively full and beautiful. However, I was still disturbed by the thought that my anatomy should be different because I have darker skin.

Earlier in the evening, Kate had stayed close to me while she undressed for our chunky dunkin'. While she undressed she chanted, "I'm fat. I'm fat. I'm fat...."

"Kate! Stop that. You're fine," I admonished.

She looked over at me, "You know, I never thought I was fat until a kid at school told me I was a month ago."

Isn't that how our road to the tortures of low self-esteem begins? By some generous someone telling us their low opinion about who we are or what we represent to them? I am always shocked by the cruelty of children... and adults, for that matter.

Aghast, I looked at Kate. "Well, that was rude of him! You should tell him to keep his comments to himself."

When I got out to Evelyn in the lake, I told her what her daughter was saying about herself. "You know," she said, "I've told her she will never be skinny. She has my stocky build and she knows how I struggle with my weight. I've told her she needs to learn to accept her body the way it is."

Many parents don't have that conversation with their children. *Don't worry about what/who others think you should be, accept what/who you are.* It's an important conversation to have. Evelyn gave a good rebuttal to a nasty childhood verbal knock.

I was a super skinny little girl. When I was a teenager, I prayed and begged God to bless me with some weight. Well, guess what – I'm keeping my mouth shut from now on! He's given me a ripe, bountiful body that looks as if it could nurture a whole community! I'm trying to appreciate, manage and maintain it to the best of my ability.

Kate is a very athletic child. She's swims in the lake two to three times a day, weather permitting. She rides her bike, walks with her mom and jumps on a trampoline for hours at a time. If she sat around eating all day without activity, I would be concerned about her weight. However, her stockiness is natural. I don't think she should feel bad about that.

Not every word is a good word

I don't know too many people in my church. It was my desire to stay focused on learning the Word, receiving the message and getting grounded in my new church home before allowing members to put their spin on what I was learning. The first time I stayed after service, nearly a year after I'd started attending, was to speak with a church member I had met on one of the outings.

I had spoken to him briefly on a few occasions before, but for some reason that day I let myself get roped into a conversation. Somehow he got my activities with Jazzy Media out of me regarding my body image workshops. He said something to the effect, "You know Pastor So-n-So has a strong opinion about fat people. What do you think?" First of all, I don't know why people automatically jump to the word FAT when I mention BODY IMAGE or SELF-ESTEEM! *Anyway....*

I told him I wasn't too familiar with the opinion he mentioned. He enlightened me. I have since heard this particular pastor voice this particular opinion several times. Basically, this pastor thinks people are fat because they want to be fat. If they simply stop eating, they would lose weight. *Ta-da!* They're skinny. From the way the church member ran this down, I could tell he was in agreement. I wasn't sure, however, if he was calling *me* fat. So, I told him what I thought.

"If you line up five *fat* people in front of you, are you able to tell which one is fat because of a medical condition? Which one because of emotional overeating? Which one because of heredity? No. There's no way you can tell by looking at someone why they are the way they are. So, who are you to judge? Who are we? That's not our place."

I tilted my head in the direction of a group of ladies. "If you bring over one of those petite, skinny women and stand her next to me, she may look up and think, 'Wow, she's huge! She's fat!' Compared to a short, petite woman, maybe I am. But I'm not looking at myself from her perspective or anyone else's for that matter. I'm only concerned with my own self-perception."

He nodded as if he were listening then went on another tangent, but to me, it was all ignorance. He was speaking from a closed-minded perspective. He offered an opinion from a judgmental view-point based on someone else's closed-minded judgment. There was no empathy or interest in individual humanity. He just offered a sweeping judgment on a group of people he and his pastor thought didn't look as *they* thought they should.

People will try to pour their negative words and energy into you, no matter who you are, where you are or what you do. No matter who we are, where we grow up, or who we grow up around, we all battle insecurities which are brought to us by others, sometimes in the name of love. It's hard to ground yourself and almost impossible to get your roots down before others start planting their own image of you into your mind.

Yeah, my butt may look like the dark side of the moon to you, but it looks just fine to me. Before we finish talking you're going to know some of the positive things I think of myself. You're also going to know that your image of my body has very little power to sway how I see myself.

Meditation Verse: Psalms 139:13-14

For You formed my inward parts; you covered me in my mother's womb. I will praise You, for I am fearfully *and* wonderfully made; marvelous are Your works, and *that* my soul knows very well.

This Is Why I'm Hot...

I'm hot because I'm me.

If you've been paying attention so far, you may have recognized some of my issues deriving from my business, my self-esteem and self-development. After nearly two years in New York City, I felt as if I were receiving more than my share of life lessons. I needed a break. I headed to Mexico City, where an old friend was doing a graduate study abroad.

Lauren and I have known each other for more than half our lives, in many capacities: co-workers, manager/employee, roommates, travel companions, and friends. We know each other's life stories and idiosyncrasies and have been witness to one another's worst behavior, yet we still love each other. And occasionally, we still try to participate in one another's life. After a couple of nights together in Mexico City, we finally had time to sit, talk and catch up. Lauren stated at one point during our conversation, "Shawnda, I'm so glad you're you again! When I got your Christmas card and letter after you arrived in New York, you sounded so depressed and it just made me so sad."

Such a statement would have given me pause had Lauren not been the third friend that week to welcome me back to myself. None of them know each other, by the way. Earlier that week, I had shared some drama about my job with Andrea and how I'd handled it. In response, she shouted, "Oh, my goodness! The old Shawnda is back! They don't know you, girl, they don't know!" After that call, while talking to another friend, Leila, about something else, I got a "Shawnda! Where have you been?"

I know where I've been, and I don't want to go there anymore. My first couple of days in Mexico City, I was very pensive about my absence from myself – the things, behavior and ill treatment I put up with because I was too beaten down and worn out to stand up for myself and assert my interests. For a long time, I ignored my perspective as much as others did. It was time to let people know I valued me even if they didn't!

During those days of reflection, I looked within and without and realized I had been looking at my life primarily from the perspective of my attractiveness. I hadn't felt too attractive since moving to New York. When people asked me about men and dating in the city, I usually replied, "Blah, nothing here." I wasn't feeling anything on any level. I felt less attractive because I had put on weight, because I had reached thirty-one without being settled in life, because I didn't have a family of my own, a home of my own, no permanent employment, my start-up was a failure.... The list went on and on. These numerous negatives told me I was undesirable and shouldn't expect to be of value to anyone. It wasn't until I stepped away from my everyday life and had a moment to reflect that I realized I didn't feel hot because I wasn't happy.

Snap!

Just like that, my mind shifted. My focus and perspective changed. Today, I will tell you, I am hot because I am happy! It was necessary for me to remind myself what happiness is. It is not material or physical. It's not a person or a circumstance. Happiness is a state of mind. I haven't lost weight, I haven't gained a whole bunch of financial stability, and generally, many other areas of my life are just as troubled as they were when I moved to New York. Though I have made incremental progress everywhere, the landscape of the big picture hasn't changed much. What has changed is the way I think. I have a renewed mind. Something about my inner joy and happiness makes me feel sexier and more attractive than anything else I can name. Knowing that God made me as I am keeps me pretty confident! He could have made me any way He wanted, but He chose my components as they are for a reason.

My Creator God has graced me with a measure of joy I've learned to appreciate and cultivate. I challenge you to ask yourself why you are hot.

Meditation Verse: John 17:11-13

Now I am no longer in the world, but these are in the world, and I come to You. Holy Father, keep through Your name, those whom You have given Me, that they may be one as We *are*. While I was with them in the world, I kept them in Your name. Those whom You gave Me I have kept; and none of them is lost except the son of perdition, that the Scripture might be fulfilled. But now I come to You, and these things I speak in the world, that they may have My joy fulfilled in themselves.

Speak Power and Prosperity into Your Life

The catalyst for my July 4th trip home that started with four days at Prudence's U.P. cottage was me quitting my job. I refused to focus on what I was letting go of; I focused instead on the relationships I wanted to embrace. I visited many friends who have been more like family than my family has been to me. Friends who have improved the quality of my life with their presence and their acceptance of me.

You gotta know when to hold 'em...

Some people you click with, some you don't. Who knows how chemistry works? I don't. However, I know you have to hold on to the people you have chemistry with. I think I have a special bond with everyone I saw during my week back in Wisconsin. I felt a need to reaffirm my appreciation for everyone in my life.

Prudence's cottage is one of the most peaceful places I've ever been. The sun sets in her back yard. I was in need of rest and my, what a glorious environment to rest in.

I was looking forward to waking up to watch the sun rise, chatting with my old friend over coffee, sitting out by a campfire in companionable silence and just generally enjoying the company of someone who knows and loves me. I hadn't made any connections with anyone in New York City. Even the old friends who had followed me to the big city seemed to fall off. I wasn't clicking with neighbors, co-workers or managers.

Within six months of relocating, I landed a senior administrative position in a posh private entertainment bank on Park Avenue. My manager and I had a very strained and uncomfortable relationship. Every day I stepped in the office I felt as if I needed to gird myself for battle.

During my first conversation with Prudence at her cottage, I told her I had put up with the negativity as long as I could. The situation wasn't improving and I felt more and more corroded the longer I was exposed to the maliciousness in that office. When I told Prudence my manager had asked for my resignation three weeks before I quit because none of the people I supported liked me, she said I should have replied, "You may not like me, but there are many people waiting to see me who like me a lot!" She was so indignant and offended on my behalf, it cheered me a bit. How dare they talk to her LaShawnda like that! I had forgotten what a supporter I had in Prudence! It's always refreshing spending time with her. It was great hearing how her family has grown through grandchildren and new friends. And I enjoyed sharing stories of all the living I had stuffed into the years since I'd last seen her.

Sometimes life is a simple matter of what is put before you. Other times it's what you make of it. No matter your outlook, the people in your life will dictate the quality of your life. I know and love some wonderful people and I am truly blessed because they know and love me back!

Know when to fold 'em,
Know when to walk away;
And know when to run...

Working for Mean Jack was torment. He made it known early that he did not like me. He hired me because I was a referral from a hotshot relationship banker he had recently hired. Not only did I support Mean Jack, he was the manager in charge of all New York operations for the bank. When he set himself against me, the rest of the office followed suit. The environment was so hostile, I became agitated, stressed and angry. When I started responding to them the way they were treating me, I decided it was time to walk away.

When I folded on my job, I walked away from yet another situation that was damaging to the person I want to be. Some people called me brave. More felt sorry for me. A few congratulated me. Others thought I caved in prematurely. I didn't resign when my manager had asked me to, I resigned when I couldn't take any more of the environment he created in the office. I viewed my walking away from that position as something I had to do to breathe easier. The people in that office had the intention and potential to make my days miserable. That's not a paranoid suspicion; they informed me of their intentions.

I tell people all the time to speak positively into themselves and their lives, yet there I was diminishing myself into a role I was far too big for.

I decided to take some of my own advice. I told myself repeatedly, *My name is LaShawnda Demetrius Jones. I am a child of God and I will fear no man. This job does not define me. I was provided for before this and I will be provided for after.*

I can't tell you how much that affirmation straightened my spine and lifted my head. Power. It's inside all of us. Sometimes it's latent or ebbing, other times it's roaring and bursting from us. I tried to subdue myself by turning mine off. Or rather, I thought I had turned it off while attempting to conform to Mean Jack's idea and expectation of who I should be as an employee. Despite the effort I put forth to dim my light, I apparently couldn't hide it. Jack and his minions saw it. They attacked it by trying to feed me fear – in this case, fear for my job and livelihood. Threats were levied on a regular basis and mini-conspiracies were created for the smallest issue. Fear doesn't taste good, nor does it wear well.

Staying in that environment was detrimental to my development. My spirit was constantly under attack. Working for Mean Jack was my first full-time permanent employment in New York City. I was hired after six months of spotty short-term work around the city, so I truly resisted quitting my job. Even when Mean Jack and his Number Two asked explicitly for my resignation, I said *no*. I had no intention of giving up my job and thereby my income. I wanted to hold onto the financial security that job represented to me. However, eventually I began to feel as if I was questioning my faith by holding on so stubbornly. Or rather, I began to feel as if I had more faith in a job than I did in my God's promises. New York is a hard city to survive and thrive in, everyone knows that, but I can do anything through Christ, who strengthens me! It wasn't my job keeping me afloat in New York City, it was my dependence on my Heavenly Father to provide for me, to protect me and to make all my trials work to my benefit. I kept telling myself, *I have not been brought this far to amount to nothing. I will accomplish what I am meant to accomplish. I'm still building and my foundation is becoming solid. God will complete the work He began in me!*

So, I tossed in my hand and got up from the table. Mean Jack and his minions were not my fight.

You never count your money when you're sittin' at the table.
There'll be time enough for countin' when the dealing's done.

Sometimes, I find myself resting in a hand. Tallying up my costs and experiences, then projecting their effects and consequences on my life. Often, I have to remind myself the game is not over. The race is not done. Sure, I need to keep track, mentally, but I don't need to tally as if I am going home just yet. Richard Bach's words come to mind during these low times: "Here is a test to find out whether your mission in life is complete. If you're alive, it isn't."

There it is. Mean Jack's rejection of me was taken personally. I lost confidence in my professional prowess and value as an employee. However, the rejection did not retire me. I'm still here; with experience to grow on!

Meditation Verse: Philippians 1:3-7

I thank my God upon every remembrance of you, always in every prayer of mine making request for you all with joy, for your fellowship in the gospel from the first day until now, being confident of this very thing, that He who has begun a good work in you will complete *it* until the day of Jesus Christ; just as it is right for me to think this of you all, because I have you in my heart, inasmuch as both in my chains and in the defense and confirmation of the gospel, you all are partakers with me of grace.

They Say I'm Lucky...

They say I'm lucky.... Those were the first words I shared with Mrs. Fogarty when I walked into her bed and breakfast on Saranac Lake in upstate New York. Last fall I took a breather from the city and headed to the Adirondacks. I was seeking peace and beauty and luckily for me, New York State has an abundance of natural beauty on display. My plan was to see the fall foliage decorating the mountains and reflecting off of lakes. Though I arrived at the bed and breakfast hours later than expected, Mrs. Fogarty stayed up to guide me to her door step via the phone after a wrong turn in the pitch black mountain night.

As she welcomed me into her home, she took my coat and told me to sit and rest as she proceeded to ask about the travails of my travel. After I shared my aggravations, she looked at me with wide eyes and said, "You're more than lucky! You must have multiple angels instructing others on how to help you."

I smiled. "That too."

"No, really! You shouldn't even be here. You were lucky just to get the car rental."

"Yeah, that's what the girl at the counter kept saying." This turned out to be very true.

That weekend was the first time I had rented a car in New York. I won't even begin to itemize all the trouble I had with getting a car to drive. I've been renting cars for over a decade all over the country. I have a frequent renter account with the company I rent from on most of my trips. This was the company I made my reservation with. They refused to give me a car because in New York, they only rent to people who place a credit card on file. I haven't had a major credit card since college. That's when most of my bad financial habits got their start. I've never had problems doing, going or getting anything or anywhere with my Visa Check Card. Never. So, after going back and forth with the car rental agency and their three alternative suggestions to get around their rule, I started asking the other car agencies, at the small regional airport I traveled to pick up the car, for a rental. One was out of cars. One required me to be traveling in and out of the airport. A woman at the third rental agency said she just needed to see an itinerary (flight or train) in order to rent me a car.

This is where my weekend mantra of *"Don't cry, don't cry, don't cry"* came in. I didn't realize how frustrated I was in general and how much I truly needed to get out of the city until being denied a rental car brought me to tears! I'm telling you, I've had much more difficult moments in life than that....

For some reason I had decided to buy a one-way train ticket for the twenty-minute ride from Harlem (in Manhattan) to White Plains (north of the City) to pick up the rental car at Westchester County Airport. There was no train itinerary to show because Metro North is a commuter rail. The car rental agent suggested I go to one of the airline ticket counters and ask for an itinerary. I thought it was prudent to point out I had only traveled from the city via Metro North, a commuter rail. She assured me they would be able to help.

The ladies at the airline ticket counter looked at me like I was crazy. "Are you flying?"

"No, I just need an itinerary. The lady over there said you'd be able to help."

"No. We can't just print you an itinerary....."

I walked away to go sit on a window sill and think about my next steps. I would be charged for the bed and breakfast if I didn't show because they would not be able to re-book. I had a day off work to get away and relax. I decided I was not going home to sit in my apartment for the weekend. I called Trailways to see if they had a bus up to Saranac Lake. Next bus was Sunday at 8:25AM. It was Saturday, 1:00PM. I called Amtrak to see if there was a train to the "neighborhood" of the lake I wanted to get to. Nothing even close. I hadn't realized I had picked such a remote location. Then I remembered I was at a regional airport. I went back to the ticket counter. "Do you all have any flights to Saranac Lake?"

"Sara-what?" She had never heard of it, but looked it up. None of the airlines at Westchester County Airport went to Saranac Lake. "What exactly are you trying to do?" The same lady who had looked at me like I was crazy earlier asked me.

"I'm trying to get away for a 'relaxing' weekend,'" said with air quotes. Then choking up, "But this is more stressful than I need right now."

"So, you were trying to rent a car?"

"Yes."

"What did they say you need?"

"An itinerary. But I got here on Metro North. They don't give itineraries. It's just a ticket and the conductor took the ticket."

"I'm not telling you this, but call our reservations number. Book a flight; tell them you'll ticket at the counter and I'll print you an itinerary."

"Really?"

"Yes, but you didn't hear this from me." I did as I was told. Booked a flight to Boston, returning on Tuesday. She did as she said she would and printed that itinerary. The car rental agent accepted the itinerary and gave me a car for the weekend. The young woman there told me, in future, I should call her directly for my rentals. It's laid out clean and easy for you here, but all the back and forth took about two-and- a-half hours.

Fast forward to Monday morning, I checked my checking account to make sure everything was in order for my trip back and found out my account had been drained into multiple negative numbers since before the weekend. ConEdison (gas/electric company) had debited my account many times what was due them and every transaction I made since Friday received an insufficient funds fee of thirty-five dollars. I almost fainted when I looked at my negative balance. Saranac Lake was a five-and-a-half hour drive away from Westchester County Airport; I had only a tank of gas, no cash, and no access to cash. Long story short, I was on the phone with my bank and ConEdison for over an hour trying to get that transaction reversed and the fees removed.

ConEdison customer service representatives are notoriously rude, but I'm telling you, by the end of my sad, whimpering and somewhat incoherent call, they were assuring me everything would be alright. "Ms. Jones, don't worry. We'll straighten this out for you! Everything will be clear in three to five business days."

"I need to go home today! It wouldn't be an issue if I was home. But I'm up in the mountains trying to get home and pay for my stay at a B&B and my car rental. This is horrible."

Because of the way ConEdison took out the money, they had to reverse the transaction. My bank claimed they couldn't do anything in regards to reversing all the fees until ConEdison corrected their mistake over the next few business days. Again, I tell you, three to four phone calls and multiple departmental transfers later, I had enough money showing positive on my account to withdraw funds from an ATM for lunch and tolls.

Halfway through my return drive down state, I had calmed down enough to chuckle at my situation. I must say, I was in some awe myself!

I skipped a part of my three-day weekend: I drove up to Montréal, Quebec on the second day. The afternoon in Montreal was by far the highlight of the trip.

I thanked God for all he does for me the moment I realized that from Friday on I had no available funds in my account (mind you, everything was fine on Thursday when I checked). Unbeknownst to me, my account was showing negative when I went through the hassle of renting the car. It was empty when I checked into the B&B Saturday evening. I was completely and blessedly oblivious to my lack of available cash when I crossed the Canadian border to go shopping in Montréal Sunday afternoon. Had no idea, as I spent my last twenty dollar bill on the worst dinner I've had in ages Sunday night, I would regret spending that bill in more ways than one.

Rhetorical question: How many of your things work when they're technically broken?

Wow, You are Awesome, Father!

There was never any doubt that I was going to have my weekend away. My focus was on *what do I have to do to get it?* What I learned from the weekend is I will receive those things I want, but they won't come without some aggravations (tests). No matter how uncertain things may appear, I'm not in charge of the outcome. My God is driving and He is going to get me to where He wants me to be when He wants me there.

So, yes, I let a few tears slip out. They weren't tears of worry that things would not work out, but tears of frustration that I couldn't have a smooth ride. Even a simple weekend away became a trial.

One of the biggest lessons I have learned over the last few years, a lesson that has changed the way I look at my past and live my present is: an easy life is not worth living. Romans 5:3-4 says *we glory in tribulations, knowing those tribulations produce perseverance and our perseverance produces character.* Reading that verse was a turning point for me. I struggled through my twenties hoping and expecting difficult times to morph into carefree ease. In my opinion, a life such as mine was due a comfortable respite here on Earth. I thought an easy life equaled a good life. I'm glad I've learned differently. If there are no detours or hardships on the road, what have you really learned on your journey? It has come to me in fragments, but I finally understand the devastation and troubles that have rocked my life could have destroyed me, but instead my Father used them to edify me. I've learned to appreciate the woman He is building. The process is painful, but more than worthwhile.

During my drive downstate, my last trip to London started looping through my mind. I had planned to stay four to five days in London a couple of winters ago. The purpose of the trip was to meet a plus-size fashion designer who had promised clothes for a *VoLux Full-Figured Calendar* photo shoot. The outcome: I never met the designer and had to return home early.

The sequence of events was something like this: Day 1 – Land in London, check into hostel, walk around neighborhood, stop to eat, reach for wallet to pay for food, realize wallet is gone.

Yeah, the first few hours in London I lost my wallet. I retraced my steps as I had just stopped in a music store and bought Corinne Bailey Rae's CD. No luck. I had just enough British pounds on me to pay for my meal. Literally, I think I got like five pence back from the bill. I didn't panic immediately. I walked back to my room to think about next steps. I had prepaid the hostel bill for the full stay. I called my bank to cancel my card. I am not a fan of cash, I use my check card for everything, but when I leave the country I pack money in both currencies for emergencies. My plan was to make withdrawals via ATM as needed for local currency. I try to be a savvy traveler. I also keep my ID and passport separate. My wallet, which was more like a card pouch, had my driver's license, work ID, metro pass, check card and all my emergency cash (US and British).

What would you do? I arrived on a Saturday; my appointment with the designer was on Monday. I decided to stay till Monday and leave after the appointment.

I went to the front desk, explained my situation and asked if I could have a cash refund for my last three days. Mind you, I was staying in a youth hostel, so it wasn't like I could be fancy free with the cash refund. They agreed and immediately refunded me. I spent the rest of the day and all day Sunday being a tourist. I visited Kensington Palace, Piccadilly Circus and St. Paul's Cathedral. On Monday I tried to meet up with the designer, but her assistant was not the best with directions. Their address was extremely difficult to find. The bus driver hadn't heard of the street. I tried a taxi, no luck. I walked into a real estate agency and they put the address into their system and came up with nothing. I called the office via pay phone at about which time it began to pour cold, stinging rain. I had no umbrella and was dragging my luggage with me. Naming streets, buildings, landmarks, subway stations – none of that helped the assistant help me find them. After an hour and a half of walking around (this after getting off the bus *in* the neighborhood) asking various shop owners and locals for directions to this street or address, I gave up and hopped on the closest train to the airport.

The airline ticket agent refused to waive my ticket change fee, for my early return, until I filed a police report for my lost wallet. The agent's questions were as suspicious-sounding as customs, but she soon directed me to the airport's police desk, where I filed the required report. Upon returning to the ticket counter, I received my updated ticket and was put on the next flight to New York City.

Dianna was staying with me during that time. When I shared the details of my troubled trip, she burst into riotous laughter. It stung painfully. I repeatedly told her I saw nothing funny about my situation. It was a wasted trip; I didn't achieve my goal, not to mention being financially stranded in a foreign country with no one to call for assistance (not even her and she was living in my apartment). When she finally caught her breath, she said, "Jones, can't you see how ridiculously funny this is? You're the only person I know who can leave the country, lose her wallet on the first day, chill for a couple of days and come back with cash in her pocket!"

I had about $16 left over from the London hostel refund when I walked into my apartment. I admitted I didn't know anyone with a story like mine either.

I had $2 left over from my weekend in Saranac Lake after three hundred miles, lunch and tolls. Anyone else thinking fish and masses here? God provides. It may not be what you think you want or when you think you need it, but if you rely on the Lord to get you through your days, He'll carry you through your troubles too.

Meditation Verse: Romans 5:1-5

Therefore, having been justified by faith, we have peace with God through our Lord Jesus Christ, through whom also we have access by faith into this grace in which we stand, and rejoice in hope of the glory of God. Not only *that,* but we also glory in tribulations, knowing that tribulation produces perseverance; and perseverance, character; and character, hope. Now hope does not disappoint, because the love of God has been poured out in our hearts by the Holy Spirit who was given to us.

Forged in Adversity

Nothing easy
No simplicity
Known only strife
Wouldn't know how
To enjoy a walk in the park
Could never accept
A free lunch
Reciprocated love
Saddest joke
Family loyalty
Bestselling fiction

As difficult as it's been
I feel strain from an
Upward climb
No longer descending
This vast valley
Is turning
I feel it
Debilitating hope
Soon to be rewarded
At some point
All this adversity
Will be a boon
And a blessing

Every Day is a Big Deal

Within six months of joining a church in Harlem, I signed up for a baptismal ceremony. It was important to me as an outward commitment to my renewed biblical study and spiritual growth. I had been baptized in my youth and remembered the experience well. It's my belief that God has held me all these years because of my acceptance of Him as a child. My faith and commitment to the Word of God is in my heart and expressed by the way I treat others and live my life.

I was surprised by three friends who were offended I didn't invite them to my baptism. They claimed I should have informed them in enough time to allow them to make travel arrangements. It didn't cross my mind that any of them would have been interested in attending, let alone travel for the event. It was just another day in my life.

I told one friend the day before and another right after the ceremony. Sure, I would have loved having friends and family there taking pictures, meeting the church folk I spent so much time with that year, but that was not the reality of my day-to-day. My daily reality is: I live alone, act alone, and travel alone. I make decisions by myself. I hurt by myself. I heal by myself. I'm a solitary person thinking and planning from a solitary point of view. If these same people have little interest in sharing a regular day with me, why would I assume they would put themselves out to share a not-so-regular day with me?

I've asked for help with various things in my life on many occasions. Help on things that didn't require much effort at all and certainly no travel; just a little of their attention and time. I've asked for their presence just to talk and hang out. Rarely have people followed through. If you won't spend five minutes to an hour on a request from the comfort of your home, why would I think you would be willing to travel five hours for a one-minute ceremony?

My friends and family have become part of my week- to-week and my month-to-month. They are part of my landscape, but not necessarily part of my details. I am lonelier for that. I truly desire relationships I have a daily stake in. I want nothing more on Earth than a companion to share my details with. For many years, my friends were satisfactory companions, but their lives progressed to other stages. They've joined with their life partners and started building their lives as wives and mothers. I've noticed over the past few years that I've put more energy into sharing in my friends' lives than anyone has put into sharing in my life. I've come to appreciate reciprocity because I haven't really experienced it. I can spend days on end talking to friends, helping them with something in their home, playing with their children, sharing meals at their table, but at the end of the day I return to a dark, quiet apartment that doesn't hold similar experiences or memories. I commit to the day-to-day requests and the special occasions when able. My commitment to putting time into my relationships is a declaration of how important the individual is to me.

My friend Nadine insisted she would have flown the four hours from Phoenix for the baptism. I sort of felt bad hearing her insistence when I spoke to her after the ceremony. The conversation wasn't even about the baptism. Nadine called while I was grocery shopping after church, she asked about the service and the rest of my afternoon. I told her about the sermon and, as an after-thought, mentioned the baptism that took place after the service. She insisted my baptism was a big deal and I should have included the people in my life. "People love you. We want to be there for you during big events like this. Getting baptized is a big deal."

"Every day is a big deal." I replied. "This was just another event in my life that I went through alone. There's no one here at the end of a bad day or a good day. There's no one here when I start a new job or when I'm looking for one. There's no one here to show a great purchase to. Or just to talk to. Why would I think someone would want to be here for my baptism? It was just another day." I really don't understand the thinking that elevates one day above another.

These three girlfriends are probably as close to constants as I have. They know where I come from; they know how my experiences have shaped me and what I look forward to in my future. On average, I talk to each of them two to four times per week. I don't see them often; they live in different corners of the country, but nothing really happens in our lives without analysis and discussion. We talk about everything, but rarely show up for anything. That was my defense as they each reamed me and basically ganged up on me on different phone calls.

I held my ground: every day *is* a big deal. I told them about the baptism because it was part of my week; I discussed it like I talk about any other activity. They each in turn expressed concern about becoming informed about future life events in such a nonchalant manner.

They don't know each other, but the three of them vehemently set me straight on one issue: I better notify them in advance about my wedding. "Don't make the mistake of thinking your wedding is just another day. Too many people have invested in your life. We deserve to have notice and choice on participating in such events." I hadn't looked at it in such a way. Andrea added a threat, "You keep on letting big events go by in your life without anyone knowing. Well, I'm letting you know, me and a few other of your friends will come by and beat your butt if you get married without telling us!" I was shocked; my friends don't threaten bodily harm! Besides, she barely reaches my shoulder. I thought the comment was funny enough to share with the other two and they both wanted to know what I was laughing at. "She can take your knees; we'll take care of the rest."

Those were interesting exchanges. I was made aware of how emotionally disconnected I had become, even with my closest friends. Living alone apparently does that to you. It narrows your perspective until you can only focus on you – your needs, your wants, your hurts and what would benefit you. It becomes more difficult to automatically think of other peoples' preferences before your own. I am not the only one guilty of this narrow, selfish perspective. My friends tell me they love me because of how I make them feel and because I'm a good friend to them. I can't say the same about all of my friends. I love them because my heart was open and they entered. Some have pulled away. Others have stayed to build relationships that have helped us through difficult days. The early development that built lasting relationships wouldn't have happened had my friends waited for the *special occasion* to show up and be present in my life. I would love for someone to show up for no other reason than to visit with me. It would be nice if people were present for events I think are important and not just those they think are worthy of their time. That was my point to my friends: every day is not extraordinary, but that doesn't make ordinary days less important.

Meditation Verse: Romans 14:5, 7-8

One person esteems *one* day above another; another esteems every day *alike*. Let each be fully convinced in his own mind.

For none of us lives to himself, and no one dies to himself. For if we live, we live to the Lord; and if we die, we die to the Lord. Therefore, whether we live or die, we are the Lord's.

Next of Kin

My phone rang early on Friday, July 13, 2007. I have been leery of early morning phone calls since I received the one informing me of my mom's death on a dark August morning in 1996. However, I had just quit my job the week prior and rushed to the phone expecting to exuberantly say *yes* to a job offer.

When my cousin Ebby's choked, sobbing voice hit my ears with, "Shawnda, I need you to sit down," I immediately thought of my ailing grandmother who had been sick for a number of years. "Is it Grandma?" I thought I would be ready for that. Honestly, I thought I could hear that.

"No, it's not Grandma. I need you to sit down." I sat.

"I'm sitting...."

"It's Antoine." He's my younger brother by sixteen months. He was thirty years old.

Somewhere in her tearful onslaught of words, she told me my brother was dead. I heard, "He was at a club... he fell... his head landed on a piece of glass... and he lost a lot of blood...." I told her I couldn't listen to her anymore. I was crying... on my knees, bent over. Sobbing. I wasn't ready to hear that. I couldn't accept that. I hung up to dial Bertha, his long-term live-in. The mother of his two daughters. My phone lit up with her incoming call while I was searching for her number. Her voice was broken, too – this big, solid woman who had told my brother repeatedly that she didn't need him – was crying in my ear.

All she managed to say was, "Shawnda..." All I could say was, "Tell me he's okay, Bertha! Just tell me he's okay...." She couldn't tell me anything. She passed the phone to her mother who struggled to tell me my brother had just died in a hospital in Gary, Indiana. They were calling me for permission to identify his body.

I was bewildered by the request. "Can't Bertha do it?" Silence. Then slowly realization dawned, "Oh, my God, she has no legal rights."

Bertha and Antoine had been an item since grade school. Their relationship has always been very tumultuous. I never got involved in their many breakups because I knew they would always get back together. They've been joking about marriage after all these years and two children together (Bertha has a total of three), but no real plans. They were the constants in each other's lives and I thought it must have been a painful knock for her to not be able to take care of his final needs. She learned in a harsh, abrupt manner that a shared life and children do not make a marriage. The State of Indiana does not recognize common law relationships. Bertha had no legal standing in my brother's life on the day he died, even though she was the woman he chose to spend his living days with.

I didn't realize until the end of that conversation that I was the legal next of kin – his children were far too young to make the decisions that needed to be made.

I had awakened that morning with a prayer on my lips. I prayed for my sister – she was living a wild life, and no one had heard from her in a while. Then I prayed for a friend who was on the verge of falling into a pit of her own digging. I couldn't help thinking I prayed for the wrong people – my overwhelming concern upon waking was not for the right person. I wasn't ready to hear that news....

Meditation Verse: 1 Thessalonians 4:13-18

But I do not want you to be ignorant, brethren, concerning those who have fallen asleep, lest you sorrow as others who have no hope. For if we believe that Jesus died and rose again, even so God will bring with Him those who sleep in Jesus.

For this we say to you by the word of the Lord, that we who are alive and remain until the coming of the Lord will by no means precede those who are asleep. For the Lord Himself will descend from heaven with a shout, with the voice of an archangel, and with the trumpet of God. And the dead in Christ will rise first. Then we who are alive and remain shall be caught up together with them in the clouds to meet the Lord in the air. And thus we shall always be with the Lord. Therefore comfort one another with these words.

One Second

Afternoon rush is ten minutes away.
It is Tuesday. 11:10 AM
And five seconds. Crew is rushing around.
A customer slumps over in lobby –
Near death or dead, with no one aware.
Afternoon rush is nine minutes away.
Someone walks past the collapsed man and sounds
The alarm, figuratively speaking.
Someone dials 9-1-1, quietly, so
Other customers aren't inconvenienced.
Here one second; gone the next. Life goes on;
The dead pass, the living stay – no pause, no
Interruption in anyone's day. No
Moment of silence; no closing of the
Doors to grieve the ultimate loss of a
Customer. The crew continued to rush;
The managers got on with their business.
The customers still swamped in line putting
In their orders, ignoring the man
Being wheeled away by the paramedics.
Ignoring the power Death has to pull
Someone, in a split second, from this world
To the next. Disrespectful, completely,
Of that power. "He must've eaten here,"
One customer joked. I guess it doesn't
Matter if you die alone or in a
Crowd – your passing is barely a nano-
Second in history's time line. Few will
Mourn a stranger. Why? What is the purpose?
Ignore it, some think, in silence, let the
Dead lie, so the living don't have to grieve
In public. The world stops for nobody.
Mourn at home – if you have the time. Or don't.

Who U Wit?

Sometimes I forget how big my family is because I have always been such a solitary figure within it. During my brothers' wake and funeral service, I met relatives I don't even recall meeting at other funerals. I heard stories about my mom's youth that were entertaining but hard to believe. It appeared my brother stayed connected. Or maybe everyone showed up to support Peewee and grandparents. Either way, my brother brought together an eclectic mix of family branches and generations.

My people, being themselves, create enough drama to entertain anyone for quite a while. But, I'll keep it brief....

Say What!

Good ole Peewee chose my brother's funeral as the time to introduce his new wife to everyone. I met her the morning of my brother's wake – three weeks before my thirty-second birthday. I'm the oldest of my mother's children. Kim, the youngest, was twenty-eight. Peewee's new wife was twenty-five years old *and* she had a three-year-old daughter. If that's not enough to make you say "What the heck," she also shares the same first name as my mother. Believe me when I tell you, every family member turned their backs on her and Peewee upon introduction. His mom, my mom's mom, his siblings, my mom's siblings... I've never seen my family unite like that! His people were still talking to him but only while she sat in the car waiting! She was not well received at all.

So the joke all day during the wake was, "Where's your stepmom?" Asked with smirks and choked laughter.

At first I was truly confused, "I don't have a stepmom". Then, after a while, I looked around and asked, "You talkin' t'me?" When everyone stopped falling over themselves laughing I replied, depending on the person, "Oh, you mean your cousin's wife! Your brother's wife! Your momma's son's wife." To which they all replied, "No, we mean yo' daddy's wife!"

Whatever! Nothing was right about that situation. Most definitely not the fact that Peewee was living with a female child again. His wife was aware of his history. I refused to support that union.

Baby Mama Drama

My sister is an instigator. She showed up and showed out. Yet still, we all pamper her because we're so happy to see her. We all have hope she will soon get her life together and take better care of herself.

Kim and I were looking through the guest registry at the funeral home during the wake and she noticed a lot of women's names. We were both impressed with all the people who showed up – the book was pretty full by the end of the day. Kim made a joke about most of those unknown women being my brother's wannabe baby mamas. Bertha, his girlfriend of over sixteen years and the only baby mama I know about, had just walked past. I slanted a look at Kim, "Don't start nothing."

Kim has never listened well. Not too long after, I walked through the chapel and saw Kim, Ebby, Bertha, and a couple of her female relatives sitting in the back pews shooting the breeze. Kim was talking about her first love, Bertha's cousin Harold, who she first hooked up with when she was twelve. Yes, my sister has always been fast. Apparently, Antoine and Bertha met because Antoine was following Kim around in an attempt to stop her from becoming a "ho" (his and her word). So, Kim is telling this story and says, "Yeah, Bertha, I'm still waiting for Harold."

"Where is he?" I asked.

Everyone looked at me like I was Boo Boo, you know, the fool. It came to me, slowly, "Oh, he's still in jail!" Kim goes back to reminiscing. "He has this many more years," holding up fingers on two hands. She sighed and lounged back on the pew. "He took my virginity."

Bertha's aunt was shocked; hopefully she wasn't Harold's mother! "What? You want it back?"

I broke in, "From the sound of it, she wants to give it to him again."

Kim sticks out her belly and says, "Yeah, wouldn't that be nice...." *And here we go....* "Bertha, how many baby mamas you think Twon has up in here?"

I almost fell out. Everyone around us got real quiet. Think of the scene in *The Color Purple* where Sophia and Harpo are dancing in the juke joint and Squeak breaks in, tapping Sophia on the shoulder. Squeak haughtily says, "I wanna dance wit my man!" All Sophia said was, "Fine by me." She was ready to turn and leave the floor. But Harpo grabbed her close and said no, he wanted to dance. So, Squeak took out her frustration on Sophia by slapping her and saying, "You ain't nothin' but a big fat heifer. *Ha, ha, ha, ha....*" The next screen shot, right before Squeak got punched clear across the room was of the piano player slamming his piano top close, getting up and saying, "Time t'go!" Bertha is Sophia, only much, much larger. Everyone else was the piano player – we were all looking for an exit. And of course, my trouble-making sister cast herself as Squeak.

Bertha looked Kim straight in the eye and said, "I was wondering the same thing. I've been waiting for someone to get up there and cry all over him."

I calmly spoke in what I hoped was a voice of reason, "Bertha, there are no other baby mamas."

She mentioned someone from Milwaukee with a child about nine years old. That was the first I'd heard that. I discounted it. Someone else said, "Well, if the child is nine, that was before you." Bertha's oldest by my brother was eight, but she had a twelve-year-old who was conceived during one of their break-up periods. Bertha replied with scorn, "No one was before me." Which is true; she was his first girlfriend. All I could do was shoot darts from my eyes at Kim, "I told you not to start nothin'!"

Just as I said that, two young women walked in, took one look at our group, i.e. Bertha, turned on their heels and walked right back out. They didn't even sign the registry.

 Meditation Verse: Proverbs 9:13-18

A foolish woman is clamorous; she *is* simple, and knows nothing. For she sits at the door of her house, on a seat *by* the highest places of the city, to call to those who pass by, who go straight on their way: "Whoever *is* simple, let him turn in here"; and *as for* him who lacks understanding, she says to him, "Stolen water is sweet, and bread *eaten* in secret is pleasant." But he does not know that the dead *are* there, that her guests *are* in the depths of hell.

Some Things About Funerals

Good

Funerals bring families together in proximity. Sometimes such proximity can be stressful, but I'm thinking about the positives right now.

During the few days I spent home in Gary that week, I focused as much energy as possible on my young cousins – some of whom have their own families. I remember my cousins' birth announcements and the excitement of holding them as babies, toddlers and young children. The growth of new generations keeps you from focusing too long on death – I wanted to pay attention to life. *Thank you, Father, for allowing me to do so!*

I have a trademark hug that usually involves a swing or repeated tosses in the air (depending on child size). Well, the youngest of my uncle's children are in their early teens. The last few times I saw them, they were climbing all over me and swinging from my neck. I was excited to see little Julian (age thirteen), because he had been MIA my last couple of trips. I hugged and squeezed him and then he asked me to swing him. I don't think I ever thought I'd get to the point where I wouldn't be able to pick one of them up. I cleared up some space and gave him a whirl or two. Then gave him my disclaimer: *Julian, I don't think I'll be able to lift you on my next visit.* I was winded! Shortly after that, little JJ (also age thirteen) came over for his hug and practically lifted me off my feet. That tickled me. I am wowed by the way time passes. One day I'm picking up babies, carrying toddlers on my hip and the next day I can't lift the kids and the teenagers are nearly picking me up.

Bad

When confronted with death, many become short tempered and short sighted. Fear and anger become accelerants. I was on fight alert the whole week. A break-out was so expected that the police commander I spoke with offered me a police presence for the wake and funeral. No one knew what to expect. My cousin Ebby wanted to give Peewee's wife an old-fashioned beat down because the wife successfully clocked our Uncle Vinny on the head with an iron in Ebby's house. So, on GP (general principle), Ebby felt she had to beat the girl down for disrespecting her uncle and her house. Ebby had just turned twenty-five, same age as the new wife. She also grew up with me more in the role of a big sister than a cousin and she still seeks my opinion and approval.

When she picked me up from the airport, she immediately started telling me what went down at her house. My sister Kim was in the car and said, "Ebby, I'm telling you, don't tell Shawnda!" Apparently everyone told Ebby not to tell me. Her mom and Vinny told her to just handle her business and tell me why it all went down later. They call me the Peace Maker – they don't really care for peace. Vinny later said (the biggest compliment of my life was intended as an insult), "Telling Shawnda something is like telling God. She's your conscious. She's not going to let you do anything wrong." My sister also offered her own form of high praise. After Ebby caught me up on the drama, I replied simply with, "Do you." (As in: do what you want to do.) Kim started jumping up and down in the back seat, "Oh! Oh! It's *onnnn*! You got the Don's approval!" I clarified by adding, "It's not my blessing or approval, just my statement that I'm not getting in the middle of anything. I'm here to focus on taking care of Antoine."

As much as my family has ostracized me over the years, during family trials they express a high opinion and expectation of me. They would have accepted me had I been more like them – had I chosen to travel the worst paths, living immorally and eagerly learning from parents, aunts, uncles and cousins how to do more dirt. However, I have always lived according to my conscience, my spirit. I made a lot of hard, lonely choices that didn't appear to do me any good at the time but in the long term have benefited me immensely. Each choice continues to be a building block for life. I am so glad I have been able to feed my spirit good, moral and clean things in the midst of a polluted environment.

Three of my uncles took me back to the airport. During the ride, we discussed two of my teenage female cousins. One was pregnant and thought she had to give up a full ride to Indiana State that fall. The other was having difficulty living with her mother and asked if she and her toddler could stay with me. I couldn't take her at the time, but told her maybe in a couple of years I'd be able to. So, my uncles and I were discussing their daughters and I shared what I would do in either situation. One uncle looked at me and said, "But Shawnda, you were blessed."

"Yes, I agree. I have been blessed with opportunities, but no more than the next person."

I can't say that I have always made the right choices, but I can see a positive progression in my life based on my decisions. I'm not living a dream life, but there is no place I would rather be right now. That says a lot, because I have been in places where I wanted to be anywhere but where I was.

Everyone feared Grandma Bessie was going to go Wild, Wild West on us. She threatened to go get a gun (she's currently restricted from owning a handgun in Gary) and take care of the person responsible for or suspected of my brother's death. It may sound funny, but she's restricted for a reason....

Everyone was watching everyone else, especially those with tempers. I'm always charged with watching Grandma Bessie because she's her calmest around me. I sat her next to Granddaddy and she was cool after that (they've been divorced for decades, but he's still the love of her life). So, it came as a shock to everyone, especially me, that I was the one whose anger exploded at the funeral.

Sad

Putting a loved one to rest is life altering for those left behind. Life is put into a different perspective. A lot of things just don't seem so important any more. I tend to focus more on the present when death comes around. When my mom died, I got rid of everything I owned and hit the road. I didn't want to be tied to anything on the land. When my brother died, I realized how much energy I had been putting into my hopes for my future – a prosperous business, comfortable home, loving husband, healthy children, overall joy and happiness. At that point only the occasional moment of joy and happiness were part of my life. I found myself guilty of not appreciating and enjoying my present in preference of working on a vision for my future. Today was all about work and laying the ground foundation, no time for gentle breezes and soft talk. I had to change that. I wanted today to be as much of a celebration of my singledom as tomorrow will be with my husband and children. I will only ever be who I am in this moment. The week of my brother's funeral, I said goodbye to a lot of things I wanted in a future I was not promised. Sometimes our hopes and wishes can be heavy baggage slowing us down. I did not let go of all my hopes, but I most certainly let go of thoughts that have borne no fruit.

With death, we are confronted with how truly fragile and temporary life is.

That week was also the first time I had seen my sister in nearly three years. She's been keeping herself from me, even though I have assured her I will love her always, no matter her circumstances. But her appearance depressed me a bit. She was not taking care of herself and it showed. She didn't look healthy or rested. It crossed my mind that here was a breathing person who had just let her life go. I wondered why she didn't reverse a choice at some point on her journey, "This isn't working for me, let me go back and try something else." It is never too late to rectify our situation. We are told, even in final judgment we will have to give an accounting of our lives.

Glad

Death is the final curtain call on this portion of our existence. When you see it up close and personal, you come away with resolutions – if you've been paying attention. Your life may get a little more organized and purpose filled. You rejoice in what you have – your life – because you're still here. You still have time to get your life in order. Please, use the time you have to get your life in order. Offer your life in service to God, your family, your community. Use your life as a conduit for love. Present yourself as a holy example of living. Honor the breath and spirit moving through your lungs.

Your life is the greatest gift and opportunity God has graced you with. Don't let it go. Don't give it up. Don't take it for granted. Don't destroy it. Bless it and rejoice in it!

Meditation Verse: Revelation 20:11-15

Then I saw a great white throne and Him who sat on it, from whose face the earth and the heaven fled away. And there was found no place for them. And I saw the dead, small and great, standing before God, and books were opened. And another book was opened, which is *the Book of Life*. And the dead were judged according to their works, by the things which were written in the books. The sea gave up the dead who were in it, and Death and Hades delivered up the dead who were in them. And they were judged, each one according to his works. Then Death and Hades were cast into the lake of fire. This is the second death. And anyone not found written in the Book of Life was cast into the lake of fire.

Best Things in Life

The best things in life are the gifts of *love, friendship, grace,* and *forgiveness.*

    The night of my thirty-second birthday was a humbling night, yet wonderfully surprising. I went to bed with a full heart. A heart overflowing with thanksgiving. I can't recall going to bed with such fullness before. I had the best birthday I've had in eleven years and it was through no effort of my own – I guess that's why it was so special. That month marked the eleventh anniversary of my mothers' death and my brother had just died the month before. I was set to be a wreck for the whole summer. Two of the three people who always celebrated my presence on this Earth were gone and I thought it would be the loneliest birthday ever. However, my friends pulled me through; they all helped save a wreck that day.

    My friend Jemini and her children were true godsends that bright August day. I don't know how her three-year-old twins kept the secret, but they all threw me a surprise birthday party. That was the best gift of the day – a celebration with people I love. It wasn't expected, I had actually hoped to spend my birthday weekend away with friends, but no one was interested. The last thing I wanted was to spend my birthday alone, but I resigned myself to another quiet weekend at home doing just that. Blessedly, I was remembered. It's affirming to have your existence acknowledged. Birthday wishes came via web comments, emails, texts, voicemails, phone calls and breakfast with my surrogate family - Jemini and her four little munchkins.

    I was overjoyed that I was able to spend the day with people who love me and whom I in return love immensely. The cherry on top of that was receiving a call from my sister and nieces. They rarely call and never return my calls. As a result, I went to bed that night not feeling like the emotional orphan I had come to believe I was, but satisfied and full with my blessings.

    Again, I say to you, the people in your life make all the difference.

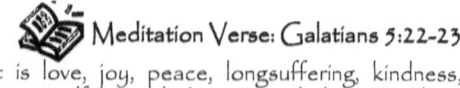

Meditation Verse: Galatians 5:22-23

But the fruit of the Spirit is love, joy, peace, longsuffering, kindness, goodness, faithfulness, gentleness, self-control. Against such there is no law.

Can I Love You?

In 2009, I realized I had been on a love-quest, searching hungrily for people to love. It was more difficult and labor-intensive than I anything in my life. Why? Because I tried to love everyone and everyone doesn't know how to accept love.

Meditation Verse: Mark 12:28-31

One of the teachers of the law came and heard them debating. Noticing that Jesus had given them a good answer, he asked him, "Of all the commandments, which is the most important?"

"The most important one" answered Jesus, "is this: 'Hear, O, Israel, the Lord our God, the Lord is one. Love the Lord your God with all your heart and with all your soul and with all your mind and with all your strength. The second is this: 'Love your neighbor as yourself.' There is no commandment greater than these."

The following passage, from *Beauty for Ashes* by Joyce Meyer, resonated with me because it illustrates behavioral traits I've observed in people who have rejected me and my habits of love. As I read, it struck me that I seem to search out and embrace people who reject others for fear of being rejected themselves.

Fear of Being Rejected Causes Rejection of Others

If you cannot believe that you are basically a lovable, valuable person, you will be unable to trust others who claim they love you. If you believe that you must be perfect to be worthy of love and acceptance, then you are a candidate for a miserable life, because you will never be perfect as long as you are in an earthly body.

You may have a perfect heart, in that your desire is to please God in all things, but your performance will not match your heart's desire until you get to Heaven. You can improve all the time and keep pressing toward the mark of perfection, but you will always need Jesus as long as you are here on this earth. There will never come a time when you will not need His forgiveness and His cleansing blood.

Unless you accept your value and worth by faith through Christ, you will always be insecure and unable to trust those who want to love you. People who have no capacity to trust suspect the motives of others. I know this is true because I had a real problem in this area. Even when other people told me they loved me, I was always waiting for them to hurt me, disappoint me, fail me, or abuse me. I just could not believe anyone would want me just for myself. There had to be some other reason!

I felt so bad about myself, was so full of shame, condemnation, self-hatred, and self-rejection, that whenever anyone tried to show me love and acceptance, I thought to myself, "Well, if this person likes me now, he won't when he gets to know the real me." Therefore I would not receive love from other people, or from God. I deflected it by my behavior, which became more and more obnoxious as I set out to prove to everyone that I was as unlovable as I believed myself to be.

> *Whatever you believe about yourself on the inside is what you will manifest on the outside. In my case, I believed that I was not lovable, so that is how I acted. I was very difficult to get along with. I believed that other people would eventually reject me, and so they usually did. Because my attitude was manifested in my actions, I could not sustain healthy, loving, lasting relationships.*

Reading that passage brought one question to mind, a question I imagine God asking me – asking us all: *Can I love you?*

I am a beggar. Are you?

Some people beg for love. Others beg for the opportunity to love in hope of reaping such devotion. I used to beg for love by offering love. Have you ever found yourself begging someone to let you love them? *Can I love you?* seems to be the common unspoken question in all my relationships. My way of loving is giving. Giving of myself, my time, and my resources. I open my heart, my home, my life to people. I focus on their needs, their comfort, and their situation. *Can I love you?* is the hidden question when I ask *What can I do for you? What will make your day better? What do you need in your life? Can I love you?* is what I'm asking when I open my ears and my heart to your troubles. When I embrace you in greeting and farewell. When I offer to fill a need you haven't even recognized yet.

Can I love you? sounds so pathetic, I think, when heard with ears not filtered by the Love of God. Some of my beggar years were painful because I didn't want to appear pathetic, I didn't want to appear needy. I didn't want to appear ridiculous begging someone to allow me to love them. Those shameful days of hiding my need to love are over. I'm open and unapologetic with my loving now. I'm okay if you don't want to receive it. I won't break down if you don't know how to reciprocate it. I no longer expect an answer to my question. Like any other beggar, I've learned that many will cross my path, a few will stop and make a deposit into my life, and some will pause to share a kind word. Others will glance my way while continuing on theirs, but throngs will never notice me at all. The life of a beggar is hard; it's thankless. But we still give thanks for each person we touch and double thanks for each person who reaches out to touch us back.

Can I love you? I want to love you. I want to share the light and grace God has blessed my life with. His love is so wonderfully magnificent I can't contain it. Neither can you. You can't hoard it. You can't wrap your mind or your heart around it. But you can channel it. You can pass it on. You can share it. You can give it. There are no requirements, no rules, no standards. You can bestow your gift of love on family, friends, neighbors, co-workers, strangers – anybody and everybody. That's the beauty of it - it multiplies with use. You lose nothing by living in love but you gain so much with each interaction.

Don't be too proud to beg – it'll do your spirit good!

Family and Friend Relationships

Words, Part One

I know I am well-loved
My mother swore she loved me
My brother and sister, they love me
My dad says he will always love me
Friends love me
Employers praise me
I know I am well-loved
But love does not have positive representation

My brother resents me
My sister deserted me
My dad molested me
My mother stood by my dad
All my friends make me feel disposable
Employers often mistreat me
Yet they all assure me, I am well-loved

They all may as well have hated me,
Despised me,
For their love has branded and maimed me

Now there's this man
Whom I want to share every moment with
And I do, in my thoughts
People tell me I am in love
I don't believe them
Love is too insignificant a word
It has no value for me
No consistency
No truth
Love is a false positive
So I sit here, searching for words
Wanting to put sound and form to these feelings
My longing, desire
Need to see him, touch him
Hear his voice, look into his eyes
My expectation to hold him
No, I don't love him
My feelings are deeper than that
He is well-respected,
Highly honored, profoundly favored
And still these words
Only scratch the surface
Of my feelings for this man

Defining Family and Friend

I could have avoided many hurts in my family and friend relationships if:
1. I would have simply understood the definition and word history of the words *family* and *friend*;
2. I had appreciated that very few people operate with the knowledge of definitions;
3. I had known that the impact and importance of a relationship is rarely seen until the relationship has been destroyed

That being said, nothing changed the way I operated within my relationships as much as learning that God is my friend. Had I known that from the beginning, I would not have put up with so much mistreatment from people who claimed to love me, yet didn't know the definition of love. God *is* love *(1 John 4:7)*. God *is* my friend *(John 15:14)*. If you don't love me like He does, I don't want what you call "love." If you aren't interested in being a friend like He is, I have to call you something else. I have begun the practice of loving others as God loves me and being a friend to them as He is a friend to me. I am not perfect, but I am working on perfecting my life walk lesson by lesson and relationship by relationship.

family
1. All the members of a household under one roof
2. A fundamental social group in society typically consisting of one or two parents and their children
3. Two or more people who share goals, values and have long-term commitments to one another

Word History – "servants of a household," (Latin); familia "household," including relatives and servants, from famulus "servant," of unknown origin. The modern sense of "those connected by blood" is first recorded in 1667.

friend
1. A person whom one knows, likes, and trusts; whom one is on good terms with
2. A person attached to another by feelings of affection or personal regard
3. A person who gives assistance

Word History – A friend is a lover, literally. The relationship between Latin amīcus "friend" and amō "I love" is clear, as is the relationship between Greek Jamesos "friend" and Jameseō "I love." In English, though, we have to go back a millennium before we see the verb related to "friend." At that time, frēond, the Old English word for "friend," was simply the present participle of the verb frēon, "to love." The Germanic root behind this verb is frī-, which meant "to like, love, be friendly to." Closely linked to these concepts is that of "peace," and in fact there is a German noun the root, frithu-, meaning exactly that.

relationship
1. An emotional or other connection between people
2. A state of connectedness between people
3. Connection between persons by blood or marriage

Based on the above definitions, I can say I am God's family, He is my friend and we are in an eternal relationship. With the Trinity, I have a faithful teacher in Jesus, a Holy Spirit who helps me and a Creator who deepens our connection with every word He speaks to me.

Meditation Verse: John 15:9-17

"As the Father loved Me, I also have loved you; abide in My love. If you keep My commandments, you will abide in My love, just as I have kept My Father's commandments and abide in His love.

"These things I have spoken to you, that My joy may remain in you, and *that* your joy may be full. This is My commandment, that you love one another as I have loved you. Greater love has no one than this, than to lay down one's life for his friends. You are My friends if you do whatever I command you. No longer do I call you servants, for a servant does not know what his master is doing; but I have called you friends, for all things that I heard from My Father I have made known to you. You did not choose Me, but I chose you and appointed you that you should go and bear fruit, and *that* your fruit should remain, that whatever you ask the Father in My name He may give you. These things I command you, that you love one another.

Covenant of Friendship

I pride myself on paying attention to life and looking for my lessons. Even before I began to study God's Word, I was aware He was working in my life through my connections with people. This *Family and Friend Relationships* section chronicles my most important lessons about friendship. The teachings were not provided all at once, they were spread out over many years and dispersed within many relationships.

Meditation Verse: Ecclesiastes 4:7-12

Two are better than one, because they have a good reward for their labor. For if they fall, one will lift up his companion. But woe to him who is alone when he falls, for he has no one to help him up. Again, if two lie down together, they will keep warm; but how can one be warm alone? Though one may be overpowered by another, two can withstand him. And a threefold cord is not quickly broken.

Trinity

1. Union of three persons (Father, Son, and Holy Spirit) in one Godhead, or the threefold personality of the one Divine Being.
2. A group consisting of three closely related members.
3. Any union of three in one; three units treated as one; three people considered as a unit

Your interpersonal relationships can be your personal Trinity - *Teacher, Helper and the Lord.* Jesus came to teach us the ways of God. When He left we were promised the Holy Spirit to comfort and help us. And God promised to never leave us nor forsake us. If our LORD God is the central figure in our interpersonal relationships, primarily friendships, then we are members of a trinity. At any given point within the life of a friendship we are either a *Teacher* or a *Helper* and God is there between us.

Covenant

1. The agreement between God and the ancient Israelites, in which God promised to protect them if they kept His law and were faithful to Him.
2. An agreement, usually formal, between two or more persons to do or not do something specified.
3. A promise.

Friend is a covenant term. It's Biblical. Did you know that? I didn't know until I got deep into my study a couple of years ago. I have friends who have been telling me for years that I expect too much of them. They made me feel guilty for holding them to supposedly high standards and expectations. Or more correctly, I felt guilty until I learned God is my friend and Jesus taught to us as friends rather than servants. When I found that out, I realized my standards had always been far too low. I had been putting undeserving people on par with God when I called them *friend*.

Worldly Friends

I've always been popular with people, but I have rarely done the popular things. I have learned that people are attracted to my strong sense of self and my independent individualism. I am drawn to the same type of people. Meaning, I have always been myself by myself and I don't mind hanging out with you as yourself. I'm not interested in *LaShawnda Pleasers* or *Other People Pleasers*. I want to know the *you* who is true to your inner being.

I have called people "friend" who came around only when they needed me, but were hard to track down when I needed anything. There have been "friends" who offered assistance in anticipation of what would be done for them in return. I've learned that the term "friend" is used very loosely in today's society. People who appear "nice" and "kind" and perform a favor are almost immediately given the honor of being addressed as your friend. If we don't take the Trinity casually or fling promises around with no regard for our words, why are we so casual about calling undeserving people *friend*?

True friends do for one another because it pleases them to help their comrade.

Casual "friends" are only interested in good times, commonly known as *fun*. But friendship is not meant for amusement, it is meant to provide support. We are meant to be helpers to one another. That is not to say you cannot enjoy your friendships. Of course you can, but that is not the primary purpose of friendship. Support can be offered in many ways; it can be expressed in the physical, emotional and/or spiritual realms. Your relationship will determine what is needed and when.

When I first started my business, I had a "friend" who loaned me one thousand dollars. Initially, I felt blessed. I thought, "Wow! What a great friend!" But she wasn't really. She was foolish. She didn't believe in what I was doing and offered money as a way to avoid offering her time and energy. She wanted to *show* support, but she didn't want to *give* support. I would have much preferred to have her believe in me and my effort. She reinforced for me that your presence in someone's life is worth much more than your money. Had I known before she loaned me the money that she didn't believe in what I was doing, I would not have accepted her offering. True friendship is indeed its own reward.

Back to Basics

Blood is thicker than water is a phrase we misunderstand today. When I first heard my pastor correct the congregation's interpretation, I felt as if the true nature of all my relationships had been revealed to me. Rearrange your thoughts on this with me: the blood bond of the COVENANT is thicker and stronger than the water ties of the WOMB.

My relationship with those I am joined to in covenant has more value than my relationship with those I am connected to through the womb. If this is your first time hearing this, it may strike you as ridiculous. But think on it.... Jesus's blood washes us cleaner than any water. He was a blood sacrifice for our sins; baptismal water alone does not do for us what His blood does. Therefore, any covenant relationship we have is going to have a stronger bond than our family ties. If you are honest and review your relationships, you will see a definitive difference between your covenant relationships and family relationships. Covenant relationships are usually you and God, you and your friend, you and your spouse. Covenant relationships are greatly valued, require constant effort, and inspire a deep commitment. Faith, loyalty and love are also implicit. Our family relationships are usually filled with strife and covered with scars. That is not to say, however, that relatives cannot become covenant friends.

David and Jonathan's Example

Friendship, like love, can be one-sided. Also, like love, it's so much better when reciprocated. In *1 Samuel*, David becomes the champion of Israel much to the rage and jealousy of Israel's King Saul. Saul's son, Jonathan, befriended David and hid him from his father the king. Jonathan actually questioned his father about his desire to kill David and then went to inform David of his father's intentions. Before they parted from that meeting they made a covenant of friendship, promising not only to be friends for life but promising their descendents would be friends for eternity. They acknowledged God as witness to their covenant. That is powerful to me! I have friends, good friends and better friends but I haven't had one yet I would bind to my descendents for eternity.

Meditation Verse: 1 Samual 20:12-17, 42

Then Jonathan said to David: "The LORD God of Israel *is witness!* When I have sounded out my father sometime tomorrow, *or* the third *day,* and indeed *there is* good toward David, and I do not send to you and tell you, may the LORD do so and much more to Jonathan. But if it pleases my father *to do* you evil, then I will report it to you and send you away, that you may go in safety. And the LORD be with you as He has been with my father. And you shall not only show me the kindness of the LORD while I still live, that I may not die; but you shall not cut off your kindness from my house forever, no, not when the LORD has cut off every one of the enemies of David from the face of the earth."

So Jonathan made *a covenant* with the house of David, *saying,* "Let the LORD require *it* at the hand of David's enemies." Now Jonathan again caused David to vow, because he loved him; for he loved him as he loved his own soul.

Then Jonathan said to David, "Go in peace, since we have both sworn in the name of the LORD, saying, 'May the LORD be between you and me, and between your descendants and my descendants, forever.'" So he arose and departed, and Jonathan went into the city.

Levels of Teaching

Sometime during my twenty-something to thirty-something evolution I began to look at everything in my life as a lesson. Everyone who crossed my path became a potential teacher. More than ever, I began taking my self-representation very seriously and engaged in the process of pruning away certain influences within my environment. The below excerpt from Marianne Williamson's *A Return to Love* clarified quite a bit of grey area for me.

Teachers of God

"Therefore, the plan includes very specific contacts to be made for every teacher of God."

Relationships are assignments. They are part of a vast plan for our enlightenment, the Holy Spirit's blueprint by which each individual soul is led to greater awareness and expanded love. Relationships are the Holy Spirit's laboratories in which He brings together people who have the maximal opportunity for mutual growth. He appraises who can learn most from whom at any given time, and then assigns them to each other. Like a giant universal computer, He knows exactly what combination of energies, in exactly what context, would do the most to further God's plan for salvation. No meetings are accidental. "Those who are to meet will meet, because together they have the potential for a holy relationship."

The Course says that there are "three levels of teaching" in a relationship. The first level is what we think of as a casual encounter, such as two strangers meeting in an elevator or students who "happen" to walk home from school together. The second level is a "more sustained relationship, in which, for a time, two people enter into a fairly intense teaching-learning situation and then appear to separate." The third level of teaching is a relationship which, once formed, lasts all our lives. At this level, "each person is given a chosen learning partner who presents him with unlimited opportunities for learning."

Even at the first level of teaching, the people in the elevator might smile at one another or the students might become friends. It is mostly in casual encounters that we are given a chance to practice the fine art of chiseling away the hard edges of our personalities. Whatever personal weaknesses are evident in our casual interactions will inevitably appear magnified in more intense relationships. If we're crabby with the bank teller, it will be harder to be gentle with the people we love the most.

At the second level of teaching, people are brought together for more intense work. During their time together, they will go through whatever experiences provide them with their next lessons to be learned. When physical proximity no longer supports the highest level of teaching and learning between them, the assignment will call for physical separation. What then appears to be the end of the relationship however is not really an end. Relationships are eternal. They are of the mind, not the body, since people are energy, not physical substance. Bodies joining may or may not denote real joining, since joining is of the mind. People who have slept in the same bed for twenty-five years may not be truly joined, and people who are many miles apart may not be separate at all.

Often we see a couple who has separated or divorced and look with sadness at the "failure" of their relationship. But if both people learned what they were meant to learn, then that relationship was a success. Now it may be time for physical separation so that more can be learned in other ways. That not only means learning elsewhere, from other people; it also means learning the lessons of pure love that come from having to release the form of an existing relationship.

Third-level, life-long relationships, are generally few because "their existence implies that those involved have reached a stage simultaneously in which the teaching-learning balance is actually perfect." That doesn't mean, however, that we necessarily recognize our third level assignments; in fact, generally we don't. We may even feel hostility toward these particular people. Someone with whom we have a lifetime's worth of lessons to learn is someone whose presence in our lives forces us to grow. Sometimes it represents someone with whom we participate lovingly all our lives, and sometimes it represents someone who we experience as a thorn in our side for years, or even forever. Just because someone has a lot to teach us, doesn't mean we like them. People who have the most to teach us are often the ones who reflect back to us the limits to our own capacity to love, those who consciously or unconsciously challenge our fearful positions. They show us our walls. Our walls are our wounds – the places where we feel we can't love any more, can't connect any more deeply, can't forgive past a certain point. We are in each other's lives in order to help us see where we most need healing, and in order to help us heal.

During a conversation with my friend Sierra, I mentioned a man, Rakeem, whom I had recently met at a dinner party (*Man Friend Lessons, p. 217*). He impressed me with his conversation – a married man informing single women about their mistakes in relationships. Sierra's response was, "You always have really deep conversations wherever you go and with whomever you meet." Oddly, her comment gave me pause. In my mind, conversations are exchanges of ideas and perspectives. They're discussions about your life and experiences. When you're sharing, you should be receptive to what's coming back to you. The give and the take are equally important. The reverse of her comment implied people normally have meaningless conversations with people they meet. Perplexed, I replied, "I don't have much time for frivolous talk."

The autumn I moved to New York City, my friend Andrea came to visit me for Thanksgiving. I hadn't seen her in many months, if not a couple of years, so I didn't answer my phone much while she was visiting. She commented that she couldn't recall me ever answering my phone whenever she has been around. I replied calmly, "I hardly see you. I talk to people on the phone all the time." Meaning, if I picked up the phone at that moment while she was in front of me or later when she wasn't, the person on the other end of the phone was still going to be on the other end of the phone. Why shouldn't I honor the presence in front of me? I think that's what all my friends love about me; you can ask them. I like giving my attention to them fully. They know immediately when I'm distracted, have visitors or am not able to speak freely, because I have always made time for them whenever they call or visit. That's a life skill I actually learned from my first job – *Be here now!* I try to be fully present in everything I do.

Practicing this principle, I have benefited from many casual encounters, coming away with amazing insights, perspectives and messages. I have had meaningful exchanges with people I passed in crosswalks, sat next to on public transportation, chatted with on planes, shared elbow space with at receptions, and during many other such God-opportunities.

My poem *Priscilla on the 5* (p. 121) is about one such casual encounter on a Bronx subway platform (*Journal: Friday, January 13, 2006, p. 119*). I don't think that woman spoke one word that was her own. At that moment and even looking back, I believe God was speaking to me through her. I was in one of the deepest depressions of my life and that eternal five-minute conversation with the stranger Priscilla gave me hope to push through my darkness.

Most of my relationships are at the second level according, to Marianne Williamson's book. I had a crisis point a few years ago and felt I had to disconnect from many who were attached to me. I have grown a great deal over the past few years due to my separation. It's been a difficult growth process, but necessary for the work God is doing in my life. Today, I am okay with my journey being separate from others. I'm not interested in force companionship or mutual growth. I am, instead, focused on what I *need* to do for me and what I *can* do to help you along your road.

There are two third-level relationships that drained me nearly unconscious. I don't like either of the people and years ago did not have a nice thought regarding them. Over the years, I have gotten to a point where I not only pray for them, but can claim to love one of them and working on expressing love to the second. Getting to this point has released my dad's and his brother's hold on my energy in untold ways.

May you be willing to accept all God's blessings and love through the people he sends to sow into your life!

Meditation Verse: 2 Corinthians 2:14-17

Now thanks *be* to God who always leads us in triumph in Christ, and through us diffuses the fragrance of His knowledge in every place. For we are to God the fragrance of Christ among those who are being saved and among those who are perishing. To the one *we are* the aroma of death *leading* to death, and to the other the aroma of life *leading* to life. And who *is* sufficient for these things? For we are not, as so many, peddling the word of God; but as of sincerity, but as from God, we speak in the sight of God in Christ.

God of Good and Evil

A year after I moved to New York City, one of my social acquaintances from Milwaukee relocated to the Big Apple. Zoë said she was inspired by my move and my hardiness. She stayed with me for a week while she searched for a job and an apartment. Within four days she had both. I was impressed with her success in taking care of her needs so quickly. Though I was happy for her on one hand, on the other overwhelmingly heavy hand, her success incited a great deal of negative feelings in me for my apparent lack of success in the city.

Shortly after Zoë moved to New York, I had an unprecedented fit of jealousy, bitterness and frustration. I started dialing friends and got a hold of two, Andrea and Dianna. As soon as they picked up, I told them what I was in the grip of, "I'm a bitter bitch right now and I need to vent." My goal was to embrace all the negativity and push it out of myself.

They both listened raptly, as I had never described myself as either bitter or a bitch before. What started out as a jealous fit on the surface turned into a rail against God and my lot in life, because I was doing yet another thing I never do: comparing myself to someone else. When I measured my situation against Zoë's, I came up short and disadvantaged.

Andrea and I considered our friendship a spiritual relationship. She's Muslim and very strong in her faith. Everything we talk about from men, work, education, family, politics, etc. is tempered by what is right by God.

Dianna is a model I met when I modeled. We didn't hit it off until after we worked together. She was a friend who wanted to be a better friend to everyone she called friend. However, when I look back on our experiences together, I see a very cosmetic relationship. We were good when the surface looked good. Without fail, whenever I am around her, I feel guilty for putting more than two bites of food in my mouth. If we're working out and I finish before her, she calls me lazy. "Come on, Jones, we didn't come here to talk."

Don't get me wrong, I believe people are in our lives for different reasons; to fill different needs. I have come a long way with Andrea supporting and reaffirming my faith, values and morals. I have also come a long way with Dianna insisting I take better care of my body and my physical appearance. "It won't kill you to put on a little make-up, Jones."

When you get to a point of examining the things that really matter to you – like, trying to understand why something is happening, who you are, or what you are becoming – you may realize that even your friends aren't equipped to help. They aren't equipped to offer advice. They aren't even equipped to understand.

Several years ago, I watched a sermon by Dr. Myles Munroe. He had powerful, enlightening words that struck chords throughout my being. He spoke about the purpose of individuals. He pointed out how we all relate to purpose. We wonder what our purpose on Earth is. We question our purpose. We seek to fulfill our purpose. Then he said we are dealing with our purpose incorrectly. "No one but the Creator knows the purpose of the creation," he expostulated. He said we are too busy trying to define ourselves. We're too busy seeking validation and approval from others to fulfill this need we have.

Dr. Munroe's words came to mind after my girlfriend conversations. They had both given me unsatisfactory answers to the issue I called them about. Dianna focused on the surface jealousy and said that everything won't always be so difficult. Andrea also focused on the jealousy, but called it a spiritual battle I was losing. "That's not God," she told me. "That's you. Nothing that negative comes from God. You need to check yourself and see how all this is getting into you."

At those words, I stopped listening. I don't believe everything negative in my life is instigated by me and everything positive is of God. I believe *everything* derives from God – all things we consider to be good and evil. He delegates choice to us. We are able to decide how we deal with situations. We reap the consequences and rewards of our choices. My fit of jealousy and frustration came from watching people continuously progress in life while not necessarily being filled with neighborly love. They weren't bad people per se, but they weren't interested in the straight and narrow either. At the same time these others were progressing, I was consciously making good, moral decisions and working diligently on being the best person I could be. Yet my struggles never ceased, and there never appeared to be any ease in my life.

On the day I called my friends, I had seen just how easy and rosy some people's lives are and I didn't understand. I didn't want to understand either. I wanted just one thing to come easy to me. I wanted to lie in the sun without worrying about getting burned. I wanted to go shopping without worrying about bouncing a check; pay rent without foregoing three other bills.

Dianna told me, "Jones, go buy yourself something. A nice pair of shoes should do it. Maybe a pedicure…. It works for me when I'm down." And Andrea angrily snapped, "You're a better person for your struggles. Struggle builds character. You're able to stand on your own two feet. If everything was just handed to you, you wouldn't be half the woman you are now." None of that helped, their words only made me want to scream. It wasn't what I was looking for. Not what I needed.

My fit was short-lived. I can't say I had an epiphany and received the right answers. My feelings were resolved by me calling them what they were, confronting them and dealing with them. I didn't ask to feel the way I felt nor did I like feeling that way. But I chose to deal with it by talking it out of myself.

Around the time of this episode I had watched the PBS documentary *Kingdom of David*. I have heard the Bible stories all my life and seen re-enactments hundreds of times, in addition to reading a good portion for myself. However, there were two things that stood out for me during the first hour regarding the beginnings and endings of Moses and David. We all know Moses spent forty years in the desert. I had never concentrated on the fact that he never set foot into the promise land, Israel. He dedicated his life to getting his people there but never completed the trip himself. The story of David is one of a man highly favored by God who gained more in life than he had ever dreamed, yet the way he went about bedding and wedding Bathsheba darkened and damaged his legacy.

Both men were devout in their faith. They communicated with God and followed His instructions. They both reaped rewards from their diligent practice and follow-through as servants of God.

We're told Moses didn't get what he wanted here on Earth, but he got to meet God. Being King went to David's head and the choices he made later in life reaped enormous consequences. We're told God claimed responsibility for it all. You do this, I'll do that. You do that, you get this. So, yes, all the good things and bad things are God-given. We believe it in the Bible stories but don't want to believe it in our own lives. He doesn't punish just those who have done wrong, we all have our time and cycle of ups and downs. Rather we recognize the cycle for what it is or not. We may take the good times for granted and not be able to cope with the rough spots. We may be so used to adversity that we don't know how to enjoy the easy moments. We are all varying shades of skeptics, non-believers, true believers, realists, optimists and pessimists. There is some of everything in all of us. There comes a point in time when we need to accept that our understanding is not going to be complete. We have to accept who we are and recognize we have all been given the divine power of choice. With that, we can live our lives intuitively, fully, and completely.

Meditation Verse: Job 1:6-12

Now there was a day when the sons of God came to present themselves before the LORD, and Satan also came among them. And the LORD said to Satan, "From where do you come?"

So Satan answered the LORD and said, "From going to and fro on the earth, and from walking back and forth on it."

Then the LORD said to Satan, "Have you considered My servant Job, that *there is* none like him on the earth, a blameless and upright man, one who fears God and shuns evil?"

So Satan answered the LORD and said, "Does Job fear God for nothing? Have You not made a hedge around him, around his household, and around all that he has on every side? You have blessed the work of his hands, and his possessions have increased in the land. But now, stretch out Your hand and touch all that he has, and he will surely curse You to Your face!"

And the LORD said to Satan, "Behold, all that he has *is* in your power; only do not lay a hand on his *person*."

So Satan went out from the presence of the LORD.

Emotional Side Effects of Friendship

One March a few years ago, several of my friends shared their personal madness with me all at once. The deluge was emotionally draining. I am a deeply empathetic and compassionate person who is sometimes overwhelmed by other people's problems. That March I shared my friends' pain and burdens. Unfortunately, taking on heavy burdens from multiple people at once can cripple you. They zapped me of my energy – physically, mentally and emotionally. In the span of a week, these three friends bombarded me with all their anxiety, frustration, anger, bitterness, unhappiness, helplessness and uncertainty. None of them knew each other, and each one expected me to have more positive energy and insight to give to them than I was able to provide. They wanted more encouragement, more advice, support, love, hope. More light for their darkness. I could only dredge up a bare minimum. I answered the phone. I listened. I showed up. I held my tongue, giving my opinion only when asked.

Motherhood: To Be or Not To Be

My goddaughter Blossom's birthday is in early March. I decided to visit her for her tenth birthday. Before flying back home, I spoke with Chloe, Blossom's mom, to confirm times and activities for the weekend. Chloe wasn't thinking in the present as much as she was reliving the past. I imagine she never thought she would hold on to her daughter for anywhere close to ten years. In a rare moment, she dropped her know-it-all bravado and expressed a regretful, sad introspection. She asked me if she had made the right decision in keeping her daughter. She said perhaps Blossom would have been better off had Chloe given her up for adoption at birth. Chloe has never had an easy or comfortable time during her adulthood and, honestly, motherhood has multiplied her troubles. She confided in me that the family who had been waiting in the delivery room would have been better material providers for her daughter than she had been.

Chloe and Blossom have always weighed on my heart and will always be special to me. Yet, the only words I had to share were, "That family wouldn't have been able to give her *your* love, Chloe, your history or your experiences."

Marriage: P.O.W.

I flew into Chicago and drove to Milwaukee for my March visit. Tosha called me just as I was easing onto the interstate out of O'Hare International Airport. I don't drive at all in New York City; I miss the ease, freedom, and mobility driving offers. Therefore, I was looking forward to the quiet drive to Milwaukee from Chicago. However, Tosha stayed with me for the entire ride with her heavy topic – divorce.

Tosha had been in divorce proceedings for a year. Her husband had asked for the divorce but had been fighting it since he filed. Unfortunately for him, she took his desire for a divorce to heart and decided her life would be better off without him in it. Once he filed, she let go and moved on... to Florida. He hadn't expected her to let go or to move fourteen hundred miles away. He attempted to delay her leaving and dragged his feet for a year. When she called, I heard so much joy in her voice. I can't recall the last time I heard her so happy – not even in the beginning of their courtship or marriage. He had finally signed the papers! They were faxed to her that morning and she had signed and returned them immediately. Her divorce would be final that week. She was bubbling with happiness; I pictured her jumping up and down in her excitement. Eventually she noticed I wasn't sharing her joy or offering effusive congratulations. She calmed enough to express her disappointment, "No one is sounding happy. My mom was the first person I called and she didn't sound happy. You don't sound happy for me either."

"We are happy you're happy. But I don't think any of us thought there would be a day that you would be happier with the end of your marriage than you were on the day you made your vows."

Life: M.I.A.

I had called Leila a week before I arrived. I hadn't spoken with her since her thirty-eighth birthday the prior October. During that conversation, I had a sharp disagreement with her long-term live-in boyfriend a.k.a. the daddy of her children. I don't recall what we argued about, but I know I was adamant in my viewpoint, and I thought maybe she took offense because each time I called her following that conversation, she brushed me off with some excuse and rushed off the phone. The last time I spoke with her that fall, she said she was out shopping and would call me when she got home. So, you can say several months later, on my March weekend visit, I was still waiting for her to get home.

My stubborn streak is so thick, sometimes I can't hide it. After a few weeks of not hearing back from her, I decided she could be mad if she wanted to be; I wasn't the one to chase after her to cajole her.

Seven days before I was due to arrive in Milwaukee, my spirit urged me to call Leila. I balked. *"No. She needs to call me; I'm not making any more moves."* The voice persisted, *Call Leila.* I went about my day, but Leila did not leave my mind until I picked up my phone and dialed her number. Out of service. I tried her cell. Disconnected. I almost panicked. In the eight years I had known her, I've always been able to reach her.

That night I searched my apartment for old address books to look for her mother's number. Couldn't find it. Then I looked for her boyfriend Sam's number and called what I had. His number had been reassigned. Now I was worried. The next morning, I looked up Sam's business website, called the number listed and emailed him. "*Hi, just checking on you all. Couldn't reach Leila via phone, could you have her call me?*"

He called me back within five minutes. "Didn't you know we broke up?"

"No. I thought you were reconciling."

"She's acting a straight-up fool towards me with the kids." He continued to run down all her transgressions over the past few months. He was clear in stating that his current twenty-six-year-old girlfriend came along *after* the break-up. He shared that Leila was living with her mom. When I asked for the number and address, he evaded my question. "No worries," I told him, "I'll find her."

Saturday afternoon, I pulled up to her mothers' house just as her mom was coming home from the grocery store. "Hey, LaShawnda," she called out, like I was just down the street for the past couple of years, "Leila's upstairs. Does she know you're here?"

"No." I went up the stairs, rounded the corner just as she was coming out of one of the kids' room. She dropped what she was holding and started jumping up and down. "Shawnda! Shawnda! Is that really you?"

"It's me. Apparently, I'm still waiting for you to get home for that return phone call. I don't know why I have to roll up on people just to see how they're doing." She gave me the tightest hug ever and wouldn't let go for a good minute. We chatted only for a minute; she was taking care of her children. Immediately, I confessed to contacting her estranged ex-boyfriend in order to get her whereabouts. I decided to nap before getting her side of the story. It was hours before we were able to talk.

The gist of the story: Leila was tired of waiting for Sam to start *acting* like a father. He had sired five children total by three different women. His youngest two were with Leila. Her son was the only one of the five to receive dedicated time and attention from their daddy.

When I arrived at her mother's house, Leila's ex-boyfriend's two oldest kids were staying with her. Their mother had custody, but Leila had been their refuge and caretaker for four years. When their mother wasn't feeding or clothing them or sending them to school, they call their dad. When they got sick of waiting for their dad to come for them, they called Leila, who used to make their dad go and get them. This time they waited three weeks for their dad to pick them up or drop off food. They had told him they were hungry, there was no food in the house, and they were trying to make pancakes out of flour and water. Their dad told them he was on his way. After three weeks of waiting, they called Leila, now Dad's ex-girlfriend, to come and get them.

I was flabbergasted. I was so pained my heart was clenching.

Shortly after I had arrived, I asked her, "What can I do for you?"

"You don't need to do anything."

"I want to do something. Do you need money?" The ex had stopped supporting her months before and she wasn't working. She had been an at-home mom since delivering her first child nearly six years prior.

"You can give me something to put in the offering plate tomorrow at church."

I didn't argue. I put the contents of my pocket in her bedside Bible.

Later as I helped with the grooming of the children and listened to their firsthand account of their recent trials, I told Leila, "I'm not leaving without doing something for you. I'm not talking about doing anything for your church; I'm talking about you and your kids. We can argue about this, but I'm not backing down. Tell me something you need."

She thought for a moment and said, "If you could buy Skylar a pair of shoes, I would be grateful. She's wearing my son's shoes and underwear."

I hung my head. What type of person would call himself father and not provide the barest necessities for his children? Skylar, age twelve, was Sam's middle child and was reduced to wearing her five-year-old brother's underwear.

I took Skylar shopping and got her an overnight bag to put all her grooming materials in so she could carry her basics with her wherever she goes. I cried as I took her around the store. I couldn't understand how a man could neglect his own children, especially when he was able to provide exceedingly and abundantly for them. But then, I don't want to understand such a man.

I couldn't wrap my mind around this situation. It was too much for me. I got through the visit with my usual energy, but I shut down emotionally as soon as I boarded the plane home. It took a long time for me to recharge emotionally, primarily because Leila updated me almost daily for weeks following my visit. The updates didn't stop until she lashed out at me in frustration.

"*Ooooh*, I hope you never need a friend like this, because you'll find out people just start acting *fun-ny* when you fall."

"Are you saying I'm acting funny?"

"You're acting different."

"How am I supposed to act in a situation like this? I'm listening. I'm trying to help. And for your information, I have needed friends in life who never showed up. I don't need a situation like this to know that people will fall away. But I learned not to judge friends by what I would do for them. The greatest mistake we can make is expecting our friends to be everything we need in all our times of need. We're not equipped for that. Maybe the friends who are acting funny are acting that way because they don't know what to do to help. I'm stressed out from your situation--"

"I don't want you to be stressed –"

"Well, I am. But I'll get over it. I'm just saying if you're expecting something else, I just don't have the energy for it...."

Leila has no concept of the impact of her words. In her mind, her venting should not negatively affect her listeners. Her words and her overwhelming emotions engulfed me. I was struggling in the dark with her and had no idea how to pull either of us out. The song *Love Them Like Jesus* by Casting Crowns helped revitalize my flagging spirit and provided direction.

> *The love of her life is drifting away*
> *They're losing the fight for another day*
> *The life that she's known is falling apart*
> *A fatherless home, a child's broken heart*
>
> *You're holding her hand, you're straining for words*
> *You're trying to make sense of it all*
> *She's desperate for hope, darkness clouding her view*
> *She's looking to you*
>
> *Just love her like Jesus, carry her to Him*
> *His yoke is easy, His burden is light*
> *You don't need the answers to all of life's questions*
> *Just know that He loves her and stay by her side*
> *Love her like Jesus*

This amazing song helped me shed stress and anxiety from my friends' burdens. If you are the sounding board for your loved ones, let this song minister to you. I felt as if I were shortchanging my friends with my few words, my exhausted presence, and the little else I had to offer. But, not quite…. They are all in my heart and prayers, but I trust Jesus is better able to handle their burdens, as Proverbs 18:24 says, *There is a friend who sticks closer than a brother.*

Meditation Verse: Psalm 103:1-5

Bless the LORD, O my soul; and all that is within me, *bless* His holy name! Bless the LORD, O my soul, and forget not all His benefits: Who forgives all your iniquities, who heals all your diseases, who redeems your life from destruction, who crowns you with lovingkindness and tender mercies, who satisfies your mouth with good *things, so that* your youth is renewed like the eagle's.

Importance of Words

When Dianna decided to move to New York City the year after I did, I was quite excited. I thought I would have a good friend nearby with whom to share this portion of my life. Before she relocated, she visited for a week in order to search for employment and housing.

That week was one of our better times together. By the time she visited that autumn, I was over the depression, anger and bitterness that tried to consume me when I moved to New York City. It helped that she was on her good behavior – she didn't harp so much on what I ate or how I looked. The night before she returned home, I treated her to dinner in Times Square. On our way back to my apartment, she apologized for her poor treatment of me when I returned from Paris earlier that year (*Practicing What I Preach*, p. 28). During that time, I told her I couldn't take her hard talking anymore as it was doing more harm than good. I never brought up her hurtful words again; I just stopped sharing the more intimate details of my life with her. While waiting for the train at 42nd Street after dinner, we joked about how we cope with our problems – my Paris trip came up.

Dianna exclaimed, "I was thinking [at the time], 'Damn, she ain't doing that bad, she just picked up and went to Paris for a week!' I didn't handle that situation well; I wasn't a good friend at all."

I agreed. Not in a bitchy or snippy way, but simply, "No, you weren't. And thanks for that."

Words mean a lot to me. A lot of kids grew up shouting "Sticks and stones may break my bones, but words will never hurt me." I wasn't one of those kids. Perhaps I shouted it once, and someone said something that did hurt me. Perhaps as a result, I never uttered the mantra again. Words hurt more than sticks and stones, yet they heal better than medication and time. One of my good habits is thanking people for their words. I think it's only fair since I also tell them when their words are not appreciated.

I have always told people how they make me feel: happy, courageous, safe, intelligent, like I could do anything and go anywhere, invincible, wonderful, amazing, sexy, pretty, beautiful, magnificent, included, a part of something bigger than myself, like I matter. It's been rare that I've felt truly loved, though many have claimed to love me.

The people in my life have not been good representatives of love. It took a long time for me to separate and distinguish between their love and the love of God. It was extremely difficult for me to accept God's love when I began learning about His nature because the word was so tainted by the people in my life.

Humans are rarely aware of the impact of their words. We all need to be careful how we use our words, as our usage has the power to build or destroy.

For a time, I thought Dianna had learned how important words are. That belief elevated my excitement over her imminent move. I was so happy at the prospect of having Dianna in the city with me. She had a job offer within a couple of days of leaving. She decided to return immediately to start working. I offered to share my studio with her for a few weeks while she looked for an apartment. It's hard to tell who was happier, her or me. I had been truly lonely. Though I had been praying for companionship of a different kind, I went ahead and chuckled with God for answering with a friend instead!

Meditation Verse: Deuteronomy 32:45-47

Moses finished speaking all these words to all Israel, and he said to them: "Set your hearts on all the words which I testify among you today, which you shall command your children to be careful to observe—all the words of this law. For it *is* not a futile thing for you, because it *is* your life, and by this word you shall prolong *your* days in the land which you cross over the Jordan to possess."

Hindsight: Seeing Friends as Something Else

The joy of having Dianna around did not last. Neither did the illusion of our friendship. Seeing how truly cosmetic our relationship was, was a painful experience.

Hindsight is a wonderful tool to aid you in life.

Over the years, I have taken note of Dianna's regular reply to people's question on how she and I met. Her response was usually similar to, "We met on a nine-month road tour. When I first met LaShawnda I knew we were going to be cool – *after* the tour! I couldn't mess with her while we were on the road – the bus was too small and her personality is too big." Then she'd turn to me and say, "Shawnda, you know how you get!"

No, I really don't know how I get. Her description of our beginning never struck me as flattering. The first time I heard her say it, I questioned her because it didn't jibe with my own recollection of our meeting and interaction on the tour. I actually liked her from the first meeting and thought we would be cool immediately, however, once we hit the road, she stayed away. I didn't have an outsized personality in the beginning. I was quiet and kept to myself. That was my first modeling job; I was too busy trying to learn from other people to be a personality. The other people were too busy alternating between teaching me and laughing at me to benefit from my personality, anyway. Dianna always had a joke ready. She was the goofball. I was just being myself.

I know myself pretty well. Usually, I am an astute judge of character too. Yet, I over-estimated Dianna's integrity in relation to me. The initial terms of my offer were one month no rent, I didn't ask her to contribute financially to anything in my home. I told her I preferred she save her checks to get into her own apartment. Honestly, I didn't think she would use the whole month on offer, certainly I didn't think she would take more.

One month prior to my move to New York, I also visited to explore my options. During my four day trip, I secured an apartment, but could not secure a job. Within a week, Zoë had secured both an apartment and a job. During Dianna's pre-move trip she had secured a job. In my mind, an apartment was a week or two away.

Two weeks later she was still chilling in my spot and hadn't mentioned one apartment she had gone to see. I checked in on her and told her I couldn't believe she hadn't found anything yet. It didn't jibe with my experience of the city. Anyone can get an apartment if they're showing money. And she had no gap in employment. She finished her job in Las Vegas on a Friday and started her new job in New York on Monday. She assured me she was looking, but I don't believe she actually started her apartment search until I approached her a week prior to the end of the rent-free month I had offered her. At that point, she told me she didn't have any money to get into her own place because she had sent money to her brother.

Do I need to tell you I was somewhat livid? She was planning on taking more than I was willing to offer without even disclosing her actions. I felt as if she had no regard for me at all.

Shortly after that conversation, I told her she would be charged a daily rate up to half of my rent, due weekly after the month I had offered her was up. She ended up staying another two full weeks and only paid me enough to cover my monthly subway pass and lunch for a week. Though I really wasn't bothered by the money, I was hurt by her ingratitude. I will tell you honestly, I have yet to receive a simple thank you for sharing my one-room studio apartment with her for nearly two months. She gave me a high-five when she left and avoided me for nearly two years.

Before Dianna moved to New York, I told her, and everyone else, not to depend on me. I even told Dianna that if she came my way we would be two broke-down sistas crying together. I was honest about where I was in my life. I was an emotional and spiritual mess in search of *me*. If my process of self-discovery was threatened by what people wanted from me, then those people were going to be dropped. It was a time for me to put myself first.

Dianna later told me, after she had overstayed her welcome, that she heard what I said but thought I was talking about everyone else. It didn't cross her mind, she said, that I would also put my interests before hers. Whenever I remember that comment, I am astonished by her incredible arrogance. It says a lot about what she expected of me despite my situation and her own selfishness.

Eventually, I concluded our relationship did not survive because I expressed my unwillingness to inconvenience myself for her. Hence, my unwillingness to be taken advantage of rendered me useless to her.

After seven years of "friendship," I finally saw Dianna's nature and her strategy for keeping it hidden. Dianna will keep you laughing and entertained. She expresses more interest in the cosmetic aspects of life than the nitty-gritty growing pains. She doesn't talk – she feeds and regurgitates. In close quarters, her smoke and mirrors didn't work for me.

I am not oblivious to the fact that I may have hurt her feelings by putting my foot down and insisting she stop taking advantage of me. I acknowledge my own selfishness in making my feelings a priority. Perhaps I didn't help the situation, but the situation helped me let go of a relationship that was not benefiting my life. Her cavalier treatment of me told me how she really felt about me.

Just as I was honest about where I was and told Dianna what I was willing to do for her, she had always been honest about the low priority our relationship had to her. In her own words, she was fine not building or nurturing a relationship with me for nine months after meeting me because she had no need for me; therefore I had no value to her. Unfortunately, I was fooled by her easy humor and mistook her for a friend when her treatment of me labeled her as something else.

Meditation Verse: Philippians 3:17-21

Brethren, join in following my example, and note those who so walk, as you have us for a pattern. For many walk, of whom I have told you often, and now tell you even weeping, *that they are* the enemies of the cross of Christ: whose end *is* destruction, whose god *is their* belly, and *whose* glory *is* in their shame—who set their mind on earthly things. For our citizenship is in heaven, from which we also eagerly wait for the Savior, the Lord Jesus Christ, who will transform our lowly body that it may be conformed to His glorious body, according to the working by which He is able even to subdue all things to Himself.

And Me?

Family claim I am their rock
My strength comforts them
They do not fear lack
As long as I have
I am dependable safe shelter
They love me, so they claim

Friends praise me
My voice cheers them
My generous spirit
Embraces and reassures
I season their days with joy
And lightheartedness
They value me
And praise me on good days

Men call me beautiful… and sexy
My body inspires them
My smile lifts them
They want to grab hold
And possess me
Lay waste to my body
Control my life with their seed
They want some of me
Sometimes more of me
But never *all* of me

And me?
I don't understand
Why I have friends who aren't friends
Family who don't value me
Men who want a piece
But don't want to share my peace

I don't understand
How I can brighten so many days
Lift so many hopes
Support so many structures

Lust for fewer than lust for me
And still have no one
By my side when I'm in need
I simply wish to share my life
With loved ones

I don't understand
The many lonely birthdays
Holidays and milestones
Or how I can fill so many empty spaces
Yet remain so barren
How my light can touch on so many
While darkness prevails in me
Or how my *joie de vie* is a balm to others
Yet a depressing strain for me

I don't understand
How the strength of a child
Could be the downfall of a woman
But I am beginning to understand
How the strength of a woman
Corresponds to her solitude

Don't Grow Weary of Doing Good

During my self-exploration, I often lamented my nature, specifically, the part of me that wants to reach out and assist others. I learned from hard lessons that part of my nature usually attracted negativity from people.

My mother was my example of sympathetic, compassionate nurturer and nearly everyone she came in contact with took her kindness as weakness. If you asked and she had, she gave. I was well into my twenties before I realized people often ask for things for which they have no need. Some people will take whatever you offer with no thought of the people your resources could be a boon to. Some people will use you up before exerting effort for their own benefit. After a while, I tried to change my level of open generosity by attempting to suppress my nature. I had concluded that my nature left me vulnerable to a lot of hurt and rejection.

During the years prior to my cross-country move, I thought my struggles stemmed from giving to and doing for others. This theory evolved after many hours of solitude and self-reflection. I had reached a point in my life where I wanted to change. Ideally, I wanted to give only to those who were giving to me. Exchange energy with people who were sharing positive energy with me. I wanted to focus on and build only those relationships and withdraw from the relationships that were not reciprocating my effort.

At the time, I thought I was on the right track. I thought my thinking, reasoning and feelings were sound. However, I may have been too strict in overhauling my nature so harshly. The fable of the *Scorpion and the Frog* kept coming to mind during this time. It's one of my favorite fables and I quote it quite often. But, I used to only apply it to the negative nature of people.

My friend Jemini helped me during this flux period. One night, I was lamenting my personal issues and said something out of character to the effect of, "I just wish I could be this way and/or do that." She looked at me and shook her head, "But that's not in your nature, Shawnda." Then she quoted Forrest Whitaker's character's adaptation of *The Scorpion and the Frog* in *The Crying Game*. It was something of an *ah-ha moment* to have someone give words back to me with a different perspective. I realized that the bulk of my complaints and troubles stemmed from my attempt to change who I am. I was fighting my positive characteristics – open heart, generosity, nurturer and giver – with as much resistance as someone would fight their negative characteristics.

People gravitate to me for all sorts of reasons, but they stay around me for my warmth, gentleness, selflessness and objectivity. Only a few take extreme advantage of those characteristics. Ill treatment by a few such people created a chain-reaction that had me ricocheting off walls of self-doubt, anger, frustration, and worthlessness for several years.

It wasn't until the end of this rinse cycle that I began to embrace myself fully in conjunction with protecting myself. Today, I am quick to stop someone from taking what I'm not willing to give. That was the crux of my problem with myself – I was allowing people to use and discard me. Rather than correct that one component, I lost heart and grew weary of doing what I could for others.

Jemini continued with, "Don't be weary of being a kind, considerate and thoughtful person. It doesn't necessarily mean you're a pushover because you are willing to give way to other people's needs."

I agree. Perhaps my vision cleared or maybe my practicality pushed forward. Why fight my nature? I enjoy life so much more when I am sharing and giving of myself.

 Meditation Verse: Galatians 6:8-10

For he who sows to his flesh will of the flesh reap corruption, but he who sows to the Spirit will of the Spirit reap everlasting life. And let us not grow weary while doing good, for in due season we shall reap if we do not lose heart. Therefore, as we have opportunity, let us do good to all, especially to those who are of the household of faith.

Things Women Do and Say

One Sunday morning while getting ready for church, I was blessed to come across Pastor Jamal Bryant in an interview. He was talking about how we have to change our environment in order to grow. "God moves us from one place to another in order for us to grow, receive Him and perhaps fulfill our purpose," he said. A few weeks later, I heard the same message from another pastor. His words were, "The people we associate with can be detrimental to our development."

This message was powerful and right on time for me. I had transitioned drastically from pre-New York life to New York life. I had just survived a phase of attempting to change *who* I was to better fit *where* I was. This message reassured me that my change of environment was going to benefit my quest to live more fully as myself.

Honor among women

My early adulthood environment was very supportive, strong and nurturing in many ways. I was surrounded by strong, direct, independent women (family, friends, teachers, and employers). My oldest friend, Tosha, and I grew into our womanhood together. Our friendship became the prototype of the kind of friendship I seek to build with others: open, honest, direct, and free of malice and petty jealousies. Tosha's mother moved to Florida shortly after we started college. On our first winter break to visit her mom, we were greeted with our own personal tour guide and chauffeur (i.e. her mom recruited a young man from church to take us around safely). Robert was attractive, charismatic and older (twenty-six to our nineteen and twenty). During our second day hanging out with him, he pulled into a gas station and got out to pump the gas. Tosha and I turned to each other with arched brows. I spoke first, "Can I?" My question had more to do with whether her mother flip if she found out I was trying to romance her church friend.

Tosha said, "You can, but I'm in too."

"Really?" My excitement dropped. We had never shared an interest in a man before, or since.

She put out her hand and said, "May the best woman win."

We shook on it. She won. I bowed out. She had fun. There were no hard feelings. We have always dealt bluntly and directly with each other. In recent years, we've had bigger problems where our bluntness hasn't worked as well as it did in our youth, but our foundation is such that we will always recover. We've been friends for twenty years now. We have a true, sincere, sister-like friendship. I believe our honesty has a lot to do with it.

My problem with other women has been assuming all women take woman-to-woman talks and agreements seriously. I've learned some women take what you say to use it against you. Some tell you one thing and do another. Others build you up to your face while tearing you down behind your back.

It's been a hard lesson, but I've learned it well – there's very little honor among women.

The company you keep

I have always thought of myself as a person who knows her mind. I have never thought myself to be someone to give in to peer pressure in school, work or friendships. However, when I look at my dating life I see most of my dating activity stemmed from pressure women put on me. Women, more so than men, have given me the impression that I should share my body quick, fast and in a hurry with any available Tom, Dick or Harry.

What'cha talkin' 'bout, Shawnda?

I'm talking about the women who make single women feel unnatural for being single. The women who make childless women feel unnatural for not procreating by a certain age. I'm talking about the women who criticize other women for having high standards for their lives. The ones who say you will never get a man if you don't give him something to come back for. You'll never keep a man if you don't do what the hookers on the corner do for a couple of dollars, or the girls in the club do for a drink. Those females who masquerade as women masquerading as friends, mothers, sisters, aunts, and cousins. They are the ones who spurred me on to accept date after date in search of someone I wouldn't mind lying down with. To fit in. To be acceptable. To enter motherhood and *fo' real sister-circlehood.*

All the strong, independent women I knew were living life on their own terms. Not all were sexually active outside of marriage. Some had gone untouched for decades – I thank God for showing me polar opposites among my circle of influence. For every female in my life who insisted my life would be better with a regular rotation of casual sexual partners, I knew another woman who was waiting on God to present her with her husband. That being said, it was still women overall who called me prudish for my standoffishness with men. Men didn't call me names when I rebuffed their overtures. By and large, the men who were interested in me exerted more effort to entice me to do what they wanted me to do.

I am entreating women to stop making other women feel as if they have to subjugate their sexuality to men. Stop telling your sister her standards are too high. Stop telling your friend she's too picky. Stop telling your daughter no man will have her the way she is. God is in charge. However He created us to be, we need to trust He also created a counterpart for us. Mind you, this philosophy is spirit and character based. Asking for a rich man won't be as much of a blessing on your life as asking for one who will provide for you.

I admit to having weak moments and giving in to peer pressure once in a blue moon. Every so often, I have accepted a couple of numbers and possibly some dates just to see if I was actually missing anything. My acceptance of the dates had very little to do with the men asking me out. Variations of the question, "What's wrong with you that you don't have a man?" have been thrown at me numerous times over the years. Years ago, someone actually asked me if I was barren because I had reached my late twenties without getting pregnant. Such questions take a toll on you after a while. I started thinking maybe something was wrong with me. Maybe I wasn't trying hard enough. Maybe I wasn't as open or approachable as I could be. Maybe my life would be better with a man.

How's that for "rites of passage" socialization?

Over the last few years, I have learned to shut out the voices and shut down the questions. I've learned to ask my own questions. How's your husband? Are you happy in your marriage? What are you doing for your anniversary? This is one way to determine who is happy in their marriage. First of all, women who are happily married are not going to tell you to throw yourself down for any man who will have you. I have found that most of the scenarios I mentioned have been instigated by women who not happy in their own relationships or are not happy with themselves. This is why I turn my hearing off to women who don't love themselves or their husbands. I can't learn about love – love of self or spouse – from them. I have learned to assert that I am okay being with myself. I'm working on me now and want to enjoy the process. No longer are others able to make me feel unnatural for abiding by God's timing.

Not all advice is good advice

When I reflect on advice and comments women have given me through my teens and twenties, I realize every word affected and conditioned my way of thinking towards men. Their experiences reinforced my own negative experiences. This was a very discouraging realization.

When I talk to women, especially younger women, I speak to encourage them to protect their femininity and sexuality. There is honor in preserving yourself and rewarding one special man rather than giving yourself to many and losing bits and pieces of yourself along the way. Casual sex and serial monogamy (sex without commitment and short-term, committed sex with successive partners) ravage us – emotionally, spiritually, psychologically, and physically. Several verses in the Bible inform us that immoral sex murders the soul. We have to honor our bodies, thereby protecting our soul, as well as the Holy Spirit housed within us. First Corinthians 6:15-20 informs us *"all other sin is committed outside our bodies, but sexual immorality is a sin against our own body" (v 18)*. We have an obligation to honor and respect our bodies as temples. We are exhorted to do so as our bodies belong to God and house the Holy Spirit *(v 19-20)*.

Can I bypass the frogs?

A word for the women who think the natural course to romantic bliss is to kiss many frogs en route to your prince: I am not interested in the prince, then! I have no desire to reap the consequences – warts, slime, croaking – of aligning myself with frogs. That's my natural inclination. I only bemoan my singledom when I look at my status through someone else's judging eyes. When I attempt to conform, I am more miserable for the effort. I know God is working on someone magnificent for me. I have no wish to forfeit my blessing. So I will sit and wait on him… enjoying my life in the meantime!

Pastor Bryant also said, "We have a tendency to think that if we are walking right we will have an effect on the people around us. That's not always true. More often the people we are around have a negative effect on us." That's the crux of the message. That little morsel is the reason why it is so important to continually prune your environment of unhealthy relationships and associations. Yes, I will remain diligent in reviewing and analyzing my family and friend relationships. I will continue to monitor my environment and weed out those who don't nurture my nature before they adversely affect what is natural to me.

Meditation Verse: 1 John 4:1-6

Beloved, do not believe every spirit, but test the spirits, whether they are of God; because many false prophets have gone out into the world. By this you know the Spirit of God: Every spirit that confesses that Jesus Christ has come in the flesh is of God, and every spirit that does not confess that Jesus Christ has come in the flesh is not of God. And this is the *spirit* of the Antichrist, which you have heard was coming, and is now already in the world.

You are of God, little children, and have overcome them, because He who is in you is greater than he who is in the world. They are of the world. Therefore they speak *as* of the world, and the world hears them. We are of God. He who knows God hears us; he who is not of God does not hear us. By this we know the spirit of truth and the spirit of error.

Dichotomy of Jemini

Jemini is my newest friend, yet our relationship is perhaps the closest friendship I have formed in my adult life. She's an everyday friend. She's present to discuss the details of my everyday life. We've been knitted together by a sense of belonging. She and her whole family embraced me. For three years, I felt as if God had placed me with a family to reciprocate love with; a family lifted to great value in the absence of my childhood family. Their brand of familial love was akin to entering a lush garden after years of living in a solitary desert wasteland. Jemini's kindness, generosity and sharing of her family lured me into an incredible sense of comfort and inclusion.

Jemini's outward face is gentle, sweet, loving. Her voice is soft, motherly, soothing. Her words are usually about family and sacrifice.

I needed such kindness and gentleness in my life.

However, being exposed to the other side of Jemini was a brutal shock to my system and our friendship.

Jemini's hidden face is ravaged with bitterness, resentment, and self-hatred. We can assist one another with almost anything, but we are ineffective assisting others who aren't honest with themselves about their internal conflicts. We as individuals have too many levels of consciousness and a myriad of events which combine to form our perception of our experiences.

During the round of holiday celebrations last year, Jemini said horrible things to me on three separate occasions within the span of a week. In and of themselves, the words could have easily been dismissed. Actually, I did dismiss her words and behavior the first two times. I was hurt and perplexed but excused her. The third time, I took her words to heart. They pierced me deeply. Once her third set of words rooted in me, all of her prior words that week became injurious as well.

Each time, I immediately questioned her about her word choice. Each time she gave a flippant response. After her third attack, I withdrew, intending to get my hurt feelings under control and talk to her calmly about the effect her words had on me. It was two months before I could speak to her.

When I contacted Jemini to speak about her verbal assaults, she claimed she had just been speaking out the "side of her mouth." Not only did she not mean the words she spoke, she claimed she didn't remember saying them. She called me a liar when I repeated her words to her. Then she claimed that I misunderstood her. Next, it was her husband's fault for putting demands on her. Finally, she informed me he was jealous of our friendship and he didn't want me around on one particular holiday because he wanted to be alone with his family. She didn't feel comfortable telling me that, so she withdrew her hospitality altogether and would not accept mine. The words she used were quite harsh, and I recognized them instantly as lies.

 Meditation Verse: John 8:42-47

> Jesus said to them, "If God were your Father, you would love Me, for I proceeded forth and came from God; nor have I come of Myself, but He sent Me. Why do you not understand My speech? Because you are not able to listen to My word. You are of your father the devil, and the desires of your father you want to do. He was a murderer from the beginning, and does not stand in the truth, because there is no truth in him. When he speaks a lie, he speaks from his own resources, for he is a liar and the father of it. But because I tell the truth, you do not believe Me. Which of you convicts Me of sin? And if I tell the truth, why do you not believe Me? He who is of God hears God's words; therefore you do not hear, because you are not of God."

I was hurt and confused and didn't understand what had happened or why. Eventually, when we talked, I rejected her lies and excuses as such. I've always known her husband resented the time I spent with his family. For this reason, I have always encouraged her to spend time alone with her husband. She refuses to do this because she "doesn't want to be bothered."

Jemini has taught me important lessons during this rough patch of our friendship. I learned:
- *Like others who have claimed to love me, she cannot because true love does not reside in her*
- *She was used to waylay and distract me on my walk*
- *Small lies are still lies, and they still destroy*

A couple of months before our friendship stumbled, I met Papadou in Bryant Park (*Big Girl, Little Closet, p. 138*). He is the wise, insightful man quoted on the back of this book. One of the things Papadou told me was that I will eventually find my people. Though I heard him in that moment, I wanted to tell him that I had already found some of them. When Jemini revealed her true face and rejected me and my friendship, her actions told me that she and her family were not my people.

I knew I was attached, but I hadn't realize how wrapped up I was in her illusion of family until she unceremoniously kicked me out of her family circle.

Her family became surrogates for so much of the good things in my life – mother, sister, nieces, and grandmother.

For the two months I stayed away, every time I thought of the way she betrayed my emotions, my trust and my dependency, I cried. The only way I can explain my state of mind is this: I am a single woman who has lost her immediate family (mother and brother to death, sister to drugs and prostitution, and my dad removed himself from my life). I moved to a city of eight million people with no one. I work all day and return to a dark, empty apartment at night. When I met Jemini and her children, they latched on to me with hugs, kisses and soft touches. They asked me how my day was, fed me at their dinner table. Called to say good morning and sent me home well-fed and feeling well-loved with a good night. They were everything that was painfully absent from my life. They gave me people to talk to and love on and reciprocated in a marvelous way.

Then one day after nearly three years, for no logical reason, I was told I was not welcome. I was devastated. Had she told me simply that she and her husband wanted time alone with his family, I would have understood and given them space. Instead she lied to me. The lies were so much worse than the truth. The lies made me feel as if the whole relationship was a lie. As if I had no value whatsoever to Jemini or her family. As if I was completely dispensable.

When she and her husband decided they were ready to invite me back, I was chastised for my foolishness in thinking they meant such things as their behavior indicated. They thought I wanted a break, that's why I had stayed away so long! Surely, I was having fun with my single friends and living the city life! She hadn't called in all that time because she thought I was too busy to talk...so she said.

During one of our "friendship recovery" conversations, I told her that the only way I could understand her actions was to apply them to the devil, the father of all lies *(John 8:44)*. He is able to suggest thoughts and use people as mouth pieces. He has been after me for life (he's after you too), trying to find a way to get into me. I am very selective with my hearing and my friendships. However, I have been so completely open and vulnerable with my new family, they became my weak spot. I told her I had concluded he gave her words that had the ability to damage me and she chose to speak them. I forgave her and told her I still loved her, but I could not think of any other reason such hateful words would come out of her mouth to me.

She adamantly insisted she did not allow the devil to use her to hurt me. She started crying, claiming to be deeply hurt by my analysis.

"The only alternative is that you spoke what was in your heart." Matthew 12:34 says, *'Out of the abundance of the heart the mouth speaks.'* "If it wasn't Satan, it was you. You basically told me I was not welcome in your life. And you have yet to give a reason for your words."

"There *is* no reason," she insisted. "I didn't know what I was saying. Sometimes, there's just no reason for anything, Shawnda."

Not in my world. In my world there is a reason for *everything*. Romans 3:4 says, "Let God be true and every man a liar." Meaning, if I have to choose between her words and God's, I'm going with the word of God. I simply reiterated, "Out of the abundance of the heart the mouth speaks."

During a follow-up conversation several weeks later, after her failed attempts to make me feel guilty for the consequences of her actions, she finally admitted to an extreme amount of self-hate. I had turned her conversation around on her, I attempted for a third time to explain why words that meant nothing to her hurt me so deeply. She still didn't get it. I choked up and told her, "I won't apologize for protecting myself. I'm glad you don't understand."

"What? Why would you say that?"

"I am glad you don't share my experiences that make self-preservation part of my nature. I am glad you don't understand why I was so hurt by your rejection. I'm glad you haven't had experiences that would allow you to understand my feelings." By this time I was crying, she was hugging me and claiming to love me like a sister. I don't need that type of love. Love isn't spiteful, hateful, jealous, or manipulative. It was after that exchange that she admitted to hating herself. There's nothing about herself that she has ever loved and she had no idea how she could be that way when the people in her life have only loved and pampered her throughout her entire life.

I had long suspected Jemini did not love aspects of herself, but I thought it was only her body composition she held contempt for.

When she told me that, I finally understood it was not about me at all. I recognized her truth when she spoke it. I hadn't done anything. I had been in agony thinking I had caused offense with a word or deed. Or perhaps I had overstayed my welcome. It even crossed my mind that she didn't like her children being so attached to me. She wasn't rejecting me as much as she was creating a situation for me to reject her. Then she could be the sad, friendless martyr to her family. Not only did she sacrifice herself and her life for their every whim, but now she had sacrificed a good friend! A close confidant. Now, wasn't she the best mother and wife ever?

She admitted to self-hate, but she wasn't ready to start loving herself. She wasn't ready to use words positively to build herself and her relationships.

We have been awkward and tentative around each other most of this year, despite our soul-diving conversations. I've been listening to her with a filtered ear and seeing her with filtered shades. Love may cover a multitude of sins, but it doesn't hide them. For a long time after our reconciliation, everything about her felt false...contrived. Her words didn't ring true or sincere. Putting in work to mend a relationship is fine by me, but there has to be a mutual agreement and effort. During one of our early recovery conversations, I told her we would either come out of this much stronger or as nothing. My vote is always for stronger.

The moral of this story is: When dealing with people, believe their treatment of you over their words to you; but don't allow their treatment to dictate how you channel God's love. That was my struggle during this rough patch – how much of myself do I leave open to Jemini?

My pastor taught on love this past spring. He highlighted points that answered my questions quite clearly:

> - God is love
> - God loves through us
> - God's love is supernatural

- God's love is unconditional
- God's love is one sided

Everything happens for a reason. I was placed with this woman and her family for a reason. I am a well-trained, well-oiled, well-fed, well-loved vessel of my Father God. He is using me to love on my sister Jemini. The love that healed my hurt feelings and granted understanding of her internal pain is supernatural. It's not me. It's God. We're to love each other in good times and bad. Me loving her is not dependent on her loving me back.

This is a test and only a test. Jemini is strengthening my love walk.

Meditation Verse: Matthew 12:33-37

"Either make the tree good and its fruit good, or else make the tree bad and its fruit bad; for a tree is known by *its* fruit. Brood of vipers! How can you, being evil, speak good things? For out of the abundance of the heart the mouth speaks. A good man out of the good treasure of his heart brings forth good things, and an evil man out of the evil treasure brings forth evil things. But I say to you that for every idle word men may speak, they will give account of it in the day of judgment. For by your words you will be justified, and by your words you will be condemned."

Healing Graces

During my *Midwest Family and Friends Visit* in January 2007 I spent time with family in Gary, Indiana and friends in Milwaukee, Wisconsin. I stayed with my brother and his family while in Gary. That was his first time hosting me. It turned out to be the last time I saw my brother alive. I am grateful to report it was a good visit. My brother and I got along quite well. He would've told you it was because he didn't speak his mind. I'll tell you it was because I held my tongue. Either way, he did manage to tell me he was sick of me claiming to have no one in my life.

"Even though you may feel that way, it's not true," he claimed. "You have me," he said, thumping his chest. "You have me! You can't claim to have no one when you don't reach out to anyone."

I gave him that point after telling him his aggressive speech didn't inspire me to bare my heart and soul to him. I told him I would work on reaching out more that year. Indeed, the more I practiced reaching out, the more open and insightful our conversations became.

I drove to Milwaukee for the second half of my long weekend. I stayed with Leila. During my stay she echoed my brother's sentiments.

Leila is seeking; trying her hardest to live her best life in faith. She was conflicted and asked me during our conversation, "As a friend, Shawnda, what do you think I need to work on?"

Leila forces her kindness on people. She gets offended if you don't accept what she's offering. As stubborn as I am in some situations, I always back down with her. There's a lady from her church who was helping Leila with her children. The lady came over for a couple of hours a couple of days a week to sit with Leila's baby, which allowed Leila to run errands she normally wouldn't have time or energy for.

During my stay that weekend, I witnessed Leila arguing with her sitter the way she argues with me. She was trying to pay the lady; the lady repeatedly refused payment. Leila still wrote out a check and tried to force it into the lady's hand. The lady said, "No, Leila, I can't take it! I don't feel right. If you insist on paying me, I can't do this anymore. I just enjoy helping you; and the feeling I get from that... well... I would pay you for that...." She pulled cash from her jacket pocket Leila had forced on her the week prior and said, "You gave me enough last week for a month! It hasn't come out of my pocket. I don't plan on spending it. I don't want it."

Leila still didn't back down. She pressed the check into the lady's hand. The lady waved the check in Leila's face and said, "I'm not going to cash it! And you're going to have a reckoning!"

This exchange came to mind when Leila asked what I thought she should work on. "Listen to people, Leila. People tell you what they need or want, and you insist on giving them what you think they should have."

Leila insisted she doesn't want to take advantage of her sitter. She insists on paying because it's her way of showing the sitter she is valued. I pointed out that she and I have had the same argument repeatedly – it seems that she's always trying to force money on me too.

She told me I was burnt up (her term for tough cookies). "I'll go along with what you said about the sitter, but not about you. You were sitting in the dark without electricity before you asked anyone for help! You let things get too far gone before opening your mouth. So you're going to have to take what I give, when I give it. Otherwise, who knows what type of trouble you're going to get into."

I hadn't realized her motivation with me was my inability to ask for help in a timely manner. I assured her she had the same problem. In her quest to feel good about what she does or receives, she makes others feel bad about their actions and gifts. I reminded her of what her sitter had said, "I don't feel right taking money; if you persist, I'm going to have to stop coming over."

"Leila, you're going to miss out on a good thing because you don't listen," I told her. "You don't have to return a kindness to the person who gives one to you. You shouldn't force your brand of gratitude on people, either."

I pass kindnesses on. I appreciate that the person helping me may not need my assistance, certainly not in the same way they gave it. However, their assistance enables me to better assist someone else. Leila does practice this, however, she didn't recognize it until I pointed out the things she does for others.

My 2007 *Midwest Family and Friends Visit* was a very healing trip. The wonder was in letting go of old hurts and being bathed in new joys. I learned about things I could do to help build relationships I had had to walk away from a short time before. It had been a while since I spent time with my friends and family. I thank God for taking me there and allowing the healing conversations with my brother. I am grateful we finally reached a peaceful place in our dialogue. That visit blessed me with the healing grace family and friends bring into our lives.

 Meditation Verse: Proverbs 18:17-18

The first *one* to plead his cause *seems* right, until his neighbor comes and examines him. Casting lots causes contentions to cease, and keeps the mighty apart.

Eulogizing Antoine

My younger brother Antoine was a good, imperfect person. We were close as children, but our adult relationship was strained for a number of years because he thought I resented him for his inability to help me during our childhood.

I was sexually abused by two adult male family members over the course of four years. I prayed for the abuse to stop, and one day I was guided to our neighborhood police station. I have always seen my Lil' Bro Antoine as the little boy who held my hand as we walked through our apartment complex, across a field and over a bridge into a parking lot that held our neighborhood police outpost station. He was with me that day, the most important day of my eleven years; the first time I took control of what happens to me in this world. My ten-year-old brother was the only supporter I had at the time in my family.

Several months before he died, we got to talk openly and honestly. We cleared up misconceptions and old hurts. A lot of the strain in our adult relationship developed from the way our childhood ended. He finally opened up and told me he felt guilty for what happened to me. He thought he should've done more. He believed he should've stopped it. In his mind, for all those years we struggled to communicate, he felt shame for his inability to protect me from two adult males who actually held that responsibility.

I'm so grateful for that conversation. I was able to finally tell him that he did more than enough. I told him just by being there for me, he was my hero. Yes, I got to tell my brother how much he meant to me before he died, before I knew I was going to lose him. I am so glad I had that opportunity and took it! You are not learning anything Antoine did not know.

Antoine was a son, brother, nephew, grandson, cousin, friend...but I think he was most proud and happy being a father. He loved his family. And he tried. Like anyone else, he tried to do right, he tried to support and provide.

I'm sad. I'm so sad that I lost my brother, but I'm even sadder knowing my nieces lost their father. They are so young. I'm so sad they have to live the rest of their lives without their father being physically present. No fussing, shouts or discipline. No hugs, no kisses, or laughter. No bike rides or back rides, no advice about the boys on the block, no homework help and no dancing at the girls' weddings. He won't be around for any of that. I'm sadder still because their memory of him may fade. I don't know what their best and most lasting memories will be, but I pray they will know and remember that their father, Antoine Jones, loved them more than anybody. He loved his girls. He was proud of his girls.

Sometimes in life, my lovely nieces, knowing you are loved is all you need to know.

Meditation Verse: Matthew 7:11-12

If you then, being evil [imperfect], know how to give good gifts to your children, how much more will your Father who is in heaven give good things to those who ask Him! Therefore, whatever you want men to do to you, do also to them, for this is the Law and the Prophets.

Journal: Friday, January 13, 2006

I first saw Jeremiah 29:11 paraphrased on a plaque titled "Be Encouraged." *For I know the plans I have for you. Plans for good not evil. To give you a future and a hope.*

My "Be Encouraged" plaque sits in my home workspace on my desk.

The day started off well. Overall it was a very productive, relaxing and beautiful day. No stress. No anxiety. No screaming, disrespectful boss. Think I've had more energy today than any other since being in New York. But there's always an underlying darkness. Chloe called. I missed her and called her back only to get the aggravation I expected. Blossom's dad is on disability so Chloe is now collecting a monthly check sufficient enough to pay her rent. I don't envy Chloe for her situation, it's just an illustration of the angst I'm feeling. Chloe knowingly slept with a married man, resulting in a pregnancy. Her reward: reduced financial worries. She's planning and taking vacations!

Peewee and his brother Anthony molested and raped their daughters and niece. Their reward: their wives and families stood behind them in support.

Auntie Mac cheated on her first husband multiple times with multiple men during their first marriage. Lied to him about her second marriage (following their belated divorce). Her reward: he married her again and doubled the size of her diamond.

Who else can I think of? Surely, You get the idea, Father....

I've stayed chaste, praying for a loving, supportive husband with whom to build a family. My reward? Loneliness and solitude.

I spoke up and outed my abusers, freeing my cousin from her abuse as well. My reward: I'm ostracized by the family. They handle me with kid gloves as if I'm a foreign object they know nothing about.

I speak to men honestly about my interest and they steer clear of me.

These correlations do not bode well for a continued existence in the service of good rather than selfishness.

This was the course of my thoughts when a stranger named Priscilla sat next to me tonight. I had already discussed my thoughts with God and I believe she was one of His messengers.

Priscilla started off easy enough, low key enough. Waiting for a connecting train, she sat next to me on the 180th Street platform on the 5 line. She started discussing her weight and diet. I tried to utter words of encouragement, words from an old role I used to be comfortable playing. But the words must have come out rusty because she turned her questions to me. I revealed far more than I am prone to do with a stranger on a train or bus stop.

I fell off my exercise routine because I'm tired. Working out was my outlet and escape; now TV replaces it. I want permanent employment, so the temporary jobs are depressing me. This in turn keeps me tired.

She got all that on the platform. On the train, she asked if I go to church. I made a face and said I had visited one here in the city. She said, "Oh, you have something against church?"

I think I responded, "Yes." I finished with, "I do a home study."

She commended me for that and stated that self-satisfaction was all I needed.

I shook my head. "You don't agree?"

"No, I tried that."

"You need a relationship with God." Then she paraphrased Matthew 6:33, "Seek ye first the Kingdom of God and you will want for nothing."

I twisted my lips. "I have a relationship with God. Everyone wants to ask that question as if it's the key or answer to everything."

"What do you mean?"

"Believing in God, having a relationship with Him does not guarantee that everything will automatically be okay. It's not the end all, be all. There's a journey." I trailed off with hunched shoulders.

"You're right," she said. "It is a process. But haven't you achieved what you wanted in life?"

"Yes." For I have been blessed.

"Then patience. All you need now is patience."

Around this point she asked my name and told me hers – Priscilla. Then she realized she was on the wrong train. "It must've been meant for me to talk to you, I didn't even realize!"

"It must've been. Thank you."

As she got up to exit the train, she said, "Be encouraged."

Meditation Verse: Jeremiah 29:10-14

For thus says the LORD: After seventy years are completed at Babylon, I will visit you and perform My good word toward you, and cause you to return to this place. For I know the thoughts that I think toward you, says the LORD, thoughts of peace and not of evil, to give you a future and a hope. Then you will call upon Me and go and pray to Me, and I will listen to you. And you will seek Me and find Me, when you search for Me with all your heart. I will be found by you, says the LORD, and I will bring you back from your captivity; I will gather you from all the nations and from all the places where I have driven you, says the LORD, and I will bring you to the place from which I cause you to be carried away captive.

Priscilla on the 5

Once asked why had
I been forsaken.
Once believed no
God could live and
Have his child suffer so.
Faith and Grace
Came by to save me
Then it seemed they too
Tired of me.
I had just started to
Believe again
Yet was made to walk alone.

Thinking of the *Footprints*
poem; visualizing my lonely
Walk in the sand
Epiphany exposed
My error
Father was indeed
Holding me close to his chest
As I felt myself being
Cradled I heard Him
Whisper, *"You are not alone.*
It is now, that I carry you."
And I cried out, thinking
The voice a mirage during
My dry desert days
Doubt came to visit, insisting
I question Faith
"If you are indeed carrying me, Father,
Thank you. If not, forgive me my false Hope."
Perhaps it was then He realized
How truly weak in Spirit I had become
For I allowed
Bitterness and Resentment
To sit on my shoulders.

My Heavenly Father
Retaliated by sitting
Priscilla next to me one sad, lonely night
On the 180th St. Platform
Priscilla the Stranger seemed to know my Heart
She spoke in soothing tones
That salved spiritual wounds.
"Do you have a relationship with God?" she asked.
"I do."
*"Then seek ye first His kingdom
And you will want for nothing,"* she quoted.
"Just because I ask, doesn't mean I receive,"
I responded belligerently.
*"Everything is a process.
There's a middle that takes
A long time to come about."*
"Patience is to be practiced."
I nodded.
She looked me in the eye and quoted
The phrase holding me together,
"Be encouraged."
And I was. For a moment.
Then the morrow came
I lost yet another job
And Death gained a toehold in my mind
Prancing seductively before me, claiming
To be Peace.
Whispering coyly, *"Come to me and be eased."*
Strength and Courage pushed their way in
To fortify me.
I was assured of their unwavering
Support until Faith and Grace
Revisit and true Peace
Comes home to stay.

Speak Your Feelings

I used to be known for tempering my words with tact and diplomacy. Occasionally, I still do, however, lately tact and diplomacy have been difficult to dispense.

In the movie *A Few Good Men*, Jack Nicholson stunned viewers with his alpha male, domineering bark, "You can't handle the truth!" I often quote him jokingly, but it is as true a statement as any. People can rarely handle a truth, the truth, your truth or their truth. To some, truth is relative and has many nuances. It changes based on the speaker, perspective, experience, and feelings. That, of course, is a worldly idea of *truth*.

God's *Truth* speaks to your spirit. When your spirit speaks through you, you recognize the truth and so do those listening to you.

My first full year in New York was 2006. That year was one of many difficult spiritual and emotional challenges and changes. I look back on that year and see how my physical move and transition mirrored the amazing spiritual transition God was working in my life. Unfortunately, at the time, I couldn't see the spiritual. I felt everything physically and it all affected me mentally. But God made me a soldier, so I kept on striving. Even when I wanted to punk out, everything in me rallied together and pushed forward.

Part of my annual cycle is an evaluation of where I am and where I want to be. I keep a journal and review my entries around the New Year and around my birthday. On each of these occasions I write down at least one goal or highlight progress on prior goals. My New Year 2006 resolution was to speak my feelings. I am usually the quiet, long-suffering type. You know, the person who will take everything thrown at them, who won't say anything until they get fed up and shout out everything that has been bothering them. That was me. In 2006 that changed. I stopped complaining about mistreatment and under-appreciation. I started telling people how I felt and what I thought of situations and treatment. That year, I spoke a few of my truths. They weren't well received, but I evolved into a truer version of myself.

As a result, the New Year of 2007 was a major turning point in my spiritual life – I was finally able to recognize my spiritual growth. *A Road I Must Travel Alone* (p.125) covers a part of this revelation. That New Year I looked back on 2006 and noticed the personal progress I had made while speaking my feelings. Some church folks will tell you, you can't trust your feelings. Some believe the heart is a deceiver. I'm telling you, I trust my feelings. I trust and protect my heart. God lives in me and I live in God. And where God resides there is no fear, there are no lies. He speaks to me and I listen. My listening creates a feeling. An urge to speak or to take action. Believe me, trusting God has not led me astray.

Diehard Family

My dad's family is like a secret society with secret handshakes, secret whispers and a whole bunch of other secrets. Privacy is a big thing with that clan – I rebelled by telling most of my business. In January 2006, I documented my woes against my dad, his sister and his mother in a letter I sent to them all. My dads' mother and sister were very supportive of him through the years. They knew everything he and his brother had done to me, yet they claimed to not understand why I wanted nothing to do with their beloved sons/brothers. They wanted us to be the big, happy family that nothing could divide. I grew up hearing "blood is thicker than water" and was taught to believe my blood relations would be the strongest relationships I would ever have. However, my blood relationships have rarely done my life any good.

The letter to my dad, aunt and grandmother listed the things they had done over the years that stifled and alienated me – the treatment that kept me in bondage longer than I needed to be. I had tried to share most of my issues with them in past conversations, but they never listened. They always stopped me and told how I *should* feel. Then they changed the subject. My family never allowed me to *talk* about how I felt about my childhood abuse. For most of my life, I was conflicted because I loved them even as they were destroying me. I wanted to live free but I still wanted relationships with them. It was a big gamble to confront them.

My whole family turned against me. I broke rank and was spared no quarter. At the time, even my brother spoke against me. He called me evil for upsetting my grandmother before he even knew what she was upset about – she refused to talk about the issue with him as well.

If I had continued to keep my feelings to myself, that half of my family would probably still be in contact with me. I would be part of the united façade. I would also be as filled with angst and torment as I was when I wrote that letter. So, I sacrificed some family relationships for my peace of mind. They couldn't handle my truth, but I am okay with the consequences of speaking my truth. That process illustrated how I am better able to grow in God's truth when I separate from the shadows some relationships cast on my life.

Meditation Verse: 3 John 1:2-8

Beloved, I pray that you may prosper in all things and be in health, just as your soul prospers. For I rejoiced greatly when brethren came and testified of the truth *that is* in you, just as you walk in the truth. I have no greater joy than to hear that my children walk in truth.

A Road I Must Travel Alone

On my second New Year's Eve in New York City, I visited the historic Riverside Church in Harlem. I was in search of a church home and was immediately awed by the atmosphere in the nave of Riverside. The majestic gothic interior had a lot to do with my initial reaction.

I was in need of a message on that crisp Sunday morning. God, in His infinite wisdom, delivered one to me. I had been struggling with issues that were hard to put into words. I talked about the things I could speak on with those who would listen. But even those simpler speakable things were not well received by friends.

I was changing. As we all do. Not only was God reworking me in a major way, I knew it was time for me go to another level. I was ready for a change, however I had no idea how monumentally drastic it would be. In 2005, when I decided to move to New York, I told my family and friends I would not be in contact for at least six months. I thought that was all the time I needed for my personal evolution. My knowledge then only scratched the surface, and it's not much deeper now. However, after my visit to Riverside Church, I became more accepting of whatever changes were to come in my life.

God is in the Growing

Reverend Dr. R. Scott Colglazier gave the sermon that helped me over a hump that resembled a mountain at the time. There were hundreds of people in the nave that Sunday morning, yet I felt as if I was sitting face to face with the Reverend Doctor in private conversation, finally accepting words that have been offered previously but not embraced. He said, "People talk about Jesus as being constant – always the same now and forever. Though the essence of Jesus never changes, there was a time when Jesus, the man, went through change."

"I hear you," he said. "'As soon as life gets good, as soon as everything falls into place, I'll start living in God's presence.' What if the pieces are never all together? What if God is only found in the growth, in the striving, in the struggles of everyday life...? God is discovered in the growing, not the perfecting of life.... Don't miss out on sharing your gifts with the world. You're in a growing moment. You know what that's like, don't you? When you want to give up.... When you're missing home.... When you want to sob, not cry, but sob. Those are growing moments. Without vulnerability, mistakes, and heartaches – we don't grow. We don't change."

How profound is that? How did he know my heart? How did he know my fears? How did he know how to soothe me?

Of course, he wasn't telling me anything new, but sometimes we get so deep in our troubles, someone else's voice works as a beacon to guide us through our darkness.

I've been an advocate for change all my life. I've embraced it. Searched for it. Preached it to others. I had lived in four states and six cities by the age of fourteen. By the age of twenty-six, I had been to six countries on two continents and visited forty of fifty states, speaking three languages. One of my selling points in job interviews had been my adaptability to change. However, none of that, nor my positive attitude, upbeat personality, adventurous spirit, thirst for knowledge and culture or my facility with conversation was sufficient preparation for the road I am now traveling. Or rather, all that preparation has not been the focus of this portion of my journey.

Roadblocks

I have some good friends, but during my personal and spiritual evolution I discovered none of them was able to give me anywhere near what I needed, when I needed it. By the time Reverend Dr. Colglazier spoke to me, I had been re-evaluating my family and friend relationships for over a year. The night before I attended his service, I had concluded I had no true friends. I had no helpers or supporters who were available for me to call on in my need. They had all been tested in some way. My friends showed support but rarely followed through by actually giving support. They encouraged me to call on them and ask for assistance whenever I needed them, but they rarely responded to my call.

What my summary does not take into account are all the variables of life – marriage, children, mortgages, jobs, sick parents, personal transitions. When I have felt that my friends have failed me, they were championing others or caring for themselves. This may be the same situation when I have failed them. I have changed as a friend over the last few years as well. Whereas I used to make myself available in some capacity whenever I was called, I became a hermit and cocooned myself during my transition. I have said *no* to more requests for my time and space during this time than in the entire span of any given friendship. I needed to distance myself. I needed to be stripped of my sense of ease, security and comfort. No matter what type of relationship you have with family and friends, when you are surrounded by them you have a sense that whatever befalls you, someone will pick you up. Innately, I knew the people I turned to for advice, conversation, support, or just a listening ear were not people I could go through a personal evolution with.

God needed to be my focus. Solitude was necessary for me to learn to communicate with Him and build our relationship. He isolated me so I could hear Him better. It was time for me to lean on God and allow Him to lift me.

Everyone I knew, family and friends, were roadblocks to my spiritual growth. I don't mean that in a demeaning way. We all have our tests and struggles in life. James tells us to count all our trials as joy because the testing of our faith produces patience and matures us *(James 1:2-4)*. My family and friends were blocking my growth because their expectations of me kept my focus on them and their needs. Yes, it is good to help others; however, it is not good to neglect yourself. I did my best to fulfill whatever people expected or requested of me. My effort was based on my desire to be a positive influence in everyone's life. A dependable influence. Many people had let me down, and I didn't want to be the cause of anyone's disappointment or disillusionment. If I could be a representative of the good of man/womankind, then I would do all that I could. If someone asked me to bend backwards and my back was paining me, I wouldn't tell them I couldn't, I wouldn't even tell them that my back hurt. I would bend back as far as I could. I would barely recover before the next person and the next person and the next person were asking me to bend just a little bit further....

When I got tired of bending, I stood up and walked away. Far, far away....

For those who asked, I truthfully shared my desire to get to know me. I wanted to do things simply because I wanted to do them, not because something was expected or needed of me. I wanted to live without everyone else's demands, influences, and judgments.

Ironically enough, when breaking down my daily life in New York, it's not much different than my daily life in Milwaukee was. I'm a bit lonelier, but I am freer and happier overall. My essence, core, and character have not changed. I have grown more outspoken and protective of *me*, my wishes, and my boundaries. I've lost interest in being nice. I've gained a deeper interest in being right with God and true to myself.

My search for self-knowledge led directly to a deeper knowledge of and connection with God.

"I can't go back to yesterday, because I was a different person then."
- Lewis Carroll

I can't go back to who I was. Sometimes I cherish thoughts of giving up trying to live out my dreams and crawling back into the lifeless arms of my family and friends. That's a fantasy I can no longer afford. I'm not interested in hearing the *I-told-you-so's* and suggestions on how I should just settle for whatever is handed to me. Failure has never been part of my plan, but I've learned from all of my mistakes.

When Reverend Dr. Colglazier said, "You're in a growing moment. You know what that's like, don't you? When you want to give up.... When you're missing home.... When you want to sob, not cry, but sob. Those are growing moments." I felt like he was shaking me awake. He went on to say, "Sometimes change is easy and joyful. Sometimes it's painful and hard. Enlightenment is telling the truth of where you really are. Risk something this year. Risk something for yourself."

The road of spiritual growth and personal development is never-ending. I became aware of my long journey a short time ago, when my physical uprooting mirrored my spiritual uprooting. It's a lonely process, and every once in a while I've tried to pull someone onto the road with me. Not because I felt they needed to be there, but because I felt I was lacking in companionship. Or I simply couldn't stand my own company anymore. After a few steps, my path got crowded and I got cramped. I felt a different type of frustration, as if my temporary companion was obstructing my view. I would then set them aside and continue forward by myself. I later regarded these short intermissions of friendly companionship as friends "failing" me. A transition is no time to test friends or family. God will never equip others to be to you what He wants to be to you while He's teaching you to depend on Him. I wanted people to be trustworthy and dependable. Fortunately, I learned to trust and depend on my God for all things.

 Meditation Verse: Acts 9:3-9

As he journeyed he came near Damascus, and suddenly a light shone around him from heaven. Then he fell to the ground, and heard a voice saying to him, "Saul, Saul, why are you persecuting Me?"

And he said, "Who are You, Lord?"

Then the Lord said, "I am Jesus, whom you are persecuting. It *is* hard for you to kick against the goads."

So he, trembling and astonished, said, "Lord, what do You want me to do?"

Then the Lord *said* to him, "Arise and go into the city, and you will be told what you must do."

And the men who journeyed with him stood speechless, hearing a voice but seeing no one. Then Saul arose from the ground, and when his eyes were opened he saw no one. But they led him by the hand and brought *him* into Damascus. And he was three days without sight, and neither ate nor drank.

8 Wrong Places to Find Yourself

Shortly after my enlightening visit to Riverside Church, I visited another church which eventually became my church home. It stands out as the first church I became a member of. During my first year there, Pastor Terry Starks taught a series titled *8 Wrong Places to Find Yourself*. His list came as confirmation to me. I had already been working on a few of the areas on his list, but I became more diligent in cleaning up my life after he shared his list of wrong places.

1. Attending the wrong church
2. Marrying the wrong person
3. Working in the wrong vocation/occupation
4. Living in the wrong neighborhood
5. Saying the wrong things
6. Hanging out with the wrong people
7. Believing the wrong things
8. Eating and drinking the wrong foods and drinks

Growing Through Vulnerability

Vulnerability: Exposed or open to moral attack, censure, criticism, temptation, assault

Vulnerability is a hard word to live, but I'm living it and growing through it.

I have been vulnerable all my life and will remain so. However, I haven't always felt vulnerable... exposed... defenseless... helpless. My brother's death carried me immediately into a vulnerable state. It's not a bad state to be in, if you don't fight it. If you take your lessons and grow from them. I'm exposed, but I know I'm covered. I've been wounded, but I know I've already been healed. Temptation has come before me, but there's a hand guiding me. People are planning and launching attacks; after getting my feathers ruffled and briefly trying to fight back, I calm down, step back and realize there's not a scratch on me – I'm protected. I'm learning and growing, but through it all, I feel secure. I am secure. Are you?

I met with my friend Josie in Milwaukee during my July 4th Midwest trip in 2007. Josie and her husband founded and operated a children's ministry I used to volunteer for. I hadn't visited with her for some years and the ministry had a couple of hard knocks in that time. We met for breakfast and during our discussion I explained my job situation – I had quit the day before with nothing lined up, but no fear, God will provide! She looked at me with something akin to awe and said, "That's confidence – I've heard about that." She positioned her right hand over the table, "Faith is here," and positioned her left hand a foot above her right, "and confidence is up here. I've never seen anyone on that level." I gave her a questioning look, because I have always described her as a devout Christian – you know the Christian with so much zeal they can potentially get on your nerves or overwhelm you. "Aren't you confident, Josie?"

"No," she said solemnly, "I just have a lot of faith."

Sharing burdens...

I have always been a person people are comfortable leaning on. It's a combination of being the eldest daughter of an eldest daughter, having a direct personality, and a go-getter attitude. Add to that my planning and organizational skills. I didn't get a chance to cry for my mother till nearly a year after her death. I was too busy comforting and taking care of everyone else. Everyone wanted my comfort. They all expected me to take care of everything. I wanted to be the vulnerable child mourning the loss of her mother. I wanted to cry on the aunt who was crying on me. I wanted to sit in the lap of the uncles who slapped me on the back with a "Good job!" And lay up on my grandmothers who blessed me for being a good daughter. As with life before my pivotal loss, I was not allowed to be vulnerable. No one *expected* me to be. Suddenly, I was promoted to the position of family strength and backbone because that's how everyone had viewed my mother.

When I got the news about my brother that early Friday, July 13th morning, I took the opportunity to be vulnerable. I also defended my right to be so. It's amazing how you can move through your grief when you have the freedom to express it!

Too much came at me that Friday morning – my brother's death, the questionable situation surrounding his demise, my voluntary unemployment, a job offer, travel necessity, funeral arrangements and my empty bank account. Not to mention, I had just returned from a carefree weeklong vacation. There was some guilt associated with that. After two hours of crying on the phone and in between calls, I called Jemini. All I could say was, "My brother died... a job wants me to start Monday... I don't know what to do...." After her initial shock, she said, "Come here, baby, just come here." I walked outside in just my robe. She and her children were waiting for me at the top of their stairs, arms wide open. I cried on Jemini like I never cried on anyone. She and her children comforted me like no one has ever comforted me. She sat with me as I took and made more phone calls. The children took turns patting my hand, hugging me, and making us tea and toast with a bowl of strawberries. Even with the heart-wrenching sadness surrounding it, the memory of the children's effort to comfort me brings a smile to my heart.

Somehow, accepting my vulnerability with Jemini is natural. Not quite so with those who have known me before this portion of my evolution. Zoë offered to take me out the weekend following my return from my brother's funeral. She thought dinner and a movie would be just the thing to get me out the house. All I wanted to do was stay in my dark, airless apartment, but I accepted her offer. She called for a livery car to pick me up. I felt so uncomfortable accepting her generosity, especially when I was not in a position to repay it or contribute to it. Therefore, my first words after *Hello* were, "I have absolutely no money till Friday, so I won't be able to contribute to anything."

"You're not supposed to," she replied. "This is my treat."

"I know, but I'm used to helping with tips or transportation...."

"Don't worry about it. Will you just let me do this for you?"

Will you just let me do this for you? Those words shut me up and got me to thinking. Vulnerability *is* a choice. It's not a position or a situation. It's more than a state to be in. I could have continued to posture – to stand insecurely and uncomfortably on my own wobbly legs, or I could accept the help and comfort sent to me.

Despite my critiques in this volume, I know I have some good friends who pop up with encouragement when I least expect them to. They do make an effort in their own way to love on me. I've come to grips with the fact that they all take care of different needs, to different degrees at different times. I've been blessed enough to grow with some of them through shared burdens.

I got me; who got you?

Tosha received a short visit that week in Milwaukee as well. She was going through her divorce at the time and was packing up to move back in with her mother in Florida.

Tosha and I have quite a bit in common. We are self-sufficient, independent, no-nonsense, devoted, and faithful women. Her then soon-to-be ex-husband told her he never felt as if he were the center of her life; he didn't feel like her focus. As she shared his words with me, she looked at me with confused wounded eyes and said, "All this time, I thought he was my center. Apparently my independence didn't allow me to bend as much as he needed me to. Shawnda... where's the line between dependence and independence? How could I be dependent on him while still being myself?"

I answered her with one word: vulnerability. "He was just asking for some vulnerability on your part." I shared something my pastor, Terry Starks, had pointed out, "In marriage, you are to live and do for your spouse. Everything you do should be for him and everything he does should be for you. If you are both operating like that, no one will be left out or neglected. You both felt neglected. Your independence didn't allow him to feel necessary to your life."

Then I shared how I was just learning to be vulnerable. I had come a long way, but I could still see her where she was. It's uncomfortable opening yourself up, baring your emotions and feelings – exposing your soul. It could be painful. It could be destructive. But it can also be wonderfully freeing. It can be a catalyst to your personal and spiritual growth.

I consider myself a well-rounded person. Now I add to my list of credentials: giver and *receiver* of comfort. I've had burdens put on me and taken away. When the rotation flips and I am called upon to give support and comfort again, I will assume that role with happiness and endurance, because now I know how such has kept and restored me. May God bless and keep you as well.

Meditation Verse: Galatians 6:2-3

Bear one another's burdens, and so fulfill the law of Christ. For if anyone thinks himself to be something, when he is nothing, he deceives himself.

Speaking Rock

Sapling tree
encircling rocks,
colorful containment.
Rock sculpture
of human face
smiled.
Seeing God
in a rock decorated
curbside,
I smiled back.

Becoming Whole and Holy

Sacred Companions: The Gift of Spiritual Friendship & Direction by David G. Brenner was one of the first books I came across during my Holy Spirit-directed program on spirituality. It was uncovered in a library during a search for books to walk me through understanding my relationships. The below excerpt is an awesome summary of my journey, as chronicled throughout My God and Me – every time I read this excerpt I get something even more powerful and new from it.

Spirituality Grounded in Humanness

The reason I like to describe the goal of the Christian spiritual journey as becoming both whole and holy is that it reminds us that the focus of God's love and salvation is not some part of us but our whole person. Jesus does not love some immaterial or eternal part of me. He loves me. And Jesus did not die so that some part of me would be saved; He died so that in my whole being I would be made anew. Anything less than this trivializes salvation and fractures human personhood in ways God never intended.

Too often the Christian journey is understood simply in terms of becoming like God. While this is an essential component, if we only emphasize this aspect of it, we are likely to develop a spirituality that deemphasizes our humanity. The goal of the Christian spiritual journey is not to become less human and more divine; it is to become more fully human. Salvation is not to rescue us from our humanity; it is to redeem our humanity.

Tragically, some visions of the Christian spiritual journey have led people to deny entire aspects of their humanity. Some people have rejected their sexuality, others their intellect, emotions or playfulness. All who do so limp along the path to wholeness and holiness. But rather than bring their lameness to God for healing, they tend to wear it as a badge of spiritual honor.

Spirituality not grounded in humanness is no earthly good. Worse, it can actually be dangerous. Spirituality that apparently makes us more like God but fails to make us more genuinely human actually destroys our personhood. If embracing humanness was good enough for Jesus, how can we despise it? To become like Jesus and take on his character, we must – like Him – embrace our humanity and work out our spirituality within it. The authentic journey of Christian spirituality must always involve redemption of our humanity, never its denial or attempted crucifixion.

This draws our attention to the importance and interdependence of knowing both God and self. As argued by John Calvin, there is no deep knowing of God apart from a deep knowing of self and no deep knowing of self apart from a deep knowing of God. Knowing God and knowing self are both necessary for wholeness and holiness.

How tragic it is when a person invests all his or her energy in knowing God and none in genuinely knowing him or herself. And how terrifying when such a person is in a position of leadership or influence. Christian maturity demands that we know God and ourselves, recognizing that deep knowing of each supports deeper knowing of the other.

While holiness emphasizes taking on the character of God, wholeness reminds us that doing so does not make us gods or even angels – it makes us more completely human. St. Irenaeus reminds us that the glory of God is a fully alive human being. God is in the business of making us fully human and fully alive. This is the abundant life promised by Jesus (John 10:10). Our vitality, our genuine fullness of life, points back to God, the author of life. In so doing it gives God glory.

The purpose of salvation is to make whole that which is broken. The Christian spiritual journey settles for nothing less than such wholeness. But genuine wholeness cannot occur apart from holiness. R.C. Sproul noted that the pattern of God's transforming encounters with humans is always the same. God appears; humans respond with fear because of their sin; God forgives our sins and heals us (holiness and wholeness); God then sends us out to serve him. This means that holiness and wholeness are the interrelated goals of the Christian spiritual journey. Holiness is the goal of the spiritual journey because God is holy and commands that we be holy (Leviticus 11:44).

Holiness involves taking on the life and character of a holy God by means of a restored relationship to him. This relationship heals our most fundamental disease – our separation from our Source, our redeemer, the Great Lover of our soul. This relationship is therefore simultaneously the source of our holiness and of our wholeness.

Human beings were designed for intimate relationship with God and cannot find fulfillment of their true and deepest self apart from that relationship. Holiness does not involve the annihilation of our identity with a simple transplant of God's identity. Rather, it involves the transformation of our self, made possible by the work of God's Spirit within us. Holiness is becoming like the God with whom we live in intimate relationship. It is acquiring his Spirit and allowing spirit to be transformed by Spirit. It is finding and living our life in Christ, and then discovering that Christ's life and Spirit are our life and spirit. This is the journey of Christian spiritual transformation. This is the process of becoming whole and holy.

Meditation Verse: 1 Peter 1:13-16

Therefore gird up the loins of your mind, be sober, and rest *your* hope fully upon the grace that is to be brought to you at the revelation of Jesus Christ; as obedient children, not conforming yourselves to the former lusts, *as* in your ignorance; but as He who called you *is* holy, you also be holy in all *your* conduct, because it is written, *"Be holy, for I am holy."*

Rebounding

My last day working for Mean Jack was Monday, July 3, 2007. That day became a marking point, the start of *Week Zero*, for all that has followed in my life.

My equilibrium was knocked off kilter by the hostile work environment Mean Jack encouraged and more so by my brother's death the following week.

Gratefully, I was able to bounce back and reposition myself. The process of doing so left me with a better appreciation for rebound relationships. They are helpful for adjusting your mind from a damaging, painful situation to a new opportunity. In this instance, my rebound work environment allowed me the time and space to grieve.

Week Eight

I could say God showed up early, but it's more accurate to say He never left me. Eight weeks after I walked out on Mean Jack and his cronies, I was sitting pretty, albeit sad, in a cushy position with a giant global corporation (*a.k.a.* the bank). I was hired on as a temp and started working during *Week Four*. It was easy to view my temp assignment as a rebound situation because I was not where I wanted to be; I had simply landed there after hitting a hard wall. For the first time in a long time, I had absolutely no complaints about my employment. My manager during recovery was wonderful. Under her calm, gentle supervision I realized I was traumatized from bad, borderline abusive work relationships. Every couple of days I shook my head and told myself to act like I wanted the position permanently. I was a serious contender for full-time employment.

Fortunately, I knew I had entered into a quiet time – a transitional period. It was time for me to just be. To live in the moment as I was. To sit quiet and listen. To allow myself to be guided. It was time to wait on God.

Week Eleven

By *Week Eleven* I was thanking God for the paid sabbatical He had given me! *Week Zero* was spent in the Midwest reconnecting with friends. *Week One* began with an intense job hunt and ended with notification of my brother's death. *Week Two* was filled with job interviews and funeral arrangements. At the beginning of *Week Three* I started as a long-term temp at the bank. It was during my second assignment at the bank that I was placed with a gracious and respectful manager.

Through her treatment and appreciation of me, I began to see value in myself as an employee again.

Week Thirteen

By *Week Thirteen* I realized I really needed the time I had been given to reposition myself, my thoughts and my goals. I was in a truly fragile state emotionally and mentally. My spirit took some damage too. My decisions are made based on how I feel my spirit is guiding me. This period of my life was a culmination of seemingly good situations that turned out bad. Every time something went opposite of my expectations, I questioned my judgment. More profoundly, I questioned if I could rely on my listening skills. If I thought God was talking to me and took a certain action which did not benefit me in the end, then was that truly God speaking to me? I didn't stop trusting God, but I did lose faith in my ability to hear God.

During my many weeks of recovery I sat at my desk with very little work and communed with God in the way I've communed with Him since childhood – I wrote. I wrote blogs about my brother. I wrote about my hurt and anger over my former job. I wrote entry after entry of questions, uncertainty, confusion and hope. The process of being persecuted, tossed away, landing hard and bouncing back needed to be experienced in order for me to grow beyond where I was.

Lesson Learned

The temp work at the bank was well above my prior position supporting Mean Jack. *EVERY* time I leave something, I walk into something better. That's how I know God is working in my life. Even as I sit crying, He's cleansing me with my tears!

Every moment with Mean Jack felt awkward – my performance was ostracized, underappreciated and disrespected. Even so, I put forth my best effort and energy. The people in that office did not value me as a person, an employee or co-worker. God responded by placing me with someone who valued people and treated me well!

Professional dysfunction was cut at the root. Re-planting freed me of my former malaise. I identified and repaired problems I had control over. I evolved from that process rejuvenated; embracing the opportunities God place before me.

Meditation Verse: Luke 4:23-24

He said to them, "You will surely say this proverb to Me, 'Physician, heal yourself! Whatever we have heard done in Capernaum, do also here in Your country.'" Then He said, "Assuredly, I say to you, no prophet is accepted in his own country."

Big Girl, Little Closet

The opportunity to walk in the Macy's Thanksgiving Day Parade was offered to me in 2008. I walked the parade route as a clown in a group composed of Zoë, her friends and co-workers. A few weeks before the parade, the organizers scheduled a half day of clown training at the 34th Street Macy's headquarters.

Overall, it was a light and entertaining morning. It was also very awkward. Dianna was a member of the clown group I was in. We hadn't seen or spoken to one another much at all that year. Zoë and Dianna had become good friends even as my friendship with both of them had diminished. Zoë and I stayed in regular social contact – greetings and the occasional good wish. Dianna had drifted far away after she moved into her own apartment. We saw each other only when Zoë had an event and decided to add me to the guest list.

Spending the morning in the proximity of someone I once considered a good friend, who would not hold my gaze or a conversation, left a heavy weight on me. The awkwardness turned into unease. I didn't know if an overture was expected of me, but I did know I wasn't interested in making the initial move to reconnect. One thing I have been proud to say over the years is I know my value as a friend. I may be uncertain of how people value me in other areas of my life, but I know I am a good friend. So, I always knew what Dianna and others were walking away from, I was not so sure about what they were leaving me without.

After the clown training, I decided to hit a couple of departments in Macy's to see if any sales and clearances would remove the heaviness weighing me down. Mac cosmetics didn't have the eye shadow I was looking for. Lingerie looked too complicated. Linens was far too spread out to enjoy a leisurely stroll. My last stop was Macy's Woman, nothing inspired me there either. Slowly, I realized retail therapy had lost its effectiveness for me.

Exiting Macy's, I walked aimlessly down 34th Street. When I got to Fifth Avenue I turned left and started walking uptown. Usually, I stay away from the touristy areas of the city, 34th Street around the holidays is as touristy as it gets. As I turned up Fifth Avenue, I passed three middle-aged ladies, and one gushed to the others, "Do you wanna go the Empire State Building? It's right there!" I turned to follow her upward-pointing finger to look at the Empire State Building, somewhat dismissively, then oddly curious. My first thought was, *It's just a building.* My second thought, *I remember being so excited the first time I saw the Empire State Building.* The next thought, *When did I lose that excitement?*

Turning away, I continued walking. As I approached Bryant Park on 42nd Street, I decided to take a writing break. I had the first draft of the *My God and Me* manuscript with me and had planned to write in Central Park, however my walk ended there in Bryant Park, as I know it was meant to. I grabbed a table next to the ice skating rink. I didn't see the people surrounding me as much as I saw the very existentialist questions parading through my mind. *To be or not to be... does this mean I'm done?*

Realizing I had lost the joy of retail therapy temporarily took my mind away from analyzing the state of my relationships. As I sat down at the table I thought of how the front end of everything is always lovely. The back end, however, usually comes across as pointless. The train of my thoughts moved relentlessly onward: I outgrew my love of shopping => the glitter and luster of New York City has dulled => my relationships don't really exist => what's the purpose of anything => does the temporal nature of life's cycle make everything meaningless?

I used to receive genuine pleasure from my relationships with friends and family. It pleased and validated me as a person to invest in my relationships with time, effort, emotion and whatever else was needed. How much had I outgrown my life that my world now felt like a small isolating closet?

Many of my relationships have seemingly disintegrated over the last few years. I found myself asking, "Were the dead and dying relationships really relationships? What about people maintaining contact? Should I expect their presence to translate into dependability? Shouldn't the quality of interactions determine our connection? What makes a relationship real?"

Two years prior to this moment, I would have absolutely said my best relationships were with those I saw and talked to on a regular basis. Those people I could share aspects of my life with and share in aspects of theirs. Emotionally, I connect better with people in person – face to face, voice to voice, but with technological advances, I find myself communicating electronically more often. Can an e-relationship be real? Alternative forms of communication are very enlightening, but only when supplementing what you already know about someone, not as the sole, primary way of getting to know them.

Truthfully, I find myself becoming more detached emotionally in relationships where the main form of communication is electronic. I'm convinced people use emails and text messages as a way to maintain an emotional distance. I don't think it starts out that way, but it becomes an obstacle to interpersonal communication. However, I can accept some merits of e-communication in moderation.

My friend Sierra came to mind. We were roommates for a total of eleven months eight years ago. Seven of the eight years of our friendship had been maintained via the phone. I started thinking about what makes her different from the friends I live near or visit more regularly. Why does Sierra stand out?

Sierra stands out because she is very clear about wanting to know *me*. She wants to know about my daily life. No detail is too small. No thought is insignificant.

Further analysis showed the common denominator in my faltering and dissipating relationships is the fact that *I* was not important as a friend. What held value to the other person was *what* I was willing to do for them.

Our benefit to people does not have to be anything extravagant. We could satisfy very simple desires. We could be the last resort for a night on the town or a place to stay just in case they come to town. We could be an ego boost to get them through a romantic drought or the push to get them out of a difficult situation. We may be the ear listening to their complaints or the shoulder sharing their burdens. We might be our friend's conscience or their bad influence. People connect for a multitude of reasons, and they drift apart for just as many.

This analysis provided me with one answer to guide me through my relationship fatigue. A sign of true friendship is when people choose to be around you simply because you are you. There's no reason. No incentive. No measurable benefit. No purpose for loving you as a human being whose presence is special to their life.

Finding My People

While still deeply contemplating the history, present state and possible future of my relationships, an ageless Senegalese man walked over to my table and stood towering over me. Papadou, as he later introduced himself, was not a welcome interruption at first, however I have come to treasure the words he shared with me that day.

My manuscript was in the middle of the table and I had just started writing out my internal debate on a loose pile of papers. The Senegalese man looked down at me with an expression that was almost but not quite smiling, "Are you a writer," he asked.

His question created a surreal moment for me. I had self-published two books of poetry, contributed to a political blog of New York's largest circulation daily throughout the election year, and maintained my own blog with subscribers, but I did not claim to be a writer. My uncertainty on how to answer his question must've shown. He rephrased his question, "Where can I get your material?" Still I didn't speak. "Do you speak French?" Perhaps because my responses were verbalizing so slowly, he wondered if I understood his English. Or perhaps my darting eyes conveyed my desire to avoid engaging in conversation with him. He stood there, not moving, with his smiling-non-smiling face looking gently down on me.

My darting eyes noticed the lushness of the trees and the fleeting flight of twittering birds. They noted peaceful blue sky sprinkled with powder-puff clouds. In my mind's eye I saw this man walking towards me with a purpose. Then I didn't see him at all; I saw Adam and Eve in the garden. I thought of how God walked through the garden to confront them with their sin, *"What is this you have done?"* In that moment, I believed God was confronting me for doubting the purpose and significance of my existence. *"What is this you write?"* He had asked, even as my pen scribbled questions.

Slowly, I gathered words to answer him. "I speak French, but it's rusty. I have materials for sale, but I don't really sell them."

He eyed my manuscript. I removed it from the table and put it in my bag. He started reading from the sheet of paper I was writing on. "*Big Girl, Little Closet*, what is this?"

Still intent on hiding, I covered my paper with both hands. Incredulous, I asked, "You're really not going to go away, are you?"

"What is this you write?" he asked again.

I gave in. I submitted. I opened up and shared all my angst and confusion. I voiced my questions from earlier in the day and theories from days past. I concluded my purge with, "What's a real relationship and what isn't? If we can't identify reality what's the purpose of life?"

He answered me very succinctly.

"Some people want to collect things and other people, but you find joy in the simpler things, the air, the trees," he arched his hands dramatically in the direction of the trees and sky. "You will eventually find your people. Even when we don't speak the same language, we can share our humanity. That man who came over to ask you for money," another man had interrupted our conversation during my outpouring of questions, "you told him you didn't have any, but offered him your food. That was your humanity and he expressed his gratitude for it. You have a skill and a talent. When you can write and talk, you can share your experiences with a greater mass of people. Your purpose is to share your humanity."

Meditation Verse: Genesis 3:7-13

Then the eyes of both of them were opened, and they knew that they *were* naked; and they sewed fig leaves together and made themselves coverings. And they heard the sound of the LORD God walking in the garden in the cool of the day, and Adam and his wife hid themselves from the presence of the LORD God among the trees of the garden. Then the LORD God called to Adam and said to him, "Where *are* you?"

So he said, "I heard Your voice in the garden, and I was afraid because I was naked; and I hid myself."

And He said, "Who told you that you *were* naked? Have you eaten from the tree of which I commanded you that you should not eat?"

Then the man said, "The woman whom You gave *to be* with me, she gave me of the tree, and I ate."

And the LORD God said to the woman, "What *is* this you have done?" The woman said, "The serpent deceived me, and I ate."

How Are You Living?

No longer do I attempt to understand the certain *je ne sais quoi* I have with people. I've learned to embrace and share it more over the last few years.

I would like to share a beautiful email note I came home to after a weekend in Milwaukee last year. I call my Midwest visits marathons because I try to see as many people as possible, primarily the people sitting heaviest on my heart. Madeline is the mother of an old friend. Her husband died nearly two years prior to my trip after a long illness, and the last of her children moved out of the house the following year. She's a loving, quiet, soft-spoken woman with a world-weary air about her. I missed her on a visit the year before and made her a priority on this one. As always, we had a nice talk. After my departure, she emailed me:

Hi La'Shawnda,

Had to write a note to say how much I enjoyed seeing you. Every time you come by, you are even a more graceful young lady & radiant with some inner peace. Even as we talk about life's trials, that will see you through. Come back at Thanksgiving, you are part of our family.

With love,
Madeline

Madeline is a Catholic-raised atheist. She doesn't believe in or agree with organized religion. I'm not a fan of organized religion either, but more than that, she thinks depending on a higher being is like depending on an illusion.

When I joined the church in New York she was one of the first people I talked to about it. She brought up the church during our conversation that weekend, crediting it with my apparent growth and ease in my skin. "The church has helped you get through a lot, hasn't it?"

I looked at her askance, wondering how she got that impression. "No, I've had more problems with the church than solutions. I actually stopped attending and just recently went back. I needed a break, because they weren't Christ-like to me."

Jemini, Catholic raised and schooled once told me that I'm the only person she knows who lives the principles of their beliefs. A high honorable mention indeed, and nothing I would have ever thought I was close to achieving, though I do consciously try.

Radiant with some inner peace... that's what Madeline said. I didn't know my glow was so wonderful! I didn't know the light guiding my life and emanating from my soul would be visible to a non-believer. To someone who believes the God I believe in is nothing but an illusion.

But it is visible! It's visible to those close to me and those I only see once in a while. It's visible to strangers and life-long friends alike. Madeline's note reminds me that the way I choose to live my life is not a waste of effort or energy.

My former roommate, Sasha, drove into town to meet up with me that weekend. We hadn't visited with one another in quite some time. Sasha used to be one of the more self-centered people I knew, but with me she is very open and giving. She's generous, gracious and loving. Her concern regarding my life issues is always for me and not for the best in the situation. I haven't had much experience with that type of regard.

I was drooping on Sunday afternoon. All day Friday and Saturday were spent running around for another friend's wedding. Sunday morning, I went to breakfast with my goddaughter and her mom. I had paused to take a nap before the afternoon visits. As I lay on the sofa, Sasha looked at me and said, "Shawnda, you don't have to do any of this running around. This is your vacation! Do what you want."

Her words clashed with something in me. It's odd how strongly wrong her words sounded. When I moved to New York three years prior, my goal was to do only what I wanted to do for myself. When I moved to New York, I told myself I was done catering to other people and exhausting myself for their benefit. I had come full circle. Only this time, there was a deep-seated joy emanating from my actions and my desire to do for others. I spoke with a wealth of feeling and purpose, "It pleases me to please others."

On some level, I am able to put people at ease; I'm able to share my peace and joy and brighten their day. Even if it's draining to me, I know my source and am able to recharge. When I share myself nothing is taken from me, indeed, I grow from it.

Jemini and I once discussed how we have been placed with and assigned to one another. I assured her she and her family does much more for my heart and spirit than I do for hers. She replied by saying, "But, Shawnda, you don't need us. You would've been fine if you had never met us. We need you. You have brought so much into this family."

How much of yourself do you share with those around you? Not your money, not your property, not your belongings, but you – your spirit, your love, your energy? A kind word, a hug, a moment of your time with your complete attention? Your thoughts, your hopes, your goals, your dreams? Not just with those close to you, but perhaps the person in the grocery store looking at the same box of cereal you just put in your basket. It's a scary world; I'm not suggesting embracing every stranger you come in contact with, but we certainly don't need to shut everyone out either.

Some time ago, a woman sat next to me on the subway train. She started talking to me before her butt connected to the seat. I was writing in my journal and was set to ignore her or kindly put her off, but instead, I closed my journal, turned towards the lady and listened calmly to what she had to tell me. Instinctively, I knew she had a message for me. She started talking about the premiere of a new independent film, *Trouble the Water,* and suggested I go see it. But there was something more to her message. I listened intently and wrote down the words she punctuated her description with. She repeated these same words in the same order I wrote them before I left the train: *pray, watch, be ready and forgive.*

I say to you: be open and live more fully.

Meditation Verse: Genesis 18:1-15

Then the LORD appeared to him by the terebinth trees of Mamre, as he was sitting in the tent door in the heat of the day. So he lifted his eyes and looked, and behold, three men were standing by him; and when he saw *them,* he ran from the tent door to meet them, and bowed himself to the ground, and said, "My Lord, if I have now found favor in Your sight, do not pass on by Your servant. Please let a little water be brought, and wash your feet, and rest yourselves under the tree. And I will bring a morsel of bread, that you may refresh your hearts. After that you may pass by, inasmuch as you have come to your servant."

They said, "Do as you have said."

So Abraham hurried into the tent to Sarah and said, "Quickly, make ready three measures of fine meal; knead *it* and make cakes." And Abraham ran to the herd, took a tender and good calf, gave *it* to a young man, and he hastened to prepare it. So he took butter and milk and the calf which he had prepared, and set *it* before them; and he stood by them under the tree as they ate.

Then they said to him, "Where *is* Sarah your wife?"

So he said, "Here, in the tent."

And He said, "I will certainly return to you according to the time of life, and behold, Sarah your wife shall have a son." (Sarah was listening in the tent door which *was* behind him.) Now Abraham and Sarah were old, well advanced in age; *and* Sarah had passed the age of childbearing. Therefore Sarah laughed within herself, saying, "After I have grown old, shall I have pleasure, my lord being old also?"

And the LORD said to Abraham, "Why did Sarah laugh, saying, 'Shall I surely bear *a child,* since I am old?' Is anything too hard for the LORD? At the appointed time I will return to you, according to the time of life, and Sarah shall have a son."

But Sarah denied *it,* saying, "I did not laugh," for she was afraid.

And He said, "No, but you did laugh!"

Boss Lady: A Brief Illusion of the Triumph of Evil

Over the last five years, I've had three very intensely negative work relationships with managers. The environments they created were demeaning and stifling. The first relationship was in Milwaukee; I quit after eight months. The second was with Mean Jack. It started six months after I moved to New York; I quit after twelve months.

Nadine warned me at the time that I would continue to experience similar situations until I learned the lesson I was supposed to learn. Though she felt my pain, she told me quitting was not the answer. The third and most exhausting of these relationships was with Boss Lady. I started working for her seven months after I quit Mean Jack. God was gracious enough to give me a rebound period between the two!

Boss Lady was my third assignment at the bank, which lasted eighteen months. I was determined not to quit. After a year and a half, she released me and hired someone else. The reason: she felt neglected because I didn't cater to her *enough*. I received my lesson and was free to go! *Thank You, Jesus!*

During Boss Lady's campaign to replace me, I was able to observe her machinations. Despite my desire to keep my job, it was awesome to witness her masterful puppetry of her colleagues and my other two managers. Boss Lady was one of three people I supported directly, but the others were so cowed by her personality they never spoke up for me.

She was such a draining presence to be around, I was truly overjoyed to learn I would soon be removed from her attacking and repressive energy. We were in an invisible battle for months. Every day I went to work with a smile and warm greetings; whenever she spoke to me (no matter how demeaning or belittling) I'd ask if there was anything else she wanted me to do for her. Any day she didn't speak to me was a good day. The best days were when she was not in the office. Not just for me, but many others in the office. When Boss Lady informed me, a month in advance, of my impending release, I felt as if a millstone had been lifted from around my neck. There was a great relief, even with no job lined up.

By and large, I loved working in Boss Lady's group. In general, colleagues were friendly and willing to chip in with one another; teamwork was inherently built into everyone's job function. Most of all, I enjoyed the conversations. There was always someone to talk to about something in the news or in the office, on my mind or on theirs. Boss Lady was the only source of aggravation for me.

For a year, she attempted to turn our work relationship into a marriage. Early on, in a desire to "see where it was going," I went along. I can understand the basic desire was for a great partnership at work. One in which I knew her mind, anticipated her needs, took care of everything without having to bother her with the details and check in throughout the day to give her updates and get approvals. Apparently, I was the wife!

Unfortunately for me, she was not a good husband. From my first project with her, I knew she didn't have my back. She left me hanging and flapping in the wind even when she didn't need to. She wanted me to be the fall-guy for her bad decisions. The messenger she sent to give bad tidings or arrogant orders. When the backlash skipped over me and returned directly to her office, she claimed I had messed up the message. "LaShawnda didn't deliver it as instructed." Or, she hadn't told me to say anything at all.

She was fond of telling me to tell others to do something she wanted them to do. The situation was: Boss Lady sent a temp admin to tell vice presidents, directors and managing directors how to do their jobs with nothing other than her orders. I didn't have background information, knowledge of the project, nor knowledge of the subordinates' role or function. I just knew the words she told me to parrot. So, when they asked me a question, as they always did, I had to admit to not knowing the answer and direct them to Boss Lady. One time I balked; told her it made no sense to send me with her message when everyone was going to have something to say and I would have to direct them to her anyway. "I can't make these people do anything," I said in exasperation.

Oh, she was livid! "What do you mean, you can't make them do anything? I'm their boss!" See, when she spoke to me, we were one, when she spoke of me to others, I was some wayward employee.... "Yes, *you're* their boss. I'm not. This order should come from you, not your assistant."

Maybe that was the beginning of the end....

She repeatedly asked for a commitment. So much so, my inventive ways of avoiding conversation made me feel like a commitment-phobe. Boss Lady did not represent marriage or partnership well. What she represented was deceit, deviousness, disloyalty, selfishness, unfaithfulness, lack of appreciation, and emotional and verbal abuse. It saddens me to think what her own marriage must be like, based on her representation of the institution.

Three days before my last day, she announced my imminent departure via email. The group was shocked. No one was aware of her maneuvering behind closed doors. She completed her coup in as much secrecy and deception as she did everything else. She led my other two managers to believe she was working on paperwork to hire me permanently, while behind our backs, she interviewed candidates to replace me. God kept me informed. Every step she took, someone called to update me about it. She was shocked every time I shared my knowledge with her. Though I was not surprised by her actions, my feelings were extremely hurt. Despite our difficult relationship, I felt painfully rejected by her. Throughout most of her sneaky campaign, I observed her actions against me with no fear for my future. Despite pockets of bitterness, hurt and rejection, there was overall peace. God has never once failed to provide for me. Whatever happened, I knew two things for sure: I would be able to pay my rent and I would be able to eat.

After the announcement, I received numerous phone calls, desk-drop-bys and emails of farewell. Most people said the same thing: They enjoyed seeing my smile and hearing my laughter. *Love that joy, it's completely supernatural!*

I was encouraged to learn, even in the midst of battle for my source of income, my spirit was unshakeable. The stress of our hidden conflict may have manifested in my body – my skin changed, my face aged, I grew a cluster of grey hair at my crown, and solid pounds settled around my mid-section, but no one saw the effect Boss Lady had on me. Her darkness was not dimming my light.

Boss Lady felt triumphant... briefly. Until the last day, when she saw people still seeking me for a last chat or heard our uproarious laughter at the final jokes. I'm sure she felt as if she had flexed her strategic muscle and increased her power base within the group, until the group began questioning her on her decision to let me go. She has relied on her cunning, misdirection and secrets to get to where she is and obtain what she wants – that won't last.

What I've learned from the outpouring of well-wishes and appreciation is that my light is greater than any darkness attempting to suppress me. Another lesson is that I can successfully compartmentalize and manage my troubles.

Boss Lady helped me spiritually, and I'm grateful to be able to recognize her contribution. One of her Jewish account managers jokingly asked on my last day, "What? You grew closer to God by calling on Jesus every day? *Jesus, Jesus, please help me!*" He had a big laugh with that one. So did I. "Pretty much! That's how it went!"

I thank Boss Lady for her contribution to my journey. Difficult people and difficult relationships grow us exponentially. I didn't understand servitude in Christ as well as I understand it now. I truly believe that was my lesson with this placement. *Service.* A deeper, unquestioning service, with a cheerful and unchanged heart, no matter the opposition. I'm so ready to go to the next level!

Meditation Verse: Mark 10:42-45

But Jesus called them to *Himself* and said to them, "You know that those who are considered rulers over the Gentiles lord it over them, and their great ones exercise authority over them. Yet it shall not be so among you; but whoever desires to become great among you shall be your servant. And whoever of you desires to be first shall be slave of all. For even the Son of Man did not come to be served, but to serve, and to give His life a ransom for many."

Pop Culture Messiah

On June 25, 2009 Michael Jackson died. He's being called an icon, but I prefer to think of him as an amazingly gifted human being.

I confess I was one of his many doubters. It's not that I believed Michael Jackson molested a child, more specifically, I believe human beings are capable of anything. I wanted to believe in Michael's innocence, but he didn't adequately defend himself. He paid money to make a situation go away. Only, money invited more such situations. On the other hand, when the accuser's parents accepted cash as payment for their child's allegedly stolen innocence, I then doubted their claims more than I doubted Michael. Oh, what a tangled web we weave....

Yes, I was a doubter. Until the day he died. From that day on, all I can remember is his message of love, his cry for help, his screams of anguish. I remember how his words have always reverberated through me, reaching to the depths of my soul and vibrating across the width of my spirit. I was a doubter until he breathed his last, and I realized even death could not extinguish his light.

I no longer doubt Michael Jackson's innocence. One thing I know for sure is evil and love cannot co-exist. God is love. And Michael Jackson's existence was an expression of love. His talents were used to sow love around the world, he reached corners where Jesus isn't known. Even though he may not have stayed here long enough to reap the harvest of his labor, I am confident he will be graced with his eternal reward.

Meditation Verse: 1 John 4:7-12

Dear friends, let us love one another, for love comes from God. Everyone who loves has been born of God and knows God. Whoever does not love does not know God, because God is love. This is how God showed his love among us: He sent his one and only Son into the world that we might live through him. This is love: not that we loved God, but that he loved us and sent his Son as an atoning sacrifice for our sins. Dear friends, since God so loved us, we also ought to love one another. No one has ever seen God; but if we love one another, God lives in us and his love is made complete in us.

We know that God sends messengers and scouts. He sends us soldiers and prophets. Two thousand years ago He sent His only begotten Son, Jesus Christ, to teach us. After Jesus, God sent His Holy Spirit to dwell within us. His indwelling Spirit works to call His children closer to Him. Those who choose to obey His call have their talents activated and magnified for His glorification and are sent forth into the world as light-bearers, truth-sayers, love-doers, performers of His Word and servants of His will.

Perhaps, like many others, the story of Michael Jackson's life and his cultural significance is hard to appreciate from the viewpoint of his deep valleys. Similarly, we as individuals have difficulty seeing our significance from our own low points. I am guilty of growing weary. I am guilty of focusing on the ugly scars and errors in judgment received from falls and fatigue. Like every person born since Adam, I am guilty and will forever fall short of the glorious perfection of God and Christ Jesus. But that won't stop me from being the most wonderful servant of God the world has yet to see. Lack of perfection will not deter me from being a marvelous representation of my Father. I will not falter in my quest to continuously evolve my character into a mirror-image of my Creator.

Change, growth and evolution – they all hurt. They aren't easy. We witnessed all three in Michael Jackson's life and career. We didn't like the look or sound of his change, growth or evolution sometimes, but we certainly saw it. We didn't understand it, but we definitely felt it. Many of us never spent a moment in his physical presence, but our lives have always been surrounded by his music. To know his music is to know him. His music told us who he was – his music was a healing agent for those in pain and fighting disease; it told us of his love for the hungry and needy. His music spoke of memories, wishes, and prayers; it put his heart in direct communication with our hearts. That's why we love Michael Jackson.

I love Michael Jackson because of his words.

How powerful is a word?

God created the world with a word. *"And God said... and it was so." (Genesis 1:3-30)*

Jesus healed with His word. *"Lord... only speak a word, and my servant will be healed." (Matthew 8:8)*

We bind ourselves to our life partners with two words: "Do you take this man or woman...*I do."*

We are instructed to *"Speak to one another with psalms, hymns and spiritual songs. Sing and make music in your heart to the Lord, always giving thanks to God the Father for everything, in the name of our Lord Jesus Christ." (Ephesians 5:19-20)*

Words are life. They have power. *"The tongue has the power of life and death, and those who love it will eat its fruit." (Proverbs 18:21)*

Michael Jackson was not just an entertainer. He was not just a pop star. He was not just a sad, confused human being. He was one of God's messengers. His message was one of hope, love, peace and unity. That's scripture. His music was rooted deep in biblical principles. I didn't see or appreciate his message song by song, album by album, year by year. But it's something I can't miss when reviewing the whole of his life and musical catalog after his death.

God's hand was all up and through Michael's life. He was holding him, guiding him and speaking through him. I can understand how Michael may have sometimes felt bereft of His comfort; he had far too many people and distractions clamoring around him, causing him to stumble. But even in his imperfection he was the best Michael Joseph Jackson ever. He was an awesome steward of his talents. He was a loving and hospitable ambassador of biblical principles. His colossal, global renown suggests some obedience to God's plan for his life. I give thanks for the technology that keeps his voice as clean and clear as the day he first laid the tracks. I give thanks that we haven't lost him, we won't forget him and more people will come to love him for his message. Sometimes we don't notice the little flickering lights in our own lives until a stunningly bright star falls from the sky.

Some of Michael Jackson's words:

Hold me, like the River Jordan and I will then say to thee, you are my Friend. Carry me, like you are my brother. Love me like a mother. Will you be there? They told me, a man should be faithful and walk when not able and fight till the end, but I'm only Human! Everyone's taking control of me. Seems like the world's got a role for me. I'm so confused, will you show to me, you'll be there for me and care enough to bear me? (Will You Be There?)

I'm starting with the man in the mirror. I'm asking him to change his ways. And no message could've been any clearer. If you wanna make the world a better place, take a look at yourself, and make a change! (Man in the Mirror)

We are the world. We are the children. We are the ones who make a better place so let's start giving. There's a choice we're making. We're saving our own lives. It's true we'll make a better day, just you and me. (We Are the World)

Heal the world. Make it a better place – for you, for me and the entire human race. (Heal the World)

Take Me

Take me, Lord, all that I am
My heart strained by anguish
Lay open, awaiting your Love
I wrongly sought self-satisfaction
Now, I seek You. Set it right, free it…
Take my heart, Lord, and fill me with Your Love.

Take me, Jehovah, all that I am
My mind crowded with supposition
Cleanse me to receive your Word
Too many distractions in this world
Too few havens to rest in
Take my mind, Jehovah, and fill me with Your Word.

Keep me, Father, all that I am
My soul aches from bruising battles
Heal me and rejuvenate me with your Spirit.
I've never been a fighter
But I want to be your soldier
Keep me, Father, and fill me with Your Spirit.

Keep me, I AM, all that I am.
My body yearns for worldly pleasures
Calm me, soothe me with your Presence.
I've been anxious and need your touch.
Shape me, mold me, guide me, console me.
Keep me, I AM, and fill me with Your Presence.

Build it...

"Build it and he will come,"
a voice whispered persistently
inside me.
The whisper drove me passionately
across the country –
out of Los Angeles
back to Milwaukee
onward to New York.
I believed it.
Commenced building
my self
my spirit
my life
a home
a career.
Fell in love while working
on my physical self.
For a while, thought One was the *he*
until the Other had me thinking in we.
For years, I built many *its*.
Now, there's no voice,
no mantra,
no hope,
no *it*, no *he*, no *come*.

Reconciling My Sexiness with My Celibacy

Reconcile: to bring into agreement or harmony; make compatible or consistent

I've been celibate for most of my life. I've never quite been sexually active, though I did voluntarily complete the act once during my first semester of college. That one random time convinced me that the next time would be with someone I cared for. Though, I admit, it took years to come to the decision to wait for my husband.

I fought living a celibate life tooth and nail. I dated for years with the intent of finding a man suitable enough to share my body with, even if I didn't want to share my heart with him. God had other plans. I've been interested in relationships with very few men – less than five. And sexually attracted to even less. Every time I attempted to act out my curiosity and lust, something happened to prevent me. The summer I turned twenty-eight, I threw up my hands and said, "Okay, Father, I'm done trying to be a hoochie. I'll do it your way." It took two more years before I promised to wait for my husband.

During my twenties, I was intent on claiming my sexuality. I wanted to own it. I felt the only way to truly own my sexuality was to give it freely to whomever I wanted to give it. I wanted to exercise my power to *choose* my sexual partners. Remember, excluding the one time in college, my only sexual experiences had been forced on me. My greatest fear was that I would never be able to erase from my mind or body the things my violators did to me and made me do to them. I wanted to write over the residue of memories they created with sexual experiences I had control over.

Thank you, Father, You knew better! I was not ready. I couldn't have handled loveless and non-committed intimacies. I would have destroyed myself.

When I was eighteen, I wrote a poem titled *The Beginning*. In it, I expressed anger that the choice of being a virgin bride was denied me. I carried that anger through my teens and twenties. During those years, I didn't think it mattered who I shared my body with because I was already soiled. Thoroughly violated. No longer pure. I was used goods and, rather than be used by men (as a victim), I decided to use them (as a conqueror). God, in His infinite wisdom, thwarted me in all my sexual pursuits. When I sat down to think about how to write this portion, it came to me that God has not only protected me from myself and strange men, He has also purified me. *Hallelujah! I praise Your Holy Name and Most Gracious Spirit, Father!* These past few years, He has cleansed my mind from those debilitating memories. He separated my self-concept from the violations I was subjected to. He has always protected my heart from the death and malice of this world. He reminded me my *heart* has never been violated by men; my heart remains pure. My body may have been violated, but it is still His most holy temple. Through the process of living, forgiving, loving and giving, God has renewed my mind, soul and spirit *(Romans 12:1-2)*. With this, the Spirit of God informed me, I *will be* as a virgin to my husband.

Now I am free of the demons those violators attached to me. *Hallelujah!*

Can't take sexy out the girl

During my twenties, the one thing threatening to lead me astray in the wild, wild world was my sex appeal. Men were really attracted to me. Like, really.... Their age, height, ethnicity, marital status – none of that presented barriers to them. They approached representing all shapes, sizes and backgrounds. To this day, I can't put a finger on what they were attracted to in me. I've been told by various men that it's my smile, my laugh, my figure, my intelligence, independence and confidence among other things. If I were to guess, I would say my light and freshness is the most attractive thing about me. Men are intrigued by my air of innocence.

I have attempted to play the vamp, though I never quite got it right. During the years I was trying to be a bad girl, I wrote out my fantasies, which went a long way to cure me of the desire to act them out. After a while, I realized I had enough erotic poems to compile a book. With this project in mind, I asked my friend Doug to help me with a photo shoot to illustrate portions of the poems. I gave Doug a list of verses I wanted him to model for, I had certain poses in mind already as well. We had use of a small apartment for the photo shoot, however the bulk of Doug's photos were taken in the bedroom. At one point, as he lounged on the bed, I stood behind the photographer, looking at the shot through her lens, trying to see what she saw. Doug looked at me with the most amazing, smoldering heat in his eyes. With a pert arch of my brow, I asked him, "What'cha looking at?"

"I'm looking at you," he replied low and sultry.

"Oh, really," I mimicked the low and sultry and attempted to give him something to look at. Apparently, I didn't think standing in front of him in skimpy lingerie, fishnets and four-inch stilettos was enough of a tease. I lifted one of my legs slowly into the air while maintaining eye contact and attempted to lower my foot onto a nearby dresser. Perhaps I intended to adjust my stockings once propped on the dresser, can't quite recall, but I remember feeling like a vampish cabaret dancer in that moment. Unfortunately, I am innately clumsy. My foot never connected with the dresser, I missed my mark and almost fell on my face when my foot slammed to the floor and I lost my balance. Doug started cracking up as did the photographer and other model standing by. "Shawnda, you are crazy...," Doug exclaimed, "but that was still sexy as hell...."

Moral of the story: Me trying to be sexy doesn't really work. Therefore, people telling me I'm sexy never really computed because I didn't know what they were alluding to. Now, I just tell people I have a certain *je ne sais quoi*.

For many years I wore big, baggy clothes in an effort to go unnoticed because I thought men were only attracted to my breasts and butt. The men I was attracted to the most paid no attention to me at all. Deep down, I wanted someone to focus on getting to know the *Inner* LaShawnda. The girl who comes out in quiet moments and private times. The lady who responds to gentle talk and tender care. The woman who appreciates a soft touch and a firm word. The man who connects with those parts of me will be the one to claim my heart.

Two sides of the same coin

None of the men I've been attracted to got to know the *Inner* LaShawnda. I will say a couple of them worked themselves past the physical traits. I can't blame the men completely for not wanting to get to know me. There were instances, back then, when I made overtures to entice and seduce because I had started to believe the hype and myth of my own sex appeal. Out of respect for me, so they told me, they declined. Those were the only times I resented the high esteem people hold me in. I was in my mid-twenties, and I refer to that period of my life as my *Sexually Frustrated Years* – all I could think about was finding a partner to help me with a whole bunch of itches I should not have been thinking about scratching.

Celibacy was never my intention. In my mind, it was only a matter of time before I hooked up with someone and began life as a pleasure-seeking nympho. I didn't admit to being celibate until a couple of years ago, actually. For a while before that, I only committed to abstaining. There is a clear difference. Celibacy is about vows and intent; God is involved. Abstinence is a decision not to indulge particular appetites for a period of time. In my mind, my abstinence was going to be short lived. Before I admitted to abstinence, I simply told people I was waiting for a decent man to share myself with. Even in my youth, I realized and accepted I could not dishonor myself by sharing my body with just anyone.

As you can see, I had conflicting issues here. Part of me thought I was a nympho-in-waiting, however my dominant part knew my body as a temple and sacred housing. My body is a holy place – I've always felt that way, but it took a long time to acknowledge and accept the feeling as truth. From this viewpoint, I could not invite just anyone into my body.

Even during that confused, unformed youthful period, every question I asked a man eliminated him as a potential partner. Was he clean? Was he honest? Was he pure of intent? Upfront? Trustworthy? Honorable and loyal? Worth keeping around? Covenant husband material? Father material? Imagine how much more difficult it is now, when I want to know if he has a relationship with God. Can I study, pray and worship with him? Can we discuss our foundational beliefs and practices? Men with these characteristics aren't on every bus that rolls by, nor are they in every school of fish. Such men are God-given. You need to be able to recognize your mate when God presents him to you, or presents you to him – whichever way you want to think of it. Despite what many women say about waiting for a man to find you as his good thing, I prefer to keep an open mind. Ruth was directed to Boaz and instructed on how to win him. *(Ruth 3:1-6)*

Do you want a standard or a man?

Let's face it, non-committed casual sex can produce unwanted consequences. Notice I did not say *unexpected* consequences. We know what we're getting into when we engage in non-committed casual sex. My rationale has always been: if I can't stand a man for five minutes or for the length of a date, chances were we weren't going to be a successful parenting couple for eighteen years to life. Each man I have been interested in I have mentally put in the role of my husband. That may sound crazy to you. You may be thinking, "Why not just see what happens? Have fun! Enjoy yourself, you're young!"

I don't waste my time letting men enjoy themselves with me. I know what I want. My end goal is marriage and a family. Almost immediately, you become aware of what someone is looking for when you date. If a man is not compatible from the beginning with my needs, I move on. Perhaps now you can see how I *accidentally* lapsed into nearly two decades of celibacy.

I used to joke that I was only looking for a halfway decent man. Countless people throughout the years have urged me to lower my standards and take what's on offer. I am more amazed now than in the past. My standards aren't something I made up. They were set in me. There is a reason I'm attracted to a man who knows his mind and goes after what he wants. A reason I'm attracted to a man I can look up to, talk to and walk with. A reason I'm attracted to intelligence and humor, to gentleness and strength, to honesty and commitment, faithfulness and character. There is a reason for my standards. I embody certain characteristics that would not pair well with a man who doesn't know his own mind or with one who needs constant pampering. I would not partner well with someone who only thinks of himself or someone not interested in building a relationship and a life together. I am not the helpmate of just anyone. Neither are you. Lowering my standards wouldn't change me. However, it would change the course of my life, as I would then be willing to accept less than what God has prepared for me.

The question of Jazzy Media and VoLux

A couple years after arriving in New York, I decided to fold on my *VoLux-Full Figured Calendar*. Since then, I've rethought the rest of my business. To close down everything felt too much like quitting on myself. Early on, I wanted to drop the calendar because I couldn't reconcile the sexiness people see in my physical body with the reality of my celibacy. There was an expectation for me to be a siren. I couldn't deliver. I felt like a fraud. I didn't want to continue perpetuating a lie – selling sex appeal while recoiling from that imagery.

Now I am more comfortable with the sex appeal contained in my physicality. I no longer see my physical appearance or the appreciation my physical attributes receive as a contradiction of who I am. Yes, I can be sexy to man and still belong to God. I can love and adorn my body while remaining chaste for my husband.

One persistent thought helped reconcile my sexiness to my celibacy – disregarding either is disregarding something God gave me. He did not make any mistakes with my physique nor with my desire for a holy union. Neither were my business and calendar ideas developed on my own. My Father God was with me every step of the way. The ideas were planted and talents surfaced to bring the ideas to fruition. I learned and accepted a lot about myself through the development, experience and marketing of *VoLux Full-Figured Calendar*.

There's still work to do. I need to figure out how I can create as I wish, give as I am able, grow as I must, and accept all the accolades and admiration without shame or embarrassment. While continuing to operate with grace and love, taste and style, and maintain economic efficiency – all without becoming overwhelmed.

I understand my future is rooted in reconciling my sexiness with my celibacy; my physical with my spiritual. My future will be defined by how I accept and merge my many different parts, so my body and health prosper even as my soul prospers *(3 John 1:2)*. My struggle is hardest when I attempt to separate my elements. I am at peace when I prune and grow all of me together.

Meditation Verse: Isaiah 54:4-8

"Do not fear, for you will not be ashamed; neither be disgraced, for you will not be put to shame; for you will forget the shame of your youth, and will not remember the reproach of your widowhood anymore.

For your Maker *is* your husband, the LORD of hosts *is* His name; and your Redeemer *is* the Holy One of Israel; He is called the God of the whole earth.

For the LORD has called you like a woman forsaken and grieved in spirit, like a youthful wife when you were refused," says your God. "For a mere moment I have forsaken you, but with great mercies I will gather you. With a little wrath I hid My face from you for a moment; but with everlasting kindness I will have mercy on you," says the LORD, your Redeemer.

Ladies, You're the Prize!

Disclaimer: Please, don't try this at home!

Shortly after I came off a self-imposed one-year dating hiatus in New York City, I was asked out on an old fashion-style date of dinner and dancing. I was pleasantly surprised and graciously accepted. Over the years I've learned my open, exuberant nature sometimes sends out wrong signals. Though I've been working on toning it down, it bursts free on occasion. That being said, I still don't know how the guy who started with such a nice invitation of dinner and dancing ended the conversation as a balled-up *no* in my waste bin. Perhaps, he was surprised and overly encouraged by my initial *yes*, because he added, "Do you wrestle? I think it will be fun to wrestle you... I'm looking for fun and distractions."

In short, I told him, "Fun and Distractions are not part of my name and the last time I wrestled a man, was *the last time* I will wrestle a man.... My ego is too fragile."

This brief exchange reminded me of a boy-man I wrestled when I was twenty years old. His name was Lenny. We were both restaurant managers assigned to different locations. He was about my age, a couple of inches shorter than I and super skinny. He had a slimy, Casanova approach that rubbed me the wrong way. I admit I wasn't nice to him. He used to badger me to go out with him every time he saw me. It got to the point that I told him he had no chance, I wasn't interested, and he was getting on my nerves. Unfortunately for me, Lenny was paying more attention to me than I thought he was. He learned I was an athlete, enjoyed challenges at work, and I never backed down. One day he approached me with a challenge, "How about we wrestle for a date?"

"Excuse me?!?!" My response was full of irritated twenty-year-old attitude.

"We wrestle..."

"Not on your life!" I didn't want him touching me.

"No, wait! If you win, I'll leave you alone." My ears perked up. "If I win, you go out with me." All I heard was that he would leave me alone. "You'll stop asking me out?"

"Yes."

"You'll stop talking junk?"

"Yes."

"You'll stop talking to me altogether?"

"Well...."

"Lenny!"

"Yes."

"Ok. Deal!" We shook on it. He gave me his slick-looking smile, and I rolled my eyes. I was confident I would take the boy-man down lickety-split. We met one day after work in the parking lot. We crouched in our positions. I told him not to take the can of whup-ass personally, but he had it coming. Yeah, I talked junk back then, too.

Before I could do one good circle to look for a weak spot in his stance, he pounced on me. I don't remember landing. I like to think it was winter and he dropped me in a pile of snow. Or maybe it was fall and he tossed me into a pile of leaves. Whatever.... One second he had me up in the air, the next second I was on my back and he was climbing on top of me with a wide, cheesy smile showing all his pearly white thirty-two's. "When should I pick you up?"

Let me tell you, my pride was bruised. Especially, when he got up and started jumping up and down with his hands up in the air like he was Rocky Balboa. High-fiving his boys – I hadn't even noticed we had an audience.... Half the restaurant came out to watch!

Everything about him said I could take him: he was one of those fancy boys, always sweet talking the ladies; he carried a comb in his pocket to slick back his hair throughout the day; he wasn't athletic; and he was somewhat goofy and very skinny. I grew up putting my younger brother in headlocks and took boxing lessons from my older half brother. Boys didn't scare me. I could handle a boy. But Lenny gave me a lesson on respecting men. I honored my end of the bargain and went out with him.

Years later, I told this story to Andrea. Between guffaws of laughter she said, "Girl, you should've known you didn't have a chance! *You* were the prize!"

I hadn't looked at it that way, but seeing myself as *The Prize* changed the way I deal with men. Every woman should view herself as *The Prize*. With such a view point, women are less likely to sell themselves short in relationships. Lenny drove home the realization that men will do whatever it takes to gain your attention and win your favor. I didn't appreciate Lenny's interest as genuine, but the lesson I learned certainly was.

Meditation Verse: Genesis 29:15-20

Then Laban said to Jacob, "Because you *are* my relative, should you therefore serve me for nothing? Tell me, what *should* your wages *be?*" Now Laban had two daughters: the name of the elder *was* Leah, and the name of the younger *was* Rachel. Leah's eyes *were* delicate, but Rachel was beautiful of form and appearance.

Now Jacob loved Rachel; so he said, "I will serve you seven years for Rachel your younger daughter."

And Laban said, "*It is* better that I give her to you than that I should give her to another man. Stay with me." So Jacob served seven years for Rachel, and they seemed *only* a few days to him because of the love he had for her.

Men

Some men are destroyers.
Some are builders.
Which are you?

Set Apart

My body has been a barrier to a comfortable dating life. Men have been obscenely fixated on my physical form. Even when I thought sex was all I wanted from a man, if a man was explicit about his sexual interest in me he was immediately vilified. Eventually, I became able to break down what sex represented to me at that time. The sexually active people I knew had companionship and help in their daily lives. What I really wanted (companionship) was misrepresented by what I was pursuing (sex). In my ignorance, I wasted time with men who only saw a body useful for sex; they did not see a person in need of companionship. Not knowing how to bridge that gap kept me uncomfortable when dealing with men who expressed a personal interest in me.

I've had a lot of first dates, some second dates, but very few third dates. I have never been a casual dater – one to go out with someone just because…. The "just because" reasons are ridiculous to me… just because I'm bored, he has money, he's cute, he's fun, it's a free meal, etc. Not interested. I have to be open to a future with a man. That may sound like a lot, but how many of your friends have children by men they were just kickin' it with? Or they were surprised his seed took root and bore fruit despite their precautions?

I look at it this way – any man could potentially be the sperm donor for my child if I allow him access. It doesn't matter what I blame conception on – my lack of self-control or his excessive persuasion – my child would be the result. If a man enters and deposits and I deliver, then I'm stuck dealing with that man for at least the whole of my child's childhood. That's a life sentence. So, if I'm sitting on the phone or across the table from a man and I am exposed to something that doesn't look or sound like the *father* of my child, I'm done. There's no need to go further. That does not mean I look at every man and think, *I want to have your baby.* I do prefer a planned pregnancy within the confines of a healthy marriage.

Wrong Number

One of the first contacts I had in New York was through Zoë and one of her friends. They had a male friend, Clark, who was a "born and bred" New Yorker. Clark and I had been introduced via email before I relocated. He suggested I call him once I got situated in the city and he would show me around. The first phone call I had with him was the day after I arrived in New York. Prior to that phone call, Clark had never spoken to me or seen me.

My friend Nadine had flown to Milwaukee to drive to New York with me. She stayed that weekend to help me unpack and settle in. I mentioned Clark to her and asked her to meet him with me that weekend.

After we returned the rental truck, I made an introductory call to Clark. One minute into the conversation, I knew he was single, hadn't had sex in a while (which he didn't understand because he was Superman in the bed), and took care of his women with the Superman theme song playing in the background. He offered to play a sample on the phone for me. I was speechless. I pulled my phone away from my ear and looked at it as if it had shape-shifted in my hand. When I put it back to my ear, he told me he was a big man, physically – overweight – but still well-endowed. I couldn't take any more, "This is too much information!" I said before disconnecting the call.

I called Zoë in Milwaukee and asked her what the heck she had told Clark about me. "Why is he running down his sex credentials within the first minute of conversation?" She was horrified and swore she had only told him I was a good friend moving to the city who didn't know anyone. That had me thinking the man was a predator. I didn't trust the situation. No amount of apologies or reassurance that he'd meant no harm would put me at ease.

Meditation Verse: Psalm 4:3, 8

But know that the LORD has set apart for Himself him who is godly; the LORD will hear when I call to Him.

I will both lie down in peace, and sleep; for You alone, O LORD, make me dwell in safety.

Something Ain't Right

Let me tell you a story. There was this guy, Kortney, in Milwaukee that I almost "hooked up" with twice. He was four years my junior, about six feet six inches tall, creamy vanilla mocha skin that looked like it was sprinkled with gold dust. He had the most beautiful blue-grey eyes I had ever seen and dark blond cornrows. Yeah, looking at him, you wondered – *is he or isn't he…* but as soon as he opened his mouth his thick hood drawl marked him as straight black. True, he could've been trying extra hard because he was so fair, but his ethnicity didn't matter – the man was fine! Kortney was probably the only exception to my *I don't date just because* stance. I had no other reason for wanting to jump his bones than his looks. So sad, I know….

The first time we met, I was twenty-three years old working at a bank. He walked into teller line one day. Before I'd counted out his cash, I had his number. I also learned he was only nineteen years old. But again, he was that kind of fine! Fortunately for me, his conversation was a turn-off. When he eventually got around to asking me out, it was to go to his place to play video games with him and his friend.

"*Uh*, no. Catch ya later." Video games were not on my mind. Age apparently is a great indicator of where you are in life!

Several years later, while working at another bank, Kortney appeared in my teller line again. Time seemed to stand still as we cow-eyed one another. He slipped me his number, I called, he asked me over, I went. Believe me when I tell you, I was about as prime as I had ever been for a man I wanted nothing other than sex from. I was twenty-eight years old and had not been touched since my college encounter ten years prior. I thought it was time I became a real woman! I didn't tell anyone what I was doing, but I did leave a note for my roommate with Kortney's contact information in case I didn't make it back home. On some level I knew I was playing with fire. By the time I got to his house, I was congratulating myself for finally stepping into the game, *"You go, girl! Tonight, I'm bringing out the sex siren. It's about to happen for me."* I was ready to bring on my sexual revolution!

I was all smiles, breathy voice and fluttering lashes when he greeted me at my car. My whole body was vibrating in anticipation. However, something happened between my car and his front door. The revelation is clearer today.

He hugged me.

When he pulled away, I didn't see the man I was excited for, I saw something else. His features were distorted, menacing, dark, pointed and angular. I felt the bones in his chest, back and arms when my arms wrapped around him. It was like the big solid man evaporated on contact. He changed on me and to this day I believe I saw a demon spirit. When he spoke, his voice even sounded different. I couldn't place it, but the whole situation took on a supernatural feel. We ended up talking outside for an hour or so. Before we entered his apartment I whispered a quick prayer. My time in his home turned into a counseling session. Kortney was deeply troubled and dealing with some serious issues. I offered my ear, some hope and a couple of suggestions, then I hightailed it out of there.

During that period, when I went to Kortney's house, I didn't consider myself a practicing Christian. In fact, I was purposefully putting off committing to God until I had gotten some of my worldly urges out of my system. God had different plans, but He tolerated my meager attempts to thwart Him for several years. After the visit with Kortney, I gave up trying to be what I was not.

When I tell people I am protected, this is one of the examples I share. In my eagerness to become "worldly" I have put myself in several dangerous and unsavory situations. Yet, I have been prevented from aligning myself with people who mean me no good.

Commuting Casanova

David was a manager of mine a decade ago. He was a consummate ladies man at least fifteen years my senior. He never really hid his attraction for me. I admit to being somewhat attracted to him, but the age difference was a turn-off for me. However, I left the door open for persuading. We stayed in touch after I moved on to another line of work. I lived in Milwaukee; David traveled a lot but was based in Chicago. My job with him ended in May and throughout the summer we tried to get together for lunch or drinks. Both of our efforts were thwarted. He had vacation plans; then my aunt had a baby and I traveled to assist her. Finally, we nailed down a date in the fall. He was supposed to drive to Milwaukee to have dinner with me at 7:00 PM on a Sunday night. Depending on your point of measurement, no more than ninety-two miles separate Chicago and Milwaukee. At most, barring heavy traffic, travel time is about one hour and a half. I don't know what time David got on the road but he called me at 1:00 AM to say he was on his way. Though I had been in bed for some time, I was alert enough to ask, "David, what are you planning on doing when you get here?" I was perplexed because he had always been a gentleman with me.

"I'm still taking you out to eat, Baby."

"No. I don't think so. It's 1:00 AM on a Sunday night in Milwaukee. Nothing's open. If you're closer to Chicago, you should just go back home."

"I'm closer to you."

"Well, come on, but I'm almost asleep."

I didn't hear from David for the rest of the night.

The next afternoon he called and had the nerve to be angry with me. David is a successful black man with a wonderful job at a historic Chicago company. He travels seventy-five percent of the year on the company dime and banks his income. At first, I didn't think too much of him driving in the middle of the night to see me, even though he was unusually off schedule. When he expressed his anger at me the next day, I re-evaluated his possible motive for the late-night drive.

During the afternoon phone call, David informed me in a snarling voice that he had gotten arrested shortly after he spoke with me the night before.

Through his explanation of how his arrest was my fault (as he's never been arrested before) I learned what he had been doing all day Sunday that put him behind schedule. He had been called into work to take care of a delivery that had been waiting for him. He then worked on personal real estate management issues, followed by making care arrangements for his dogs for later that week when he would be traveling. He didn't say exactly when, but at some point during his busy Sunday he went to a shooting range to practice shooting his handgun. The way he told it, he was in such a rush leaving the shooting range he didn't bother putting his gun back in its case; he shoved it into his glove compartment instead.

So...when he got pulled over for speeding in Racine, Wisconsin, shortly after crossing the Illinois/Wisconsin border, the officers asked for his license and registration. He reached over to the glove compartment to retrieve his registration papers and the gun he forgot about fell out.... *Brothas and sistas, you know it was on from there!* The cops yanked David from the car, frisked him, read him his rights and took him jail.

He was angry. I had never heard him angry before. He targeted his anger at me because I was the woman associated with his fall. If it hadn't been for me, he wouldn't have been rushing or speeding; he wouldn't have even been on that highway. Certainly, he never would have been in *Wisconsin!*

Patiently and in awe, I listened to all he had to say. When he finished, I said with quiet simplicity, "David, you didn't have good intentions."

Dwelling in Safety

God has His ways, people. I know because I spent years trying to get around them. Examples like David and Kortney tell me God has something else planned for me and no one is going to be allowed to ruin what He has set me apart for. My body is not mine to do with as I please. Yes, I've tried to toss myself at a couple of men. A couple of times I jumped, hoping I would just land on something interesting. Each time, men not aligned with God's will for my life have been moved out of my way. My Father God has always sent me home untouched, chastened and ashamed of my dishonorable intentions.

I resisted joining a church throughout my twenties because I did not want to be a backsliding hypocrite. I wanted to live freely in sin. I know, that's an oxymoron, but, I wanted to live without the guilt of breaking promises to God. He didn't care for my thought pattern. The incident with Kortney was the last time I put any effort into getting "sexual healing" from a man. My King will come; I believe he is already en route. When I finally accepted that my base desires for my life were not compatible with God's intentions for me, in fact, when I realized I dishonored Him with my disobedience, I stopped fighting and started preparing.

Meditation Verse: 2 John 1:7-11

For many deceivers have gone out into the world who do not confess Jesus Christ *as* coming in the flesh. This is a deceiver and an antichrist. Look to yourselves, that we do not lose those things we worked for, but *that* we may receive a full reward.

Whoever transgresses and does not abide in the doctrine of Christ does not have God. He who abides in the doctrine of Christ has both the Father and the Son. If anyone comes to you and does not bring this doctrine, do not receive him into your house nor greet him; for he who greets him shares in his evil deeds.

Dating Anxiety

Dating is not a hobby of mine. Something out of the ordinary has to happen for me to take notice of a man these days.

I met Al (*a.k.a.* Rough Handler) on a Saturday at Macy's a couple of years ago. I was out shopping with Jemini, her daughters and her mother. We were on a lunch break in one of Macy's cafeteria-style restaurants. Al approached me with an awed expression on his face. His voice was thick with awe as well as he asked if he could introduce himself. Just from that opening, I knew he wasn't from New York. Such an approach was out of the ordinary for me. We chatted while I filled my tray; he told me he was in town for the weekend from North Carolina. A few minutes into the conversation, Jemini's girls came over to tell me they were all looking for me. Al didn't miss a beat; he immediately introduced himself to the girls as well. Because he was sticking rather close, despite my attempts to shake him, I invited Al to sit with us for lunch. He asked me out for the evening. I had plans. He asked if I would have any time over the weekend as he was leaving Monday. I told him I had a couple of hours early Sunday evening. We met up Sunday; it went well enough that he changed his ticket so he could see me again Monday night. I should have stayed home.

I know myself well enough to know that had he told me he lived nearby, within driving distance, I would have been busy all weekend with no time for him. I probably would have said I was seeing someone, but because he was an out-of-towner he was "safe." No further expectations or obligations. He would count as my date for the year.

Now, the below comments are prefaced with: I enjoyed *some* aspects of Rough Handler's company. He was a kind man and a gentleman of some fashion. Were I to list characteristics I want in a man, I would say he exhibited a couple of them. That being said, he struck out because:

1. *He didn't listen to my words*
2. *He didn't believe or respect my words*
3. *He kept attempting to push his own agenda despite my stated preferences*

Over the weekend, I received harsh criticism. Jemini thought I had been snooty and aloof during lunch with Al. I thoroughly disagreed. I thought I had been rather polite and charming, albeit a bit reserved – he was a stranger. However, he impressed me enough with his approach that I invited him to sit in on my *Jemini*

Family Time. That was extremely generous on my part. After all, I am a single woman living in the big bad city with few friends – simple love and affection with no strings is hard to come by.

"What else was I supposed to do," I asked Jemini. "Drape myself all over him?" She agreed that I was polite and charming, but she felt I should have been warmer. I disagree. I told her, "*LaShawnda's Special Treatment*, the love and attention friends and family enjoy, is not instantaneously bestowed on people *just because*...." That conversation with Jemini peeved me more than anything else. She kept harping on me about being more available to some man just because he showed a bit of interest. She wants to see me married, but I don't think *happy* and *content* in a *God-ordained union* are part of her vision.

Rough Handler peeved me a great deal as well. He complained Monday night about our Sunday night date. Though his words did not change how I behave on dates, I decided I would never again go out with someone after knowing them for such a short period of time. He was extremely ballsy in reciting his litany against me. Had Jemini not made me feel as if I were a mean, man-eating woman that did not give Rough Handler a proper chance, I never would have consented to meeting him again.

Rough Handler's criticism of me took the form of high-school bullying. He called me *scary* because I refused to go up to his hotel room while he was getting ready the first night. He had asked if he could come pick me up; I said no. Unless I feel comfortable, I don't share my address. Instead, I met him in his hotel lobby in Midtown West. He was only a few blocks away from Times Square, our destination for dinner. He asked if I was a virgin and Republican because I was far too conservative, i.e. I didn't want him hugging, rubbing and touching all over me. He told me I was bossy and apparently need to be in control because I set a curfew for myself. He didn't like my hug Sunday night – it was generic. He wanted a hug *and* a kiss. He asked for the cheek, I graciously offered the cheek, but I stopped him from slobbering all over it – in his opinion I should have let him continue soaking my face. Then he told me I am not affectionate because I didn't want him holding my hand, draping his arm over my shoulder, or gripping my arm and waist to guide my steps. When he tried to guide me across the street, I shook his hands off and told him I managed to get this far in life without someone holding my hand, I could manage to cross the street just fine. He had been enjoyable on Sunday night but he harped on me throughout the whole date Monday night. At one point I asked if he was trying to shame me into doing what he wanted me to do. "Sorry, it's not going to happen. Why do you want me in your hotel room so bad?" He wouldn't let that go either!

"I have a beautiful suite," he kept saying when I called to tell him I was in the lobby. "It has a bedroom, a sitting room, two baths with whirlpools, comfortable sofas, pull-out cot; you can come up while I get dressed..."

"Sounds nice.... It's not going to happen. Get ready; I'll meet you in the lobby." That was the start of our Sunday date. I told him my reservations had nothing to do with fear, but everything to do with self-preservation. "I will do what I am comfortable doing. I am comfortable waiting for you in the lobby and we can walk to Times Square." By the end of the date I had a headache. When I later shared with Zoë, she said she would've gotten up and walked out. I'm not that bold yet. My tactics were to speed up his eating and change the topic. At 10:30 PM, my stated cutoff from the beginning of the date, I told him we needed to wrap it up.

Later, when I spoke with Andrea about Rough Handler, she told me, "Shawnda, he didn't know what to do with you. He's probably used to women just going along with whatever he suggests or wants whether they're comfortable or not. And I'm sure he thought you would change your mind if he kept talking about stuff."

At one point Monday night, I asked him if he was using all his game on me – I was good and irritated by then. I wanted to ask what type of woman he was used to because his behavioral pattern didn't fit the type of woman I am.

"You're not touchy-feely, are you," he asked.

"Not really."

"You're not affectionate at all."

"I'm quite affectionate, but I don't know you. Can I get to know you before you start touching on me?" Why is that such a foreign concept? And why did he attempt to make me feel like a freak because I want to know the person attached to the hand holding and rubbing me? I don't mind if you look, but I do mind if you touch!

He went even more juvenile on me and said, "Well, I didn't tell you to stop touching me when you touched my shoulder and hand while you talked!" I apologized for talking with my hands. Do they ever grow up? He was forty-two years old, yet I felt like I was dealing with an over-eager, under-sexed high school jock. "We had better chemistry," he continued his petulant complaints, "during dinner than the way you ended the night. You didn't have to run for the subway after giving me a generic hug!"

"I offered to hail a cab for you!" I replied, truly trying to figure out what he expected from me. We had just met the day before!

"That's not what I'm talking about! You said I could kiss your cheek and you stopped me."

"You asked and I agreed to *one* cheek kiss and you kept on kissing my cheek." Then he grabbed me in a bear hug! We were standing on Eighth Avenue and 42nd Street two feet from the subway steps. All I wanted was for him to say good night and get in a cab. "There's no need for all that. As I told you before, you got much further than any other first date I've ever had."

"Oh, *really*. So, how do you normally end your first dates?" My ears detected disbelief and sarcasm.

"I say, *Good night*."

After the second night, I told Jemini I wasn't too pleased with her, and she had the nerve to keep defending him! "But he seemed so nice, Shawnda. Nobody's perfect...."

"*Nooooo*.... But he kept badgering me about the wrong things – deal breakers."

Late on the Monday date, Rough Handler accused me of needing to be in control; I didn't deny it nor did I explain it. By that point, my focus was on getting home, not further conversation. I'll elaborate here. I do not need to be in control of a man or a relationship. Nor do I have a desire to be. However, I do need to be in control of myself and what makes contact with my body. If I tell someone not to touch me, I mean *do not touch me*. That does not mean: don't touch me now, but you can touch me later; or don't touch me here, but you can touch me there. If a person cannot demonstrate respect for a simple request or any other preference pertaining to my person, then they are demonstrating their lack of respect for me. In that case, I want nothing to do with them.

Meditation Verse: Luke 16:15

And He said to them, "You are those who justify yourselves before men, but God knows your hearts. For what is highly esteemed among men is an abomination in the sight of God."

Good Touch, Bad Touch

Your body knows the difference between a good touch and a bad touch. I've learned to listen to my body.

Dating is torture; only those no longer willing to suffer are willing to admit it. The second and final date with Rough Handler angered me. I gave him the benefit of many doubts, primarily because I listened to Jemini and her mother. They were quite taken with Al at lunch that Saturday. They claimed to like everything about him they were exposed to and insisted I would get over my concerns if I simply accepted his human flaws. "Nobody is perfect," they insistently told me, and I should be more open to giving men chances. That was the last time I took dating advice from either of them.

My interactions with Rough Handler became increasingly disastrous. The second date could have been a good time, except he kept asking to touch me – hug me, kiss me on my cheek – followed by sly gropes throughout the night. My repeated *no*'s and pushes didn't faze him. His repeated requests were disrespectful. Every time he used some excuse to touch me – arm around my shoulder, hand at my waist, the small of my back, linking our arms in the guise of helping me up the stairs, holding my hand – I let him know his touch wasn't necessary or wanted.

"I'm a good guy; you don't have to be scared," he said repeatedly with an overly jovial smile.

"It has nothing to do with fear. It has everything to do with self-preservation." I am more comfortable in my own space. It took me years and a horrible date *(Better than You Should Be, p. 21)* to be able to enunciate that – to be succinct in my preferences. Clear. Not coy. No two ways about it. Eventually, I got to a point of not caring that a man may be offended because I stepped away, pulled away, removed a hand, adjusted a hold. It's not about their preferences and desires. It's about me feeling comfortable in my skin while in their presence.

I've been able to compare and contrast men over recent years due to some positive interactions which have kept me sane and functional with men overall.

Jay is a male acquaintance who has always amazed me because I felt comfortable in his presence from the first moment he spoke to me. Whenever he touched me – a hand to my waist in gentle greeting or a caress of my arm in goodbye or a close hug in farewell – it always felt right. His touch felt good. Sadly, I had never learned how to walk into a good touch during my formative years.

Frankly, I was astounded to experience a touch I wanted to walk into rather than jerk away from. I didn't know how to accept or reciprocate it. Experience had taught me to always be on guard against bad touches – the hurtful, destructive, invasive touches. For a long time, when I talked with Jay, it took all my concentration to simply accept his closeness and not recoil from habit. It took even more courage for me to touch back, but sooner than I thought possible (like within this lifetime) I was reaching for the skin of his arm, the firmness of his shoulder, the edge of his shirt. My response time was off by a couple of years, but eventually I felt comfortable enough to express myself with him through touch and conversation.

Jay came prominently to mind after the fiasco with Rough Handler. Over that weekend, I kept telling myself Rough Handler was a rather decent fellow, and not quite the worst date ever. He was cordial, gentlemanly, fun, and eager to spend time with me. His southern charm wasn't completely wasted on me. Yet and still, he didn't feel right. The hugs he pleaded for were hard and awkward. When he gripped my hand and shoulder it felt like he was trying to claim unearned proprietary rights.

Friends used to ask what attracted me to Jay. What, in him, drew my focus so completely I couldn't see other men? The best explanation I had was: I felt comfortable around him and loved the way he handled me. Jay is a big man, six-feet-five-inches, with a solid muscular build, but we seemed to communicate eye-to-eye from the beginning. I believed he treated me like I was precious and handled me with care and respect. He may have sensed my skittishness, but regardless, his gentleness was a lure to me.

In retrospect, it's sad that a man's gentle, respectful care was enough to woo me. Unfortunately, my exposure was limited, and prior treatment had been poor.

I'm glad for the experience to compare others to – the rough handlers, as I call them. The dates that just want to grope and touch with no regard for the fact they have no right to take such liberties.

Sometimes I wish my man would come prepackaged and ready to insert into my life without all the ridiculous shenanigans – clueless and pointless appointments. The world would be a better place if we were inundated with more men who not only respect women, but listen to them as well.

Meditation Verse: John 10:1-5

"Most assuredly, I say to you, he who does not enter the sheepfold by the door, but climbs up some other way, the same is a thief and a robber. But he who enters by the door is the shepherd of the sheep. To him the doorkeeper opens, and the sheep hear his voice; and he calls his own sheep by name and leads them out. And when he brings out his own sheep, he goes before them; and the sheep follow him, for they know his voice. Yet they will by no means follow a stranger, but will flee from him, for they do not know the voice of strangers."

And it Don't Stop!

Andrea is my dating memory. She assured me I had attracted a couple of Rough Handler-types in the past. Then she encouraged me to pray on it so God will remove or correct whatever it is in me that type of man is attracted to. These quick-to-attach men are the main reason I avoid the dating scene. Though I never suffered from the thought that I need to please a man despite my personal preferences, I know of many women who attempt to do just that. If I am known as nothing else, I want to be known as a woman who stayed true to herself and her beliefs and lived accordingly. As well as someone who lived a good life despite what others may consider strict values.

> *"Be careful, little ears, what you hear. When flattery leads to compromise the end is always near."*

Al the Rough Handler and I met on a Saturday, had date one on Sunday, date two on Monday. He left town on Tuesday. He started calling relentlessly on Wednesday. I called him back on Thursday only because I hadn't yet told him to lose my number. I had hoped not to hear from him again after he left New York. I had spent Monday and Tuesday mentally reviewing our dates and decided I was quite irritated. When I spoke with Rough Handler on Thursday, I was in wrap-up mode. I was officially done and no longer wanted to be bothered.

When he picked up the phone, his voice was petulant, and he complained about the length of time it took me to get back to him. He went on to tell me how much he missed me, my smile and my eyes. I had explicitly told him on Sunday night to drop the compliments and flattery, they weren't necessary. I was even less interested on Thursday. I changed the subject.

"How was your flight home?" Prudently, I wanted to make sure he was out of town before I started talking slick.

"It was fine." Then he started filling my ear with rubbish, how he couldn't wait to see me again and get a couple of hugs…. I changed the subject again, but I was perilously close to asking what made him think he would have another opportunity. My mind was wondering, he kept rotating the conversation back to seeing me again.

"It's not looking too promising," I informed him.

He asked if I like to travel.

"Yes, but I'm pretty much done for the year; except for two trips over the next couple of months." It was early September.

"I want to see you again, but out of your element, out of New York. Maybe North Carolina...."

"The rest of my year is pretty tight."

He paused. Then, "Do you have a male friend?"

I paused, because I wasn't interested in accommodating his attempt to beat around the bush. "I have several male friends. Female friends as well. What are you asking?"

"Do you have a male friend?"

"Yes. I have both male and female friends. What are you asking?"

He continued with his agenda. "Baby," this word in my ear from his lips was like nails on a chalkboard, "I want to take you on a golf tour with me. We'll hit *someplace* [my hearing was going in and out] and Orlando. I'll take care of your airfare and hotel –

"No."

"Wait, baby. You don't understand."

"No. I have the gist of what you're asking."

"This is no jest."

"I know it's not a jest. I get the gist… I know what you're asking and my answer is *no*."

His tone changed. Frustration or anger, either way he had no right to it. "Baby, I'm telling you, I'll pay for everything. Do you like the theme parks? Maybe we can visit a couple of the theme parks."

"I do like the theme parks. I plan on taking my nieces next year. But I am not going to put myself in the type of situation you're suggesting."

"What type of situation are you talking about? Are you in a relationship?" asked with a bit of indignation.

I spoke with more indignation, "No, I'm not in a relationship, but that would have no bearing on how I live my life. I do not live my life in a way that I would accept what you're offering."

"You don't have to be scared. I'm a good guy. Ask Jemini," he entreated after getting her name wrong twice. I assumed that's why he kept calling me *Baby* too.

Surprisingly, I maintained vocal control. "I'm *not* scared. I'm not comfortable with you. For that reason I will not be taking any trips with you. And I don't need to ask Jemini anything, she's not in my skin…."

"She can vouch for me," he interrupted.

"No, she can't. I need to vouch for you. And right now, I don't trust you." He kept trying to talk over me. "Okay. I can't have this conversation right now. I'll get back to you over the weekend. Good-bye."

"Be careful, little feet, where you go
For it's the little feet behind you that are sure to follow"

One thing I know for sure is my self-presentation is moderate and ladylike. No one who spends any amount of time with me will walk away with the impression that I'm fast and loose with my favors. No matter what type of woman you're used to, if you have to beg for a hug on the second date, there's no logical reason to believe that woman would travel to you for a third date.

Jemini continued to opine that I was too hard on Rough Handler. "Give him another chance," she urged me. "He doesn't know better; he'll learn." Each time she spoke in favor of him, my anger grew.

"I gave him two extended chances: Sunday and Monday," I repeatedly told her. Those two nights and Thursday's conversation told me he had listening and comprehension challenges, as well as respect issues. He didn't understand the meaning of *no* and his judgment was completely off. Respect and courtesy are bare minimums, prerequisites, if you will. Yes, he was courteous, but he did not respect my wishes. Multiple-choice minimums were not on offer. There's never any need to get involved with someone who doesn't respect your minimum requirements.

During the final conversation on Thursday I pushed to clarify his offer, "You want me to *travel* to *watch* you play golf?"

"Yeah, you can drive the cart," he imparted enthusiastically, as if I should be honored.

After choking back an incredulous laugh, all I could get out was, "Wow!" Add to the above list: selfish and self-centered.

Both Andrea and Jemini were laughing uproariously by the end of our respective phone calls. Andrea said, "He's looking for a maid and a mistress!"

"Yeah…I guess I was supposed to put out then clean it up, too!"

Jemini kept piling hers on. "Oh, Shawnda, it must be so hard for you! Can you blame the man for trying to grab your butt? Honestly!"

"Honestly, no. I don't blame him. I've batted away quite a few hands in my time."

"It's just sitting there; I'm sure a lot of men have a hard time keeping their hands to themselves. I can't even imagine. You have all that in back and all that in front – walking around looking like Jessica Rabbit! I had no booty and I was flat-chested; men only dated me for my brain!"

"I want to be appreciated for my brain too!"

She most likely fell off her chair laughing over that one. When she caught her breath she said, "Wow, you either have men falling all over you or ignoring you completely. Why can't we get a happy medium?"

I agree. Where's my happy medium? Perhaps the reason I'm attracted to men who want nothing to do with me is because those who attach themselves too quickly make the aloof ones look good. If the man is ignoring me, I can have a romantic focus without him focusing on me. My, I think I just had a breakthrough – I want a man, but not really!

All kidding aside, these man-opportunities, as I refer to them, educate me about their ways. I sincerely believe God has led me through these situations unscathed in order to show me I was not missing out on anything. He has plans for me. I don't know the end result, but I know it's going to be good. Even when I have believed myself thrown in the fire, He has brought me out on the other side, much better for the trouble. I have to make sure I make choices that are worthy of the work He is doing in my life. I am committed to making choices that honor and glorify my God!

It's a slow fade when you give yourself away
It's a slow fade when black and white have turned to gray
Thoughts invade, choices are made, a price will be paid
  - Slow Fade, Casting Crowns

Meditation Verse: Proverbs 26:26, 28

Though his hatred is covered by deceit, his wickedness will be revealed before the assembly.

A lying tongue hates *those who are* crushed by it, and a flattering mouth works ruin.

Sugar Daddy M.O.

Older men have always been attracted to me. One helpful older gentleman explained why, "Those young boys, they'll mess you up! But us older fellas, well, we're done messing women over. When we see a good one, we try to snatch her up!"

That's all fine and good, but I do prefer a man closer to my age. However, as with all things in my life, I sought to locate a lesson in the interactions I've had over the years. After Rough Handler graciously offered me an all-expense paid trip to Florida to caddy for him, he was added to the list of outrageous offers that have come my way.

As mentioned earlier, Andrea is my dating memory. As such, she reminded me of a couple of the below scenarios, as I am very good at forgetting men and their nonsense. When I told her about Rough Handler's proposition she laughed so hard I offered to call her back. Andrea is deep in her faith and she has been a sister in celibacy for as long as I've known her. She would never approve of me accepting any offer for my sexual favors, but she gets a kick out of joking about it. "Does he know what type of offers you've turned down? His go straight to the bottom! I'm of a mind to call him and tell him, 'Next time, bring your A-game!'" That cracked *me* up!

So, Andrea and I reminisced on three standout offers I've had over the years.

Tender Roni

A month after my eighteenth birthday, I started college in Chicago. I lasted only the first semester because I couldn't keep up with the cost. Despite scholarships, loans, and an off-campus job, the tuition payment schedule was too much. My dough was earned at Pizza Hut that semester, working as many hours as I could. Roy was a delivery man who was usually scheduled on my shifts. He was in his mid-forties, recently divorced with two children. He wasn't the cleanest-looking fellow, nor did he come across as the brightest, but on occasion he was an interesting conversationalist. One night, while he was driving me to my dorm, he promised me all his earnings if I would consider getting together with him. Since I was in his car, late at night, going through dark neighborhoods, I thought it prudent not to laugh at the offer. He must've seen my struggle, because he continued in a rush, "I have money. It's tied up in my divorce. The wife got the house, the kids and all the savings. We started a business years ago that's bringing in good money. I know I'll get at least half of the business back. I'll do whatever I can with whatever I have – it's yours. Think about it."

"Right... sounds nice, but I'm not trying to take anything from your wife. And if you have children, nothing belongs to you. You should be promising them your delivery money."

That was the last ride I accepted from Roy.

What a thought: Roy was willing to give up his last dollar for whatever he could get from me.

Glamorous Life

Rehearsal for Ebony Fashion Fair started a week after my twenty-fifth birthday. We started touring around week three. At the time, I didn't consider myself young and nubile, but looking at pictures from that period, I can certainly see how that description fits. I came into contact with many men who wanted to meet and mingle with models. Several NBA basketball players attended our Portland show. Dianna had gone to school with one of the players and he invited us to hang out with a group of his teammates and friends after the show. It was a very entertaining evening. There were ballplayers, managers, accountants, wives and friends. Michael was a friend of Dianna's friend; he attended with his wife. He was an executive for a well-known technology company and had wonderful conversation. Before the night was over I had exchanged numbers with both Michael and his wife. He was a great networking opportunity for employment after the fashion show tour.

Michael and I communicated on and off for months. I had emailed him my resume and was very clear about my interest in employment opportunities with his company when I finished the tour.

When I returned home after the tour ended, my job hunt was discouraging. Perhaps I expressed that during a conversation with Michael. During our last conversation, he asked, "LaShawnda, what are your monthly expenses?"

Admittedly, I can be naïve sometimes, but this particular time I truly didn't know any better. I had no understanding of the terms or lifestyles of a *kept woman* or *mistress*. I thought this successful black man kept in touch because he was interested in helping a young sister get a *legitimate* leg up in corporate America.

"I'm sorry.... My monthly expenses?"

"Yes, what are your monthly expenses? I can take care of them for you."

"Well, I don't really have any expenses."

"Sure you do."

I was renting a room in a friend's house. "Well, I pay two-hundred dollars for rent. My bus pass is twelve dollars a week." I was curious to see where the question would lead. "I guess if you add in miscellaneous bills and such I can reach five-hundred dollars a month."

"Come on.... That's my weekly dry cleaning bill! Seriously, what do you need each month?"

At that moment, I realized I was in over my head. I could not fathom giving a man a price for me. Was he really asking how much money I would charge for him to have his way with me?

After a quiet moment, I asked, "Does your wife know you're on the phone propositioning me?" That question ended the call. I'm sure he said more, but I was no longer listening.

After we covered Michael in our recap of outrageous offers, Andrea jokingly stated, "Do you know what type of lifestyle we could have if you had given Michael a price? We could be living it up!"

Michael's suave offer: Name your price; ask and it's yours.

No Regrets

Then there was David, an old-school playboy. I was somewhat enamored with David and I knew he was interested in me. However, he never mentioned commitment or fidelity. Those two words are rather important to me.

David had been in the same position for over twenty years, traveling around the country. Everyone who knew him knew he had regular women in many cities around the country. He wasn't flashy, but I knew he took care of his women. According to gossip, his main girlfriend was set up in a house in Chicago. When he approached me, he simply said he had a thing for me and wanted to explore it. I didn't know what to say, so I told him, "I don't know what to say."

We stayed in contact throughout my late twenties. I ran into him at least once or twice a year and we would always sit for a minute and catch up.

The last time I saw him, I had just moved to New York City. By that time we had worked together for a year and been in sporadic contact for four years. When I saw him in New York, his then girlfriend was by his side. We chatted; she spoke on his behalf through most of the conversation. I wasn't sure if he was uncomfortable or if she was just marking her territory. At some point she shared that she lived in New Orleans where David had purchased a house for her. I have no idea how that came up, but he seemed to squirm even more. I looked at him; he looked at me sideways with a quirked brow. I wished them both well when I walked away.

Andrea screamed at that tidbit, "It would probably be under water now," she gushed, "but we would have had a couple of years to chill in New Orleans!"

Had I listened to David, I would have heard: Where do you want to live, Baby?

Live and Learn

Do the temptations of Christ come to mind? Whenever I think about these men and people like them, I think of the devil working his wiles on Christ in the desert. People often talk about what they wouldn't do for all the tea in China or all the money in the world. I am able to tell you exactly what I did not do for a blank check and a free ride. I didn't turn those men down because I had so much going on financially. However, my character prospered by such moral propositions. They weren't dilemmas because *yes* was never an option for me. Those propositions didn't suit any part of my lifestyle.

Rough Handler isn't in league with the sugar daddy wannabes, but his grade school offer had me thinking of prior high school offers. He would have been rebuffed no matter what he came up with, but the fact that he offered *only* an airline ticket and wanted me to drive him around added insult to injury. He didn't even measure up to the jerks I've come across.

Rough Handler's lesson: no matter the charm or finesse a man tries to show you, you can tell what he thinks of you by what he offers you.

I'm holding out for the upper classman with the commitment and fidelity ring!

Blessedly, I am not concerned with what others think of my decisions. Public opinion doesn't sway me as much as my personal opinion. Whatever I do, I know I have to be able to look myself in the eye *every* time I look in a mirror. I need to respect myself. I need to know that a choice I made was not disgraceful to who I am.

Remember, the quality of your life is determined by the choices you make, not by the things you get by with or the people you get over on.

Meditation Verse: Matthew 4:1-11

Then Jesus was led up by the Spirit into the wilderness to be tempted by the devil. And when He had fasted forty days and forty nights, afterward He was hungry. Now when the tempter came to Him, he said, "If You are the Son of God, command that these stones become bread."

But He answered and said, "It is written, *'Man shall not live by bread alone, but by every word that proceeds from the mouth of God.'*"

Then the devil took Him up into the holy city, set Him on the pinnacle of the temple, and said to Him, "If You are the Son of God, throw Yourself down. For it is written: *'He shall give His angels charge over you,'* and, *'In their hands they shall bear you up, lest you dash your foot against a stone.'*"

Jesus said to him, "It is written again, *'You shall not tempt the LORD your God.'*"

Again, the devil took Him up on an exceedingly high mountain, and showed Him all the kingdoms of the world and their glory. And he said to Him, "All these things I will give You if You will fall down and worship me."

Then Jesus said to him, "Away with you, Satan! For it is written, *'You shall worship the LORD your God, and Him only you shall serve.'*"

Then the devil left Him, and behold, angels came and ministered to Him.

Technology Upgrade, Personal Downgrade

My Sanyo flip phone was retired after nearly seven years of service in favor of a Palm Treo upgrade. At first, I refused to get into texting. I wasn't interested in another option to avoid face-to-face or voice-to-voice communication. Not when the new option appeared more time consuming, less efficient, and unforgivably more impersonal than traditional options. Rather, that was my opinion before I met a very interesting and attractive man while hanging out with friends. We exchanged numbers on a Thursday; when I didn't hear from him by Monday, I gave him a call.

"Ah, LaShawnda.... I text'd you on Friday to thank you for the great time and to see what you were into for the weekend. When I didn't hear back from you, I figured you weren't interested."

My heart dropped – I had missed a man-opportunity because I didn't text? My girlfriends had been reaming me for a while and had a field day rubbing it in. "We told you! How can you have a computer-based business and not know how to text people?" They all made me feel like a dummy!

I told the guy I wasn't ignoring him, I just didn't realize I had a text, didn't know how to check them and had never sent one. I assured him once we got off the phone I would play with my phone and figure out how to work those features. He was a bit taken aback. Apparently he thought I was jiving him. "Are you serious? You don't know how to text? My eight-year-old son texts me all the time."

"Thanks for that. I realize children today are more tech savvy than most adults."

"Texting is an easy way for men to connect with women without the nerves of actually calling. But you don't have to learn a new skill for me."

"Oh, I didn't realize...." A man who admitted to a weakness.... Oh, my! "Well, I need to learn this skill anyway. Apparently, I'm behind the times."

He was my first text. The next text from a man trying to connect with me assured me this technology upgrade is a personal downgrade. I'm not interested in getting to know people strictly through technological advances.

A few weeks later, I met Vince at a party. What came off as confidence at the lounge sounded more like arrogance in the light of day. He struck up a conversation or rather made a series of statements and asked a series of questions. "My name's Vince. I'm an investment banker on Wall Street. Here's my number. What's your name? What do you do? Can I get your number?" After slightly rolling my eyes, I answered his questions. Sometimes men sound so pompous; I couldn't stop myself from adding, "I'm in banking too. We're not on Wall Street but we are based in Beverly Hills, perhaps you've heard of us." He had mentioned he was from California; my place of employment was a prominent private entertainment bank.

His strategy proved to be something of a no-need-to-muddy-the-get-to-know-you-game with getting-to-know-you stuff. In lieu of calling, he text'd. The first couple of times, I responded by calling and got his voicemail. He then replied to my voicemail via text and added an invite for drinks. Sure, some men are busy these days, I can appreciate that, but don't initiate anything you can't give proper attention to. I text'd Vince back. "The text situation is odd. I'll pass on drinks. Thks."

Sometimes men read too much into the statistics claiming men are in short supply. They forget they still have competition – there's another man someplace! We women do not forget our competition is any other woman breathing. Not every woman is willing to take just any man and put up with anything. We are doing quite well by ourselves these days. As far as I'm concerned, if you can't treat me at least as well as I treat myself, you're out of the running. And guess what – I respect myself. I pay attention to my needs. I listen to what I have to say. I'm not concerned with your financial situation, I'm concerned about our connection and how I feel around you.

Why do people hide behind texts and emails? Relationships are built on conversation. Conversation allows people to relate to one another, but it isn't just about what we say – it's how we say it, how we react to what is said, and our non-verbal expressions and gestures. Unless we already know someone relatively well, texts and emails are just words with no substance. They have no value. Why would someone want to build on something with no value?

Voice intonations relay as much, if not more, information than words. You can't get that from a text. I can't read a text the way I can read a voice or a face. But I can read actions, and their meanings translate the same way no matter how much technology upgrades. What are you doing to make your intentions clear?

Even though I have upgraded my telecommunications skills, I feel like regressing to the days when we only had land lines. When boys knew to call girls before a certain time and men adhered to social graces and decorum when courting women. Regressing to the days when men stated their intentions and women weren't confused about what to expect.

 Meditation Verse: Ruth 4:9-10

> And Boaz said to the elders and all the people, "You *are* witnesses this day that I have bought all that was Elimelech's, and all that *was* Chilion's and Mahlon's, from the hand of Naomi. Moreover, Ruth the Moabitess, the widow of Mahlon, I have acquired as my wife, to perpetuate the name of the dead through his inheritance, that the name of the dead may not be cut off from among his brethren and from his position at the gate. You *are* witnesses this day."

Call Me Naïve...

During my early promotion of *VoLux Full-Figured Calendar* in New York, I maintained a page dedicated to the calendar and the blogs this book is derived from on a social networking site. One spring day I opened my inbox to an email titled *YOU'RE THE REAL DEAL.* I had just posted a blog about vanity and was interested in reading the responses to it. The email completely played into the vanity I had written so cryptically about. In short, it was a sweet note written in apparent sincerity from an operator of the Black Porn Network (BPN). The email was so flowery and near pandering, my only reply was, "Don't know what to say... you have me blushing...."

The next day, when I got home and logged on, I was greeted to an email titled, *Divine beauty! Everything a plus sized woman should be!* I thought it was spam and was about to delete it when I saw a reference in the body to BPN. The writer wanted more personal contact than business-to-business email. The email was lengthy, cordial and complimentary. He mentioned his wife – which kept me reading; I figure you can't be all bad if a woman married you. He mentioned my writing, which told me he followed my blogs and website. He then stated he was a screenwriter, producer and photographer. All that intrigued me; I love creative people. The face of his profile picture was mostly covered by his hand. I clicked on his profile to see the man who was so intrigued with me in cyberspace.

What I discovered put me in a mild state of shock and an intensely flaming temper. The BPN profile belonged to Six-five. Six-five worked in my office building. I referred to him as Six-five because that's how he introduced himself. We had had friendly conversations throughout the prior several months. He was attractive but extremely outrageous in his flirtatious speech. He had never once in the many months I had known him mentioned he was even in a relationship, let alone married. He hadn't even mentioned the recent birth of his newborn son. His wife and child were there for me to see on his profile page. As was his alternate lifestyle. As I sat looking through his wedding pictures from the previous fall and the newborn pictures of his son in the winter, I recalled asking him directly if he was with anyone. He had assured me he wasn't and even allowed one of his friends to co-sign on his availability and legitimate interest in me. *Do men stand by each other no matter what?* However, despite his friend's deceitful confirmation, I told Six-five that night I could not take him seriously because he was so over the top with his approach and comments.

Call me naïve, but I was inclined to think of the cyber encounters as coincidence.

There was no mention or recognition in his emails that he knew I was one of the women at work that he'd been chatting up for months. I leaned back in my chair after looking around his page and thought about Clark Kent and Diana Prince. I used to watch *Superman* and *Wonder Woman* and think everyone on screen were idiots for not recognizing Clark Kent and Superman were one and the same. How could people not see Diana was the same person as Wonder Woman? The only differences between regular Joe/Jane and superhero were glasses and hairstyles. That was also the only difference between me as a *VoLux Full-Figured Calendar* model and me at work. I wear glasses and very little to no make-up at work. My shape, size and features are the same. Here's a naïve question: What the heck is he looking at that he can't put three images of me together as one person? Me at work. Me in a calendar. Me online.

A whirlwind of outrage overtook me. Why was he even trying to talk to me via various avenues when he was married? Call me naïve, but married means you're off the market! You're out the game. Disqualified player. You're in another league. No scouting, no squirreling away numbers, emails or future possibilities. You don't speak words to other women that should only be spoken to your wife. How could he go home and look his wife in the face – or his son for that matter? We had done nothing but talk, but I felt as if I violated his marriage vows just by being a recipient of his flirtations. Words have intent. He later claimed he meant nothing by his words, but all I could think of was, "What if my husband spoke to another woman like that?"

I told him he was a cheater. I have no idea what he had done with anyone else, but the way he presented himself as a single, eligible man implied intent to act like an unmarried individual.

Marriage is about trust, honor, integrity, respect, commitment, faithfulness, love and honesty. It chilled me to think I could marry a man and outside our home he acts like a free-willing bachelor. Six-five's behavior was extremely offensive. He's a deceiver of the worst kind: his actions expressed intent to step out on his family. There is no need to make a commitment to someone if you don't intend to honor it. Such damage and disrespect extends beyond yourself to your spouse and the third party. You, the cheater, put three lives at risk for your lack of self-control.

> *"I suppose he will not begin to doubt anything she says until he begins to doubt everything."*
> *– James Baldwin*

Years ago, in Milwaukee, I was out with a group of girlfriends. The club had just closed and we were trying to decide what to do next: go to an after party, go eat or go home to bed. I watched this guy, Chuck, approach three of my girls one after another. They each turned their back on him. I was slightly off to the side finishing up a conversation with someone when he walked over to me. I don't remember exactly what he said, but he was confused, exasperated and frustrated. He started off with, "What's wrong with your girls?"

"What do you mean?"

"Women always talk about how they want honesty, but y'all can't handle it." I arched a brow. He continued. "I'm married and I'm looking for something on the side. I'm not trying to hide my wife but I'm not trying to flaunt my girl either...."

Can I get a *WOW!*?

If a man is willing to learn; I'm willing to teach. I told him he was wrong. "Women deserve honesty. You're not doing us a favor by telling us your status; you're enabling us to make an informed decision. Just like you chose to marry, a woman has the right to decide to get involved with a married man or *not*. Just because you tell us the truth doesn't mean we're going to do what you want us to do."

"Why didn't your girls say anything to me?"

"Two of them are engaged and the other is in a long-term relationship."

"Are you saying something because you're interested?"

"No. I'm just disgusted." And I walked away.

 Meditation Verse: James 4:4

Adulterers and adulteresses! Do you not know that friendship with the world is enmity with God? Whoever therefore wants to be a friend of the world makes himself an enemy of God.

I Never Asked You Out...

Six-five spoke words that will stay with me for the rest of my single days. Granted, he could have been trying to save face after I publicly lambasted him for approaching me with lascivious intent as a married man with a newborn child, but his words still rang true. He said, "I didn't intend to lead you on. I find you attractive. I flirted and you reciprocated, but I never followed up or pursued anything else. I never asked you out."

I never asked you out. He wasn't nasty or mean. He simply stated a fact. I took his words at face value and applied them to other situations in my life.

Over the years, friends have assured me there is no reason to be confused by men because they ask for what they want. If they don't ask, they don't want. In my stubbornness I held fast to the shy male myth, believing some men needed to be coaxed from their shells, assuming some were in need of encouragement and a bit of enticement.

Six-five cured me of that belief.

Nadine refers to the talking, discovery, question-and-answer portion of mate selection as the *interview stage*. Jay and I spent a lot of time interviewing. When he entered a relationship a couple of years ago, Nadine told me calmly and dispassionately, "He simply went with another candidate, Shawnda. Don't personalize it. You just didn't pass the interview."

Easier said than felt, but the bottom-line reality of the situation was: Jay had never asked me out either.

Meditation Verse: James 1:12

Blessed *is* the man who endures temptation; for when he has been approved, he will receive the crown of life which the Lord has promised to those who love Him.

REVELATIONS

DESTROYERS
Chasing the dream of a man
broke me well before I knew
what various pieces of me were.
Men nearly destroyed me.
Not one, not two, but more than even three.
An evil-doer who attempted to lead me astray
succeeded in tainting my thoughts.
A barbarian marauder in the guise of
my champion trampled my innocence.
But the greatest deceiver in my world,
positioned to provide and protect,
stripped me of trust instead.
This, all in my early years;
they put a domino effect of damage in motion,
all in my early years.

THE CHASE
Yet and still, I thought I could
recover with the love of a man.
If only I could willingly take a man
into my body in an act of love, my
scars would heal, past violations would
have no more power. I would be
in control of my sexuality.
I've chased the lure of that thought
since before gaining my womanhood.
I have tried to show men –
not one, not two, but more than even three –
I was worthy of their love and companionship.
There was the sweet boy in high school
who called me friend.
The womanizing co-worker
who called every woman friend.
Then there was the One I wasn't even looking for.
He seemed to talk to my spirit at times. He appeared

interested in knowing my mind. But his *actions* are for
so many other women, never for me.

NEED

I prayed in tears, in earnest, in anger
I pleaded for God to send someone to ease me
to love me, to help me, to walk with me
for a decade I've been praying, pleading
and attempting to help Him help me.
"Ok, Father, I found someone.
Just make him want me."
Early on I attempted to bargain.
I don't remember what I thought
was worthy of a barter with God
but He replied, *"You belong to me."*
It took years to realize He would do with me
as He will, not as I would have Him do.
But now I know. I see his possessiveness
in the context of a creator, leader,
mother, father, husband, lover and friend.
Now, I am embarrassed to think of how
I went to Him, in all His magnificent glory and grace,
and asked for someone else.
Now, I know shame.
Now, I appreciate His sufficiency.
He has guided and shielded me
these long, lonely years.
Yet, I rejected His comfort.
In all my triumphs, I praised Him;
in all my sorrows, I sought Him;
but in the dark of night, in my cold, barren bed
I burned and begged for a mortal man to ease me.
Oh! How He must have cringed at my every plea!

DISTRACTIONS

I recall signals He sent to steer me
away from paths I wanted to travel.
Oh! How He must've shaken His head
when I executed my will before His Word.
Acting on desires I didn't understand,
asking for a life I wasn't ready for.
And He whispered to me intermittently
"I'm all you need."
Maybe that was a ringing in my ears –

Who's all I need?
I looked around and saw someone
who was pleasing to my eyes
and in my human ignorance
assumed that man's spirit was speaking to mine.
Oh! How the Father must've contemplated
letting me go! Instead, He has prodded
me these past seven years,
"If you build it, he will come."
I got to work.
Started building a life –
continuing higher education, creating a home
structuring a career, chasing men
who were physically more than I ever dreamed.
I was building various pieces of me
to support the life I envisioned.

RECKONING
Then it all unraveled and I fell apart.
The home got vandalized
the career got downsized
the men kept leading me in circles.
What good was education, anyhow?
I was left to wonder:
What did I do wrong?

He was more succinct this time,
*"If you build your relationship with God,
He will come."*
All my errors were revealed to me.
I was working on the outside
when I should've been building my foundation.

Now, I'm building.
Building upon the words of my mother
the lessons of my ancestors
the life and history of the Bible.
I'm building my relationship and nurturing my spirit.
Now, I am feeling loved, worthy, protected,
well provisioned and well within my soul.
At last, I know I am complete in Him.

Preparation for the

Marriage Relationship

If I were the Author of my life

If I were the Author of my life
I would write me a love story
Sampled through with romance
With minimum suspense
No horror or tragedy to speak of
And just enough drama to spice the retelling

If I were the Author of my story
I would write a Hero companion in every scene
With minimum conflict
No hate or misunderstandings to speak of
And just enough friction to flavor the experience

If I were the Author of this script
My happy, laughing children would be
An active piece of the formula
Learning the ways of their mother and father
Obedient to God's plan; keepers of one another
With just enough rivalry to keep them thriving

At the end of the scene
The sun would come up, the road ahead
Would be endless and my loved ones and I
Would be linked arm in arm as we walk

Just when I think my story is done
My Hero companion swoops down to
Carry me on to new adventures
He marvels with new visions
Energizes with new ideas
Encourages me to live again

If I were the Finisher of my life
I would know and understand
I am who I am
Exactly where I am supposed to be
My life is not an error
My errors are experiences
My experiences lead to my path
This path is not a mistake
Each stop along my path is a lesson
My lessons are for my training
My training is preparation
My preparation is for my ministry
My ministry is part of my purpose

My purpose is part of my assignment
My assignment is the reason for my placement
My placement is why I am where I am supposed to be
But sometimes my understanding is limited
Hurt expands
Doubt floods
And I am attacked by negative energy
In those moments, I want to rewrite my life
Redo my story
Provide an alternate middle for my script.
It's in those sad, lost moments the
Author & Finisher sweeps me off my feet
Calms my heart
Dries my tears
And gently blows a caress through my hair
As he reminds me:
Not only is He Father to the fatherless and protector of widows
Not only do I belong to Him
But He is all I need
And I am His bride whom He is preparing for a Homecoming
He abides in me as I abide in Him
And He will never leave me nor forsake me.

What else is there to write?

25 Things to Think Twice About Before You Marry

Pastor Terry Starks teaches that your mate is a choice of your intelligence – whatever you think of your spouse reflects back on you. A couple of years ago he taught a marriage series, alternating his focus between specific lessons for married couples and singles. He encouraged married couples to work on the relationship they have and avoid falling into the trap of thinking they married the wrong person, thereby breaking their covenant with God and their spouse in order to search for someone else. He cautioned singles to consider their potential mate carefully before committing to a marriage relationship. I am passing on his list of twenty-five things singles should carefully consider before marrying.

As Pastor Terry fondly said, we not only need to find the right mate, we need to be the right mate. Our diligence will keep us clear of #2 on the *8 Wrong Places to Find Yourself (p. 129)* list.

1. Think twice if you do not see continual progress or improvement.
2. Think twice if you can't trust him/her to pursue God without your constant encouragement.
3. Think twice if they refuse to sit consistently under the Word of God.
4. Think twice if they ignore worded counsel in their life.
5. Think twice if s/he does not have a passionate desire to be with you. The proof of love is the desire to spend time.
6. Think twice when it's obvious you will never become their focus or assignment. Your spouse is your assignment.
7. Think twice if they feel inferior *or* superior to you. Marriage is an equal partnership.
8. Think twice if you can't trust him/her with your most painful memories.
9. Think twice if you can't trust him/her with your greatest fears and secrets.
10. Think twice if small problems unleash a mountain of anger.
11. Think twice if they embrace an accusation against you before knowing your side of the story.
12. Think twice if an atmosphere of unbelievers excites them.
13. Think twice if they have an obsession to attract the opposite sex.
14. Think twice if they refuse to get a job. Productive women excite productive men and vice versa.
15. Think twice if s/he doesn't respect your time or schedule. If a person doesn't respect your time, they won't respect your wisdom.

16. Think twice if they continuously give you counsel *contrary* to the Word of God.
17. Think twice if they are unwilling to follow your personal advice and value your counsel.
18. Think twice if you're not excited about introducing them to loved ones.
19. Think twice if their parents have contempt for you.
20. Think twice if there's continuous strife between them and their parents.
21. Think twice if their pastor is not impressed with them.
22. Think twice if you can't trust them around your closest friends.
23. Think twice if you can't trust them in your absence. Trust is the foundation of every relationship.
24. Think twice if they can't be trusted in the area of their own personal finances.
25. Think twice if they aren't thankful. Ungrateful people give hard lessons but learn very little.

Absence of desire to be with you means you are not their assignment (# 5 & 6)

These two knocked me for a loop. Historically, I have been attracted to men who either have no interest in me or men fond of categorizing me as their "last woman on Earth" option just in case their first million choices were to dry up. At that point they may *possibly* consider a relationship with me. In the past, any small amount of attention from those men had the power to keep me hanging on to hope for ridiculous amounts of time. I handicapped myself with this tendency. I really, really want to be wanted! I deserve to be wanted for who I am. Eventually, I grew tired of my availability, blatant attraction, hope and presence being taken for granted.

Doug, an old wannabe flame, got married a couple of years ago. In my opinion, there was a bit of drama about the way I was informed. Doug and I know a few people in common and I was very direct about my interest in him back in the day (i.e. everyone around us knew). Apparently, these people thought (or hoped) I would be crushed by news of his pending nuptials. Dianna, a mutual friend at the time, gleefully told me he had gotten engaged right before she told me he had been interested in me but she told him it would never work out. She shared this with me at dinner with other acquaintances shortly after she moved out of my apartment. All I could think about were the times she told me I was "too much woman" for him and other things that made me doubt the quality of a match with Doug. I responded to her news with a calm request for her to let me know when he finally spoke his vows. I felt a bit catty, but I was dealing with a cat. A month after Dianna informed me of the planned nuptials, Doug emailed me, "You've probably heard it through the grapevine but I'm getting married in November".... blah, blah, blah.... he closed with, "I got the calendar at Christmas...even after all these years we still look good together." It also seemed obvious that he expected Dianna or someone else to tell me with the further expectation that I would call him to confirm. For some reason he was hesitant about giving me the news. That irritated me, but I was more hurt learning Dianna actively and purposefully fed each of us misinformation during a time we were both considering the other for a relationship.

Dianna isn't to blame, though. As I said, I was very vocal and demonstrative about my interest in him for nearly a year of living and working in close proximity and he never asked me out, to quote Six-five. He never pulled me aside to discuss the possibility of us. We were buddies, we had great conversations. He told me he respected me and enjoyed hanging out with me. I fed off his morsels of attention, and then got to watch him chase or succumb to seemingly every other woman within his radius.

He had no passionate desire to be with me. That was a hard fact to swallow. When I finally accepted that I would never be a focus for him, I was able to let go. As much as I want to give of myself, I want to receive from my partner as well. Reciprocation is not only appreciated, it's necessary!

Shortly after Doug sent his email update, Dianna and I ended up dining together with a group of acquaintances. Doug called her to shoot the breeze while we were waiting for a table. She went all giggly and started gushing and repeating everything he said. I was talking to someone else in our group when I heard her say, "Yeah, Shawnda's here.... I'll tell her." I turned to her with my hand out, "Give me the phone, he can tell me himself."

"Dang, Shawnda, did you just snatch the phone from Dianna?" he exclaimed after I greeted him.

"Yes, I did. You're doing your man-thang and I'm hearing about it from everyone else. I know you're walking around with your chest all puffed out n'all, but I wanted to congratulate you since I'm still waiting on you to return my last call."

"Ahh, man, Shawnda...."

"Oh, my fault. Maybe you're not home yet. Remember, you were traveling a couple of months ago and said you'd call me when you got back home. When are you getting home?"

"Girl... okay, I'm sorry! I've just been so busy."

"So, I've heard...." I also heard in his voice that he was happy and hopeful. And he was planning. I can't knock anyone for finding joy in their lifetime. I wanted to take the opportunity to personally and publicly tell him I was happy for the joy he was receiving and embracing in his life. I didn't like thinking he was uneasy expressing his joy to me. I am grateful for the things I've learned about myself because of him. There is no way I could resent our association.

You can't trust others, if you can't trust yourself (#22)

My friend Nadine came to mind with Number 22. She has a strict rule to never introduce her girlfriends to her man. She was engaged when I met her, and my inquiries about her fiancé were met with, "I keep my man and girlfriends separate. Women can't be trusted." This was an odd concept to me. When I make friends, I get friendly with the whole family. Separating your friends from your life partner keeps both in isolation, which in turn keeps you in isolation. It's like you're hiding a huge part of yourself from your friends and your partner. Nadine explained this was a lesson her mother taught her and exhibited while she was growing up. For most of the time I have known Nadine, following her break-up with her fiancé, she only sought and interacted with married or otherwise committed men. She has repeatedly set herself up for a world of hurt and self-destruction. I've witnessed exactly why she does not trust women around her men – she is not a trustworthy woman.

Unfortunately for Nadine, at some point during her life she decided a measurement of her worth was the willingness of a man to leave his wife for her. They all promised some form of that, in some way, during some heated moment. A couple eventually divorced their wives – long after they had stopped seeing Nadine. But none of them ever called her to rekindle any flame or to proclaim their undying love or to ask for her hand in marriage.

Nadine is a life-long Baptist and has been active in her church most of her adult life. Though she tries to walk right, she inevitably acts wrong. I was in denial about her nature for a number of years. During one conversation a couple of years ago when she spoke about an interest in yet another married man, I cautioned her and quoted the Bible as a warning. That was around the time I began getting deep into my study and found I was able to apply scripture with nearly all the advice I dispensed. Nadine claimed she was not committing the sin of adultery because *she* was not married. The men she cavorted with were guilty of adultery. *They* were breaking their vows; *they* had to deal with God, not her. I was appalled at such a thought pattern. I told her God had threatened death to a man who didn't even know he was lusting after a married woman *(Genesis 20:1-7)*. Yet, she was acting in full knowledge, how did she expect God to deal with her? She asked for the scripture, I pulled out the book.

 Meditation Verse: Genesis 20:1-7

And Abraham journeyed from there to the South, and dwelt between Kadesh and Shur, and stayed in Gerar. Now Abraham said of Sarah his wife, "She is my sister." And Abimelech king of Gerar sent and took Sarah.

But God came to Abimelech in a dream by night, and said to him, "Indeed you are a dead man because of the woman whom you have taken, for she is a man's wife."

> But Abimelech had not come near her; and he said, "Lord, will You slay a righteous nation also? Did he not say to me, 'She is my sister'? And she, even she herself said, 'He is my brother.' In the integrity of my heart and innocence of my hands I have done this."
>
> And God said to him in a dream, "Yes, I know that you did this in the integrity of your heart. For I also withheld you from sinning against Me; therefore I did not let you touch her. Now therefore, restore the man's wife; for he is a prophet, and he will pray for you and you shall live. But if you do not restore her, know that you shall surely die, you and all who are yours."

Did you notice God said *He* prevented Abimelech from sinning *against Him* by not letting Abimelech touch Sarah? That's powerful! The marriage covenant is man, woman and God. You are not exonerated from violating the marriage covenant even if you are not aware of it. Nadine has not brought up married men to me since that conversation.

As open as I am with my friends and family, I've decided very few will have access to my marriage. Definitely, anyone who does not respect the sanctity of the covenant marriage relationship will not be privy to anything involving my union.

Some have asked why I still call Nadine friend – simply, because she needs a friend.

Ungratefulness bears its own fruit (#25)

I love my girl, Andrea, despite our regular disagreements. We are always amazed after a heavy debate that two opinionated loud-mouths have remained close friends for so long.

My greatest pet peeve with people is ungratefulness – lack of appreciation. Can't stand it! Some time ago, I shared with Andrea details from a good date I had had. She knows all about the bad ones, and it's very rare that I have a good experience on a date. Everything was easy and comfortable. The man took care of everything: plans, transportation, and finances – it was so smooth, I didn't feel right taking my wallet out! He told me to put it away anyway. Our conversation was also enjoyable. It was a good time and I told him so.

We discovered we were both early risers when we shared a grumble about the late hour the date ended. It was raining hard when he dropped me off and started his drive home to New Jersey; I asked him to call me once he arrived home safely. He did, but it took him double the time he had estimated, and I had long since fallen asleep by the time he called. He teased me in his voicemail. I felt no shame. Anyone who's around me for any length of time quickly learns I will fall asleep between two blinks of an eye, especially after a certain time, like say, 10:00 PM. I called him back the next morning, attempting to save face. I told him I stayed up for the twenty minutes he said it would take him to get home, but after that I lost control of my eyelids. He forgave me. We chatted and I thanked him again for a nice evening. His easy company was a pleasant and welcome surprise.

Andrea was horrified. She chastised me for expressing my gratitude. "It's your due," she told me indignantly. "You can thank him once, but you certainly don't have to thank him two or three times! It's like telling him you're not used to good treatment!"

I'm not! Where has she been during all the bad date discussions?

I sat there in stunned silence, because I never imagined it would be inappropriate to thank someone more than once. As I've mentioned before, dating is not my hobby of choice, so sometimes I turn to my girls to decipher men. Wrong! Don't do that to yourselves, ladies! I've had better interactions with men since I stopped taking women's advice on how to deal with them.

I stood my common sense ground with Andrea. "If a lot of women think the way you think, that's probably why we're confronted with so many jerks." If the men who are making an effort to be gentlemanly are confronted with unappreciative women, then guess what? They are probably going to reduce that effort or eliminate it altogether. If women are liberal and expressive with criticism and expectations, we should be just as liberal and expressive with our praise and appreciation.

So, THANK YOU to all you gentlemen out there who know how to treat ladies. I am grateful and very appreciative!

Meditation Verse: Psalm 37:1-6

Do not fret because of evildoers, nor be envious of the workers of iniquity. For they shall soon be cut down like the grass, and wither as the green herb. Trust in the LORD, and do good; dwell in the land, and feed on His faithfulness. Delight yourself also in the LORD, and He shall give you the desires of your heart.

Commit your way to the LORD, trust also in Him, and He shall bring *it* to pass. He shall bring forth your righteousness as the light, and your justice as the noonday.

Foolish of Me

For many years, I claimed men never state their interest with me. They tiptoe around me and then disappear. However, a chance reconnection online with an old college interest a couple of years ago reminded me of a time when men were very straightforward with their intentions for me. Yes, I had experienced the phenomenon of a man not only stating his intentions but spending time and effort following through on them. There were two men, in particular. In my own defense, I made them aware that I was not ready for what they had on offer – commitment, marriage and possibly love.

Persistence does not always pay off

Dot was the most persistent man I've ever encountered. He is probably the reason I shoot every man down as he approaches and ask questions later. Dot didn't understand *no*. Granted English was not his first language, but he assumed *no* was a *negotiation*. Unfortunately, he passed through my life during my early twenties. I tell people he set me back four years in development, because I didn't date anyone for about two years after I managed to drop off his radar. The problem with Dot was twofold: 1) I liked him; 2) My mom had just died.

In an effort to rebuff him lightly, I told him, "Listen, I like you, but I can't deal with a relationship right now. If you give me time and space, I'm sure I will come around. But I can't give you what you want right now." His actions told me he understood my words to mean: if he badgered me more, I would come around quicker. He started popping up at my job, insisting on taking me to dinner after my shift. He would pop up on my college campus to take me to lunch between classes. When I started switching routes and shifts, he called repeatedly until someone dragged me to the phone. My co-workers thought he was the most romantic man, so if I tried to hide in the stock room and told them to tell him I had already left, they would calmly sit him down, get him a drink and tell him I would be right out. I couldn't shake him until the end of the summer when classes were over. I also started a new job and moved into a new apartment.

Why was I avoiding Dot?

He wanted to marry me. Marriage was not an institution I saw myself committing to during my early twenties. I wanted to experience life – as an individual. I wanted to learn who I was, what I wanted, what I liked, what worked for me. Dot's personality was overpowering. I didn't sense his interest was in me as an individual as much as it was in the idea of me as his wife. To date, he is the only man I've ever dealt with whom I could see myself losing pieces of my identity in order to live the life he wanted me to live. That scared me more than anything. Even then, as a young woman just learning her way, I knew I wanted to be with someone I didn't have to lose or change myself to be with. Dot was single minded. Anything I said that was not in alignment with his end-goal was not acknowledged. He mentioned marriage on the first date, meeting his family on the second and how he wanted our children to have my hands and feet on the third. It was too much, far too fast.

Every once in a while, when I feel sad for not yet having children, I think about Dot. In the vision, I'm barefoot in his homeland of Nigeria and pregnant with our eighth child. The vision quickly snaps me out of my melancholy mood!

Selective honesty can be good

Pisces passed through my life about two years later. I call him that because his horoscope sign is the reason I gave him for why we wouldn't work well together.

We went on a couple of dates, but only one night is clear in my mind. The night I told him we would not work out. He had already admitted to having a jealous nature, so being a Pisces was strike two. It was only a matter of time before strike three put him back in the dugout. He was incredulous and outraged at my summation. What I chose not to share with Pisces was that Peewee and his brother were both Pisces with violent natures fueled by jealousy and rivalry. I had not yet reached a point where men I encountered were able to stand on their own merits and credentials. Sadly, I saw all men as a variation of my violators until they proved themselves otherwise.

I feel silly even thinking about that conversation with Pisces, but the premise was a truth to me at the time. Oddly enough, I don't remember the details of our courtship, but I remember the thoughts I had about him. He was intelligent, ambitious, thoughtful, caring, supportive, sweet and kind. His approach was strong and direct with a hint of shy reserve. He was honest, respectful and thoughtful. I appreciated, above all, feeling like a prize he was determined to earn and claim. Unfortunately, that appreciation would not manifest for several years.

I think it's unfortunate Pisces passed through my life so early. The memory of him was overshadowed by less worthy men. My *ah-ha moment* came when I realized everything I now claim to want in a man was actually at my fingertips with him. At that stage of my womanhood, I did not know what to do with a man of character, how to embrace him, how to love and honor him, or how to respect him.

I don't regret not moving forward with Dot. He didn't want me for me. He wanted me because I fit his image of a wife and timetable for his life. He would not have allowed me equal partnership in a marriage. I know this by the way he did not respect my voice and preferences while dating.

    Dot and Pisces provided me with opportunities to fortify my womanhood. I may have bumbled some interactions, but I am better for the exposure. My hope is that I didn't set either back in their search for their mates. I have derived much from my encounters with them. It would be a grave disservice for them to be hindered by my youthful ineptitude, lack of insight, and foolishness.

 Meditation Verse: Proverbs 14:8-10

The wisdom of the prudent *is* to understand his way, but the folly of fools *is* deceit. Fools mock at sin, but among the upright *there is* favor. The heart knows its own bitterness, and a stranger does not share its joy.

Life Isn't Fair, Dream Anyway

In 2006, Lifetime television network aired a movie called *Human Trafficking*. I recorded and watched the four-hour mini-series in one sitting. Though I enjoyed the storytelling, it was a depressing topic. The movie explored women and children being abducted and forced to become sex slaves. Another term is sexual exploitation of women and children. However, kidnapping and rape are simple words that explain the situation just as well.

Two of the main characters, Elena and Nadia, fell into their horrific abductions and forced prostitution while trying to pursue their dreams. Elena was a young, single mother who lived in Prague. She met a handsome, charming man who expressed interest in a future with her and her child. She was floating in her own fairy tale. She even told her young daughter that she may have a new papa. Elena was hopeful because her new beau said he loved her and wanted to take her on a trip to commemorate the relationship. He took her to another country and took her passport.

Nadia was a sixteen-year-old girl aspiring to become a model. She attended a model call in Vienna and was "selected" to go to the United States to work for a modeling agency. Her mother was deceased, and she didn't tell her father about her opportunity because she didn't think he would understand. Nadia's father was extremely protective, and she believed his extreme protectiveness prevented her mother from living out her dreams. So, she ran away to become a model. The agency she ran to was a front for a forced-prostitution ring. Nadia was taken to the United States and relieved of her passport as well.

Life isn't easy. Nor is it intended to be. The Bible is a set of instructions on how to persevere through our Earthly hardships. Instead of telling these truths to children, especially young girls, we are told fairy tales – stories with tranquil beginnings, difficult middles and happy endings. We go through life thinking we are on the road to meet our Prince Charming, who is busy building our house with a white picket fence encasing a yard large enough for our enchanting brood of children to run carefree. That's a dream we all chase even when we don't realize it. Even when we don't want to want it.

Deadlines are implicit in such tales, though. They are coded in our culture. The summer I turned thirty, I sincerely felt as if I had reached an expiration date. I felt as if my usefulness as a young, fertile woman was nearing an end. Add to that the fact that my story has always been a difficult one. I didn't have a tranquil beginning, and I am perpetually in the thick of a difficult middle.

People are used to telling others their fairy tales, they aren't so interested in sharing their unpleasant truths. They speak of whirlwind courtships, romantic proposals, princess-worthy weddings, professional upwardly mobile husbands, and the new houses in the nice cul de sac or suburb. I used to sit and listen to my friends tell their tales with something approaching envy. I was happy for them but I felt I was missing out on a major part of life because I didn't have a family of my own. Given time, though, the façade always cracked. Some people began sharing the raw, uncut version of their tales. Others stopped talking altogether.

One of my college friends unraveled before my eyes. She and I developed our friendship shortly before her marriage. I had an official function in her wedding, helped clean her house during her pregnancy, and became a regular babysitter for her first two children. By pregnancy number three, she was a wreck. She had never wanted children and thought she would never marry, until she met her husband. Her husband wanted a big family and she was in love. Each pregnancy was extremely hard on her body. It was during her second pregnancy and a near breakdown that she shared that her charming, lovable husband was verbally and physically abusive – more of a bully than a wife beater. Either way, he intimidated her. She told me she had a plan to leave him but couldn't fund it because he made and controlled the money. She was an at-home mom who started drinking through the day just to make her outlook rosier.

Another friend distanced herself from her family early in her engagement and marriage because of embarrassment, shame and frustration. Soon her friends were peripheral as she attempted to merge with her new upper-middle-class in-laws. It took her a few years, but she eventually realized her husband had no respect for her, her mother, or her friends. She praised him more for his earning power than anything else. As a result, he did what he wanted in the marriage and placated her with ultimatums and expensive gifts.

Of all the women I know, I am hard pressed to think of more than one who is happy in her marriage. They all entered their relationship because they believed they could author their own fairy tale. They stay because they hope their story will turn into one.

My friends' experiences have jaded me a bit. Seeing so many fall short of being honorable and worthy of someone else's love and admiration is discouraging. It also scared me; I steered clear of men for quite a while. I focused on my business, thinking it would be a far more rewarding dream to chase than romantic love and familial contentment. To my untried mind, focusing on building a business wouldn't hurt as much nor disillusion me.

I've since learned different. I've learned that when you give yourself completely, to anything or anyone, the prospect of failure is more excruciating than anything you can imagine. Then the failure itself becomes debilitating.

Though I cannot begin to speak on the pains and sorrows of my girlfriends, I can speak on mine. I have often felt unworthy of my goals and sometimes felt unworthy of people, but I have never felt unworthy of a dream.

It is not my intention to deter you from following your own ambitions and dreams, or designing your own utopia. I share to make you firmer in your resolve to live the life you envision. There are a lot of dreams floating around. Pursuing the American dream destroyed Nadia, and letting Prince Charming sweep her off her feet killed Elena in *Human Trafficking*. Through the years, my friends have become women who don't care to look at themselves in the mirror. I've struggled in other ways, but as hard as it has been to put substance to my ideas, I wouldn't trade my experiences for the world – or a premature man.

Life isn't fair. Getting what you want in life takes persistence, perseverance, fortitude and compromise. Nothing is going to fall into your lap and stay there. I'm reminded of one of my favorite plays, *Into the Woods*, a parody which picks up on several fairy tales where they leave off. In it, Cinderella confronts Prince Charming after catching him returning from a tryst in the woods with one of her stepsisters. He looks at her disdainfully, as her eyes well with tears and huffs of breath burst from her. He shrugs his shoulders, adjusts himself in his pants and says, "I promised you happily ever after. I did not promise you fidelity."

Meditation Verse: Genesis 37:5-11

Now Joseph had a dream, and he told *it* to his brothers; and they hated him even more. So he said to them, "Please hear this dream which I have dreamed: There we were, binding sheaves in the field. Then behold, my sheaf arose and also stood upright; and indeed your sheaves stood all around and bowed down to my sheaf."

And his brothers said to him, "Shall you indeed reign over us? Or shall you indeed have dominion over us?" So they hated him even more for his dreams and for his words.

Then he dreamed still another dream and told it to his brothers, and said, "Look, I have dreamed another dream. And this time, the sun, the moon, and the eleven stars bowed down to me."

So he told *it* to his father and his brothers; and his father rebuked him and said to him, "What *is* this dream that you have dreamed? Shall your mother and I and your brothers indeed come to bow down to the earth before you?" And his brothers envied him, but his father kept the matter *in mind*.

Fascinating Womanhood: What does he see in her?

I believe God placed me in an accelerated marriage curriculum in order to instruct me on his intended purpose for the institution. He has used books, movies, and sermons. He has positioned me with couples in their natural habitats to witness practical Biblical applications or the lack thereof within their marital relationships.

Helen Adelin's book *Fascinating Womanhood* provided an amazing example of nurturing sentiment and behavior in your children. The simplicity of the message left a deep and lasting impression. Appreciation – a poorly practiced common word.

What does he see in her?

There was a woman in our neighborhood that had everyone puzzled. She was not beautiful, was overweight, and always dressed a little dowdy. There wasn't anything about her that was above average, at least not that anyone could see on the surface, yet her husband seemed to adore her. What on earth was it? Everyone wondered.

One evening I was in their home about dinnertime. She was busy in the kitchen putting the final touches on the dinner when her husband came home from work. This happened to be payday. He came into the kitchen, kissed her, and handed her his paycheck. She immediately stopped what she was doing, put her arms around him and said, "I know how hard you have worked for this… how many long hours. Thank you for providing us with so many comforts, and making it possible for me to stay home and care for the family."

But this was not enough. She went into the living room where the children were all playing on the floor. She made them all stop and stand up. "Look," she said as she held up the paycheck. "See, your father had worked hard to earn this money. Now, Jane, this means you can have a new pair of shoes, and Johnny, you can have your bicycle fixed." The father stood there beaming. Not only did his wife appreciate him, but she taught their children to. In his eyes, she was a beautiful woman.

I'm not sure she did this every payday, but I know that here was a home where the man was appreciated for his daily efforts. This ordinary woman was not so ordinary. She knew how to appreciate a man, and this is why she was beautiful to him.

Meditation Verse: Proverbs 31:26-30

She opens her mouth with wisdom, and on her tongue *is* the law of kindness. She watches over the ways of her household, and does not eat the bread of idleness. Her children rise up and call her blessed; her husband *also*, and he praises her: "Many daughters have done well, but you excel them all." Charm *is* deceitful and beauty *is* passing, but a woman *who* fears the LORD, she shall be praised.

So, what are you really saying?

Does your word choice represent what you really want? Do your actions speak to what you need? Do the people you push away really mean nothing at all, or are you fighting because they matter too much?

Is this a negotiation? Or something that'll only work on your terms, in your time? With rules only you know about?

What's going on? What about me? What about you? Why isn't there an *us*? Am I being hyper-sensitive or too obtuse? I thought I had it, but I really don't get it. Maybe it's hormones. Maybe it's frustration or exhaustion. Most likely it's a combination of everything that represents you and me.

Is this communication really fulfilling to you? Satisfying? Does the avoidance really work for you? I would much rather talk to you face to face. With your arms wrapped around me – I love the way that feels – with your nose nudging mine as your words make their way into my listening heart. I would much rather listen to your touch and read your face. I want to be much more than an influence; I want to be your helper and supporter.

What's so scary about that? And why are you so willing to gamble this away?

If we weren't connected, I would believe every no-contact message you send. But it's not my depression trying to drown me. It's not my sadness bringing me to tears. It's yours. Light shined on my darkness long ago. If I must hurt with you, why won't you let me help you work through it?

Who's to say anything about the future? Yet we have power over the direction we take today. Making no decision is still a choice you're responsible for. Silence *is* a response. Even if I choose to ignore it for a while, I may one day accept it as a final reply.

I appreciate and respect inner struggle – I recommend it for character building. But, all I'm saying is: *Invite me in.*

Meditation Verse: 1 Peter 3:8-9

Finally, all *of you be* of one mind, having compassion for one another; love as brothers, *be* tenderhearted, *be* courteous; not returning evil for evil or reviling for reviling, but on the contrary blessing, knowing that you were called to this, that you may inherit a blessing.

Prepare for Marriage?

"The real seeker of truth never seeks truth. On the contrary, he tries to clean himself of all that is untrue, inauthentic, insincere - and when his heart is ready, purified, the guest comes. You cannot find the guest, you cannot go after him. He comes to you; you just have to be prepared. You have to be in a right attitude."
— Osho

I have a confession: I no longer dream of a lavish, over-the-top wedding. That dream faded some moons ago. Now the dream is of something simple, inexpensive and efficient. Simple like: me, the groom, pastor and two witnesses.

Sister2Sister Magazine published an article titled *Preparing for Marriage not the Wedding*. Andrea brought it to my attention, and we discussed the two main points the article highlighted: pre-marital counseling and conversations. We made the observation from our own circle of friends that many couples put more thought and planning into the wedding festivities than they do the intricacies of marriage partnership and longevity.

Andrea and I are now witnessing separations and divorces among our friends who eagerly entered matrimony in their twenties. Our girlfriends put in three years, five years, seven years. He left. She left. They didn't work out.

We also have girlfriends who are intent on maintaining their marriages. They've been in it for twelve years, fifteen years, twenty-five years. Refuse to leave. Can't imagine he would. Don't want to continue living under his thumb, disregarded, overlooked and underappreciated. These women married in their twenties too but have stuck it out in hopes things would get better.

 Meditation Verse: Genesis 2:24

"Therefore a man shall leave his father and mother and be joined to his wife, and they shall become one flesh."

Married Woes

I am lucky to have married women friends who speak honestly about some of their marital problems. Two of them included me in one of their conversations a while ago. At the time, one had been married for thirteen years and the other was fifteen years into her second marriage. Both are stay-at-home moms. Both of their husbands are highly successful in their professional fields. Neither husband helps with the child rearing and discipline on a daily basis. I look at these women and think they are glorified single moms because their husbands are hardly ever around. The one wonderful difference between their status and a single mother is they don't have to worry about bringing in the income in addition to everything else. I remember thinking, *if that is what's in store for me, I'll just take the sperm, please, he can keep the ring.* Who wants a partner who's never around?

One of the women shared events that happened in her marriage. They were horror stories to me, but just regular episodes in the course of her fifteen-year marital relationship. In one story, she said her husband dotes on their children when he's home. When she tries to keep order in the house among the children, he tells them to disregard her fussing and to do as they please. The children take their father's directive to heart and disregard their mother, who replies by simply cleaning up the mess the children leave behind. In another story, she said her husband moved his mother in without discussing it with her first. She found out when her mother-in-law started shipping boxes to her home. While living in her house, the mother-in-law continually disrespected her and told her husband lies about her. The husband claimed he didn't believe the lies but refused to check his mother. My friend was alienated in her own home. Adding insult, her husband complained she was overreacting even as he coddled his mother.

Horrified, I asked her two questions: *How does he sleep peacefully at night? Don't you have a skillet?*

I cannot imagine being joined to someone who encourages and enables everyone in our life to disrespect and disregard me. That is not a union or a partnership, how can they call it a marriage?

My gaze shifted to the other woman. "Okay... so I need to be specific about my parenting expectations in my marriage contract: *You will participate, you will be present, you will sometimes take care of your children without me being physically present.* And, most importantly, your mother is not part of our marriage!"

The second woman looked at me with an arched brow and said, "Yeah, you go ahead and put that in your marriage contract." Her tone told me it wouldn't matter if I did or not...

After a minute, though, she admitted she and her husband never discussed how they would raise their children. When they married, they were both working. After her first pregnancy, she stopped working; their life unfolded the way it unfolded. Now, he is rarely home and she's overburdened with the responsibilities of a large household.

First Comes Love

I don't want to live a haphazard life, yet, I am aware that even well-planned futures have a way of falling down. All I can do is work on me. When my partner comes along, we will work on our partnership. I pray to be directed in a covenant marriage where we are both in sync with our instructions, goals, plans, and execution. In my opinion, many families fail because the *managing partners* work at cross purposes. They don't communicate, they avoid one another, avoid uncomfortable topics, they prefer work to home. Most times the managing partners each believe their own role in the partnership is more important than the others.

In an ideal world, I want to be an at-home mom for the first few years of my children's lives. Two children, two years apart, or better yet, one set of twins. By this plan, I would be out of the workforce for five to seven years. Ideally, I would like for our household income to support however our family grows. It would not do for my husband to think he runs everything because he's the sole income earner. Just as I shouldn't think everything that happens under our roof is my decision since I'm home all the time. Unfortunately, that's the trend people's attitude take when they get caught up in the importance of their individual contributions to the family unit. By deciding to stay home to raise our children, I am not diminishing nor forfeiting my partnership status. My primary function has simply changed; not our marriage and family goals. I would trust my husband to provide for me and our children, just as he would trust me to support him and to nurture our children. In most of the relationships I have observed, recognition of the nuances of give and take is missing.

Thank God for His intervention! The power struggles I've witnessed could have had me running for the hills.... far, far away from matrimony, but He has fed me and educated me in baby steps. He has renewed my mind and given me a vision of love I am eager for Him to fulfill!

Meditation Verse: Proverbs 16:3, 9

Commit your works to the Lord and your thoughts will be established.

A man's heart plans his way; but the Lord directs his steps.

Talking Isn't Always Communicating

Though Leila and Sam never married, their relationship had problems similar to a marriage. After seven years together they had a mortgage, two children together and three others from his prior relationships. When they decided to call it quits they had to discuss property, financial disbursement and child custody. Leila had been at home for nearly the full seven years they were together. When they separated, she fully expected Sam to continue paying the bills. Sam expected Leila to get a job.

Throughout the span of their relationship, I have been a sounding board for their problems. They regularly asked me to mediate and assign blame. Each time I listened to them argue their sides, I told them they were both to blame. Neither of them listened to the other. Neither appreciated the other's contribution to the family. Each thought he or she was more important to the family unit than the other.

To have Leila tell it, Sam wouldn't be able to function without her – she takes care of his clothes, food, children and bills. To have Sam it, Leila couldn't do anything without him – he earned the income that financed everything she did for the family. They were in agreement on how to raise the children. She told him what was going to happen and he followed through. However, when he made large ticket purchases without her approval, it created a whole new fight. In his mind, he didn't bother her about her childrearing decisions, so she shouldn't have a say on how he spent his money. They were operating at cross-purposes. I still don't understand how a person can claim they want to be with someone, yet continue to think as an independent individual in a relationship.

Singles vs. Marrieds

Andrea and I discussed the article and our friend examples. Afterwards, we asked each other why *we* wanted to get married. Her imam had told her it was unfair of her married friends to share their bad experiences without balancing them with good ones. I agree. I understand people don't complain about good things – they savor them, but if they share the bitter, they should share some sweet as well.

Following the discussion with my married friends, my outrage was on full display. They then rushed to reassure me that the friend whose husband tore her down in her home to their children and his mother was actually a good man who loved her. She insisted her marriage was good. I was not convinced, but it's not my place to be so. If she wants to choke the words out and believe them, that's her prerogative.

Many of the issues mentioned boil down to the quality of pre-marital conversation, counseling and personal revelations.

> *"True religion is real living; living with all one's soul, with all one's goodness, all one's honesty."*
> *- Albert Einstein*

I haven't been privy to much of my friends' pre-marital conversations, but I know Tosha well enough to know what she most likely did not discuss in detail. Her lack of honesty about her desire for children contributed to her divorce. Her husband didn't want children; he was adamantly opposed to the idea for medical reasons more than anything. When they got married, she wasn't fond of children and perhaps thought the stipulation was no big deal. Four years into the marriage, suddenly, she wants nothing more than to have a child. At some point she claimed she thought it would bring them closer together because he had been growing distant. She pleaded with him, bargained with him, and after a while she was trying to conceive on the sly. He stopped coming home. They stopped being intimate.

Someone missed or disregarded a very pertinent piece of information in that relationship. Tosha swears she always wanted to have children. She swears they discussed it before they married. I'm doubtful. Tosha and I were best friends in high school. I learned more about my feminine hygiene and menstrual care from her and her mother than from my own relatives. We shared very intimate details about our lives for more than ten years. She never once mentioned a desire to bear children. In contrast, from the moment they got serious, within the first year of dating, we all knew he had no desire to father children. And he was very clear about his reasons with all their friends and family.

A couple of years ago I went on a date with someone. We exchanged two snippets of information during our dinner conversation. I wanted children. He didn't.

I had shared a story about Jemini and her children. He picked up on my enthusiasm and said, "Sounds like children are important to you."

For a moment, I considered giving a flippant response, but luckily I answered honestly on the off chance the dating went further, "They are."

"You want children?"

"Yes. You?"

"No."

There may be other reasons, but I had no desire to see him after that. I am not a woman who thinks she can change a man's mind. I'm not interested in trying. I'll meet you where you are; I can't meet you where I want you to be.

We make decisions based on what is important to us. Are you being honest with yourself about your priorities? If you're not honest with yourself, you can't be honest with your potential spouse. Family is important to me. I want someone to share and build a life with. If your top priority is status or money or just having a spouse, well, you may continue dating someone after they baldly state they don't want children. Tosha did. Her main priority was financial stability, and her husband represented that to her. How do I know? Because she told him that plenty of times in front of their friends and family. I told her early on to stop telling her husband she married him because of his earning potential. When they were going through their divorce she didn't miss his income, she missed him. Truthfulness and openness would have helped her a lot.

Be honest in your motives and desires. People will feed you what you say you want. If your cravings go unsatisfied, ask yourself if you were honest about what you hungered for.

Seeking Satisfaction

I awoke one morning from a dream that did not immediately appear to be a direct message for me. However, after some introspection, I understood it to mean I have everything I need, I just have to claim it and be satisfied with it.

Then again, perhaps the dream was meant for you....

The setting was my home; though not any home I have lived in to date. A good friend was visiting me for several days. Every day of her visit I did something special for her. On the last morning, I got up and cooked a big breakfast. My friend walked into the kitchen and stepped up behind me to look over my shoulder. As she took in the elaborate spread of food, her hungry eyes opened wide with eager appreciation. Her awed, wistful voice spoke in my ear, "Wow! That looks good! I wish there was enough for me...."

Perplexed, I turned to face her, "Why wouldn't there be enough for you?"

"You didn't tell me I could have any," she said, "so I thought you were just cooking for yourself."

"That makes no sense, there's so much here!" My hand made a sweeping motion towards the banquet-like fare I had prepared for her. "If you're waiting for me to cater to you in a different way, it's not going to happen. Assuming none of this is for you is like God causing it to rain and then asking you if you want rain. Or making the sun burn bright and, as an afterthought, asking if you want light. Or sending the wind, only to ask if you want air. All you need has already been given. If you're not satisfied, you need to go to Him and tell Him."

Meditation Verse: Isaiah 58:8-12

Then your light shall break forth like the morning, your healing shall spring forth speedily, and your righteousness shall go before you; the glory of the LORD shall be your rear guard. Then you shall call, and the LORD will answer; you shall cry, and He will say, 'Here I am.'

"If you take away the yoke from your midst, the pointing of the finger, and speaking wickedness, If you extend your soul to the hungry and satisfy the afflicted soul, then your light shall dawn in the darkness, and your darkness shall *be* as the noonday. The LORD will guide you continually, and satisfy your soul in drought, and strengthen your bones; you shall be like a watered garden, and like a spring of water, whose waters do not fail.

Those from among you shall build the old waste places; you shall raise up the foundations of many generations; and you shall be called the Repairer of the Breach, the Restorer of Streets to Dwell In.

Man Friend Lessons

If you're waiting for a man, you're wasting your time!

A couple of summers ago, I met a very forthcoming man, Rakeem, at a neighbor's backyard party. Rakeem was celebrating his fifth wedding anniversary. He sat down at my table which was occupied by another single woman and a dating couple, all in their thirties. I have no idea how the conversation started but almost immediately Rakeem started schooling us ladies on the ways of men. Ladies, I wish I had a tape recorder! I would love to be able to share verbatim. Everything he said was pretty much something I needed to hear!

He started off talking about crappy, ill treatment women take from men in hopes of things eventually getting better. For example: multiple children from multiple women, men moving their mom in, or needing years to figure out if they want to marry you or not. "I'm telling you now," Rakeem said, "Don't take it! Don't start off taking it. You deserve better. From a man's point of view, it's great that so many women are willing to put up with our shit. But from a woman's point of view, I'm telling you, you're selling yourself short!

"When I met my wife, I could see my children coming through her birth canal," he continued. "I was living with someone at the time, but there was no way in hell I would have a child of mine come from that woman and I told her so. She wasn't the one. She was comfortable. Within three weeks of dating my wife, I told her I was going to marry her. She brushed me off, gave me a line or two and told me we were just kicking it. A year and a half later, we were married. A man knows. You don't have to be with him for six months, three years, or five years.... all that is a waste of your time. God put something in us that give men the ability to recognize our wife. This isn't something you women can change a man into knowing or accepting. Don't waste your time!"

The other ladies at the table and I were truly awed with his directness. The other man at the table was nodding in agreement. Rakeem paused after a while, looked around the table and said, "I don't know why I'm sharing all this...."

"Because we need to hear it," I chimed in, hoping he wouldn't stop talking! "Your directness is refreshing!"

Double check your signals, your tail light might be glaring!

School was in session for me that week. I had a very adult conversation with my trainer, Don Juan. Don Juan was sexy, flirtatious and straightforward. The week prior we were supposed to meet for lunch near my job in Tribeca. A couple of hours before our appointment, Don Juan texted me to ask if I meant it when I flirted with him or was I just playing.

People tell me my penchant for honesty is as much a weakness as it is a strength. I didn't want to lie, but I certainly didn't want to put myself out on a limb, blowing in the wind for lack of reciprocation. My reply was circular and wordy, "I would say it depends on whom I'm flirting with. I don't think I'm as flirty as I used to be. So yes, perhaps I do mean it.... Which isn't the same as knowing what to do about it or as follow up."

"How about when u flirt with me?"

"Short answer: I mean it."

Don Juan piqued my interest in part because of his directness. I knew immediately he was attracted to me. I wasn't subjected to months and months of wondering and speculating. He put his desire out there and sort of demanded I be just as forthcoming.

We ended up talking on the phone in lieu of lunch. He wanted to know what he was coming to lunch for. Quite honestly, that's a bit *too* direct for me (and tacky), but I prefer to find out on the front end rather than down the line. His first questions were, "Where are you? What are you looking for?"

I've never been asked directly about my status and interest by someone I was interested in a status with. In that moment I was over the moon with anticipation. I had imagined eventually having that conversation and had pre-formulated very ambitious replies, none of which came to mind. I hemmed and hawed for a moment, not sure about how much to share. Unfortunately, I had grown used to men running away from me, when I relayed what I wanted, as if a woman who knows what she wants is the worst thing they've ever encountered. After a couple of false starts, Don Juan told me, "Go ahead, be bold."

He wanted me to be bold! Remember that – that's me coming full circle.

"I'm not interested in anything casual. That's not me." Wait! That was not what I imagined I would say! It was a hot summer and I believed I would be willing to compromise for someone I was interested in. I had imagined I would be giving him a time and location and greet him at the door with some skimpy lingerie. As the words left my mouth, I looked heavenward and asked, "Father, why do you test me like this?"

I asked Don Juan, "So, where are you?"

"Can I be blunt?"

"Sure."

"I won't mess up our friendship by saying what I have to say?"

"Oh, my... let me brace myself." I took a breath. "Okay. Go ahead, we're cool."

"Well, you just answered my question. I thought you might be interested in playing around." Yes, he said *playing around!* "Because, you know... I'm otherwise committed."

"Wait. Stop. Did you just say *committed*? You're in a relationship?"

"Yeah, I told you that!"

"You did not!"

"I did! Remember when...." He gave some convoluted explanation, even noting my attention was diverted elsewhere – about how he told me he had a girlfriend. Perhaps he did tell me; perhaps he mumbled his comment under his breath several feet away with his back to me. There's no way I would have missed such an announcement intended for my ears, especially, since I had been trying to figure out a way to ask him without being obvious about my interest. Are we ever *not* obvious?

"Don Juan, had I heard you say 'I'm in a relationship, I'm with someone, I have a girlfriend, I'm not available,' whatever, I would've stopped flirting right away."

"Well, I'm glad you didn't hear it, then. You're being far too intense."

"I've heard that before. But I feel as if I've been poaching on someone else's property."

"It's not that serious. We've been off and on for a while. It's complicated. You aren't poaching. I don't believe you can take something that isn't for you anyway."

"I agree, but I could've been interfering with something that was developing into something more."

"Not at all."

"You must think I'm a hooch or something. Is that why you're propositioning me?" Then I mumbled, half to myself, "I have to tell the girls I presented myself as a hoochie...."

"Now you're being ridiculous! And this is an A and B conversation; no friends. You've only ever been professional and ladylike. But I thought the attraction was mutual."

"It is...."

"Thanks for that. I thought you heard me when I said I wasn't available, so I thought you were interested in having some fun."

"Having some fun.... Thank you for your honesty. I think I've been in this situation several times in the past and never knew how to get pass it. I assumed the men weren't interested or that I had misread the situation. It's nice to know it wasn't me.... Yeah....well...if casual is all you're interested in...."

"I didn't say that's all I'm interested in; I thought that's what you wanted."

Clearing up that situation was somewhat euphoric. My feelings weren't hurt. I wasn't angry. I was happy he hadn't wasted my time or energy. That conversation had me thinking about Doug, Jay and Jay's early competition, Distractor.

Meditation Verse: Proverbs 17:3
The crucible for silver and the furnace for gold, but the Lord tests the heart.

A fool and her words won't be taken seriously

I used to call Doug my awakener. It felt like my body was asleep before he crossed my path during my twenty-fifth year. He was a sweetheart of a man. We became good friends, and then I decided I wanted more. When I was getting to know him, whatever crossed my mind also passed my lips unedited. Doug was appalled at how I turned into a sex-hungry-maniac around him. I couldn't control my hormones. I was a late bloomer, but extremely articulate. I wanted to make up for those seven adult years I hadn't been sexually active! Doug was the first man I recognized as a potential sexual partner. I started telling him where my aches were and what he could do to help me out. Unfortunately, there were witnesses.... Our co-workers got a few laughs from watching me proposition Doug every few days. I remember telling Doug, "Listen, this can be any way you want it. With strings or without. I don't really care. I just need to take care of what's going on with my body." Yes, I've always been rather pragmatic – ever the problem solver....

Doug, however, was more sensitive. He gasped out a horrified, "LaShawnda!" Picture him clutching his heart then crossing his arms over his chest and privates. He later told me, "I respect you too much." His respect translated, to me, as, *I'm not attracted to you at all*. "Go take a cold shower and go to bed," he told me one especially heated night. "You won't feel the same in the morning." I resented his words for so long. As time passed and my attention focused elsewhere, I became extremely grateful for his gentle chiding and instruction.

All attractions are not equal

A couple of years later, Jay and Distractor crossed my path. Believe me when I tell you, I have yet to encounter any more fantastic specimen of manhood than either of these two men. Not in my travels, not in any work environment, not on land, air or sea, on this continent or others. The finest movie stars you can think of have nothing on either one of them. Distractor received my attention first. His bronze Adonis beauty blinded me to anyone else in the vicinity. That is, until Jay opened his mouth and spoke to me. Jay commanded all of my attention from the moment he first started a conversation with me.

I've never been one to sit back and wait for things to happen. Action was in order. I needed research to better perform a self-evaluation and self-improvement before taking action. I called Doug and asked, "What was it about me that turned you off?" The goal was to improve my chances with the new man-opportunities by avoiding mistakes from a former one.

"What are you talking about?"

"There's someone I'm interested in, but I don't want to make the same mistakes I made with you. So, what was it about me that turned you off?"

An awkward chuckle sounded over the line. "Shawnda, nothing about you turned me off. You're great!"

"*No-o-o-o.* Something about me didn't interest you. Something was a turn off."

"Seriously, Shawnda, you're great. You're a lovely person; I love your spirit, your laugh. I love talking to you. There's nothing wrong with you."

"So you say *now* [a few years after we met and I had shamelessly thrown myself at him]. Okay, how about one critique? If there were one thing I should work on... what would it be?"

"Okay, okay! If I were to critique one thing... *hmmm*...it would be...," some hemming and hawing, "well... you know... well... you're... a *bit* aggressive."

"You think I'm aggressive?" I chewed on that.

"Just a *li'l* bit..."

"I was just direct and honest with you, Doug, but that was too much for you?"

"Sometimes...."

Doug messed up my confidence with that critique. I shouldn't have asked. Most certainly, I shouldn't have taken him so literally and done an about-face. I've never been one for half measures. I'm either full on or full off. I steered clear of Jay and Distractor for nearly a year after the conversation with Doug, attempting to control my exuberance (which I thought was the root of my aggression). That was the beginning of the circle I mentioned. I stopped being bold. I became timid around Jay and Distractor. Also, I stopped being open and honest about my feelings. My mistake was assuming all men were as squeamish as Doug. My natural bold self-expression deteriorated to a point that I tried to hide my femininity and sexuality. In retrospect, I saw that suppressing one part of my nature blocked my ability to tap deeper emotions for their truth.

If you're sweet enough, long enough, they'll eventually want a taste

Even though my libido was moving forward, a part of me thought I would always be sexually attracted to Doug. Luckily, I was tested in a most memorable way: choosing between something I had begged for (lust of my eyes) and something I couldn't see (a pull on my heart). Several years after I had last seen him, Doug traveled to Milwaukee to help me with a photo shoot for my first book of poetry. By that time, I was completely besotted by Jay.

On his second day in Milwaukee, Doug took a leaf from my old book and asked, "So, d'ya wanna have sex?" His broad chest closed in on me as he leaned towards me with a lascivious leer.

"No." I tried to soften the refusal with a gentle pat to his chest, "That's not going to happen," I said, as I stepped around him to continue doing whatever I was doing.

I don't know who was more shocked at my refusal! In the back of my mind, I thought if he ever turned his *no* into a *yes* I would be all over him. His dumbfounded expression told me he had believed so, too.

We are the sum of our parts, real and imagined

Over the years my pseudo-relationships each had their own overwhelming identifier. During my early twenties I learned how to be present. Dot and Pisces exposed my tendency of hiding myself in order to better observe. My dealings with them taught me confidence in being present as myself. During my mid-twenties I learned how to give and get information – I'm still learning how to use what I learn, though.

Doug represented a pure, fiery lust. Distractor was an object of idolatry; I was obsessed with his masculine beauty. Jay was outside my realm of understanding. His presence overwhelmed me. I could feel him in a building before I saw him. Seeing him brightened my outlook for days. After talking to him I walked on clouds until our next meeting. From the beginning, Jay had an effect on me I found difficult to wrap my head and heart around.

I needed all these experiences. I learned very important lessons from these men through their silence, conversation, interest and lack thereof. I believe their presence in my life nudged me through intensive emotional development and growth during times I would have otherwise been stagnant.

Your mate will be different than anything you expect

Rakeem told us about the moment he realized he was in love with the woman who became his wife. He admitted to being a mac throughout his twenties and early thirties. They had been active in the same social circles for years. One night she saw him while she was on a date she wanted to escape. She asked him if he would mind helping her out – he didn't mind. She went back to her date and told him he could leave because Rakeem was going to take her home. Rakeem was impressed. He said in the back of his mind he was thinking he was just going to put her in a cab and send her on her way. However, they ended up talking for the rest of the night; he ended up walking her home and taking a cab back to his place. He said the next morning when he woke up he realized something had happened. He wanted to call her, talk to her, and see her. She was busy; he asked to tag along. She agreed. He said he sat next to her petrified she was going to guess how he felt about her! He looked at everyone sitting around the table, "This love thing is crazy!"

When Rakeem spoke about the crazy swings his personality took, I was intrigued that I could relate. He talked about his fears and how he wanted to run. I ran. I high-tailed it away from Jay because he caused a disturbance in me I could not explain and was not equipped to address. Yet there has always been a fervent hope that he would follow...

 Meditation Verse: Proverbs 14:1, 18

The wise woman builds her house, but the foolish pulls it down with her hands.

The simple inherit folly, but the prudent are crowned with knowledge.

Preparing for Marriage
Learning from Bad Examples

How many good examples of marriage have you been exposed to in your life? Within your family and friend circles? Not simply long marriages, but partnerships full of mutual respect and love, maintained with open communication. I have not been privy to one of those.

There were times when I thought I had crossed paths with such a couple, usually, people I knew before they married. Perhaps they operated well as boyfriend and girlfriend or they presented a great façade when they lived together pre-matrimony. Maybe they thought marriage would be no different than the relationship that preceded it. The couples I thought were on the yellow brick road to matrimonial bliss provided me with a panoramic view of some of the heartbreaks endured in marriage from the painful stages of growth and adjustments to buildups and fall-downs. All of which should be expected, however, many enter marriage believing it to be a cure-all, full of joy and happy moments. Very little allowance is given for the regular rotation of pain and sorrow. The quitters tend to forget their vows on the down cycle. They lose sight of the fact that partnerships are successful when both partners are working together for one another and for the marriage. Uniting with a common mind, bond, goal, and purpose will bring success to your labor.

I have been privy to decent unions where, perhaps, only one spouse was miserable. I have also seen unions that appear better off than the partners think they are. More than any other, I have been exposed to sad, bad and horrendous marriages – unions that were never partnerships or meetings of the mind. My best examples of what not to do in marriage are from my own family. It's important to take note of good and bad examples alike. There are far too many mistakes to be made to repeat the ones you know about. When people ask me what I want in a man, I am able to answer with what I *don't* want.

Deuteronomy 10:19 tells us, "Do not plow with an ox and a donkey yoked together." My pastor added his own extension, "Because the ox is going to want to work and the ass just wants to play."

Meditation Verse: Proverbs 4:20-23

My son, give attention to my words; incline your ear to my sayings. Do not let them depart from your eyes; keep them in the midst of your heart; for they *are* life to those who find them, and health to all their flesh. Keep your heart with all diligence, for out of it *spring* the issues of life.

If one spouse is the breadwinner, the other should be the caretaker

I watched my mom cook dinner every day, then get ready for her overnight shift taking care of two elderly sisters. While my mother worked at home and outside, Peewee sat on the sofa watching TV all day or ran the streets with his associates in the evenings. He didn't have any positive contributions to our upbringing. He was there, but I sincerely wish he hadn't been.

Often I consider my current status: thirty-something, single, childless. Every month some bills go unpaid. I shake my head in amazement when I think of my mother supporting a family of five on a salary I surpassed sometime in college. I can't imagine how she kept us clean, clothed, fed and content with what we had. She was like a one-woman industry.

Watching mom work for and take care of us ingrained a solid sense of independence in me. I have no problem with a woman bringing home the bread, especially if that's the only way it's going to get on the table. However, if the man is in the house, then he should cut and serve the bread. He should contribute in another way. Peewee never got that concept – *partnership*. Even with a wife and children, everything was always all about him. Him first, him now, him last.... He was a taker, never a giver or provider.

Meditation Verse: Genesis 2:15, 18, 20-24

Then the LORD God took the man and put him in the garden of Eden to tend and keep it.

And the LORD God said, "*It is* not good that man should be alone; I will make him a helper comparable to him."

So Adam gave names to all cattle, to the birds of the air, and to every beast of the field. But for Adam there was not found a helper comparable to him. And the LORD God caused a deep sleep to fall on Adam, and he slept; and He took one of his ribs, and closed up the flesh in its place. Then the rib which the LORD God had taken from man He made into a woman, and He brought her to the man.

And Adam said: "This *is* now bone of my bones and flesh of my flesh; she shall be called Woman, because she was taken out of Man."

Therefore a man shall leave his father and mother and be joined to his wife, and they shall become one flesh.

Staying together for the children is a disservice to them

Peewee was not a good man, husband or father. My mother was a good woman, wife and mother, and I used to tell her she could do so much better than what she was holding on to. She could be with a man who treated her well, respected her and honored her. Wouldn't it be wonderful to have a supporter and provider for her and her children; a father in practice, not just deed? I started my divorce campaign when I was twelve, shortly after I reported Peewee to the police for child molestation. Even with full knowledge of his actions against her daughter, my mother chose to stand by her man. Today, I view her decision as a choice to honor her marriage vows. For many years, I couldn't begin to comprehend *why*....

Mom listened to my arguments against her marriage and waved me away. She was committed to her vows. She didn't think it would be right for another man to raise her children. She continued to give her husband all the chances he asked for.

As for me, my brother and sister, we would have appreciated having a positive example of fatherhood in our youth, even if he was not our biological father.

Extramarital affairs last longer than the sex

In 2000 my sister and I met with Peewee for the first time in twelve years. He had recently completed his prison sentence in Arizona and relocated to Upper Michigan. Our mother had died four years prior, and I felt a need to reach out in forgiveness as a tribute to my mother. Kim and I met him in Gary, Indiana in the presence of both grandmothers. She and I were interested in exploring a possible adult relationship with him. I took everyone to lunch at a buffet restaurant. Kim enjoyed her food, as she always has done. Peewee made a comment about her needing to slow down before she got as big as our server, who was a large woman. I looked at him and said, "What would be wrong with that? That's the type of woman you like."

His eyes bugged out. "What are you talking about?"

"Teresa."

"Teresa?"

"Yes. The woman you lived with for three months in Arizona. I was about ten or eleven."

He almost choked on his food. Both my grandmothers *tsked* and looked away.

"Damn, girl! You have a memory!"

Kim chimed in, "Shawnda doesn't forget anything!"

"I guess not! I didn't even remember the girl's name."

"You didn't remember the name of the woman you left your family for," I asked with an arched brow and perhaps a sneer....

"I didn't leave you guys. Your Mom put me out. I needed a place to stay; Teresa had a place. How do you know about her?"

"I was with Mom when she dropped your stuff off at Teresa's house."

You would think my Mom would've divorced him after that, but then she never put him out for his cheating. I can't say what she got fed up with that time, but she always took him back. His effort to make promises outweighed his tendency to break them all.

Mom could've left Peewee on grounds of unfaithfulness and sexual depravity, but she claimed she stayed because she loved him.

Meditation Verse: Proverbs 5:20-23

For why should you, my son, be enraptured by an immoral woman, and be embraced in the arms of a seductress? For the ways of man *are* before the eyes of the LORD, and He ponders all his paths. His own iniquities entrap the wicked *man,* and he is caught in the cords of his sin. He shall die for lack of instruction, and in the greatness of his folly he shall go astray.

Honesty is good, but being right is better

As much as I would like to be married, I refuse to be pressured into a commitment, especially since I have seen the effects of a bad man on a good woman.

Peewee has never been financially sound because he's never been interested in working. Yet, somehow, he has always been able to attract women and have them feel honored to cater to him. I've seen it with my own eyes. He's a spoiled, selfish man who will not eat a feast set before him unless someone fixes his plate. He visited me once in Milwaukee a couple of years after our reunion in Gary. He had a live-in girlfriend, at the time, who chose not to travel with him. He complained all the first day that he was hungry. He called me at work repeatedly asking when I would be home. I kept telling him to fix something to eat, as I had stocked the cupboards and fridge. On the second day, his girlfriend called me at work to tell me how to take care of him so he would eat. "I'm not about to cater to him, this is ridiculous! He's sitting in my house with a cabinet full of food and won't eat because no one is there to fix him a plate? He's a grown man!"

"I know. I know. I just do it so I won't hear his mouth."

As despicable as Peewee is in many respects, I can say this for him: he doesn't hide his nature from anyone. He doesn't woo women then switch his game. If he's with someone and interested in someone else, he tells them, "Yo, I'm with someone. If you want in, fine, this is what I expect.... If not, keep it moving." His brothers are the same.

Uncle Vinny has never worked a job in his life (for any substantial amount of time). He doesn't sell drugs or any other paraphernalia, as far as I know. He uses them, though, Vinny can smoke, drink, curse and party you under a table. He has more sneakers than I have shoes, always in the latest fashion. His clothes stay pressed and clean, mostly '80s and '90s-style hip hop gear. He's truly fly, I have to give it to him; he stays sharp and usually has an old-school pimp-style car. He lives well from woman to woman. The main woman may not know about the many others (chances are she does, though), but the others are all trying to outspend each other to become the main woman.

How do I know? Because I grew up on some of his lessons. Uncle Vinny told his daughter and nieces not to be like the women he deals with. In the next breath he bragged to his brothers and nephews about his most extravagant conquests.

The main lesson I learned from Vinny, that colored some of my interactions with men I dated, was: A man doesn't have to spend money on me. I can finance my expenditures, but he better not ask me for money. I am not interested in financing a man's expenditures.

More disheartening are the effects of a bad woman on a good man.

Peewee's younger sister was the biggest mac I have ever come across. *Ever!* I think the reason I wanted to be a party girl was so I could make my aunt proud by leaving men panting in my wake. Like she did. Something about her had men begging to do things for her. Admittedly, I believed her assertions that men gave her extravagant gifts without so much as a kiss in return. I started to doubt her claim later in my twenties. Looking back, I can see how she could have gotten by with just her beauty. Until her beauty started to age, fade and spread. By the time she hit her late thirties I knew she was doing more than just smiling at men for their shrinking gifts.

Auntie Mac met a wonderful man in her mid twenties. Unfortunately, she didn't consider him her type at all, but she married him because he worshipped the ground she walked on. He praised her; she could do no wrong. Her word was law in the household, even when it was spiteful and mean-spirited. I felt sorry for her husband, but I believed they would live happily ever after simply because she wanted to be worshiped and he wanted to worship her.

Even though he continually looked the other way when she slighted him, she eventually walked out on him on the grounds of his inability to satisfy her sexually.

On Peewee's side of the family, most relationships boil down to sex. They have very high sex drives and are extremely active. This isn't necessarily held against them by their mates, the mates just try to hold on and keep up. Honestly, I've seen this manifested in Peewee, his two brothers and his sister, my brother, sister and two female cousins. None of them has ever been faithful in relationships or marriages.

This excessive exposure to sexual misconduct, misdeeds, infidelity, perversions and promiscuity by married family members painted a skewed picture of marriage for me. I grew up thinking it was something people did "just because." By high school I thought of marriage as a phase of our social lives. During my twenties I viewed marriage as a means to an end (legitimate children and a family unit) and convenience (regular sex source and companionship).

It was not until I began my Holy Spirit-directed study of marriage, in my thirties, that I began to look at marriage as a covenant relationship entered into with sacred vows. It is my belief that God had withheld my husband because I was not ready to be a good man's good thing *(Proverbs 18:22)*. I needed cultivating, pruning and relearning.

Meditation Verse: Proverbs 21:2-3

All a man's ways are right in his own eyes, but the LORD weighs the heart. To do what is right and just is more acceptable to the LORD than sacrifice.

Your fantasy mate is a figment of your imagination

Auntie Mac's husband always referred to her as his fantasy woman. His ideal wife looked like my aunt. I'm not sure which attributes, but I must admit my aunt was a hot mama in her day! She was a petite caramel dream with great legs, a beautiful, dimpled white smile, sparkling eyes, and personality for days.

One day Auntie Mac walked past him in a mall and he rushed into a store to buy an ink pen, then ran after her and asked for her number. She wrote it down for him. He pursued and wooed her into marriage. Uncle told me about their first meeting whenever I asked him why he put up with her ill treatment in the marriage. He would say, "Your aunt is the most beautiful woman in the world. When I saw her walking that day, it was like she had just walked out of my dreams. She was everything I had ever dreamed of having in a wife. Not many men get to marry their fantasy woman." As a teenager, it sounded like a wonderfully romantic love story. As a woman of God, I realize neither of them mentioned God or love in their story.

Uncle was a decent Christian man, and it was hard to believe his fantasy woman had no substance. Auntie Mac has some wonderful qualities – she's generous and supportive for starters, but her best qualities were not presented to her husband.

Meditation Verse: Proverbs 19:22

What is desired in a man is kindness, and a poor man is better than a liar.

Sex should strengthen a union, not divide it

Leila and Sam never married, however they owned a house and had two children together. Sam had three children from two prior relationships, two of whom often lived with them. They were together for seven years. Each fought for control for the majority of that time. Her weapon of choice was sex, his was money.

Several years ago, Leila told me she put Sam on a sex restriction because he wasn't acting right, i.e. doing what she wanted him to do. The first time was for a year. She refused to have sex with him and told him it was over if he had sex with someone else. I sat in amazement at this revelation. How could you not only expect your man to take an extended sex punishment, but demand he not go to someone else? My experience with my brother and uncles told me Leila was delusional. A year of no whiff, no look, no touch and she thought he remained faithful? Okay.... but if she believes it, who am I to question?

It's not funny, but I couldn't help but laugh in amazement, "Did he cry when you finally gave him some?"

"Girl, yeah… but I couldn't talk about him. I was in need too."

When she shared this snippet, I thought back to a visit with them a couple of years prior. She had had her first child some months before and her butt was still sort of *there*. I was tickled to see her with a butt – she's naturally a very slender, petite size 2/4 – when she walked past me I smacked it with a, "My goodness! Look at all that!" Sam was sitting on the sofa and his eyes glazed over, "Shawnda, can you hit it again? For me? Please!"

"Why won't you hit it," I asked him.

"She won't let me touch her."

"You're kidding! You can't even smack her butt?"

"Nope. Can't even see her in her panties."

"So sorry.... Come here, girl, one more smack."

Again, not funny, but I laughed really hard! During our revealing conversation, I asked her, "Was that during the one-year restriction?"

"Yep, it sure was!"

They have since broken up and have been in a vicious custody battle for the last two years. Before the breakup, they had one last make-up. When he got back in her good graces he put a tighter control on the money and other things he was the sole source for. She fought back by restricting sex again, and he stepped out with someone else. When Leila found out, she moved back in with her mother.

Meditation Verse: 1 Corinthians 7:1-5

It is good for a man not to marry. But since there is so much immorality, each man should have his own wife and each woman her own husband. The husband should fulfill his marital duty to his wife, and likewise the wife to her husband. The wife's body does not belong to her alone but also to her husband. In the same way, the husband's body does not belong to him alone but also to his wife. Do not deprive each other except by mutual consent and for a time, so that you may devote yourselves to prayer. Then come together again so that Satan will not tempt you because of your lack of self-control.

Scandalous

This past spring, I met a couple who were very much in love. They met in high school over twenty years ago and dated for a short period afterwards. He asked her to marry him within eight months of dating and she said yes. That should have been the beginning of their happily ever after, but in the man's words, at that time, he wasn't ready to be a man. He wasn't ready for commitment and family responsibility, so he disappeared within a month of asking for her hand in marriage. He stopped calling, stopped coming around. No word. No explanation.

A few years later he saw her on the street walking with another man. He shouted her name. She looked back and saw him, but her then-boyfriend had a strong grip on her hand and didn't slow down. During the retelling, she said she remembered that moment and how she wanted to yank away from her boyfriends grip and run to her former flame. But she didn't.

Fast forward to this past January, the two star-crossed lovers' paths intersected again. Sparks flew. Flames ignited. Love was undeniable. Life became too short to let another chance at happiness slide away. This time they each wanted to hold on to their incredible connection. This time neither wanted to allow the other to walk out of their life.

The woman told me she kissed him the first night they were reunited and knew everything she needed to know. He interjected, in fond remembrance, "Yeah, that kiss made me forget my address!"

Looking between the two, I chuckled, "Really?"

"Yeah, really," she nodded in confirmation. "He was getting into a cab at the time. After I kissed him, he couldn't tell the cabbie his address! They both looked at me but I wasn't any help – I didn't know where he lived!" I was impressed by such skill. It crossed my mind that one day I may be proud to toot such a horn of feminine wiles.

The man later said, as he placed a proprietary hand to the back of her neck, "This woman here... the best way I can explain it... is... she's my buddy. With benefits."

"Yeah that's what got us in trouble the first time," she said

"How so?" I asked.

"We outlined our relationship so casually. We were friends with benefits. When he asked me to marry him, I was in love but had no idea he loved me. I kept telling myself I was stupid for falling in love with a hook-up."

"Did you love her?" I asked him.

"I did, but I never told her. I asked her to marry me but never mentioned love. Then I got cold feet and disappeared."

"That was dirty," I exclaimed. "I disappear on people, but I don't ask them to marry me first!" They both agreed he was wrong then. "Do you love her now?"

"Yes!"

"Does she know that?"

He looked over at her, "Yeah, if she doesn't know it by now something's wrong with her!" She sent a dimpled smile his way.

If this was the only part of their story I had heard that night, I would have gone home with stars in my eyes. Their story represented the triumph of true love. It would have stood as an example of endless cosmic connection. Undeniable. Never ending. Complete unity. Soul stirring. Amazing. Luckily, I'm not as naïve as my wide eyes mislead people to believe.

That portion of the conversation was the last thing I learned about them. They shared their background after dinner on our walk to the train station. Hearing about their beginning made them human, completely fallible and somewhat tragic. Their whole story was really sad. Even though there were some elements of awareness, learning and growth, overall it did not appear they were acting progressively. They were clinging to one another because they each represented the happiness of a carefree time to the other.

The man shared his two regrets in life: 1) he hadn't married her their first time around and 2) they never had children together. They both have children and neither is able to reproduce. Imagine knowing your whole adult life that you had met the one person you wanted to share your life with but you walked away from them out of fear of the unknown. The only thing stopping my heart from bleeding for them was one of the first things they told me. Before I learned their names, but *after* they shared photos of themselves in semi-nude, sexually explicit positions.

We were all guests at a birthday dinner of a mutual associate. We had a private room in a restaurant with less than fifteen people in attendance. I admit to being a bit nosy sometimes. The man and woman had made quite a boisterous entrance. Shortly after arriving, I noticed they were standing behind me, flanked by a few women. Everyone was looking intently at a phone in the man's hand. I craned my neck to see between the shoulders of two of the flanking ladies. When I realized what I was looking at, I let out a squeak. "Excuse me! Is that a nipple?"

"Yes." The man looked up with a smile.

"And was that your mouth near the nipple?"

"Yes."

"Okay." I turned back to my food. This is New York, after all. You never know what people are doing or for what reason. In short order I learned I was sitting across from the photographer of the photos the man was showing off on his phone. So, assuming all was innocent and perhaps I had just seen a portion of an *art* photo of a man's mouth approaching a woman's nipple, I asked the man if I could see his photos. As he handed me his phone, he said the photos were for his blog. *Oh, work related, I can deal with that,* I thought. [Bear with me, please; I know I'm slow sometimes!]

"What type of blog?"

"Sex from a man's perspective." By this time I was already scrolling through the photos trying to keep my mouth from dropping open. Each photo was progressively more lewd and suggestive of imminent intercourse. Indeed, after several photos he snatched the phone out my hand and said, "That's enough. You don't need to see the next one." I started to ask what would be worst than what I'd already seen. Thankfully that question stayed behind my teeth.

A lot was going through my mind, but I couldn't understand why a man would show such photos of his wife, especially to her associates and friends. Or how she could stand next to him and profess pride at the beauty of the photos. This is a network of people I've done events and promotions with for Jazzy Media. I could tell by a couple of freezing faces and crossed arms I was not the only one taken aback by the couple's presentation.

For some reason, part of my mind thought such exploitation could be explained within the confines of marriage.... Like, he took such photos with his wife rather than a model or prostitute to illustrate a message he was writing about. (My mind works hard to explain human behavior.) "Are you two married?"

"Yes," he said. I sighed with relief. "To other people," he finished.

"Excuse me? You're kidding, right?"

"No. We're both married to other people."

"What do they think about this?"

"They're not too happy."

I had to step away for a minute on that one. The woman came to sit by me and I asked her why she took the photos. She gave me a blank look. I pressed on, "Are you... selling them?"

"Oh, no!"

"Well, he mentioned a blog...."

"Oh, no, we just wanted to take the pictures. But they're not for a web site or anything. I think it was something great to do. I got to see myself how others see me. When we got the photos back, I kept thinking, 'Wow! I'm hot!' I'm so glad I took them."

"Okay...." I still couldn't understand *WHY*.

The party hostess later told me with a sad shake of her head, "LaShawnda, before she got with him she was a good Christian woman. That's all I can say." Everyone at the table nodded in agreement.

At one point of the evening I was in a small group with the birthday girl and a couple (who were married to each other) discussing the photos. The birthday girl's parents were in attendance (they've been happily married for over thirty years) and the birthday girl was rightfully outraged that such photos were shared not just at her party but while her parents were present. She kept asking, "Why would someone take out photos like that and just pass them around?"

I offered my observation. "Once you take one step outside of decency you rapidly lose your sense of what's right. They no longer have a sense of decency."

As we left the restaurant, a group of us were wrapping up a dating conversation. Some of the ladies were schooling me. The man walked up and tried to interject his advice. I stopped him and told him we were talking about me finding a good Christian man. His neck jerked back, "So? What does that mean? Some of the biggest freaks I've been with have been in the church! Every Sunday they were in church!"

The woman also took offense at my claim of wanting a good Christian man. She mimicked her companion. "Yeah, being a Christian man don't mean nothing!"

The other ladies shut them and the conversation down after those comments.

The group dispersed. The man and woman were the only two walking in my direction. After searching my brain for an excuse *not* to walk with them, I gave up, looked heavenward and told God to stay with me, then fell into step with them as we headed uptown. During that walk I got the beginning of their story.

I don't like to judge people and I can forgive most anything immediately and the remainder of things after some time, but when they so nonchalantly stated their adulterous relationship, I found myself turning up my nose a bit. I was truly scandalized! Their attitude blatantly disregarded the matrimonial relationship. They have three children apiece and had no concern for the example they were setting, nor the damage they were causing. Lack of self-control and extreme lust does not exonerate you from the responsibility of your vows. Sometime before the dinner had ended, they also shared they had both gotten nipple and tongue piercings together. I can only imagine how wide my eyes grew as I uttered, "You two are freaky!"

He replied with a chipper *yes*, but she took exception. "I'm happy I have this at my age! We're great together! This is exciting! And we do plan to marry! We're going to work out this time."

May God bless them and have mercy on their souls. I don't know what's in store for them, but Bible stories tell me their union will not be blessed.

Shortly after meeting them, I watched the story of Jacob on the Gospel Channel while reading along with some of the scenes. I used to think the story of Jacob and Rachel was very romantic, after all, that's how it's usually taught. Jacob worked for seven years to earn the right to claim Rachel. *Wow!* I would be impressed! She had to know she was loved! Even after he was tricked into consummating his vows with her sister, Leah, which made Leah his legal wife, he worked another seven years to earn the right to make Rachel his second wife. He wanted her that much. He claimed to love her that much. But seeing these words acted out with the addition of colloquial conversation, I began to see something different in Jacob and Rachel's story. I saw a man who believed in the God of his father Isaac and grandfather Abraham but didn't seek his God's direction. This time I reread Jacob's story and saw a man who was driven by a selfish need to satisfy himself – his lusts, his needs, his wants, and his greed. Nothing he did in his early story was for the benefit of others. Just because he was not aware he married Leah (who stood in her sister's stead) did not make his commitment of his life and his body to her any less valid. However, his resentment of her and his situation caused him to neglect her in favor of his second wife, Rachel. His favoritism and his unwillingness to honor his first wife moved God to produce in his rightful marriage and withhold in his second.

And when the Lord saw that Leah was hated, he opened her womb: but Rachel was barren. (Genesis 29:31) Leah went on to birth six sons and one daughter. Leah bore the line of Christ. She's the ancestress of the priesthood and the king. I hadn't noticed before how much the Lord blessed her union with Jacob. The hated wife became the blessed mother.

On the other hand, Rachel and Jacob had a contentious relationship. *And when Rachel saw that she bare Jacob no children, Rachel envied her sister; and said unto Jacob, Give me children, or else I die. And Jacob's anger was kindled against Rachel: and he said, Am I in God's stead, who has withheld from you the fruit of the womb? (Genesis 30:1-2)* Later, God opened her womb and blessed Rachel with Joseph and Benjamin. But God's blessing and promise to His nation was delivered through her sister Leah's marriage and womb.

My prominent thoughts while speaking with the adulterers was: Marriage is a covenant. It's a pact. It's a promise. The main witness standing for your committed relationship is God. He takes His role seriously as the creator of the institution and us.

Dr. Myles Munroe described marriage in wonderful terms in *The Purpose and Power of Love and Marriage,* "Marriage is the highest of all human relationships, and friendship is the highest level of that relationship.... Marriage is an earthly, fleshly picture of the relationship in the spiritual realm between not only God the Father, God the Son and God the Holy Spirit, but also between God and mankind whom He created."

How would your view and handling of your marriage change if you saw your spouse as a representation of God?

When I separated from the adulterers at the subway station, I had a mental summary of their situation: they were violating two spouses, two marriages, two families and one God. All the interactions of each of those relationships have a ripple effect. They were bringing ruin to many lives, most especially to their individual selves. If marriage represents another level of connection to God, then by violating their marriage relationships weren't they also violating their connection to their God?

My pastor made a radical statement a couple of years ago. He said, "People are walking around thinking they married the wrong person. I'm here to tell you, you didn't. Whoever you married is the *right* person."

That clanged harshly in my ears, because I knew some people who weren't working well together. A better understanding of his statement revealed marriage is less about the *who* and more about the *commitment*. On the front end, you need to make sure you are not committing your life to someone you will have difficulty maintaining your vows with. However, once you promise to love, honor and cherish till death parts you, God is taking you at your word. You need to remain faithful to the end, no matter what (excluding Biblical exceptions).

My pastor also insisted during that lesson that a man seeks to protect his wife's reputation above all things (see Ruth and Boaz's story). Perhaps remembrance of that part of the lesson was why I couldn't wrap my mind around the inconsistency of a man claiming to love a woman and wanting to marry her, while portraying her in a whorish light before her associates and friends.

I didn't see any love in the adulterous relationship. I saw decay and destruction. They smelled of it as well.

Meditation Verse: Matthew 19:1-10

Now it came to pass, when Jesus had finished these sayings, that He departed from Galilee and came to the region of Judea beyond the Jordan. And great multitudes followed Him, and He healed them there.

The Pharisees also came to Him, testing Him, and saying to Him, "Is it lawful for a man to divorce his wife for *just* any reason?"

And He answered and said to them, "Have you not read that He who made *them* at the beginning *'made them male and female,'* and said, *'For this reason a man shall leave his father and mother and be joined to his wife, and the two shall become one flesh'*? So then, they are no longer two but one flesh. Therefore what God has joined together, let not man separate."

They said to Him, "Why then did Moses command to give a certificate of divorce, and to put her away?"

He said to them, "Moses, because of the hardness of your hearts, permitted you to divorce your wives, but from the beginning it was not so. And I say to you, whoever divorces his wife, except for sexual immorality, and marries another, commits adultery; and whoever marries her who is divorced commits adultery."

His disciples said to Him, "If such is the case of the man with *his* wife, it is better not to marry."

Marriage: Work It!

There is one good example of marriage I will cite. I cannot vouch for much, because I have come to realize that couples truly content in their marriages don't speak much about them. My friend Sierra appears to be living her fairy tale. I used to tease her about her stand-by-her-man-ride-or-die practices. If she could have joined herself to his hip, she certainly would have. She's supportive of everything he does, yet she still manages to work in some of her own goals and ambitions. From all appearances, after six years, a house and a child, their relationship is healthy and sound. There's love, commitment, communication, faithfulness, loyalty, respect and a lot of mutual support.

A couple of years ago, I told Sierra I would stop teasing her about her dedication to her husband. She was upset with him about something, which is truly rare for her to be upset enough to talk about it. She recalled some of my teasing jokes to support her irritation and I had to stop her. I told her, despite my jokes, I plan on taking a chapter or two from her book on *How to Treat Your Man Right!*

Sierra and Rex are also an example of a couple that works despite distance, character and personality differences and any other seemingly insurmountable obstacle. They've been together for over eleven years, married for six. Sierra was my roommate when I modeled for the Ebony Fashion Fair show. When we met, she had dreams of being a supermodel (*a la* Tyra Banks) slash television action hero (*a la* Zena). In pursuit of those dreams, she left her native Tampa, Florida and moved to Los Angeles, California. Rex, her boyfriend at the time, went with her as a demonstration of his support. Rex is a laid-back, casual, reserved fellow in love with his native Florida. He didn't care for Los Angeles at all and left after a few months. Sierra eventually followed him back to Tampa. Six months later she was offered a phenomenal position with a government agency in Los Angeles. Rex agreed to move back with her, but for a set term this time. Though living in Los Angeles, they married in their hometown of Tampa. A year or so after the wedding, Rex, who still had not acquired a taste for Los Angeles, moved back to Florida before the time they had agreed upon. He cemented his move by accepting a position of his own in Miami. Sierra tried to stick it out and wait for an official job transfer to Miami, which depended on vacancies. Months passed and she was still separated by thousands of miles from her man. Eventually, she chucked the job and moved to Miami to reclaim her husband. Perhaps, you can see where the teasing comes from? I called them my Bi-Coastal Couple – pick a state already!

In the conversation where Sierra expressed a rare bout of frustration with her husband (note: even during all the transnational back and forth she didn't speak in frustration against him), I told her there's a bond between the two of them that can't be damaged by someone preying on one of their insecurities. "You have some couples who can be divided by their own thoughts or by a third party's words or actions. Say for instance, someone tried to speak against how you feel about Rex. He would wave them off with a 'Man, please! Do you know what this woman does for me?' You back up how you feel and what you want for the two of you with action. You love him; he knows it because you show him he's important to you. What he wants is important to you. What he likes is important to you. He knows where he stands in your life. And vice versa."

Sierra puts her love in action. Sometimes, to the exclusion of others, but that's okay – *others* aren't part of her marriage. Also, what she did to get him, she does to keep him. He is pretty consistent with his treatment of her as well. There is a foundational care and respect that has always been exhibited between the two of them in full view of others. I haven't heard of any instances where their friends and family have imposed on their marriage. Their priority is clearly one another, their marriage and their growing family. They welcomed their second child this past spring.

Sierra is focused. That's the best way to describe her. She has single-minded determination regarding her husband – keep him happy and be happy with him! She has taught me quite a bit.

When their first child was seven months old, they were still struggling to maintain their social calendar and couple activities. One night we were talking and she said she and Rex were going to a sports bar called Daisy Duke's to watch a pay-per-view game. I choked on laughter at the mention of Daisy Duke's, especially when she explained, "It's like Hooter's, only different."

"Right…. So their focus is booty, not boobs!"

She chuckled. "He wants to see the game, he asked me to go, so I'm going… and taking the baby." Remember, I said ride-or-die!

"How are you going to manage that?"

"We have the baby on a schedule. By the time the game starts she should be fed and asleep. We also get in our movies this way."

All I could say was, "Work it!" Then, just out of curiosity, "Why don't you just send Rex to see the game on his own?"

She basically said she didn't see why she had to. He asked her to go and she enjoyed the sport. Then she mentioned a co-worker of hers who continually sends her husband out to hang with the guys. The husband always asked her to do stuff and she didn't want to be bothered. "I don't know what's wrong with her," she said. "She's sending her husband out alone all the time, basically begging other women to make moves on him. Rex has his guy time and he has the time he wants to spend with me; I don't mind making adjustments to make that happen. So what, it's at a sports bar or movie; it's doable."

Sierra impressed me! She had a full-time job on top of being a new mom and could have easily cried exhaustion. But she hasn't lost her focus. It expanded with the baby, but the premise is still the same: stand by my man, keep him happy and be happy with him.

My, what a concept.

I shared this story with every exhausted and frustrated mom I knew. As you can imagine, I received many evil looks and suggestions to update them when Sierra had to juggle two, three or four children. As they suspected, Sierra started showing signs of wear sooner than later. Well before the baby turned two, Sierra was noticeably irritable and crabby. She was losing patience with everyone, me included. She was also pregnant with her second child, still working full-time, and still fitting in social activities with her family. I know she was exhausted during her second pregnancy – chasing a two-year-old around and working up to her due date. Every time we communicated during her second pregnancy, I asked if she was resting or had scheduled rest. She kept reassuring me she would rest during her maternity leave. Indeed, she enjoyed her maternity leave so much, she didn't want to return to work!

I am extremely glad I have a friend going before me in the way I wish to go. Sierra is very focused on her family. Her focus makes her an admirable wife, mother and friend.

Meditation Verse: Proverbs 19:14

Houses and wealth are inherited from parents, but a prudent wife is from the LORD.

Tell Me You Love Me

Whitney Houston asked in one of her 1980s hit songs, "If somebody loves you, won't they always love you?" My young vocal cords strained to hit the notes in tandem with her. Such a philosophical question can probably have many philosophical answers, however, I'm inclined to say a straight *yes*. Yes, you do always love those you once loved. The nature and intensity may wane, but the love doesn't completely disappear. Even if your emotions corrode to hate.... the love is still underneath the hard feelings, because whatever you loved about that person is still in them.

> *Where do broken hearts go?*
> *Can they find their way home;*
> *Back to the open arms*
> *Of a love that's waiting there?*
> *And, if somebody loves you*
> *Won't they always love you?*
> *I look in your eyes*
> *And I know that you still care*
> *For me*

The HBO series *Tell Me You Love Me* was about four couples in various crisis stages of their relationships who were seeking counseling. Three couples were married, one was engaged. May, the therapist, was part of one of the married couples profiled. The potential crisis to her decades-old marriage was the sudden availability of an old lover. May's old college flame, John, was the rival her husband, Arthur, vanquished for her hand in marriage.

This triangle was profiled in Episode #7. John called May's house out of the blue and asked to meet with her. His wife had recently died and he was setting up his life as a widower. May was conflicted because her husband had always been a bit touchy about John, but Arthur urged her to meet John to see what he wanted. They were both aware John was intent on breaking up their marriage and taking May back.

May met John at his new apartment. Their conversation took place on his sofa after he poured them both a glass of wine.

May: Sigh... "You know this is a lot to face. A new apartment.... It's tough starting everything new so quickly."

John: "I don't think of it as starting new." He looked at her suggestively. "More like coming back..."

May: "I thought a lot about us since you called...about what we've held on to all these years...."

John: "And...?"

May: Sigh... "I think I owe a lot of my marriage to you... to the thought of you... the fantasy of us."

John: "This isn't a fantasy. I think it's about regrets. Living a life that is *not* filled with them."

May: Nodding her head in agreement, "That's why I'm here. The thought of us together again was something I used to get myself through the difficult times with Arthur, with myself.... And if you hadn't come back now, I think I'd still be using it.

John: "Don't talk yourself out of this...."

May: "No.... I care more for you now than those mornings when we couldn't bear to leave each other. Ironically, though, it's the thought of you that has kept me with the man I love." She paused. "That's a good thing."

John: "Then why are you here?"

May: "Because I think endings need to be treated with as much care and gentleness as any other part of a relationship."

I agree with May. What a powerful line, *"I think endings need to be treated with as much care and gentleness as any other part of a relationship."* I have witnessed some very temperamental and painful break-ups. All the temper appears to be a waste of energy because couples more often than not get back together – even if briefly. I always wondered how temperamental couples could stand to look at each other with all the angry, painful words they exchanged during their fits of temper. I also wondered why those people did not choose to end their relationships with dignity and respect, even if only so they could cross paths in the future without shame or regret.

Wouldn't it be easier, more accurate and humane to look at your unwanted partner and say, "Yes, I still love you, I may always love you, but I no longer want to be with you..." Something along those lines.... It's not a discussion; it's a statement. It's not an argument; it's a decision. You're not demeaning the other person; you're acknowledging the shared experiences, love, and time. Gracefully letting go and walking away is much better than laying waste to everything you two built together.

 Meditation Verse: Proverbs 10:30-32

The righteous will never be removed, but the wicked will not inhabit the earth. The mouth of the righteous brings forth wisdom, but the perverse tongue will be cut out. The lips of the righteous know what is acceptable, but the mouth of the wicked *what is* perverse.

#1 Predictor of Divorce

According to Diane Sollee of SmartMarriages.com, the number-one predictor of divorce is the habitual avoidance of conflict. She also reports the reason married couples avoid conflict is because they believe conflict will lead to divorce. Talk about a Catch-22!

> It's like the cartoon where the couple explains to the marriage counselor, "We never talk anymore; we figured out that's when we have all our fights!"
>
> In the beginning, we avoid conflict because we are so much in love and we believe that "being in love" is about agreeing. We're afraid if we disagree or fight we'll ruin our marriage. Later, we avoid conflict because when we try to deal with our differences things get so out of hand and our fights become so destructive and upsetting we simply shut down. After a few bad blow-ups we become determined to avoid conflict at any cost.
>
> Successful couples are those who know how to discuss their differences in ways that actually strengthen their relationship and improve intimacy. They don't let their disagreements spill over and contaminate the rest of the relationship.
>
> While it's true that we don't get married to handle conflict, if a couple doesn't know how – or learn how – to fight or disagree successfully, they won't be able to do all the other things they got married to do. Couples are often so determined to avoid disagreements that they quit speaking.
>
> Research has found every happy, successful couple has approximately ten areas of incompatibility or disagreement that they will never resolve. Instead, the successful couples learn how to manage the disagreements and live life "around" them – to love in spite of their areas of difference, and to at least develop understanding and empathy for their partner's positions.
>
> The divorce courts have it all wrong. "Irreconcilable differences" – like a bad knee or a chronic back – are part of every good marriage. Successful couples learn to dance in spite of their differences. If we switch partners we'll just get ten new areas of disagreement, and sadly, the most destructive will be about the children from our previous relationship(s).
>
> In addition to skills for handling disagreements, we also have to learn to welcome and embrace change. When we marry, we promise to stay together till death parts us – but, we don't promise to stay the same! We need skills to integrate and negotiate change along the way.
>
> The good news is that the skills or behaviors – behaviors for handling disagreement and conflict, for integrating change, and for expressing love, intimacy, support, and appreciation – can all be learned. Couples can unlearn the behaviors that predict divorce – that destroy love – and replace them with behaviors that keep love alive.

Andrea visited me over Memorial Day weekend a few months ago. When she asked if she could come, I told her I was not the best company. My job situation was depressing and tainting my outlook on life. In addition, relations with Andrea had been strained for a year by that time. Our relationship was one of the relationships I felt was dying. She had steadily become more and more distant in conversation.

I felt her withdrawal immediately. I called and asked her directly what was going on and explained how I felt about her withdrawal – hurt, angry and rejected. We hadn't had a fight or disagreement to lead to this shift. I was truly in the dark about what was wrong with our relationship. Each time I mentioned her changed behavior, she laughed it off with a joke. Each time she ignored my concerns.

When Andrea confirmed she was coming for Memorial Day weekend, I determined to bring up our strained relationship in person, where I couldn't be put off with a plea of no time and a busy schedule.

Unfortunately and perhaps by design, we never had that conversation. Admittedly, I wasn't comfortable bringing it up too soon during her visit. Friday night passed in a blur. Saturday we were invited to brunch at Dianna's. Sunday morning started off with a ridiculous statement that escalated into a huge fight later in the afternoon.

The incident was an illustration of our relationship as a whole and a microcosm of many of my other relationships. The whole situation was extremely revealing for me.

The most amazing thing about the argument was the way it ended. She put words in my mouth. She called me a liar. She told me to go to hell. She kept trying to talk over me and when I insisted on defending myself, she threw up her hands and walked away snapping, "I'm done talking! You won't let me get a word in. I'm getting upset and this is turning negative!"

I was flabbergasted and deeply offended. But not interested in pursuing an argument that made no sense to me. It was such a ridiculously petty argument!

I rarely have guests; when I do, I get quite excited and go into overdrive on the hostess tip. I was buoyed about cooking a tea brunch for her and invited Jemini and her family to share the meal. I gladly handled all the preparations, cleaning, cooking and set-up and asked only one thing of her that morning – cut the watermelon. She joked and teased about people putting her to work on her visits for over an hour. Why couldn't she just lay around and get fed, she laughed! A couple of hours after I asked her to cut the watermelon she claimed she didn't feel comfortable cutting it. I replied, "You'll feel comfortable eating it, won't you?"

"In that case I won't eat any either. I don't cut watermelon."

"If you didn't want to eat the watermelon, why did you have me buy it?"

"I'll give you the money for it."

"That's not the point."

That was the first installment. The second installment happened after the brunch. She attempted to broach the subject as a joke to tell me how my attitude took her aback. I didn't think it was a laughing matter at all. I told her the whole situation was a micro-study of my life and relationships. "I got up this morning and started cooking all this food for you as my guest. I cleaned and set up my patio in preparation to serve everyone outside. All I asked for your help with was to cut the watermelon. A very small task and you wouldn't even do that for me." Shaking my head slightly in bemusement, I concluded, "In every relationship I have, it doesn't matter what I do for anyone, no one is willing to do the smallest thing for me."

She had a number of excuses why – she didn't know how, she wasn't comfortable, she would have made a mess, it wouldn't have been perfect....

"The end result is you didn't do it," I replied. "You didn't even try. You could've said any of that from the beginning rather than joking about how you didn't want to do anything, which painted the picture of why you didn't do it in an entirely different light."

She told me I was being ridiculous and just creating a different situation in my head. She ended with a rant and walked away.

I got up in further bemusement and walked in the other direction. She left the following morning, never once bringing the subject up again. In fact, the rest of our conversation for the evening was strained.

My first thought after she left was: *she's going to have a difficult marriage.* She's not willing to hear opinions other than her own and her perspective is her only truth.

That was the last full conversation I had with Andrea. After ten years of a friendship where we talked to one another up to five times a week for hours at a time, we had been reduced to short texts perhaps three times in the three months following her visit.

Friendships are precursors to marriage relationships. You can get an idea of someone's behavior in marriage by how they deal with their friends. For example, Andrea couldn't handle a disagreement over watermelon, how much more difficult mortgage, employment and childrearing issues will be for her to discuss.

She avoids conflict by ignoring issues. Her unwillingness to talk things out has carried me to a point of being unwilling to fight for the relationship.

We are headed towards a friend divorce (a broken friendship covenant) and it could have been avoided by addressing disagreements rather than avoiding them. But, alas, it takes two in agreement.

Meditation Verse: Romans 12:9-13

Let love be without hypocrisy. Abhor what is evil. Cling to what is good. Be kindly affectionate to one another with brotherly love, in honor giving preference to one another; not lagging in diligence, fervent in spirit, serving the Lord; rejoicing in hope, patient in tribulation, continuing steadfastly in prayer; distributing to the needs of the saints, given to hospitality.

You're Being Prepared Anyway, Why Not Focus?

Since 2007 I have willingly and eagerly spent much of my free time reading about marriage and hanging out with families.

My friend Chloe is the antithesis of my idea of a mother. She and Blossom came to visit me in New York a couple of summers ago and watching her behavior up close after so long away was disturbing. One of my other friends asked me, "Isn't it ridiculous that anyone can have a child and mess them up? Yet we have to have a license to drive a car and be a certain age to drink.... There should be restrictions on who can have children!"

Her statement got me to thinking about other things we prepare for and two major things we normally don't prepare for: marriage and children. The *Sister2Sister* article *Preparing for Marriage* added fuel to my thoughts. The article stated that some states were trying to tighten marriage laws. They're contemplating adding requirements to obtain a marriage license, one such requirement would be pre-marital counseling. The Army offers a twelve-hour marriage-education course. Former president George W. Bush funded a department to promote healthy marriages. I was encouraged to read about agencies and government attempts to help build stronger foundations for marriages. There is a real need in our society to focus on preparing for and improving marriage relationships.

Examples of Preparation

Think about it for a moment, drivers take drivers education and pilots go to flight school. We are trained for any job we take. We prepare for life starting in grade school. We attend head start, pre-school and kindergarten in preparation to attend first grade and first grade in order to attend second grade and so on. Our education is a repetitious cycle until high school or college graduation. Upon completion we attend a *commencement* ceremony. I was confused by the word *commencement* at the end of years of education. I get it now – life was just beginning.

Even cooking is a learning process. Even if you follow a recipe you may decide to adjust it to your tastes. Before you make that perfect dish, your signature dish, you dig out the recipe, shop for ingredients, lay out your utensils and cookware and then begin preparing your dish in the steps outlined in the recipe. Your signature dish was not perfect the first time you made it. It became perfect through trial and error.

In sports, doesn't it seem like you practiced more than you ever played in an actual game? Depending on the sport, you had to attend practice four to six days a week for about two to three hours a night. Even if you had one game a week, it usually didn't last more than two hours and most likely you didn't play the whole time. Doesn't it seem unfair that most of the season was about *preparing* to play the game? However, each game you play is an exhibition of the skills learned in practice. Your performance showed how prepared you were for the game.

Don't you want to be an All-Star? Wouldn't you love being one of two Most Valuable Players in your marriage? I do. I've taken my preparation quite seriously.

My Marriage

The appearance of things change according to the emotions and thus we see magic and beauty in them, while the magic and beauty are really in ourselves.
-Kahlil Gilbran

People think their attraction to someone is all they need for a successful marriage. When I first read the *Sister2Sister* article I had no idea writing about my ideas concerning marriage would uncover so many negative subconscious associations (*Preparing for Marriage: Learning from Bad Examples, p.224*). I was unaware that the relationships I had grown up around tainted my judgment and ideas. It was therapeutic writing out all the hidden issues from childhood that distorted my view. I can't tell you what type of husband my husband will be, but I can tell you what kind of man I am attracted to. My tastes are changing, possibly to ensure the type of man I become attracted to will be the kind of husband I will be able to commit to. That being said, he is not my worry or concern. He's being molded and prepared for me as well – hopefully he's paying attention. I can only concern myself with my preparation. As Yolanda Adams sang, *I'm going to be ready!*

Jemini has been married for over fifteen years. She was twenty-three years old when they met, he was thirty-eight. In her house, his word is law and she carries it out because she's used to doing what he says. She resents his authoritarian rule. She has reached a point where she wants to assert her opinion and have him respect it. I ache for her; he loves her but she has gone so long without standing up for herself she feels she has no voice in her marriage. We were talking one day and she looked over at me and said, "You must think I'm a sad case indeed to be in such a situation."

I thought about her statement for a moment. Yes, I am independent and have my own mind. I know how to use my voice and assert my opinions, but I am a woman in the purest, sincerest, most natural and traditional ways. I love to nurture and take care of people. I enjoy making people happy. I enjoy doing for people. I enjoy loving people. I looked at my friend and said, "Honestly, had I married anytime before the age of thirty, I would be where you are. If I am a nurturer in general, how much more so would I be to a man in my care? If I don't like to see people upset how much more would I jump to make my man happy? *What can I do for you? What do you want? Just tell me...I'll do it...."*

I think that's where we, as women, lose ourselves – in our men. In their ambitions, preferences, desires, goals, intentions, ideas, visions, dreams and general wants. *Whatever* and *anything* for them. We smother our men with our unconditional love and support from the beginning of the relationship. We don't give them the opportunity to reciprocate early on, because we are taking care of everything – their needs and ours. Therefore, they never learn how to reciprocate – to give us what we need, in general. So when we run empty, they are at a complete loss. When we get fed up, burned out and worn down they are just as frustrated as we are. *What's the problem,* they ask. *What's different today from yesterday?* We don't condition them to be sensitive to our needs, desires and wants. However, we condition ourselves to anticipate their every need and want. When our husbands don't know how to hear our yearnings, our dreams, our hopes, or our ambitions, it's because we've enabled their selfishness.

So, what's changed since I turned thirty? I've become very well acquainted with LaShawnda – who she is, what she wants, what makes her happy, what makes her sad, what's comfortable and what isn't. I know what things I am willing to compromise and what things aren't up for discussion. I am not willing to hide who I am to secure a relationship. Nor am I willing to allow my prospective mate to hide himself from me.

I believe in beginning as you mean to go on – from the first conversation to the end of our association, everything is a building block. To that end, I check a situation when I find myself enabling behavior I wouldn't want to put up with for the rest of my life.

I am very glad that I have been exposed to men who have made me feel gloriously feminine. Perhaps, not the type of feminine they wanted, but certainly a type of feminine I have learned to accept. I've learned to accept different parts of me through my attractions over the years. I know as I accept more of me, I will have more to share in my daily life, with others, but more importantly in marriage.

Meditation Verse: Proverbs 4:4-7

"Let your heart retain my words; keep my commands, and live. Get wisdom! Get understanding! Do not forget, nor turn away from the words of my mouth. Do not forsake her, and she will preserve you; love her, and she will keep you. Wisdom *is* the principal thing; *therefore* get wisdom. And in all your getting, get understanding.

Girl vs. Woman

A girl leaves her schedule wide open and waits for a guy to call to make plans.
A Woman makes her own plans and suggests he get in where he fits in.
A girl checks him for not calling.
A Woman is too busy to realize he hadn't.

Girls worry about not being pretty or good enough for their guy.
Women know they are more than enough for any man.
Girls ignore the good men.
Women ignore the bad boys.

Girls recklessly chase the object of their affection, despite his lack of interest.
Women realize sometimes it's not meant to be and move on without bitterness.
A girl gets hurt by one man and lashes out at all men.
A Woman walks away assured *that* man was not for her.

A girl is afraid to be alone.
A Woman revels in her solitude and uses it to work on herself.
Girls try to monopolize all their man's time.
Women keep their friends and don't mind him kicking it with his.

A girl wants to control the men in her life.
A Woman knows her Man wants to please her.
Girls try to make him come home.
Women make him *want* to come home.

A girl thinks a crying man is weak.
A Woman embraces her Man for as long as he needs.
Girls want to be spoiled and treated like a queen by all their men.
Women only accept their queenly homage from their rightful King.

Note: This poem is derived from an unsourced email forward I've read several versions of under different titles. I took creative license with one version and made it my own by rewording and restructuring.

girl vs. WOMAN

Physical Woman

Physically, there's no denying I'm a woman. My feminine curves are ridiculous to me, amazing to others. Fortunately, womanhood is judged by other attributes, not subjective to various perceptions.

What's with the fascination society has with youth? Women want to be called girls, maintain their girlish figures, and be some man's girlfriend. Who will speak to our womanhood? Where are the men who wish to partner with women?

I am a Woman. It's taken some time to say that loud and proud; there's censors all around. Feminine confidence is threatening to many people. Others think strong, confident women have no need or desire for a man. It takes time to become a woman, but it's not just time that makes a woman. I have matured into who I am physically, emotionally and spiritually. I wouldn't take anything for my journey now and I look eagerly towards the remainder and continued growth.

In no area of my life do I desire to experience my girlhood again. My youth was dark and uninformed. There was very little guidance, and I doubted what I believed. I have learned from every ripple in my life. I've made better decisions with each successive fork in the road. I have grown from every pain and loss. You may not want lines or creases, but I've earned every crease on my face, every dimple in my thighs, and all the gray in my hair. Every apparent imperfection paints a lifescape of where I've been and how I've born up under pressure.

I admit to not being ecstatic about flab piling on, but I will tell you, I have grown more confident in my femininity with each pound. You could say I have a slight fear of becoming too much woman!

Years ago, when I accepted that I couldn't control the spread, I decided to manage it to the best of my ability. I remember talking with my aerobics instructor at the time. He had grown thick and paunchy over the years and he worked us out in his classes like he was being chased by a Tasmanian devil. He conducted multiple body conditioning, aerobics and dance classes a day no less than four days a week. One day we were discussing how our weight continued to pile on despite our exercise routines. I remember telling him I had come to an acceptance of being a woman of size. When I was a 12/14 I thought I was fat. Why? Because I allowed other people's perception of me to color my perception of myself (i.e. fashion, media, family and friends). As my dress size got larger over the years I've had a great dissatisfaction on some level – the very shallow social level. However, in a very elemental and primal way I have marveled at my body. I cop feels here and there, amazed by my large, nursing breasts and wide, sheltering hips. Knowing my belly is a comfort and my backside a beacon. There is a reason for my solid girth. I'm not here to suckle men as their playthings. I'm here to birth babes and raise a nation. I'm here to nurture a world. I'm about my Woman's business.

Emotional Woman

The year Leila and Jemini turned forty, they both shared a substantial amount of their relationship frustrations with me. Whenever I had a word for them, I shared it. I couldn't help thinking that on the surface I should have nothing to tell them. They are both stay-at-home moms with long-term relationship experience, born in a decade prior to my own. However, they recognized on some level they were still acting and speaking as children spiritually and it manifested in their lives. Their relationships are fraught with struggles for control, selfishness, neglect, bitterness, anger, frustration, jealousy, resentment and a complete lack of understanding and desire to know their mates.

My one consistent piece of advice for Jemini has been to spend time with her husband. He begs for her attention and acts out when he doesn't get it. She always shoos him away and claims to be too busy with their children to focus on him. One fall evening that year, she told me proudly there had been a change in her marriage. She said she woke up one day and thought of how she treats her husband and felt remorse. She didn't like the way their relationship had deteriorated because of her selfishness and neglect. She took steps to remedy her errors. She gushed at me that night, "Shawnda! All I did was this and that and you wouldn't believe the change in him! He's been so responsive! He agreed to do this, that and the other. We're getting along much better; we're not fighting. It's only been a couple of weeks, but this is great progress!"

At the time, Leila had been in a custody battle with her ex for a year and a half. She wanted to control every aspect of her ex's interaction with their children. She was bitter before the break-up and afterwards, well.... Had she been conscious during her decision to be with Sam, I don't believe she would have chosen him to father her children. But she wasn't paying attention to her life at that time; she was content to see where everything would lead, hoping for the best. Her bitterness has hardened into frustration, anger and resentment. After several court hearings, Sam won joint custody of their children. Their interactions grew more combative with the desire to hurt one another. One of Sam's weapons is his presence, or lack thereof. He has become a habitual no-show during his court-appointed time with his children.

My piece of advice to Leila has been to stop fighting for the sake of depriving him. The more she petitions the court to minimize his parental rights the more he throws into the fight to subdue her, to defeat her, to destroy her. He's not fighting because he wants joint custody – he's fighting because he doesn't want her to have what she wants: full custody. He's not interested in pleasing her; he's interested in making her feel his pain. She didn't want him and she's all he wanted. He has a lot of anger from her rejection and the more she fights, the more his anger is fueled. Incidentally, as a result, she enables him to hurt the children she's trying to protect.

Though I have no wish to experience the marital and relationship pains my friends have gone through, I do pray the insight God has graced me with to aid others proves to be a boon in my own marriage.

Spiritual Woman

Don Juan reinserted himself into my consciousness several months after he propositioned me with the all-too-easy-to-refuse offer to have "fun" with him. I don't deny being attracted to him, but I was interested in a relationship, not a casual fling.

After months of dodging and avoiding him at the gym, I ran into him. He didn't look well, so I asked about his health. He told me his sister had recently died and he was having difficulty coping. I offered him my listening ear if he needed to talk. Over the course of three days and two very short text exchanges, he propositioned me twice more. The first time I ignored him, suggested he go workout or go to church and otherwise enjoy his day. The second time I was peeved enough to tell him to forget I asked about his welfare altogether. I attempted to drop the conversation, exit gracefully and hopefully never talk to him again. He wasn't done pleading his case. What followed was disturbingly mind boggling for me and I am still astounded he sought to take advantage of my sympathy.

Don Juan made the mistake of thinking I was a girl. Down for whateva from around da way. Someone he could holla at, who would holla back. A homey, lover and part-time friend. He mistook my kindness for a weakness; my single status for open availability. How do I know? Because at some point, before the conversation deteriorated I asked him what he was looking for. He replied, "I'm ready for a girl." His speech told me he has never heard a word I've spoken and he has certainly never seen me as a woman.

Quite a bit looped through my mind as he chattered in my ear about letting things be what they are. "Why are you so uptight? Why can't you just relax and have fun? You're acting like an old lady. All you need is some good lovin'."

Sure, I thought, I could use some good lovin', but you're not the one I associate with that thought. If I were a mean-spirited person, I would have told him that. I was heated and not the way he wanted me to be! What made him think his lovin' was good? He wanted to use my body as a receptacle to dump whatever angst was spewing forth from his. He didn't want a relationship with me. He didn't want to know me. He wanted to leave a trashy residue in my life! Apparently, he thought I put as little value on myself as he did. I recoiled from the center of my being at the thought that in his desire for a playmate, someone to pass time *around*, his eyes rested on me. That's how he saw me?

I'm somebody's wife! This thought roared up from my midst and screeched through my head.

I reigned in my anger enough to enunciate, "I am not taking you into my marriage. I have no desire to have various men run up and through my body and then present myself to my husband in such a way."

He agreed, I shouldn't sleep around, that wasn't his point. "Why can't you just give me a try?"

I thank God I wasn't completely blinded by his summer charm and was able to see his character more clearly through the falling leaves of autumn.

I'm thankful my heart wasn't exposed and he didn't waste my time or energy.

I'm thankful he didn't have enough finesse to romance me into giving away what he was so crudely after.

I'm grateful I'm able to stop myself from walking any path that could end with me being bound to an undesirable man because I allowed him to carelessly leave his seed behind.

I'm grateful for the *power* of my womanhood. Although it attracts many such hounds hoping for scraps to be tossed their way, the power of my womanhood keeps me safely out of their reach. I'm protected and live securely in the knowledge that only he who is invited will bask in the bounty and glory that is me.

Yeah, Don Juan mistakenly thought me a girl and I mistook him for a man. Maybe, and this is a long shot, but possibly, if he had met a twenty-something LaShawnda he could've convinced her casual sex was the rite of passage into womanhood and he was offering a free ride on his fast moving, deep-driving, safety-tested *Good Lovin' Machine* to get me there. Perhaps, I would have fallen for something so lacking in substance when I was girl. Most likely not, as God has guided and positioned me my whole life through.

As we live, we learn….

I thank God for the place He has brought me to. I am grateful for the wisdom and understanding He has graced me with. I am happy for the discernment He allows me. I am truly ecstatic when He reveals deeper aspects of myself to me. I have grown from a girl with no real hope or expectation for a lasting marriage into a woman with heart knowledge of the man of God my Heavenly Father has set apart for me. We are both being made ready for one another. My hope is to be a virtuous woman, a worthy helpmate, an equal partner and an attentive wife to a man who models his life after Christ, who loves me as Christ loves the church, who honors and values me above all others, and who has put away all childish things – physically, emotionally, and spiritually.

Meditation Verse: 1 Corinthians 13:11-12

When I was a child, I spoke as a child, I understood as a child, I thought as a child; but when I became a man, I put away childish things. For now we see through a glass darkly; but then shall I know even as also I am known.

where r u?

"You're funny, my dear."

I sensed a gentle smile
Soft chuckle through the stark text.

That email, a memory
Probably long forgotten by sender
Reading it brought a smile to my heart
That long ago winter day
Remembering it brought a tear to my eye

"And you're far too cruel, my love."

The summer breeze scattered my words
Across the Hudson towards Jersey.

Imagining Life

I'm the first to admit: I live inside my head and my heart. They are the most idyllic places and provide a setting for a wonderful life.

The Promise Comes by Faith

There's a man at work, Sahib, who makes a point of teasing me, when he sees me, about my imaginary life. Until he called me out, I didn't pay attention to my habit of speaking of things that aren't as if they were *(Romans 4:17)*. The business world calls this type of projection dressing for success or performing for the position you want, not the one you're in. In our social circles, it's referred to as faking it until you make it.

It's been brought to my attention that I live my life based on my inner sight rather than physical or worldly boundaries and limitations. Before Sahib pulled me up short with his mocking, my friend Andrea made many comments about wanting to be rich like me. The last time she said that, I took a moment to think about what her comment implied – I have money. It's a common misunderstanding among those who have observed my life. I live from check to check, like most Americans – I don't feel rich. Her comment bothered me for a couple of weeks. Eventually I touched on why she would feel disadvantaged and poor and why I feel as if I have just enough or more than enough depending on the day.

Andrea has a poverty mentality that focuses on money. In her mind, she never has enough. She's always short; she always wants more. So she's working for the dollar and getting very little satisfaction from it. What she calls me living like I'm rich is my wealth mentality - I feel as if I always have an abundance of something. No matter how low my finances may be I know I always have something to share and give to others. If it's not my love (I am still working on my love walk!), it's still a kind word. It could be something in my house, my time, my last dollar. It doesn't matter. Whatever I have has been provided for me, knowing that, I have no problem giving away anything that may be necessary provision for someone else. I can't recall a time when I went without something I *needed*. I'm able to cover others, because my faith covers me.

The situation with Sahib had me thinking about that conversation with Andrea. I can't pinpoint the moment I stopped seeing my future as a single individual, it was an unconscious development that became a conscious certainty. After tripping me up one day, Sahib started greeting me with a mocking smirk, "How is your imaginary life today, LaShawnda? Your imaginary husband is well? And your imaginary children? I hope they are healthy! Did you have imaginary food for the holiday, too?" He rarely gets out his questions without several chuckles at my expense.

Some times I go along with him, "Life inside my head is quite nice!" But he has more fun teasing me than I have being teased. Eventually, I throw my hands up in exasperation and ask him about his home life.

This situation grew from a conversation the prior summer when he attempted, in a roundabout way, to get my status. He shared his philosophy on marriage in an open office conversation. In short, he didn't feel obligated to be faithful in his marriage. He said his wife should not expect fidelity from him, although he has never shared that opinion with her. However, he expects her to be faithful. The other married men in the group turned their backs to him and went back to work. None of the other family men put another word into the conversation. Seeing that reassured me about men's integrity. As I turned on my heel to walk away, I said, "It doesn't look as if the other husbands share your opinion. I will make sure *my* husband doesn't speak with you at any company events; I wouldn't want him tainted by such thoughts."

He replied in astonished disappointment, "You're married?"

"Not yet." I'm sure I blushed. "But, hypothetically speaking, my husband would not be allowed to speak to you."

"So, you're saying I would not be allowed to speak to your imaginary husband?" He laughed richly at that thought, which irked me.

"Can I speak with your wife and share your philosophy with her? Perhaps she would like to take a lover."

He stopped laughing. "Not possible. She's not allowed."

Open Hearts, Open Family

After spending a year in close proximity with Jemini and her family, her middle daughter declared to me, while squeezing my waist with all her might, "Shawnda, I love you! You're like a second mommy!" The declaration stunned both me and her mom. Jemini's initial reaction spoke volumes, "You don't have any second mommies! Shawnda can be your aunt!" I do believe she turned her nose up in the air with a glare directed at both her daughter and me.

Jemini's whole identity is wrapped up in her children. I understood instantly how she could feel slighted by such a declaration. She takes care of their needs 24/7. All I do is visit them, hug and kiss on them, play with them and listen to whatever they want to tell me. Even though I truly felt like a part of the family, I hadn't realized we had all gotten so attached.

After her daughter's declaration, Jemini and I took a short break from one another. The declaration of love depressed me. That's a hard word for me to accept from people, because no one has ever treated me well who claimed to love me. And the part about being a second mommy... the only thing I yearn for more than my own child, is my own husband. I used to tell Jemini spending time with her family gave me the dose of family I needed to maintain my equilibrium. Eventually though, sitting in on someone else's life lost its power to satisfy me. When Jemini's daughter made her declaration, I suddenly saw my real life as an imitation. I saw myself as a fake sister and a fake mommy. I was an honorary inclusion, but felt like a nothing exclusion.

I felt a need to step away because it was safer to imagine a life than expose myself to a family I had no place in. My difficulty lies in figuring out how to transition from living an imitation to bringing my imagination to life. I was disheartened by the thought that my mothering experience would ever only consist of in-case-of emergency-back-up for everyone else's children.

Jemini came out of her slump before I did and started referring to her children as "our children." *"Look at our babies, Shawnda!"* The children clamoring over me soothed my heart long before her peace offering did. But her offer allowed for all-around acceptance and reciprocity. It's an amazing thing when we allow our hearts to open and merge!

After a couple of weeks away, I re-entered the family fold to a jubilant reception. My first night back, Jemini's youngest daughter whispered in my ear while clinging to my neck and waist, *"Never leave me, Shawnda."*

I was speechless and near tears because I couldn't think of any soothing words for the four-year-old. I couldn't twist my lips to promise to be around always. My "imaginary" family is separate from Jemini's family, and I may or may not be removed from their physical proximity. So, I stayed silent and held her tighter, too.

Andrea is fond of explaining people's response to me with, "It's all that love, girl! You have so much love in you, we all need our Shawnda. So, I guess, if we have to share you, we'll share you. I'm telling you though....if I were a man.... *gurl!* I have no idea why you're still single!"

My friendships go through their cycles of strengths and weaknesses, ebbing and flowing. When they aren't as strong, I start thinking perhaps that part of my life was an imitation as well. I become short-sighted in those low moments. Andrea and Jemini remind me often that love powers my relationships. Love is far-sighted and far-reaching. It's not imaginary. It may be invisible, but it creates very tangible things in our lives.

Even though I enjoy my imaginary life, I am able to soak up the blessings in my physical life at the same time. I can usually appreciate that what I sometimes call an imitation of life is very real indeed. For what is life without love? What is love without a giver and receiver? We are the products of our relationships, real and imagined. What we share of ourselves we get back in amazing abundance. I do experience happiness wherever I am in my life, not because any given moment is all I hope it will be, but because I believe in making the most of *now* in order to reap the best of what's to come. We can't set a steeple on top of our temple without first laying a foundation.

Give love every day and God will make sure you get it back.

Meditation Verse: Romans 4:13-25

For the promise that he would be the heir of the world *was* not to Abraham or to his seed through the law, but through the righteousness of faith. For if those who are of the law *are* heirs, faith is made void and the promise made of no effect, because the law brings about wrath; for where there is no law *there is* no transgression.

Therefore, *it is* of faith that *it might be* according to grace, so that the promise might be sure to all the seed, not only to those who are of the law, but also to those who are of the faith of Abraham, who is the father of us all (as it is written, *"I have made you a father of many nations"*) in the presence of Him whom he believed—God, who gives life to the dead and calls those things which do not exist as though they did; who, contrary to hope, in hope believed, so that he became the father of many nations, according to what was spoken, *"So shall your descendants be."* And not being weak in faith, he did not consider his own body, already dead (since he was about a hundred years old), and the deadness of Sarah's womb. He did not waver at the promise of God through unbelief, but was strengthened in faith, giving glory to God, and being fully convinced that what He had promised He was also able to perform. And therefore *"it was accounted to him for righteousness."*

Now it was not written for his sake alone that it was imputed to him, but also for us. It shall be imputed to us who believe in Him who raised up Jesus our Lord from the dead, who was delivered up because of our offenses, and was raised because of our justification.

Gratitude

He said,
"Thanks for thinking of me."
Silly man, I thought,
That's like thanking me
For breathing.

Family Man

The time I worked with Bosslady was also spent working with a very lively group of men. Our office was primarily populated with men from around the world. Quite a few of them were family men. Several of their acts of fatherhood left an impression on me. Listening to their conversations educated me about male thought patterns and behaviors beyond anything I could have imagined. It's encouraging to have positive male examples to write about. These family men have left me with a warm, fuzzy feeling! I thank God for the positioning and the exposure!

Father Time

Mr. Bob is sixty-something and sports a dapper crop of silver hair. He's been married for nearly thirty years and has two daughters in their early twenties. All over his office, one can see photos featuring him and his family throughout the years. When he talks about his daughters, he beams – his face lights up, his smile widens and his talking hands get more energetic. Two events stand out in my memory in regard to his interaction with his daughters.

On Valentine's Day, he sends his daughters flowers. The first Valentine's I worked with him he was rather anxious. The weather was really bad, and he was nervous his delivery would be delayed, so he spent the morning calling the florist for updates. When he told me about this, I told him it was one of the sweetest things I had ever heard! But he wasn't done! He continued to share that he has always gifted his daughters on Valentine's Day, even when they were younger. His intention was to set a standard in their lives that other men would have to exceed in order to impress them.

I told him he was in danger of being daddy-napped. I am one of many women who would greatly appreciate having a standard-setting father.

Coach Dad

Andre is a real manly man. I like asking him girly questions just to see his lips curl in disgust. He's all machismo, in a wise-cracking way. He has two young boys who are quite active in their little league sports. The summer I worked with him, he took off a number of Fridays in order to drive his sons to tri-state tournaments for their leagues. During one conversation I marveled at his dedication to his children's schedule. "My goodness, Andre, all this driving! I can see you coaching your boys, too," I said. He bashfully ducked his head and muttered, "I'm an assistant coach for their team."

One Friday afternoon he packed up early so he could get home. I teased him about sneaking out the door at one o'clock. He shared that it was the last weekend for his sons' league. "Do you have a lot of driving this weekend?" He let out a long, tired sigh, "Yes, but this drive isn't so long though."

I just looked at him in wonder. "Andre, I think you're awesome. What a great father you are."

"I wouldn't say all that," he said quietly.

"Not too many people can say that. But, your boys will remember this."

No Fizz Pop

Scott is one of the most straight-talking, hard-nose, no-nonsense, get-down-to-business people I've ever worked with. It took me months to pick up on his jokes; his humor is not just dry, it's deadpan. He is also a hardcore family man. If you asked him, I think that would be the way he self-identified first. His job is just a job. He's not emotionally involved with his work. He's in the office to take care of his family. His conversation is colored by that. No soft mushy talk, none of that. Just clear-cut, this is what it is.

When his wife brought their two-year-old son into the office one day, it was one of the most interesting (and instant) dynamic changes I've witnessed in a person. The hard lines softened. His usual impatient tone seemed endlessly patient for his son. It was like watching someone flip a coin with two completely different designs.

He impressed me early on with a conversation I was ear hustling on. By virtue of having an open office space our conversations become everyone's conversations. In the beginning the fellas used to check to see if I was listening; soon though, they just spoke freely.

This particular conversation was a discussion about a wedding invite they had all received from a former co-worker. At the time, Scott was the only married man participating in the conversation. Someone asked him if he planned to take his wife to the wedding. My ears perked up. Scott stopped what he was doing and said, "You want me to bring my wife to an event in another town, where she will know no one and everyone I know is sitting around getting wasted?"

"Yeah! Wouldn't that be fun?"

"No offense, but that's why you're still single. There's no way. Even if I was stupid enough to ask her, I would never hear the end of it. You don't take wives to events where all your buddies are getting drunk and there are no other wives."

I picked up the phone, called one of my girlfriends and said, "Oh, my goodness! They do have sense! I never would have believed it, if I hadn't heard it with my own ears!"

Pastime Dad

Allen has been married seven years and is the proud father of a two-year-old and four-year-old. A smile comes to my heart when Allen talks about his kids. There's so much love and dedication in his speech. Allen took his children trick-or-treating for Halloween. The following Monday he relayed his weekend activities to me. "I spent a lot of time with my kids," he said. "I took them trick-or-treating on Friday. We hung out on Saturday. We all had something of a play date that afternoon. Me, my wife and kids went over to a friend's house, who has kids the same age, to watch college football."

"That's cool. So the kids got to play while you watched football."

"Well.... actually...my wife watched football while I hung out with the kids."

I couldn't contain my peal of laughter! Simply adorable!

We all need father figures. They add a dimension to our lives we can't get from anyone else. I thank God for allowing me to experience Him as my Father, most especially in the absence of an earthly one.

 Meditation Verse: Proverbs 20:1-7

Wine *is* a mocker, strong drink *is* a brawler, and whoever is led astray by it is not wise.

The wrath of a king *is* like the roaring of a lion; whoever provokes him to anger sins *against* his own life. *It is* honorable for a man to stop striving, since any fool can start a quarrel.

The lazy *man* will not plow because of winter; he will beg during harvest and *have* nothing.

Counsel in the heart of man *is like* deep water, but a man of understanding will draw it out.

Most men will proclaim each his own goodness, but who can find a faithful man? The righteous *man* walks in his integrity; his children *are* blessed after him.

Galaxy Quest

If I'm sunshine
You must be my galaxy quest
Life is great
I'm good
Just fine, in fact
No complaints
But two words from
You and my joy
Bubbles over
Something about seeing your whole
Countenance brighten
And glow
When I walk into a room
Causes my smile to eclipse my face
I've spoken of wonder
Before
Experienced it
Though not quite
As transcendent as this
Light years have passed
In this quest
Some spent dodging asteroids
Some years traveled in deep, dark cold space
Some were illuminated by countless stars
Yet others were spent resting peacefully on planets
Soaking in and reflecting solar rays
Your infusion into my life
Is like a supernova explosion
Startling, blinding, fiery
Consuming

A Happy Marriage is No Accident

Several years ago someone loaned me a couple of Dr. Myles Munroe's tapes. It was several years before I found one of his books, but the lessons on his tapes never left my mind. Below are excerpts from *The Purpose and the Power of Love and Marriage*, the first book placed in my path from this insightful and blessed minister.

Knowledge Overcomes Marital Illiteracy

One of the biggest challenges facing couples today, whether married or unmarried, is marital illiteracy.

The marriage relationship is a school, a learning environment in which both partners can grow and develop over time. Marriage does not demand perfection but it must be given priority. It is an institution peopled exclusively by sinners, and finds its greatest glory when those sinners see it as God's way of leading them through His ultimate curriculum of love and righteousness.

Marriage has the potential of expressing God's love to its fullest possible degree on earth. The will of the couple is the critical factor. A marriage relationship will express God's love only as far as both partners are willing to allow the Lord to really work in and through them. This is a totally unselfish love where the husband and wife "submit to one another out of reverence for Christ" (Ephesians 5:21); where the wife respects her husband (v.33) and submits to him "as to the Lord" (v. 22); and where the husband loves his wife as himself (v.33), "just as Christ loved the church and gave Himself up for her" (v.25). When two totally different people come together and live and work as one, giving unselfishly of themselves and loving, forgiving, understanding, and bearing with each other, outside observers will see at least a little bit of what the love of God is all about.

A Christian marriage is the total commitment of a husband and wife to each other and individually to the person of Jesus Christ, a commitment that holds nothing back in either the natural or the spiritual realm. It is a pledge of mutual fidelity, a partnership of mutual subordination. Marriage is one of the refining processes by which God shapes men and women into the people He wants them to be.

Roleless Partnership

Marriage is a roleless relationship. It can be no other way if the marriage is truly grounded in sacrificial love. Sacrificial love is unconditional love – love without reason. True love has no reason; it just is. Unconditional love loves regardless of the behavior or "loveableness" of the ones loved, and whether or not they return that love. The New Testament defines this love as agape. It is the kind of love that God exhibits toward a sinful human race, the kind of love that Jesus Christ demonstrated when He willingly died on the cross for that sinful race.

God does not need a reason to love us; He loves us because love is His nature.... Agape makes no demands, holds no expectations, and carries no guarantees except to guarantee itself. The Lord guarantees that He will love us regardless of whether or not we return His love.

The love of Christ is a roleless love based on responses rather than expectations. His death on the cross was His love responding to humanity's need for forgiveness. Jesus placed no expectations on us as a pre-condition to His sacrifice. He gave His life freely with no guarantee that any of us would love Him back. The only expectation Jesus had was His own joy and exaltation before His Father... His is an unconditional, open invitation... Jesus had no guarantee.

Love that looks for a reason is love with conditions attached. Conditions give rise to expectations. By expectations I mean those mundane and routine jobs, functions, or activities that husbands and wives automatically expect each other to do because it is their "role," such as washing the dishes, cooking the meals, cleaning the house, cutting the grass, making the bed, bathing the children, and so on. Expectations lead inevitably to disappointment. Disappointment leads to arguments, which strain the relationship, which then endangers fellowship.

What does all this have to do with a roleless relationship in marriage? Marital love is supposed to be like the love that Jesus has for His Church: unconditional, sacrificial, and without expectations or guarantees. Fixed roles create expectation, and expectations imply guarantees. For example, if a wife sees mowing the lawn as her husband's "role," that role creates in her mind the expectation that he will cut the grass when it gets tall. If he does not, he has violated the "guarantee." Her expectation turns to disappointment or even anger, and conflict results. If a husband believes that meal preparation is his wife's "role" he will be upset if supper is not on the table when he gets home from work. His wife has not fulfilled the "guarantee" implied in his expectation, which is based on his perception of her "role."

The upshot of all this is that love without reasons is love without expectations. If there are no expectations, there are no fixed roles. Marriage then becomes a relationship based on responding to needs rather than adhering to rigid preconceptions. If a husband and wife have no rigid role expectations of each other, neither will be disappointed. A response-based approach to marriage will bring a deep, fresh, and new dimension to the relationship. Married couples will experience greater success and happiness the more they learn how to relate without fixed roles.

Temporary Responsibilities, Not Permanent Roles

A roleless relationship in a marriage does not mean that nobody does anything or that the couple takes a random or haphazard approach to their home life. On the contrary, it is important for a husband and wife to come to a clear and mutual understanding of how things will be done. A relationship without fixed roles does mean that each partner will respond according to need, ability, and opportunity.

A role is a temporary responsibility that is based on the ability of the one who responds. As such, roles can change from one day to the next, from one minute to the next, and from one person to the other depending on the need of the moment. What needs to be done? Who can do it the best? Who is in the best position to do it right now? It is a matter of need, ability and opportunity. That's why it would probably be better to refer to marital tasks as responsibilities rather than roles. Whatever the need, whoever is able and available at the time is responsible.

Relating without fixed roles is a natural outgrowth of a marriage based on agape and in which the husband and wife truly are equal partners. Agape seeks to serve rather than to be served.

Agape expresses itself in conscious response to recognized needs. It is not an automatic or unconscious reaction to stimuli based on conditioned habits or attitudes. Agape doesn't look for roles; agape responds to needs.

Husbands and wives who approach their marriage from a roleless perspective assume full ownership of every aspect of their life together. There are no "his" and "her" roles, only "our" responsibilities. Who does what and when, depends on the specific circumstances. Each couple should arrive at a mutual agreement as to which of them has the primary responsibility for each task or need, understanding as well that ultimately they share all responsibilities together.

Assignment of marital responsibilities may depend on each person's training, abilities, or temperament. Who should prepare the meals (primarily)? Whoever is the best cook. Who should manage the family finances (primarily)? Whoever has the best head for figures and bookkeeping. Who should do the house cleaning? Whoever lives in the house. Who should wash the dishes? Whoever dirties them. Who should make the bed? Whoever sleeps in it. Who should mow the lawn? Whoever has the time and the opportunity.

Clear assignment of primary authority and responsibility between a husband and wife establishes order and helps prevent chaos and confusion. At the same time, rather than producing rigidity in the relationship, it allows for flexibility so that either partner can do what is needed at any given time Whoever can, does; whoever sees, acts.

So then, what is the husband's "role" in the marriage? He is the "head" of the home, the spiritual leader responsible for the spiritual direction of the family. He is to love his wife in the same way that Christ loved the Church, sacrificially and unconditionally. What is the wife's "role"? She is to respect her husband and submit to his headship. In the practical matters of home life they both should respond according to their need, their abilities, and their availability.

Meditation Verse: 1 Peter 3:1-4

Wives, likewise, *be* submissive to your own husbands, that even if some do not obey the word, they, without a word, may be won by the conduct of their wives, when they observe your chaste conduct *accompanied* by fear. Do not let your adornment be *merely* outward—arranging the hair, wearing gold, or putting on *fine* apparel — rather *let it be* the hidden person of the heart, with the incorruptible *beauty* of a gentle and quiet spirit, which is very precious in the sight of God.

Beautifully Imperfect

The movie *Forgetting Sarah Marshall* left a great impression on me. It was an ordinary relationship story with extraordinarily naked emotional honesty.

I was bedazzled by the human frailties and imperfections laid out in all their naked glory in the film. Jason Segal starred as the main character, Pete. He also wrote the screenplay. The emotional depth and sensitivity of his writing was touching. I felt his sensitivity through the laughs, through the half-hearted jokes, and the not-quite-there fronts – and I thought it all was beautiful.

Pete's romantic idea of everlasting love was represented by Dracula. At one point Pete said, like Dracula, he wanted to love someone forever, but when he thought he had that love and it was taken away all he wanted to do was die. However, also like Dracula, he couldn't just die. That idea connected with me.... The refrain of a song he wrote and sang in the movie was *"Die...die...die...I can't...."* That line was hilarious for some in the theater, but truly sad for me.

Shortly after the movie started, Pete walked onscreen completely naked. He was pale, flaccid and oddly shaped and the audience roared with laughter. It was obvious the shot was edited to garner laughter, after all, we have been conditioned to take muscle-strewn, lean, athletic bodies seriously, not bodies like Pete's. Still, by the end of the film I just wanted to hug him. Halfway through the movie, I realized there weren't any "perfect" Hollywood-type bodies or faces in the movie. All the actors had visible flaws. They all had their own sparkle and shine. Everyone was unique. They were all average, everyday-looking people. That was another element that made this a good movie for me. There was nothing extraordinary about anyone's looks, body or emotions, and those elements were absolutely beautiful to me. No glitz, no sugar-coating, no perfect wrap at the end. It was truly a slice-of-life film.

I went to see a break-up comedy – got it. I returned home with a new depth of introspection. When we first saw Pete cry over his break-up, the audience erupted with riotous laughter. When he attempted to have sex with a string of strange unknown women... more riotous laughter. It wasn't long before I felt that all the things causing a riot in the theater really weren't funny in their starkness; in their truth. It was an illustration of how we express ourselves, cope with our feelings and try to heal our hurts.

I left the movie with ideas to revitalize my life based on the following questions:
Why are we too scared to just jump in?

Why do we assume where we are is safer than where we're going?
Which do we fear more: a healthy relationship or the possibility of a failed one?
Why does fear of either keep us from sharing our best selves with our partners?
If honest communication is appreciated, why is it so hard to practice?

 Meditation Verse: John 4:7-10

A woman of Samaria came to draw water. Jesus said to her, "Give Me a drink." For His disciples had gone away into the city to buy food. Then the woman of Samaria said to Him, "How is it that You, being a Jew, ask a drink from me, a Samaritan woman?" For Jews have no dealings with Samaritans.

Jesus answered and said to her, "If you knew the gift of God, and who it is who says to you, 'Give Me a drink,' you would have asked Him, and He would have given you living water."

Our Nakedness

Every once in a while I meditate on Biblical relationships. Whenever I meditate on Adam and Eve I come away with something new. Last winter I focused on their attempt to hide their nakedness after eating the forbidden fruit in the garden. My thoughts looped around their nakedness being less a physical exposure than an emotional one.

Meditation Verse: Genesis 3:4-13

Then the serpent said to the woman, "You will not surely die. For God knows that in the day you eat of it your eyes will be opened, and you will be like God, knowing good and evil." So when the woman saw that the tree was good for food, that it was pleasant to the eyes, and a tree desirable to make one wise, she took of its fruit and ate. She also gave to her husband with her, and he ate. Then the eyes of both of them were opened, and they knew that they were naked; and they sewed fig leaves together and made themselves coverings. And they heard the sound of the LORD God walking in the garden in the cool of the day, and Adam and his wife hid themselves from the presence of the LORD God among the trees of the garden.

Then the LORD God called to Adam and said to him, "Where are you?"

So he said, "I heard Your voice in the garden, and I was afraid because I was naked; and I hid myself."

And He said, "Who told you that you were naked? Have you eaten from the tree of which I commanded you that you should not eat?"

Then the man said, "The woman whom You gave to be with me, she gave me of the tree, and I ate."

And the LORD God said to the woman, "What is this you have done?" The woman said, "The serpent deceived me, and I ate."

Their action exposed their doubt over the sufficiency of God's provision for them. They were acting as if they did not have knowledge already. As if God had not revealed Himself to them. It was the doubt they tried to excuse. "Well, the woman You gave to me gave me the fruit! Honestly, Father, I wouldn't have eaten it otherwise." "Yeah, well, I only gave it to him because the serpent in our garden said it would be okay." With their pointing fingers, they sought to exonerate their greedy desire to obtain more without paying any consequences. They were grabbing for something they already had, because someone else repackaged it and presented it as something out of their reach. Adam and Eve were the agents of their own downfall because they didn't take personal responsibility for their knowledge or for their actions. In conversation with the serpent they did not assert absolutely *that* particular tree, in a garden of amazing bounty, was off limits. And when God approached them and asked what they had done, they did not confess their sin.

Before the fall, Adam was proud of and pleased with the helpmate God had provided him with. *They were both naked, the man and his wife, and were not ashamed. (Genesis 2:25)*

Some argue that Adam and Eve knew no shame before the fall because they were innocent. The argument suggests they had no knowledge of good and evil. I think that's rather simplistic. Adam and Eve were made in the image of their creator. They were connected to their source. They had all the knowledge they needed and access to whatever they wanted.

Adam and Eve were joined as one flesh as man and wife. Their joining created a unity and an emotional transparency that didn't survive the enemies challenge. They became divided after the conflict with the serpent. Eve shared with her husband, and Adam willingly took what his wife offered. There was no remorse or shame in the receiving and eating. That came as an afterthought when God appeared in the garden to question them. At that point they both sought to hide and protect themselves. In this sense, they not only lost their direct connection with God, but the completeness of their union was damaged. Both attempts of covering themselves with leaves and hiding in the trees are examples of division and separation.

The first thing Adam said to God when God called to him was, *I heard Your voice... and I was afraid because I was naked; and I hid myself.* In other words, *I was exposed and I couldn't face you. I didn't want you to see me - not like this.* Adam and Eve didn't hide simply because they ate the fruit. They hid because of the emotion associated with their action; the shame of having doubted and disobeyed God and they feared judgment. Adam's fear speaks of his disconnection from his source more clearly than anything, as we are told in *1 John 4:16-18*, quite clearly: *God is love. Whoever lives in love lives in God, and God in him. In this way, love is made complete among us so that we will have confidence on the day of judgment, because in this world we are like him. There is no fear in love. But perfect love drives out fear, because fear has to do with punishment. The one who fears is not made perfect in love.*

In *2 Timothy 1:7*, we are told explicitly that *God did not give us a spirit of fear (timidity), but rather a spirit of power, love and of self-discipline (sound mind).* When you know who you are and you are secure in your place, position and relationships (with God and people), reminding yourself of this fact is sufficient to check yourself when doubt creeps in.

Adam and Eve should have presented a united front and protected one another. Instead, they selfishly sought to please and protect themselves. We are told in *1 Peter 4:8, Above all things have fervent love for one another, for love will cover a multitude of sins.* I think, perhaps, that's where the bulk of their shame came from. Not only were they caught doing something they knew not to do, they compounded their disobedience by not protecting their partner – they did not provide covering for one another. They didn't defend or stand up for each other. *There is no fear in love. Fear has to do with punishment. The one who fears is not made perfect in love.* Adam and Eve started off perfect in love. Their love could have covered their sin. Instead they chose not to take responsibility for their actions and passed blame in fear of punishment. Their choices speak directly to their separation from one another.

Their story is an illustration of a relationship in its perfect state. Two people joined as one flesh, caring and providing for one another. They were emotionally open and available to one another; they were naked together and unashamed. Their story is also an illustration of the destruction a relationship is susceptible to when influenced by outside forces and internal selfishness. They lost sight of one another's best interests. They sought to shield themselves from the other.

Relationships are still susceptible to all the nuances that caused Adam and Eve to fall. We are in danger of destroying ourselves and our relationships when we build up defenses and guard against intimacy with our partner. There is danger when we blame our partner or others for our shortcomings and insecurities. When we hide our true selves from view in hopes of escaping judgment and recriminations. There is great danger when we fear our nakedness and our emotional vulnerabilities. We are constantly endangering ourselves and our relationships.

I've seen many relationships fail because the parties were so interested in what others have to say about their relationship that they sought input from outside sources. I've seen other relationships fail from lack of trust. In others, I've witnessed selfish self-pleasing within the relationship. In all the failed relationships I have been exposed to, the individuals chose not to love their partners fervently and allow their love to cover their spouses' sins.

With Adam and Eve's relationship, these characteristics were implicit in their joining and in their nakedness before the fall. Trust is implicit when you expose and open your heart to someone. It's not something to be manipulated, taken for granted or set aside. Our nakedness is sacred and should be honored as such.

In *Proverbs 4:23* we are admonished to guard our hearts above all things. We may be gifted with a spouse, but it is our choice to continue day by day, hour by hour and minute by minute in performing our love for our partner. So, be careful you are not giving away pieces of your heart before you get to your assigned spouse; only your spouse should benefit from your emotional nakedness.

Meditation Verse: Genesis 2:18, 20-25

The LORD God said, "It is not good for the man to be alone. I will make a helper suitable for him."

But for Adam no suitable helper was found. And the LORD God caused a deep sleep to fall on Adam, and he slept; and He took one of his ribs, and closed up the flesh in its place. Then the rib which the LORD God had taken from man He made into a woman, and He brought her to the man.

And Adam said: "This is now bone of my bones and flesh of my flesh; she shall be called Woman, because she was taken out of Man."

Therefore a man shall leave his father and mother and be joined to his wife, and they shall become one flesh. And they were both naked, the man and his wife, and were not ashamed.

Lover & Lovee

So husbands ought to love their own wives as their own bodies;
he who loves his wife loves himself.
Ephesians 5:28

Lover to Lovee

Can you feel me?
Hear Me?
Hold me? Take me?
I'm yours, Lovee, love me.
Giving you my all
Consummating my promises
With my body
How's this kiss?
And my thrust? Gentle enough?
Ah, harder you say... deeper, my pleasure....
Ah... your lips are clinging
Oh... your nails just marked me

This mutual claiming is exquisite.
Your skin... soft, smooth like warm butter
Scented vanilla, mocha-flavored earthiness...
Heavenly.
You are the sweetest banquet...
Every nibble encourages exploration
Each bite begs a larger commitment
Even with you on my tongue
I hunger for more
I'm insatiable, Lovee
My desire is to feast on your bounty forever

Lovee to Lover

My Lover, my heart... I'm yours
Receive my life, claim my body
Our Father planned and ordained
Our Union.

I am blessed and
Overwhelmed with our joining
Continually thanking our Father
For blessing me
With such a wonderful man
As you
A manly man
A gentle man
A loving, caring man
Spiritual, gifted, sensitive
My lover man.
Filling me, expanding me, growing with me
You're planting generations in my womb.
Deeper, make sure they're well-seated!
Ah, the scratch of your beard is driving me wild!
Tickling my neck, tantalizing my breasts
Breasts grown to fill your hands and nurse your babes
Welcome your embrace and comfort your resting head
I love your build. I love your strength.
I love the way you handle me with reverent gentle care.
But hold me tighter, now! Pull me closer....

I'm melting into you
Skin to skin, intertwined limbs,
One body, one breath
One heart, one love, one hope.
My souling forever.

Can I feel you?
I am you. You are me.
And we are greater than you and me.
Your thoughts, mine. My voice, yours.
I'll never let you go.
I'm yours, Lover, love me.

Appendix

Self-Image Workshop Exercises

Things I Don't Like About Myself

Negative reinforcements diminish our self-esteem. Low self-esteem limits God's power to work in your life. When we diminish and limit ourselves, we destroy ourselves in ways we rarely realize. Identifying the negative words you speak into your life is a step towards highlighting your positive habits.

Write down all of the negative things you think of, believe about and say to yourself.

Body - Physical

Self – Non-Physical
(personality, character, habits)

Things I Absolutely Love About Myself

When we accentuate the positive, we build our self-esteem. Building self-esteem eventually brings us full-circle in our lives. After a while, we are no longer protecting ourselves in order to build self-esteem, our self-esteem is protecting us from situations in our life. Positive self-esteem guards against damaging negative influences. The more you highlight your positives, the better you will see your connection and contribution to the world around you!

Write down all the positive things you think of, believe about and say to yourself. Filling your heart from outside the lines is fine!

If I Could Kiss It....

We all love something about our bodies, openly or secretly. That *something* may get too much attention or too little, but if you could show your appreciation with a kiss, where would you kiss yourself?

Write your answer below. Don't let the short line limit you! If your list is long, keep on writing!

I'll go first: I would kiss my butt! I love my high, tight curve of flesh!

I would kiss my

_____

Evaluating My Life Balance

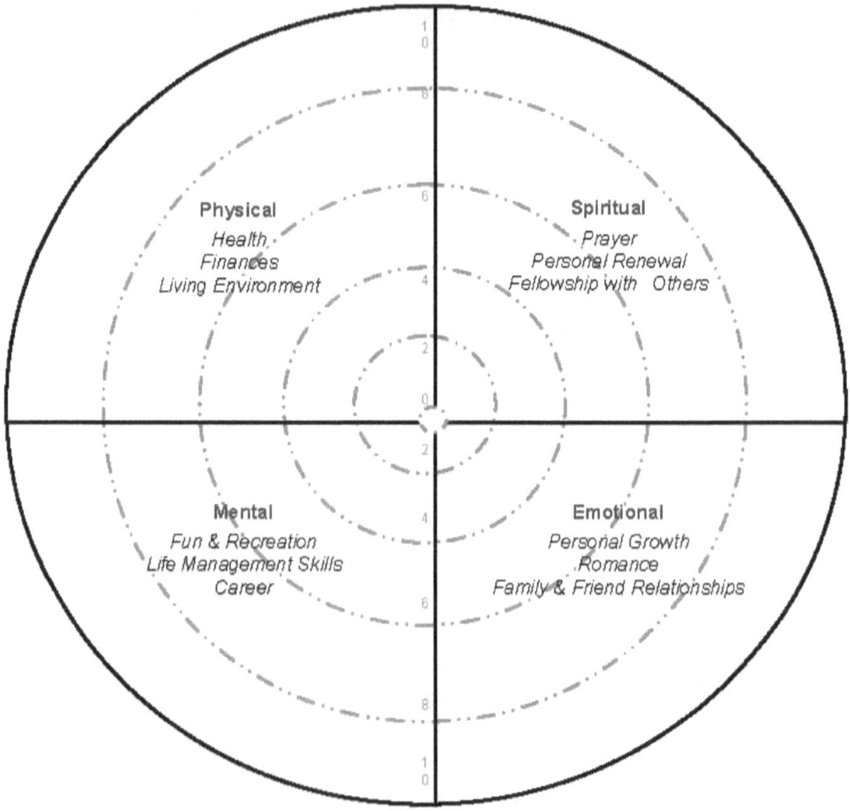

Physical
Health
Finances
Living Environment

Spiritual
Prayer
Personal Renewal
Fellowship with Others

Mental
Fun & Recreation
Life Management Skills
Career

Emotional
Personal Growth
Romance
Family & Friend Relationships

Area(s) I am Balanced in: P S M E   Area(s) I Need Balance in: P S M E

Something I can do to achieve Balance:

_____
_____
_____
_____

Self-Image Survey

In General   *Excellent=1, Good=2, Okay=3, Poor=4, N/A=5*

1. My body image is…	1	2	3	4	5
2. My overall self-image is…	1	2	3	4	5
3. My self-esteem is…	1	2	3	4	5
4. How selective are you when choosing/creating your personal environment (friends, employment, classes, extra-curricular activities, etc)	1	2	3	4	5
5. How are you at protecting your sensibilities when others attack?	1	2	3	4	5

Words and Treatment   *Yes=1, No=2, N/A=3*

6. Do you praise, compliment, reward yourself…	1	2	3
7. If yes, does it make you feel better about yourself?	1	2	3
8. Does your significant other praise, compliment, reward you…	1	2	3
9. If yes, does it make you feel better about yourself?	1	2	3
10. Do your parents praise, compliment, reward you…	1	2	3
11. If yes, does it make you feel better about yourself?	1	2	3
12. Do your friends praise, compliment, reward you…	1	2	3
13. If yes, does it make you feel better about yourself?	1	2	3
14. Do you have an emotionally painful relationship with your parents?	1	2	3
15. Do you have an emotionally painful relationship with your siblings?	1	2	3
16. Do you have an emotionally painful relationship with your significant other?	1	2	3
17. Do you have an emotionally painful relationship with your children?	1	2	3
18. Does your self-worth mirror how others treat/value you?	1	2	3
19. Does your cultural background contribute positively to your self-image?	1	2	3
20. If you could change anything about your body, would you?	1	2	3

21. If you could change anything about your character, would you? 1 2 3

22. Are you satisfied with who you are? 1 2 3

23. Do you feel validated when others acknowledge your accomplishments? 1 2 3

24. If an accomplishment is not acknowledged by loved ones, do you feel less accomplished/proud? 1 2 3

25. Do you compare yourself to perceived societal standards (beauty, weight, height, size, complexion, etc.)? 1 2 3

26. If yes, is comparison   Favorable   Unfavorable   Neutral

Your Stats

27. Age   28. Height   29. Weight   _____

30. Do you know your measurements (B/W/H)?   _____

31. What is your dress size?   _____

32. What is your ethnicity or race?   _____

33. What do you think your stats say about you?

_____

34. What do you know about yourself?

_____

35. Notes to self...

_____

_____

_____

How Much Do You Know About Marriage?

1) Between 1979 and 1987, according to Justice Department statistics, what proportion of intimate violence against women was committed by husbands?
   a) 1%
   b) About 50%
   c) Less than 10%
   d) 33%

2) On average, how much more likely is a single woman to die than a married woman of the same age.
   a) 50% more likely
   b) No difference
   c) 200% more likely
   d) 10% more likely

3) How many years does a parent's divorce knock off the life expectancy of their children (according to a study sample of gifted, white, middle class individuals).
   a) No difference. Parenting is most affected by income
   b) 6 months
   c) 4 years
   d) 2 years

4) Husbands make more money than bachelors, but marriage reduces women's earnings.
   a) True
   b) False

5) More married people cheat than couples who live together
   a) True
   b) False

6) Marriage makes men happier, but women more depressed.
   a) True
   b) False

7) Single people are more likely to be "very happy" than married people.
   a) True
   b) False

8) Single mothers usually develop unusually close relationships with their children.
   a) True
   b) False

Answers:
1. *C.* 9% of violence by intimates was committed by husbands.
2. *A*
3. *C.* Non-marriage is one of the largest behavioral health risks people voluntarily assume.
4. *False.* Husbands and wives earn more than bachelors. Childless white wives receive a marriage wage premium of 4%; black wives earn 10% more than comparable single women.
5. *False.* Co-habiting men are four times more likely to cheat than husbands; co-habiting women are eight times more likely to cheat than wives.
6. *False.* Married men and women are less depressed, less anxious, and psychologically distressed than singles, divorced or widowed Americans. By contrast getting divorced lowers both men and women's mental health, increasing depression, hostility, lowering self-esteem, sense of personal mastery, and purpose in life.
7. *False.* 40% of married people say they are "very happy" with life in general, compared to about 25% of singles or co-habitors
8. *False.* Adult children of divorce describe relationships with both parents less positively than children of intact marriages. On average, adult children of divorce are about 40% less likely than adult children of intact marriages to say they see either parent several times a week.

Scoring – each question is worth 1 point:
6-8: You are a Marriage Maven
3-5: Average Knowledge. Study to improve and prepare.
0-3: You are a Marriage Pessimist. Cheer up, there is such a thing as wedded bliss!

Quiz from *The Case for Marriage* by Linda J. Waite and Maggie Gallagher

Building a Firm Foundation
10 Stones to Start With

You've already read about preparing for the relationship you want. As a matter of fact this whole book is about preparation! In The Purpose and the Power of Love and Marriage, Dr. Myles Munroe takes us further with a discussion on *building*. Below are his ten foundation stones for a solid relationship.

Love
Agape is a self-denying and self-giving, sacrificial love. Love in marriage is more than just a feeling or an emotion; it is a choice. Love is a decision you make anew every day with regard to your spouse.

Truth
Truth is fundamental in marriage. Truthfulness between husband and wife is an indispensable part of a successful marriage. No one's interests are served if spouses are not honest with each other. Honesty, tempered and seasoned with love, foster an environment of trust.

Trust
Trust is closely related to truth. Trust enables a husband and wife to enjoy a relationship characterized by openness and transparency, with no secrets or "locked rooms" that are kept off limits to each other. Trust is also an essential element of commitment.

Commitment
Few people who marry plan for their marriages to fail, but neither do they specifically plan for success. Those who do not plan for success are virtually guaranteed to fail.

Commitment is the lifeblood of marriage. Part of our problem is that we do not understand the nature of the covenant. Marriage is a "blood covenant" of sorts and lasts a lifetime. A blood covenant is not entered into nor broken lightly. It is, first of all, a commitment to the institution of marriage and, second, an exclusive commitment to that person we have chosen to love and cherish for life.

Respect
To respect someone means to esteem that person, to consider him or her worthy of high regard. God created man – male and female – in His own image. He created them equal in every significant way. Husbands and wives who see each other as made in God's image will never have any problems with respect.

Submission
Healthy marriages are also built on mutual submission. Properly understood, there is nothing demeaning about submission. It is chosen freely, not imposed from without. Essentially, submission is the willingness to give up our right to ourselves, to freely surrender our insistence on having our own way all the time. Submission means putting the needs, rights, and welfare of another person ahead of our own.

Knowledge
Couples enter married life with no clue as to what marriage is or is not. They carry unrealistic and unreasonable expectations of themselves, their spouse, and their relationship as a whole. Couples considering marriage need time to get to know one another. They need time to talk about their dreams, their desires, and their expectations. They need time to study and learn the spiritual foundations and principles for marriage that God has given in His Word.

Faithfulness
Marital faithfulness involves more than just sexual fidelity. Being faithful to your wife also means defending her and affirming her beauty, intelligence, and integrity at all times, particularly before other people. Faithfulness to your husband means sticking up for him, always building him up and never tearing him down. Marital fidelity means that your spouse's health, happiness, security and welfare take a higher place in your life than anything else except your own relationship with the Lord.

Patience
Patience is another essential foundation stone for building a successful and happy marriage. Why? Marriage brings together two totally different people with different experiences, different backgrounds, different temperaments, different likes and dislikes, and sometimes even different cultures. Because of these differences, both partners will have to make major adjustments in their lives and attitudes if their marriage is to succeed. Some bumps and bruises along the way are inevitable. They may have conflict regarding expectations, money management, use of leisure time, sex, parenting – any number of things. The critical key in dealing with conflict and adjusting to difference is patience.

Financial stability
The time to think about finances is before the wedding – long before. A couple should discuss the matter frankly and honestly and have a clear financial plan in place before they take their vows. Financial failure is one of the main causes of marital failure. Never underestimate the importance of financial stability to a successful marriage.

Tips from *The Purpose and Power of Love & Marriage,* Dr. Myles Munroe

Family Mission Statement

Fortune 500 companies have mission statements. Non-profit corporations have mission statements. Does your family? A mission statement helps define specific values and goals, helps to guide group decisions while encourages participation and belonging. Whether a family of two or ten, creating a mission statement gives everyone input and helps keep the family on target with their goals.

Step One
Gather all the family members that live in the same house. Include small children, children who only visit on the weekends and grandparents who might live in the home.

Step Two
Explain that together you will be creating a family mission statement. Describe the benefits of having a mission statement and how it keeps the family moving in the same direction. Describe it as a road map, rather than a list of rules or requirements.

Step Three
Define your specific family by asking everyone to suggest adjectives that fit your family. Suggestions could include funny, smart, caring, active or quirky. Make sure everyone throws out an adjective or two. Write these on a white board for everyone to see.

Step Four
Brainstorm ideas to be included in the mission statement. Allow everyone to contribute and do not censor any ideas. Start off the discussion with some examples and questions. What would a stranger think when they saw your family interact? What inside jokes or stories does your family have? What goals do you have as a family? What traits are admired and what is unacceptable?

Step Five
Put several of these ideas in sentence form. Write as many sentences that are necessary. An example might be "The Smith family accepts everyone as they are but encourages change and growth for the better. We speak to one another in respect and show consideration at all times. We value privacy and trust. We agree that there are consequences to all of our actions and we agree to take responsibility for our own actions. Together we can impact each other and our community for the better."

Step Six
Edit your statement until everyone is in agreement with both the words and the sentiment. Hone the words down to the bare minimum to express your statement.

Step Seven
Craft a family motto. This should be one sentence that encapsulates your family's mission statement. It should be easy to remember and touch on at least a few of

the points in your mission statement. It could be "Do unto others as you would have them do unto you" or "Return with honor." It also could be funny or in code, as long as your family knows what it means and represents.

Step Eight
Print out your motto and family mission statement. Have everyone sign and date it. Post it somewhere so it can be seen and referenced. As good or bad decisions are made, tie it back to the family mission statement.

Step Nine
Revise your mission statement as time passes. Perhaps every New Year or anniversary date, you might need to edit the statement to grow with your family.

Family Mission Statement from www.ehow.com *by Judy Ford*

Scripture Index

OLD TESTAMENT

Genesis
1:3-30	149	Pop Culture Messiah
1:27	32	Self-Image is Everything.
1:27-31	35	Self-Image is Everything.
1:31	34	Self-Image is Everything.
2:15	225	Preparing for Marriage: Learning from Bad Examples
2:18	225, 271	Preparing for Marriage: Learning from Bad Examples, Our Nakedness
2:24	211	Prepare for Marriage?
2:20-24	225	Preparing for Marriage: Learning from Bad Examples
2:20-25	271	Our Nakedness
2:25	270	Our Nakedness
3:4-13	269	Our Nakedness
3:7-13	141	Big Girl, Little Closet
12:1-3	13	Introduction
18:1-15	144	How Are You Living?
20:1-7	200	25 Things to Think Twice About Before You Marry
29:15-20	162	Ladies, You're the Prize!
29:31	235	Scandalous
30:1-2	235	Scandalous
37:5-11	208	Life Isn't Fair, Dream Anyway

Leviticus
11:44	135	Becoming Whole and Holy

Deuteronomy
10:19	224	Preparing for Marriage: Learning from Bad Examples
32:45-47	96	Importance of Words

Ruth
3:1-6	159	Reconciling My Sexiness with My Celibacy
4:9-10	184	Technology Upgrade, Personal Downgrade

1 Samuel
20:12-17	82	Covenant of Friendship
20:42	82	Covenant of Friendship

Job
1:6-12	89	God of Good and Evil

Psalm
4:3	165	Set Apart
4:8	165	Set Apart
18:22	229	Preparing for Marriage: Learning from Bad Examples
37:1-6	202	25 Things to Think Twice About Before You Marry
103:1-5	94	Emotional Side Effects of Friendship
139:13-14	47	Out of the Mouths of Babes: My Body, Your Image
139:14	34	Self-Image is Everything.

Proverbs
4:4-7	247	You're Being Prepared Anyway, Why Not Focus?
4:20-23	225	Preparing for Marriage: Learning from Bad Examples
4:23	271	Our Nakedness
5:20-23	227	Preparing for Marriage: Learning from Bad Examples
9:13-18	67	Who U Wit?
10:30-32	241	Tell Me You Love Me
14:1	223	Man Friend Lessons
14:8-10	205	Foolish of Me
14:18	223	Man Friend Lessons

Proverbs
16:3	213	*Prepare for Marriage?*
16:9	213	*Prepare for Marriage?*
17:3	220	*Man Friend Lessons*
18:17-18	114	*Healing Graces*
18:21	149	*Pop Culture Messiah*
18:24	94	*Emotional Side Effects of Friendship*
19:14	239	*Marriage: Work It!*
19:22	229	*Preparing for Marriage: Learning from Bad Examples*
20:1-7	262	*Family Man*
21:2-3	229	*Preparing for Marriage: Learning from Bad Examples*
23:7	35	*Self-Image is Everything.*
26:26	178	*And it Don't Stop!*
26:28	178	*And it Don't Stop!*
31:26-30	209	*Fascinating Womanhood: What does he see in her?*

Ecclesiastes
4:7-12	80	*Covenant of Friendship*

Song of Solomon
1:5-6	42	*Smoke and Mirrors: The Confusion of Fantasy*

Jeremiah
1:4-7	31	*Practicing What I Preach*
1:5	34	*Self-Image Is Everything.*
29:10-14	120	*Journal: Friday, January 13, 2006*
29:11	119	*Journal: Friday, January 13, 2006*

Isaiah
54:4-8	160	*Reconciling My Sexiness with My Celibacy*
58:8-12	216	*Seeking Satisfaction*

NEW TESTAMENT

Matthew
4:1-11	182	*Sugar Daddy M.O.*
6:25-34	39	*Reflections on Weight Conversations*
6:33	120	*Journal: Friday, January 13, 2006*
7:11-12	116	*Eulogizing Antoine*
8:8	149	*Pop Culture Messiah*
12:33-37	112	*Dichotomy of Jemini*
12:34	110	*Dichotomy of Jemini*
19:1-10	236	*Scandalous*

Luke
4:23-24	137	*Rebounding*
16:15	171	*Dating Anxiety*

Mark
10:42-45	147	*Boss Lady: A Brief Illusion of the Triumph of Evil*
12:28-31	73	*Can I Love You?*

John
1:12	26	*Who I Am In Christ*
4:7-10	267	*Beautifully Imperfect*
8:42-47	109	*Dichotomy of Jemini*
8:44	110	*Dichotomy of Jemini*
10:1-5	174	*Good Touch, Bad Touch*
10:10	135	*Becoming Whole and Holy*
15:5	27	*Who I Am In Christ*
15:9-17	79	*Defining Family and Friend*
15:14	78	*Defining Family and Friend*
15:15	27	*Who I Am In Christ*
15:16	27	*Who I Am In Christ*
17:11-13	49	*This is Why I'm Hot*

Acts
9:3-9	128	*A Road I Must Travel Alone*

Romans

3:4	110	Dichotomy of Jemini
4:13-25	258	Imagining Life
4:17	255	Imagining Life
5:1	26	Who I Am In Christ
5:1-5	57	They Say I'm Lucky...
5:3-4	56	They Say I'm Lucky...
8:1-2	26	Who I Am In Christ
8:28	26	Who I Am In Christ
8:28-30	44	Chunky Dunkin'
8:37-39	26	Who I Am In Christ
12:1-2	157	Reconciling My Sexiness with My Celibacy
12:9-13	244	#1 Predictor of Divorce
14:5	61	Every Day is a Big Deal
14:7-8	61	Every Day is a Big Deal

1 Corinthians

3:16	28	Who I Am In Christ
6:15-20	106	Things Women Do and Say
6:17	26	Who I Am In Christ
6:20	26	Who I Am In Christ
7:1-5	230	Preparing for Marriage: Learning from Bad Examples
10:1-13	20	No More Complaints
12:27	26	Who I Am In Christ
13:11-12	253	girl vs. WOMAN

2 Corinthians

1:21-22	26	Who I Am In Christ
2:14-17	86	Levels of Teaching
5:17-21	27	Who I Am In Christ

Galatians

5:22-23	72	Best Things in Life
6:2-3	132	Growing Through Vulnerability
6:8-10	103	Don't Grow Weary of Doing Good

Ephesians

1:3-8	27	Who I Am In Christ
2:6	27	Who I Am In Christ
2:10	27	Who I Am In Christ
3:12	27	Who I Am In Christ
5:19-20	149	Pop Culture Messiah
5:21	264	A Happy Marriage is No Accident
5:22	264	A Happy Marriage is No Accident
5:25	264	A Happy Marriage is No Accident
5:28	273	Lover & Lovee
5:33	264	A Happy Marriage is No Accident
6:1-4	25	Better Than You Should Be
6:4	23	Better Than You Should Be
6:10	25	Better Than You Should Be

Philippians

1:3-7	52	Speak Power and Prosperity Into Your Life
1:6	27	Who I Am In Christ
3:17-21	99	Hindsight: Seeing Friends as Something Else
3:20	27	Who I Am In Christ
4:13	27	Who I Am In Christ

Colossians

1:13-14	26	Who I Am In Christ
2:10	26	Who I Am In Christ
3:1-4	26	Who I Am In Christ

1 Thessalonians

4:13-18	63	Next of Kin

2 Timothy

1:7	27, 270	Who I Am In Christ, Our Nakedness

Hebrews
- 4:4-16 — 26 — Who I Am In Christ

James
- 1:2-4 — 127 — A Road I Must Travel Alone
- 1:12 — 188 — I Never Asked You Out...
- 4:4 — 187 — Call Me Naïve...

1 Peter
- 1:13-16 — 135 — Becoming Whole and Holy
- 3:1-4 — 266 — A Happy Marriage is No Accident
- 3:8-9 — 210 — So, what are you really saying?
- 4:8 — 270 — Our Nakedness

1 John
- 4:1-6 — 107 — Things Women Do and Say
- 4:7 — 78 — Defining Family and Friend
- 4:7-12 — 148 — Pop Culture Messiah
- 4:16-18 — 270 — Our Nakedness
- 5:18 — 27 — Who I Am In Christ

2 John
- 1:7-11 — 168 — Set Apart

3 John
- 1:2 — 160 — Reconciling My Sexiness with My Celibacy
- 1:2-8 — 124 — Speak Your Feelings

Revelation
- 20:11-15 — 71 — Some Things About Funerals

Resource List

Andelin, Helen. *Fascinating Womanhood*. New York: Bantam, 2007. Print.

Anderson, Neil T. *Victory Over the Darkness*. Ventura, California: Regal, 2000. Print.

Benner, David G. *Sacred Companions The Gift of Spiritual Friendship & Direction*. New York: InterVarsity, 2004. Print.

Ford, Judy. "How to Prepare a Family Mission Statement." www.ehow.com. Web

Jones, LaShawnda. *Clichés: A Life in Verse*, New York: Jazzy Media, 2007. Print.

Jones, LaShawnda. *Fantasies: A Metamorphosis of Sexual Attraction*, New York: Jazzy Media, 2005. Print.

Meyer, Joyce. *Beauty for Ashes*, New York: Warner Books Edition, 1994. Print.

Munroe, Myles. *The Purpose and Power of Love & Marriage*. New York: Destiny Image, 2005. Print.

"Preparing for Marriage." www.*Sister2SisterMagazine.com*. Web.

Sollee, Diane. "Number One Predictor of Divorce." www.smartmarriage.com. Web.

Waite, Linda, and Maggie Gallagher. *The Case for Marriage Why Married People Are Happier, Healthier, and Better Off Financially*. New York: Doubleday, 2001. Print.

Williamson, Marianne. *Return to Love: Reflections on the Principles of a Course in Miracles*. New York: HarperCollins, 1996. Print.

Communication is Key

If you would like to correspond with me in response to my writings or invite me to speak at an event or share your own testimony, I can be contacted via:

Website

www.mygodandme.info

Email

lashawnda@mygodandme.info

Blogs & Social Networks

Keep up with me @ www.mygodandme.info/blog
Become a Fan @ www.facebook.com/mygodandme
Tweet me @ www.twitter.com/ldjonsey

Thank you so very much for your support!
I look forward to hearing from you!
May God forever bless you and yours!

LaShawnda

About the Author

LaShawnda Jones is currently living and thriving in New York City. Her writing and publishing work range from developing volumes of poetry to designing an annual full-figured calendar. She also contributed to a daily political blog during the 2008 presidential election and an anthology of letters addressed to First Lady Michelle Obama.

LaShawnda's life is an illustration of transition – constant movement and growth from one point to another. She is ecstatic about continuing forward on her journey with the LORD. She continues to grow stronger in her faith, wiser in her knowledge and more loving to people as she seeks to mirror exactly the Christ in her.

To keep up with LaShawnda's journey, subscribe to her blog at www.mygodandme.info/blog.

www.ingramcontent.com/pod-product-compliance
Lightning Source LLC
Chambersburg PA
CBHW031236290426
44109CB00012B/312

Weaving in the agency and voices of earth and connecting the examination of the causes of their suffering to the realities of racial and economic justice, gender and sexual injustice, as well as disability injustice set up an important matrix from which to explore how systems of oppressions that limit these kinds of justices from flourishing are perpetuated. This ecowomanist lens offers a glance into the touchpoints from which to construct new modes of being and thinking toward intersectional modes of justice whereby all beings, all lives with the earth, can thrive. This is the primary goal of ecowomanism.

When we use this frame, we consider that earth justice and social justice work go hand in hand. We recognize the importance of multiple justice seekers from various backgrounds and expertise being a part of conversations for climate justice. It is not enough, for example, to hear from just the preachers from the Black church tradition, whose homiletical genius has inspired generations from the antislavery and abolitionist movements through present-day antiracist, Black Lives Matter, and black liberationist movements. We also need to hear the voices of the climate activists, scientists, and others working and weaving visions of climate justice into clustered city neighborhoods, along the faith inspired vineyards of church gardens and interfaith climate collectives, and in organizational connections across the planet working to reduce carbon emissions. We must position the voices of women, nonbinary, and queer folx into the conversation about climate justice in ways that connect queer studies with environmental studies and highlight the problematic ways in which hierarchical gendered perspectives have forced non-binary folx, women, and especially women of color around the globe to pay the highest cost for climate injustice, while often contributing the least to it. We need to hear from the antiracist scholars working to dismantle white supremacy and scholars in disability studies working to change perceptions about the dominance of able-bodiedness so that we might see all bodies, and beings, as sacred and holy.

What are we to make, for example, about the fact that Harriet Tubman, cherished black feminist, is viewed as an environmentalist who read trees, *and* did so as a disabled woman who suffered from severe headaches and narcolepsy most of her life even as she led the Underground Railroad? Was there something sacred and holy about the divine connection that she recalls having when she was in an unconscious state and able to commune with God differently?[4] How is

---

4. Tubman's ability to read trees refers to her observation of the northern direction that moss typically grows on trees. Knowing which direction pointed north likely provided Tubman with valuable information about how to lead enslaved Africans on the Underground Railroad to freedom. For more, see Deirdre Cooper Owens, "Harriet Tubman's Disability and Why It Matters," *Ms.*, February 10, 2022, https://msmagazine.com/2022/02/10/harriet-tubman-disability-democracy/.

this model of being a contemplative with and in earth helpful to those practicing environmental justice and earth honoring faith today? Are there concepts, tropes, and practices in Buddhism, for example, that lend themselves toward seeing the unconscious mind as a storehouse of "good ground" from which to nurture the good?[5] How do we explain that it was not only Tubman's commitment to the freedom of Black people but also her commitment to earth that led her to cultivate land using earth honoring farming practices?[6] Seeing Tubman's life and her work as an environmentalist from this kind of intersectional perspective opens the door for us to see connections between social justice issues and earth justice. In this sense, an intersectional ecowomanist lens helps us map the methods, understand modes of thought, and discern conceptual resources and frameworks that historical and contemporary theorists, preachers, scholars, and activists use. It also invites us to apply these methods and be guided by these values of environmental or climate justice in our everyday lives.

ECOWOMANIST CONTEMPLATIVE THOUGHT, BLACK LIBERATION THEOLOGY, AND THE AFRICAN AMERICAN HOMILETICS TRADITION AS INTERDISCIPLINARY SOURCES

In previous work, I have outlined the conceptual frameworks within African American religious thought, Black liberationist perspectives, and womanist ethics that serve as foundations for ecowomanism.[7] As for the connection between African American religion and ecowomanism, the key tenet of interconnectedness guides the conversation about climate justice to begin with the acknowledgment of a belief in a sacred connection between all beings. Reflective of African indigenous religious understanding, connecting the human, earthly, and divine realms together to shape an ethical and moral framework to cultivate climate justice, interconnectedness is a primary tenet and theme of ecowomanism. It suggests that climate justice work is accompanied by a spiritual undertone. This undertone matters in the work of climate justice because it keeps the agency of earth and nature in the forefront of climate justice, thus including the earth as a being and

---

Also see Deirdre Cooper Owens, *Medical Bondage: Race, Gender, and the Origins of American Gynecology* (University of Georgia Press, 2018).

5. See Thich Nhat Hanh, *Teachings on Love* (Parallax Press, 2007).
6. Nhat Hanh, *Teachings on Love*, 2007.
7. Melanie L. Harris, "African Diaspora: African American Environmental Religious Ethics and Ecowomanism," in *Routledge Handbook of Religion and Ecology*, ed. Willis Jenkins, Mary Evelyn Tucker, and John Grim (Routledge, 2017), 199–207.

participant on the journey toward justice. In addition, the spirituality that undergirds climate justice helps to keep activists in the movement energized and empowered to take care of themselves through practices of contemplation, reflection, and rest, and to see these forms of care as central to the wider work of justice. Alice Walker reminds us of the importance of the connection between self-care and planetary care by encouraging all activists to have a spiritual practice. She writes,

> This is not a time to live without a practice. It is a time when all of us will need the most faithful, self-generated enthusiasm (enthusiasm: to be filled with god) in order to survive in human fashion. Whether we reach this inner state of recognized divinity through prayer, meditation, dancing, swimming, walking, feeding the hungry, or enriching the impoverished is immaterial. We will be doubly bereft without some form of practice that connects us, in a caring way, to what begins to feel like a dissolving world. . . . Take some time to contemplate what sort of practice appeals to you. . . . Everything has Life, everything has Spirit! . . . Whatever it is, now is the time to look for it, to locate it, definitely, and to put it to use.[8]

Alice Walker's invitation to contemplative practice is a model worth paying attention to. Walker's invitation becomes deeper as one's eyes scroll across the page. She invites us to open the heart and invite a practice into our lives in part based on the insight that only the cultivation of refuge space within can strengthen us for the justice work ahead. That is, by cultivating a contemplative or spiritual practice by deepening our connection to Spirit and having an awareness of the divine within, we can empower ourselves for the hard work of justice ahead.

As two important aspects of contemplative thought, contemplative care and contemplative practices can help individuals engaged with social and environmental justice identify strategies to establish a sense of safety for individuals or communities, even in the midst of the climate crisis; and these two aspects of contemplative thought can help with strategies and touchpoints of hope, even in the midst of the reality of the polycrisis—the religious, cultural, social, and political unrest throughout the world. To better understand the connections, one definition of the former is, "contemplative care is the art of

---

8. Alice Walker, "This Was Not an Area of Large Plantations: Suffering Too Insignificant for the Majority to See," in *We Are the Ones We've Been Waiting For: Inner Light in a Time of Darkness* (The New Press, 2006), 88–110.

providing spiritual, emotional and pastoral support, in a way that is informed by a personal, consistent contemplative or meditation practice."[9]

Scholarship on contemplative and spiritual practice have roots in the disciplines of health, mental health and wellness, and religious studies. It gives particular attention to religious studies and a focus on skill development, method, and religious or theological underpinnings. It connects theology, pastoral care and counseling, trauma studies, community care, and healing. These connections have opened the door for study on the impact of contemplative practices such as meditation or mindfulness training on reducing the impact of eco-trauma, the development of trauma informed approaches in teaching, self-compassionate leadership, and global and community organizing. This work has paved the way for study in non-harming, compassionate practices for racial justice, nonviolent action informed by the civil rights movement, and even mindfulness work to assist veterans of war and those impacted by generational eco-personal, posttraumatic stress disorder and social trauma.[10]

Put another way, the way one feels emboldened on their path of life and also empowered to fight for earth's life through social and earth justice is by first being fully rooted. Some of the wisdom outlined in the interviews, sermons, and meditations in this text help point the way toward developing practices that help move earth justice forward. In fact, one might read *Preaching Black Earth* with a contemplative lens through which to listen for earth wisdom and wisdom from environmental activists pointing to new directions for climate justice in our day. Taking this view, *Preaching Black Earth* is a companion on the journey toward environmental justice, because it offers instruction for readers and insight from various dimensions and perspectives.

BLACK LIBERATION THEOLOGY

The theological themes of justice and liberation show up repeatedly in ecowomanist contemplative thought. These themes help shape and inform some questions regarding the experience of peoples of African descent with the environment: How have African and African American (Black) communities engaged in environmental justice historically in the United States and globally? How has the experience of navigating racial injustice and racial violence, often in collusion with white supremacist "ownership" and

---

9. Cheryl A. Giles and Willa B. Miller, *The Arts of Contemplative Care: Pioneering Voices in Buddhist Chaplaincy and Pastoral Work* (Wisdom Publications, 2012), xvii.
10. For work in non-harming, compassionate practices for racial justice, see Ruth King, *Mindful of Race: Transforming Racism from the Inside Out* (Sounds True, 2018).

overuse of nature, impacted Black people's understanding of themselves, their relationship with the earth, and their understandings of environmental justice? How are ecological reparations and racial reparations connected? How might racial, gender, economic, and environmental justice be connected in unique ways for Black environmental activists? The first theme of justice underscores the importance of creating systems of fairness that create equal access to environmental health and prompt deep imagination so that we might foster communities of flourishing wherein the earth and all beings flourish. That is, through the work of exposing implicit racial, gender, and economic biases, and naming prejudices about sexual identity and other societal stereotypes, hierarchal structures can be identified and torn down.

In many Judeo-Christian religious traditions, this idea of justice comes from the theological understanding of *imago Dei*, the idea that the essence of God as light is in all things and as such all beings are related and worthy of thriving in balanced and equitable community. Akin, in interfaith and interreligious dialogue to Buddhist understandings of interbeing, wherein all beings are connected and in flow with one another, the work of justice and environmental justice specifically is grounded by a logic of non-dualism and interconnectedness rather than logic of domination and hierarchy. Central to the work of justice, and especially racial justice in Black and Brown communities, is fighting for freedom of and justice for the earth. Because of the myth that Black and Brown communities are not interested in environmental justice, developing an intersectional approach to environmental justice is key. James H. Cone, puts it this way, drawing connections between racial and environmental justice in his classic essay "Whose Earth Is It Anyway?": "Racism is profoundly interrelated with other evils, including the degradation of the earth. It is important for Black people, therefore, to make the connection between the struggle against racism and other struggles for life. . . . What good is it to eliminate racism if we are not around to enjoy a racist free environment?"[11] For Cone and other scholars who make connections among racial justice, gender and sexual justice, economic and disability justice, and divine justice, it is fairness and equality that guide the vision for working for social justice and environmental justice. The theological claim that God desires that all of creation thrive can be derived from a biblical understanding of the creation stories found in Genesis.

---

11. James H. Cone, "Whose Earth Is It Anyway?," *Cross Currents*, 50 (1/2): 36–46.

LIBERATION: HONORING BODY, CHERISHING BLACK EARTH

For many communities of color, including African and African American peoples, experiencing liberation from all systems of oppression means having the freedom to be fully who they are. This includes having a sense of freedom in body, mind, and spirit. Whether individually or communally, this kind of freedom invites a freedom of earth through an understanding of African cosmology wherein the divine realm, human realm, and earth/nature realm are interconnected.[12]

As the earth is free, so too are the people. As the earth is free, so too are the ancestors and all existence in the spirit realm. As the spirit realm is free, so too are the humans to flourish in balance and harmony with all of earth. These connections are important for ecowomanism because they reveal a sacred connection between the peoples and the earth that supports an ethical mandate—embedded in the cultural and social and in many cases spiritual values of the peoples and their communities—to care for the earth. That is, especially as descendants of enslaved Africans throughout the diaspora whose bodies were identified as property and whose bodies were used as beings from which to extract energy and labor, African Americans have a particularly complex relationship with the earth. This is what Kimberly E. Ruffin calls the "beauty-to-burden" paradox, highlighting the complexity of African American environmental history and connection with earth being filled with history, experience, and memory that evokes trauma, climate and racial violence, as well as beauty, awe, and sacred spiritual connection.

Recognizing the depth of the extremes of these paradoxical realities for African and African Americans doing work in environmental justice is key. Our entry into the work of environmental justice is often very different and sometimes misunderstood or misperceived by well-meaning (often liberal) white people in the movement with little to no experience or knowledge about the importance of true antiracist mutual relationship. Without a commitment to anti-oppressive paradigms the work of environmental justice can be difficult. Models of ecological reparations are helpful here in dismantling structures of white supremacy and exploring exploitive and extracting practices used against people of color and the earth. These practices, such as the establishment of the Dakota pipeline, follow a logic of domination whereby communities of color and land are subject to the desire of a white supremacist and capitalist agenda. The work of ecological reparations, then, is not simply to repair

---

12. Malidoma Patrice Somé, *Of Water and the Spirit: Ritual, Magic, and Initiation in the Life of an African Shaman* (Compass, 1995).

the earth from destructive anthropocentric habits and unsustainable practices that destroy the earth: ecological reparations are also about transforming systems of domination, practices of abuse, and ways of thinking that posit one position, posture, person, or being over another to the point of utter extinction.[13] Put another way, ecological reparations deals with not only repairing the earth in all of its biodiversity but also repairing systems of oppression such as racism, classism, sexism, heterosexism, and transphobia that seek to tear at the essence of beingness and sacredness of beings of a particular race, class, gender, sexual orientation, and expression. Ecological reparations interrupts abuse and calls out abuse of power in a number of forms. From this vantage point social justice is earth justice, and earth justice is social justice. This particular perspective is held specifically from an ecological perspective called ecowomanism.[14]

Ecowomanism invites contemplative and scholarly reflection on environmental justice from the perspective of women of African descent. It takes seriously the work and scholarship of Black women environmental scientists, activists, and scholars who engage environmental justice with a focus on intersectional analysis. Ecowomanism invites us to develop skillful means through which to use and apply intersectional analysis in order to understand and glean wisdom from earth-honoring practices that help to construct more healthy, non-abusive, non-exploitive and sustainable ways of being with the earth. Similar to the Buddhist practice of looking deeply, ecowomanism looks deeply into the roots of inequity in cases of environmental racism to uncover systems in place that are helping to maintain environmental injustice.[15]

For example, ecowomanist wisdom suggests that there is something sacred and important to recovering a relationship with the earth for so many peoples of color, especially descendants of enslaved Africans who have known, or can tap into their own DNA to feel, the feeling of powerlessness and hopelessness in the face of lynching. What are we to make of the relationship between the earth that soaks up the blood of a Black lynched body and that soil's relationship with the descendants of that lynched earth being? And how are we to imagine ecological reparations regarding the repair of that community's relationship with the lynching tree, not to mention the racial repair that is still necessary between the descendants of the white people who raised the Black body to be hung and celebrated the expiration of life from that lynched Black body? How does one approach repairing earth differently, and walk into environmental

---

13. "Dismantle White Supremacy," Unitarian Universalist Association, accessed January 27, 2025, https://www.uua.org/justice/dismantle-white-supremacy. Also see Audre Lorde, *The Master's Tools Will Never Dismantle the Master's House* (Penguin UK, 2018).

14. Melanie L. Harris, *Ecowomanism: African American Women and Earth-Honoring Faiths* (Orbis, 2017).

15. Thich Nhat Hanh, *No Death, No Fear: Comforting Wisdom for Life* (Riverhead Books, 2002).

justice work constructively, with an eye toward justice toward all, when one is a descendent of African enslaved peoples? Might this approach be different than the approach toward repairing earth as one who is the descendent of white peoples who historically lynched Black bodies in the United States? What do we make of the difference between the perspective on land sovereignty and rights from the perspective of the white colonial settler (recipient of stolen land) and that of Native peoples? Other questions emerge from this eco-memory reflection on the US lynching scene, including how the ecological perspective of the enslavers of Black and African bodies whose labor provided the economic base for America and whose persons were considered property, differs from the ecological perspective of those who were considered nonhuman for hundreds and hundreds of years? Considering the vastness of climate injustice, and the attacks on democracy over the past decade, have we been taught to be willfully ignorant about the negative impact unexamined white privilege has had on building a true democracy and an environmental ethic that honors the sacredness of earth? When the systems of exploitation, extraction, and abuse litter the earth with graves as a result of climate violence, when harmful unsustainable action abounds, what are we to do with the hope of healing the earth or, at least, sustaining basic ecosystems for life for the next seven generations to enjoy?

The freedom to ask these questions and the capacity to host the courage to meet them require practice sometimes in traditional and sometimes in what religious historian Rachel E. Harding calls, "alternative spaces."[16] In 2022, I had the pleasure of working with Dr. Harding on a joint project sponsored by the Food, Health, and Ecological Well-Being (FHEW) program, which I direct at Wake Forest University, and the Veterans of Hope project. The inaugural FHEW Contemplative Leadership retreat was not only one of deep renewal for activists, scholars, and ecowomanist leaders in environmental justice. It was also a time of deep and urgent reflection on the need for self and planetary care. That is, as Alice Walker and bell hooks remind us, especially for Black women and Black communities, it is central to remember that our healing is deeply woven into the healing of the earth. Our healing from internalized and external forms of oppression, racism, classism, sexism; our healing from homophobia, transphobia; even our healing from racial trauma and intimate relational violence is connected to how we connect to the earth, put our hands in the soil, listen, and fight for environmental justice.

Ecowomanist spirituality is fully lived out in the spiritual practice, ritual, and worship life of the Root Church—a space that invites a collective of community organizers, mental health providers, and everyday folk in Durham,

---

16. Rosemarie Freeney Harding with Rachel Elizabeth Harding, *Remnants: A Memoir of Spirit, Activism, and Mothering* (Duke University Press, 2015), ix.

North Carolina, together to worship God in Creation. The Root Church is organized by leaders of The Root Cause Collective, led by ecowomanist, A. W. Shields. This vibrant nonprofit organization is a collective of mental health providers and wellness professionals who are committed to liberative, holistic healthcare services for communities of color. In October, following the FHEW retreat, the Root Church celebrated worship in a truly ecowomanist way, fully honoring the intersections of Black religious life. Shaping a worship service that was grounded in a commitment to self and planetary care and anti-oppressive and life-giving ways of being for all in the earth community, including queer folk, partners, parents, children, pets, animals, plants, and friends, this model of ecowomanist spirituality embodied elements of Black liberation theology and womanist theology. Sacred space was created out of the Black farm, ritual was performed under the shade of an old oak tree, and children were invited to name their own reflections about earth, communion, and relationships, as adults were encouraged to listen to the wisdom of the children. The service also included a baby dedication service featuring an Afrocentric Christian practice of dedication and presentation to the community. The practices of Christian mysticism, mindfulness, and ancestral connection through the beauty of multiple African indigenous religious traditions were all welcomed in the space, making the "alternative space" of worship a truly interreligious space of sacred communal and earth care.

The worship space was carefully constructed outside on a beautiful fall Sunday in October on a Black farm in Durham, and the focus of this worship service was on Elijah's farm, giving us the opportunity to reclaim our connection to the land. Bell hooks notes that one of the most vital things that we can do as Black and Brown peoples and those committed to anti-racism as true white allies is reconnecting to the land. This work can be very healing and reestablish important kinship connections between Black peoples and the land that have been severed by white supremacist ways of thinking and racist acts of violence: "when we love the earth, we are able to love ourselves more fully . . . estrangement from nature and engagement in mind/body splits made it all the more possible for black people to internalize white-supremacist assumptions about black identity. Learning contempt for blackness, southerners transplanted in the north suffered both culture shock and soul loss."[17] Developing "alternative spaces" that guide Black and Brown folks into creating spiritual faith communities that honor their own sacredness as well as the sacredness of earth helps us dive more deeply into ecowomanist spirituality and uncover the depths of

---

17. Bell hooks, "Touching the Earth," in *Sisters of the Yam: Black Women and Self-Recovery* (South End Press, 1999), 134–138.

eco-theologies informed by the sense of abundance that Rosemarie Harding and Dr. Rachel E. Harding describe in *Remnants*. Here, Dr. Rachel Harding writes,

> There is no scarcity. There is no shortage. No lack of love, of compassion, of joy in the world. There is enough.
>
> There is more than enough.
>
> Only fear and greed make us think otherwise.
>
> No one need starve. There is enough land and enough food.
> No one need die of thirst. There is enough water. No one need live without mercy. There is no end to grace. And we are all instruments of grace. The more we give it, the more we share it, the more we use it, the more God makes. There is no scarcity of love. There is plenty. And always more.
>
> This is the universe my mother lived in. Her words. Her ways. This is the universe she was raised in, by parents from rural Georgia who came up in a generation after slavery. People who lived with many terrors but who knew terror was not God's final say. This is the universe she taught me. Whatever I call religion is this inclusive, Christian, indigenous, Black, southern cosmology of compassion and connectedness. It is the poetry of my mother's life.[18]

Perhaps the greatest gift and inheritance that we receive from Dr. Harding is this gift of a theology of abundance. It is the theology of her mother, Rosemarie. She believed in a world of abundance, where there was enough for all to eat, to live, to breathe, to be. Even in the midst of battling against Jim and Jane Crow, as well as the structural racism that was a deep part of the lives of African American communities living in the south at the time of Rosemarie Harding's life, still there was a deep belief, an ethic of sufficiency, that God was an abundantly loving God and saw deep worth and value in every being and every Black life and every Black soul regardless of the daily evidence of white supremacy. A theology that both allowed for the acknowledgment of evil (white supremacy, white racial harm and violence) and a theology of resistance and divine love, this theology of abundance was much more than food or money ~ it was the wealth of being ~ and was filled with the inner knowing of one's worth and value as a full earthling, a child of God, a cherished part of the heart of the planet.

---

18. Harding and Harding, *Remnants*, ix.

Healing this heart ~ healing us ~ is not only evidence of healthy theology ~ it is proof that we are healing simply by being earth. This, being with earth and being earth, is true liberation.

AFRICAN AMERICAN HOMILETICS

In the tradition of African American homiletics, proclaiming the word and the gospel of Jesus Christ for the present-day liberation of communities of faith committed to social and earth justice is the primary purpose of sermon construction, development, and delivery. Aligned with Jesus's model of radical love, inclusiveness, and commitment to justice for the oppressed, African American homiletics celebrates a history through the great oratorical genius of Sojourner Truth, Jarena Lee, Harriet Tubman, Nat Turner, Marcus Garvey, and Martin Luther King Jr. While pressed by the realities of enslavement, and reading, preaching, and even ministering under the threat of death, these leaders and preachers used various styles to "preach the word" of justice in ways that exposed the evils of racism, sexism, and other forms of oppression while painting the path forward for justice and the beloved community for all.

For ecowomanism, it is significant that King's vision of the beloved community was in part influenced by his own witness of the environmental health hazards experienced by the Memphis sanitation workers in 1968. It was to advocate for this cause that King came to Memphis to speak out against environmental injustice and for the civil and human rights of workers.[19] King's metaphor of the vision of God as a just democracy set to words in his "I've Been to the Mountaintop" speech sets the stage for an ecowomanist vision connecting the idea of the beloved community with environmental justice.

In King's theological imagination, illustrated through his sermon, we see an arc of divine justice and an argument that God intends for humans and all beings to live in harmony with one another. Due to the sins of greed, economic exploitation, militarism, and white supremacy, King explains that American society is not living into this vision, and he urges society to move toward God's grander vision of peace and justice for all. This example of King's sermon, connecting environmental justice with Black liberation, is just one through which an ecowomanist vision expands the dialogue mentioned above by James H. Cone and deepens the call for us to consider African American preaching and homiletics as an interdisciplinary source for ecowomanist reflection.

19. Diane Glave, "Black Environmental Liberation Theology," in *To Love the Wind and the Rain: African Americans and Environmental History*, ed. Diane D. Glave and Mark Stoll (University of Pittsburgh Press, 1999).

PREACHING BLACK EARTH: LISTENING, PREACHING, AND MOVING IN AN AGE OF CLIMATE CHANGE

As an interdisciplinary volume, *Preaching Black Earth* is a collection that features sermons, environmental justice reflections, and interviews. Part I includes ecowomanist sermons from political activists Stacey Abrams, Sofia Betancourt, and Elonda Clay, as well as biblical scholar Kenneth Ngwa and meditations from the Black prophetic Christian liberation tradition by John Kinney and Otis Moss III. Deeply woven into the tradition of African American literature, this book also offers selections of eco-poetry that weaves parts I and II together. Part II opens with my own eco-poetry as a unique contribution to the field of environmental justice and includes five interview conversations with foremost scholar leaders in the field, Heber Brown, Christopher Carter, Frederick Douglass Haynes III, Larry Rasmussen, Frances Roberts-Gregory, and Gina M. Stewart.

The first interview features a conversation between me and Black liberationist pastor Frederick Douglass Haynes III about the resurrection hope alive in a vision of environmental justice that centers Black theology. The second interview features a unique conversation between me and preeminent womanist pastor and preacher Gina M. Stewart as she engages the method of ecowomanism and the tenets of ecowomanist thought. The third interview showcases the collaborative work between me and Larry Rasmussen as we discuss the significance of antiracist paradigms for environmental ethics and how this turn transforms the discourse of climate justice. In the fourth interview, I engage Heber Brown and Christopher Carter about their approaches to environmental justice, building and sustaining the Black Church Food Security Network, and invigorating programs in ecological well-being in church, seminary, and academic contexts. The final interview is hosted by Kate Common of Methodist Theological School in Ohio and engages Frances Roberts-Gregory and me in a dialogue about the arc of ecowomanism and African American environmental justice work in faith communities today. This conversation uncovers the gems and tenets of ecowomanist spirituality. The volume concludes with two eco-poems, one by young environmental and antiracist activist Liv Parsons and the other a self-authored closing mantra.

HOW TO USE THIS BOOK: MY HOPE FOR YOU

Inspiring the Reader

Preaching Black Earth is a powerful volume in that it includes sermons, eco-poetry meditations, and interviews featuring many diverse and interdisciplinary voices in ecowomanist thought and environmental justice. As a collective, these voices illustrate the depth and expansive scope of ecowomanism and signal the importance of interdisciplinary, interreligious, and intercultural approaches in ecowomanism for the work of climate justice.

My hope for the reader who desires to be inspired is that the sermons in *Preaching Black Earth* will indeed spark hope, renewal, and encouragement into the heart and mind of the reader seeking refuge and solace, even as they engage the work of environmental justice in their everyday life. My hope for the reader interested in prayer and poetry writing themselves is that they be encouraged to write their own ecowomanist prayers and poems and that the eco-poems included in the volume might inspire a new generation of environmental writers. My hope for the reader of the interviews is to be able to glean new wisdom and inspiration from the voices of political activists, spiritual and religious leaders, and scholars who are committed to social and earth justice. Each interview in *Preaching Black Earth* is unique in that it models communal, respectful, and critical conversation. These models can be used to frame other conversations and discourse at the intersections of environmental studies, theology, ethics, and climate activism.

Inspiring the Student, Activist, and Teacher

Preaching Black Earth is also an excellent addition to any classroom and can be easily adapted to courses engaging environmental studies, Black and womanist theologies, theology, ethics, homiletics, ecowomanism, and more. Teachers will find the sermons helpful for describing the theological underpinnings and conceptual frames of ecowomanist thought. Themes including interconnectedness, interdependence, earth community, and the connection between theory and praxis can be gleaned from an initial reading of each sermon. These themes could be discussed in class as a way of deepening student learning and comprehension of ecowomanist perspectives.

Theology and Ethics Courses

Pedagogical Strategies

For courses in theology and ethics, one pedagogical exercise that will assist students in more deeply understanding the major themes in ecowomanist thought is to invite students to select one of the sermons and glean three or four major themes (or points) from the sermon to write about. By describing those themes in their own words, students might reflect on their own theology and how and whether the themes in the sermon align, expand, change, constrain, or transform their own theology and why.

Preaching, Rhetoric, and Homiletics Courses

Pedagogical Strategies

A particularly helpful exercise would be to invite students to write a short three-to-five-page paper responding to one or more of the following questions: How do the themes in this sermon expand my own theological understanding of earth, stewardship, and earth community? How might my faith and my faith communities be served by hearing this sermon or a sermon like this one? What critique might I bring to this sermon? What are the sermon's blind spots? What do I wish the sermon would say more about?

Considering the dynamic and diverse use of rhetorical styles applied in each of the sermons, a pedagogical exercise specifically for classes in preaching and rhetoric would be to bring a rhetorical criticism or womanist lens to the sermon and study the sermon for uses of narrative, story, and language. Students might reflect on the question of what narratives, stories, and language used in the sermon best communicate the principles (community etc.) embedded in ecowomanism. How does an examination of the sermon reveal how preachers can speak prophetically about environmental justice, engage the biblical texts, and meaningfully engage the audience by empowering them to act for earth justice?

Ecowomanist Courses

Pedagogical Strategies

Preaching Black Earth is especially helpful for students in courses in ecowomanism and environmental studies because it models several different kinds of writings used to expand the discourse. For example, one teaching strategy helpful to students in ecowomanist and environmental justice courses is to consider the eco-poems as models to inspire their own poetry writing about earth justice. What connections can students make between their own activism and the activism they witness in the stories, sermons, and interviews?

Students can be invited to write a short poem, prayer, or reflection inspired by the eco-poetry to spark their own thinking about writing forms helpful for various audiences committed to earth justice.

A CONTEMPLATIVE MOMENT

May the earth be sustained, even as we enter a new age of climate change, and may the songs of these hearts breathe alive for a new day in which justice does roll down like water ~ throughout the earth and for the sake of all beings.

breathing earth

by *Melanie L. Harris*

breathing earth
let us
proclaim
a new way of being
interconnected
honoring
safe refuge
one to another
all
sacred
all
whole
all
free

PART I

Earth Wisdom, Word, and Active Compassion
Ecowomanist Sermons and Meditations

MELANIE L. HARRIS

The full embodiment and freedom of Black women is connected to their connection and healthy relationship with earth. As feminist scholar bell hooks suggests in her book *Sisters of the Yam: Black Women and Self Recovery*, Black women and Black peoples' freedom is deeply connected to planetary freedom because of the sacred worth and value in all beings and the eerie connection between the logics of domination witnessed in the assault on earth and the assault on many peoples of color, and especially Black lives, through hundreds of years of race-based exploitation in the United States. Noticing similarities in the logics used to justify unfair treatment of Black, Brown, and Indigenous peoples and their sufferings in the United States, ecowomanism examines how these sufferings are similar to the sufferings of the earth. The ecowomanist seven-step method can be applied for a deeper comparative view. It is an approach to environmental ethics that invites participants to take seriously their own eco-memory and helps them recall how their historical, racial, cultural, family, and individual relationships with earth connection and earth community originated. In taking this step, honoring experience, it is often the case that Black, Brown, and Indigenous people have a very different entry point or historical relationship with earth, including being subjugated by white settler colonial people and white slave-owning families to work the earth. That is, for most people of color, environmental justice is not just about recovery of the planet or raising awareness about the impact of climate change in communities of color; for many of us, environmental justice is also about racial and ecological reparations. To repair the earth, one must also be engaged in social relational building, healing, and transformation.

To this point, the sermons in part I of *Preaching Black Earth* speak directly to people of color in faith contexts, mostly Black Christian churches, seminaries, and communities wherein the message about the direct connection between divine justice and social justice are connected to earth justice. Political activist Stacey Abrams's sermon "Stewardship, Service, and Redemption: Called to be God's Ministers" opens the book by outlining a frame of Black women's activism in the environmental justice movement. She recounts her own journey into environmental justice and makes connections between this and her theological understanding of Scripture that invites us to deeply consider the impact of eco-sin on all beings.

Abrams's powerful sermon is followed by Elonda Clay's sermon "Exodus in a Warming World: An Ecowomanist Sermon," which opens from the point of recognizing the power of Black women's hands, voices, and beings in the environmental justice movement. The sermon specifically addresses issues of climate change meeting many communities of color in this moment. Strategically naming core foundations for ecowomanist thought, Clay's sermon ignites readers and thinkers to act now!

The meditative voice of Kenneth Ngwa opens with a reminder to all about what time it is on the planet. Pulling together excellent exegesis of the Hebrew text of Genesis 28:10–18 with a meditative mode that invites the hearer to truly be fully present in the present moment, Ngwa's sermon opens up dialogue about how we can maintain peace "in the midst of the storms" of climate change.

In her sermon, Sophía Betancourt demonstrates the brilliant unearthing of ecowomanism alive in the Unitarian Universalist tradition and creates room in this church to expand its notions of environment as established by Henry David Thoreau. By being inclusive of Black women's wisdom and work through a scholarly and artistic investigation into the patterns, practices, and rituals led by Black women working in Walden at the time Thoreau was writing, the sermon names the important work and voices of Black women and highlights the ways Black women have constructed environmentalism historically. Validating the work of these Black women's hands and their contributions to the environment, as well as the work of the hands of many Black peoples living and working near Walden, forces us to ask at least two deeper questions about the relevance of Thoreau's great foundations in

Part I: Earth Wisdom, Word, and Active Compassion   21

environmental thought. What do we make of the obvious absence of racial consciousness in Thoreau's work, and how might this absence obscure his insights on environmental preservation?

In a poetic acceptance speech given at the Samuel DeWitt Proctor Conference as a Beautiful Are the Feet Honoree, John Kinney's spontaneous sermon of thanksgiving allows us to see the radical eco-theological thread that weaves African cosmology into his thinking, learning, teaching, leading, and being. By reading his sermon we are awakened to a new possibility of shifting outside and beyond the colonized mind to embrace a decolonial ecology that remains embedded in many African indigenous religious traditions.

Finally, in this section, the striking and powerful words of Otis Moss III given as a TheoEd Talk at Emory University in 2022 take us on a defiant journey, inspiring us to take action by any greens necessary. Sharing the story of how Chicago's Trinity United Church of Christ Church stood up for truth and environmental justice action to spearhead its own initiative to restore Chicago neighborhoods and green spaces in communities of color, Moss engages a Black power, Black liberationist model of fighting for justice, and environmental justice specifically, by any greens necessary.

The power of the preached word in the tradition of Black preaching is deeply prophetic and enlivens new earth wisdom through the sermons you are about to read. As you read contemplatively, allow the deep confidence in these words and the historic power of the social movement building to motivate you to take action for environmental justice.

1

Stewardship, Service, and Redemption

Called to Be God's Ministers

STACEY ABRAMS

Sermon Delivered at the Festival of Homiletics, May 20, 2020

Thank you to the staff of the Festival of Homiletics, including Dr. Caroline Lewis and Dr. Don Elites. I'm grateful for the invitation to share my thoughts on this year's theme of preaching a new earth, climate, and creation. As I prepared my remarks, I hunted through the Scriptures searching for that perfect verse to speak to the challenge of our climate crisis, the scourge of environmental injustice, and the hope of redemption from our sins against the earth and our fellow inhabitants. I look to the pronouncements of Genesis, the ruminations of Ecclesiastes, the condemnation of Romans. Then my thoughts turned to the writer of Chronicles, specifically 2 Chronicles 7:11–22.

We have the obligation of stewardship, the obligation of service, and the obligation of redemption. When I was in college, I interned for two summers with the EPA, first as a junior college student working for the Environmental Criterion and Assessment Office in North Carolina and then as a new college grad working in Washington at the Office of Environmental Justice. In between, I wrote my college thesis on the issue of environmental racism, particularly in Cancer Alley in Louisiana, where industrial plants spewed toxic air, and Moss Point, Mississippi, where mills and incinerators poisoned thousands.

I grew up down the highway from Moss Point in Gulfport, Mississippi, with my five brothers and sisters, an hour's drive south from where my parents were born. It wasn't unusual for us to come home from church, change out of our Sunday clothes, and pile into the station wagon to head north to Hattiesburg. The trip had a pleasing familiarity.

Along the state highway, tea tree and holly trees crowded next to magnolia and cypress and the longleaf pines that gave that area its nickname, the piney woods. Our first stop was always to my father's family home on West Side Avenue. Railroad tracks bordered by thick foliage and a deep ravine set across the street from our grandparents' house. We'd jump out of the car, hurry up the cinder block steps, and impatiently bang on the door. Usually it was Granddaddy who teasingly barked at us, demanding to know who was at his house. The six of us swarmed inside, gathering kisses and hugs from him and our grandmother. Soon, though, I would head through the kitchen and out the back door across the yard to the squat cottage where my great grandmother Mumu lived.

During warm days, I would find her on the porch, shelling peas or snapping beans picked from her garden. I would take a seat next to her and for the minutes or hours I had of her time, I'd listened to stories about her garden, about the land. She'd come from a family of sharecroppers who had descended from slaves. But these women and men, though stripped of freedom and opportunity, tended the land with the grace that only comes from God. They understood the furrows that produced corn and cotton, greens and turnips. They cultivated the harvest, whether on another's land or on the plots they plowed themselves. Conservation of soil, of water, and of seeds came from a soul-deep understanding that they were called to preserve life. When my parents, grandparents, and Mumu gathered, they'd talk of fishing in the creeks in Forest County or off the piers on the Gulf Coast. They could name nearly every creature that swam in the region or the animals that roamed in the nearby woods. Food from sea or land was for consumption, not for sport. It was only later when I learned the language of environmental justice.

It was only then that I realized that Mumu, my great grandmother, was one of the first environmentalists I ever knew. Her teachings about respect for the land seeped into my consciousness. When I was growing up, Mumu never once used the term "environmental" to describe her connection to the earth and the sea and the sky. Instead, she spoke of the language of our shared faith, the obligations that guided stewardship, the obligation to tend to what we have been given on this earth, and how feeble sometimes our understanding of the basics may be. As Job chided his friends in Job 12:7–10: "But ask the animals and they will teach you, or the birds and the sky, and they will tell you; or speak to the earth, and it will teach you, or let the fish in the sea inform you. Which of all these does not know that the hand of the LORD has done this? In his hand is the life of every creature and the breath of all mankind" (Job 12:7–10 NIV).

This temple of God, this earth that we inhabit is sacred. Yet for centuries too many have turned their faces from the Lord. Those who would have been exemplars, models for us of how to live out the faith of David and honor the earth, have gone another way. We are confronted instead by the reality that too many are victims of the iniquities of those who worship false gods and poison this earth. The Native Americans battling an indifferent federal government to not only preserve their ancestral homes, but to protect the earth and its secrets from devastating destruction.

Indigenous cultures around the globe grapple with the horrifying consequences of invisibility to corporations and governments that seek the wealth of nations rather than the bounty of nature. Black and Brown communities are poisoned by toxic air and polluted waters because they cannot afford to escape incinerators, landfills, and a twisted corporate mantra that devalues life. And the vulnerable billions of marginalized and disadvantaged are buffeted by greed, shortsightedness, and natural disasters that decimate their islands, their farms, their coastlines, or their lives.

If we are to seek God's favor, we must tend to the earth, renewing the covenant of stewardship even in the midst of devastation. We owe this temple, the earth, our stewardship, but we also owe the Lord's people our service in the days when we have failed. This is what Solomon was warned of in the verses of 2 Chronicles. We are each of us called to tend to those who suffer, especially if we have forsaken our responsibilities and our relationships. To do so, we must acknowledge and respect our place in the universe. The Lord told Solomon, "I have heard your prayer and have chosen this place for myself as a temple for sacrifices" (7:12 NIV). I would argue that God's admonition is that our presence on this planet reflects the earth as the chosen temple, the place of worship and of stewardship. However, we cannot simply demand a renaissance where we fix the broken places. We must also fix the broken people that are assailed by the consequences of climate inaction. When I sat at Mumu's knee, my mother was a librarian, and my father was a shipyard worker. They raised us to have three responsibilities: go to church, go to school, and take care of one another. With the first pillar, they grounded us in faith because they understood how personal, how prophetic a relationship with the Lord could be for those who lived with less. When working-class poverty and casual racism scoured our sense of belonging, we could look to our spiritual lives for respite and direction. Education formed the second pillar: a call to fill our minds with the lessons of the world, to arm ourselves with capacity and knowledge so that we could navigate our way to more than we dreamed. The third pillar was service, taking care of each other. A demand that we embrace the communion of family. Family of the blood. Our band of eight and more. And also a broader notion that told us to serve others, the family of Earth.

Later, when my mom and dad answered their call to the ministry, both becoming United Methodist elders, I watched them continue to live the lessons they taught us. A faith that compelled them to pastor to the souls and the lives of others. Education that brought us to Georgia while they attended the Candler School of Theology at Emory University. And always taking care of each other, tending to the ill and visiting hospitals, helping and welcoming the homeless on Atlanta's streets who were shunned by others. Their daily example, like Mumu and her garden, demonstrated a fundamental duty to shepherd and stand for others. In these times when natural disasters beset the world, or when human-made calamities devour the ice caps or poison the poor, we must remember we are not forsaken if we are willing to right our ways again.

"At times I might shut up the heavens so that no rain falls, or command grasshoppers to devour your crops or send plagues among you. Then, if my people who are called by my name will humble themselves and pray and seek my face and turn from their wicked ways, I will hear from heaven and will forgive their sins and restore their land" (2 Chr. 7:13–14, NLT).

But so much like in these Scriptures, in the question of faith or forgiveness, the work of the righteous cannot be done without also pursuing the testament of justice. As the prophet Moses notes in Deuteronomy 16:20, "Justice, and only justice, you shall follow, that you may live and inherit the land that the LORD your God is giving you" (ESV).

My parents taught us to serve regardless of our own circumstances. And as members of that oxymoronic notion, the working poor. My parents weren't content to simply worry about us. No, they decided to show us, as they always had, that no matter how little we possessed and how shaky our situation, there were always others in our community with less. They wanted us to grow up understanding that regardless of our problems or our lack, there were those with less and it was our job to serve them.

Their faith journey led them back to Mississippi in 1993, where both of my parents pastored. By 2005, they were living in Wiggins, Mississippi, where my mother led a congregation at H. A. Brown Memorial United Methodist Church, and my father headed up their outreach ministry. In August of 2005, Hurricane Katrina ravaged the communities huddled around the Gulf of Mexico, striking even the inland town of Wiggins. Wind speeds of eighty-one miles per hour ripped up the center of the state and a tornado touched down somewhere in the county.

From Atlanta, I drove my youngest sister home to check on our parents twelve days after the storm. As we traveled down the highway, the ravages of the extraordinary hurricane spoke from every downed tree, every mangled bit of metal. The lovely piney woods of my childhood had been ripped away. In their place stood root balls that stared at the sun and the aftermath, and the sturdy pines that once brushed the sky at one hundred feet or more had collapsed into the soft, rain-soaked ground. I remember how Jeanine sat motionless as we sped past a stand of pines scattered like toothpicks. Black loamy soil seemed to beg for care, for rejuvenation. "Primary succession" is a term used most often to describe the aftermath of volcanoes when lava has burned away all natural life. But in the wake of a natural disaster exacerbated by human-made hubris, the ecosystem turned to this process to create a legacy, a future.

We reached my parents at the parsonage where the roof had been damaged by the storm. The smell of wet permeated the entire house and light seeped in through the holes visible in the roof above. In the master bedroom, the bed had been moved to the center to avoid the waterfall that came with any rain. An ominous black mold crawled along the logs on the ceiling. But rather than mourn with my parents, we joined an assembly line of church volunteers next door where donations from around the country were pouring into mom's church. The semi-trailer was deep, deep enough to fill the half court gym. We'd been home for fifteen minutes, but we got to work. Night was coming soon and we knew the next day would bring hundreds in search of aid. Before we left Wiggins a few days later, the number of hungry, displaced families seeking succor would reach nearly 1,500, and in weeks they would soar to many more thousands.

In the litany that is creation and climate, our voices must lift up the obligation of service to those who have been hurt by human inaction, especially to the poor. Famine, drought, disease, and pandemic are exacerbated by climate change, and the natural disasters that once hit infrequently now become a near constant threat. To meet these challenges of survival, we must be called into service, into action in America and around the world. Families that have the weakest grasp on survival are decimated by the shocks of climate change and by inaction.

This is antithetical to the story of creation, that God's children would be destroyed by a failure to steward the earth and serve God's people. However, we can redeem our failures and supplicate to the Lord for our transgressions against the temple.

We must acknowledge that we are at war in a great massive battle that has been waged for centuries, if not millennia. It is a war spoken of in every manner of religious text, be it the Bible, the Qur'an, the Torah. It is the internal human struggle to do right by others, to do right by the earth. It is the reason we are gathered here today. We are called to be agents of radical change in an era of revolution where only dramatic, bold action will save our planet.

But silence in a revolution is a dangerous thing. It suggests complacency and defeat and complicity. This conference exists to explore that our foes do exist, but that a redemption is in the works. The Lord warned Solomon, "And though this Temple is impressive now, all who pass by will be appalled. They will ask, 'Why did the LORD do such terrible things to this land and to this Temple?'" (2 Chr. 7:21 NLT). From your pulpits and platforms, from your stages and in your sermons, you are called upon to rise up against this mockery that we have made of the earth. To rebuke those who would ignore the dangers of unchecked energy production, who would pit science against greedy lies.

Those who see the spread of COVID-19 and worry more about the loss of dollars than the loss of lives are not those called. Pandemics—from Ebola, to SARS, to COVID-19—are cries for a unity of nations that must protect us all regardless of borders. Yet in the most prosperous nation on earth, eight thousand people have lost their lives and more than a million struggle against the infection. As unemployment rises and spirits fall we will be tempted to put aside the responsibility of climate action, but that is the wrong moment and the wrong choice. In an age of no accountability, Pharisees will lament that we cannot afford to serve the poorest of our people, to extend humanitarian aid, to cooperate on a global health security system or a global climate action.

The preaching of creation must lay bare the insidious tyranny of how our actions risk our future, and that what we face now is a foretaste of climate refugees driven from barren lands and drowned states. There is a direct connection to the challenges of today's crises and what awaits us if we do not speak prophetically about drilling off the coast into endangered waters or deforestation and chemical spills that yield persistent hunger and uninhabitable lands. Revolution and redemption demand that we speak truth to the powers that will deliver education, economic parity, health care, clean energy, and through it, environmental justice.

Today, though, too many of us are not only silent, but also our vision has grown dim. Women and men of compassion and capacity, like those joining in this discussion, have struggled long and hard, and on some days, it must seem impossible to see a better tomorrow. And here, I think, is where hope enters. Where God's offer to Solomon is that redemption is possible. As those who preach and teach a resurrection story, you know the truest path lies not in simply passing the torch. Its single promise rests in passing the torch and then standing close and sharing the light. We, in our collective human history, have never had a moment where time has broken neatly into before and after, despite the machinations of historians. Time is fluid and continuous, as is the struggle for equality for every manner of man, woman, and child. So, too, is the struggle to redeem the promise of the earth, whether in a Paris Agreement or in a voting booth in November even as we know that movements to suppress votes abound.

For this revolution, for this redemption to see its way and speak its truth, we must center on the opportunity to use small actions to show what we believe. Redemption must find its "now warriors" in the seasoned activist, and the worried grandparents, and the teenagers seeking a voice. The warriors who fight the good fight today must grab the hands of the unemployed and the unacknowledged and the unseen. Our victory lies in our minds, our voices, and our hands when applied to the actions of change.

Environmental leaders eloquently and brilliantly describe the issues facing our world. They find the heart of our struggle, and they name it, giving us not only an explanation, but also a prescription for change. And their brilliance can only be magnified when faith leaders call for testimony in their own style and fashion and take up the challenge to speak honestly about the connection between our obligations to the Word and our allegiance to the world. To take action on climate. Because we have foes who know the power of denying the truth.

You have spent lifetimes building community block by block, street by street. Your congregants have fed the hungry and registered voters and helped the drug addicted. Each of you is called into this ministry every day. The Ministry of Redemption requires that we as children of God demand what Esther demanded, that we refuse to allow the destruction of our people by those who care nothing for their survival. In very real terms, the Ministry of Redemption calls upon each of you to speak aloud about how in large and small ways we can tackle the issues of climate action and pursue sustainable development. The United Nations identifies seventeen simple goals for restoring and rescuing the planet, like donating what we don't use rather than tossing food and other items aside, wasting less, and buying only what we need and using water carefully, supporting local farmers, and recycling.

But there are systemic challenges that are intertwined with our obligations: Educate our children about what the world faces and equip them to find answers in their time. Empower women and girls to continue to expand the face of leadership and the voices of change. Speak plainly and repeatedly about the real choices we face in the coming years, in the coming days. COVID-19 will continue to take Black and Brown lives at disproportionate rates. Economic injustice leads to cycles of poverty and disrepair. To save God's creation, we must make the choice of whether we allow our families to suffer without health care when asthma clogs their lungs, or whether we shift the burden of taxation onto the weakest shoulders to force a landfill into their neighborhood. These are climate action steps that determine if we are fit and equipped to fight back.

We must choose if we want to be a nation that warehouses its poor in places devoid of opportunity or a nation that nurtures them in the wide spaces of progress and access. These questions are woven together because they tell of whether we are in pursuit of redemption or pretense. Christians and the Ministry of Creation and Climate must ask the tough questions, like: What will our silence mean for the soul of our nation? And why is it my responsibility to speak up and call for action? To be redeemed, we are required to engage ourselves in the world of government. Change cannot stand divided from the obligation of politics and government

Our collective mission must be to pool our resources to serve all as those in the Ministry of Service. We must demand of our politicians that we renew the land, protect the vulnerable, and plan for the climate refugees—domestic and international—that will need our aid. That we pass laws not based on the hysteria of the moment of energy prices soaring or on the lies told to hide how our actions have bleached the coral reefs, but that our laws be grounded in the clearest vision for how we reach our future and restore our nation and our world.

We must register citizens to vote and ask all parishioners if they have completed the census because to vote is to demand action and to be counted, to be included in the story of America, and receive the economic and political power due. Every person must be included in the 2020 census. Thus, when our politicians and public servants do not listen, we have the power to put them out of office and, if need be, take up office ourselves. When our judges refuse to use the wisdom of Solomon, then we must demand that the robes of justice be worn by women and men of good conscience and sound mind. Preaching a new Earth requires stewardship, service, and a revolutionary redemption. We have for too long made a mockery of God's temple, sinned against creation. But the joy of our faith is the constant promise of renewal, of revival.

If we are willing to set ourselves to the task and never waver, let us pray.

> Dear Lord, we meet you today
> in the space separated by distance,
> but joined by our faith.
> And we meet you in our hearts,
> where we each believe in your power and your mercy.
> On this day, we come to you
> as your daughter Ruth did,
> and we repeat her pledge
> to "entreat [us] not to leave thee,
> or to return from following after thee.
> Whither thou goest? So shall [we] go?
> Your people shall be our people."

Stewardship, Service, and Redemption

Oh, Lord, our God.
Mold us, Lord,
as you did your disciples before us,
to be as righteous as Peter,
to be as wise as Solomon,
to be as faithful as Mary Magdalene,
calling us to be your ministers
in stewardship and service and in redemption.

Gird our souls to battle
the demons of uncertainty and timidity
of complacency and apathy.
Engage our minds in the troubles of the world.
Worry us until we have no other place
than serving these, your children,
and protecting this earth.

Lift our hands in supplication
and work them to your will
to build a world
that can contain our devotion
but never contain our joy.
Fill our hearts with obedience
so that we may not rest
until there is a blessed peace.
Hold our feet steady
as we continue our life's journey
and move us in your service as your ministers.
And let us all say,
Amen.

2

Exodus in a Warming World

An Ecowomanist Sermon

ELONDA CLAY

Sermon Written for Ecowomanist Leadership Retreat, Spring 2024

INTRODUCTION

The story of Exodus has always been a beacon of hope and a compass pointing us toward liberation in our collective consciousness. It has inspired freedom songs and civil rights movements, has been etched into the sermons of Martin Luther King Jr., and has given strength to the weary and courage to the fearful. Today, as we stand at the precipice of a climate crisis, this ancient tale takes on a new relevance and urgency.

In the thick of this crisis, I invite you to journey with me through the lens of the Exodus narrative. We stand before the vast sea of change, between the known dangers behind us and the vast wilderness of uncertainties ahead of us. We are much like the Israelites, caught between Pharaoh's armies and the Red Sea, threatened by an oppressive past and an unknown future. Yet, the story of Exodus teaches us that liberation is possible, that God makes a way where there seems to be no way. The parting of the Red Sea is a symbol of hope in the face of seemingly insurmountable challenges—an embodiment of divine intervention leading us from the perils of oppression toward the promise of liberation.

But the liberation we speak of today is not just for us as individuals or communities. We also speak of the liberation for creation from the clutches of human-made destruction. Today our Pharaoh is the oppressive and exploitative systems of production and consumption, capitalism's relentless hunger for profit that feeds on the earth's resources, and the systems of power that perpetuate environmental injustice.

Like the Israelites were to Pharaoh, we are enslaved by these systems. These systems profit from our consumption, perpetuating a culture of waste and excess that is causing the rapid depletion of our earth's resources and accelerating climate change. They benefit from the social and economic inequities that they create and uphold. They make us complicit in their deeds by ensnaring us in a web of convenience, comfort, and false promises of prosperity and progress. They build mighty cities and monuments to their power while the earth groans under their weight.

This bondage is not physical, as it was for the Israelites, but it is just as real and just as oppressive. It is the bondage of mindsets that prioritize profit over people, power over justice, and domination over stewardship. It is the bondage of a culture that values accumulation over sharing, competition over cooperation, and exploitation over care. It is the bondage of worldviews that see the earth as a resource to be used rather than a sacred gift to be cherished and protected.

But like the Israelites, we also dream of liberation. We long for the promised land—a world where justice and sustainability prevail, where the earth and all its inhabitants thrive, and where the dignity and rights of every creature are respected and protected. We aspire to a world where the climate crisis is averted, where clean air, pure water, fertile soil, and abundant biodiversity are not just a distant dream but a living reality.

However, to reach this promised land, we must first leave Egypt, our place of bondage. This requires courage to confront the Pharaohs of our time—the powerful corporations, the apathetic governments, and the oppressive systems that profit from the destruction of our Earth. It demands the willingness to dismantle the structures of power and privilege that underpin these systems. It calls for repentance from our ways of consumption and waste that contribute to the climate crisis. It urges us to resist the false idols of wealth, power, and success that our culture worships.

Our journey to liberation, like that of the Israelites, is not a straightforward path. It is fraught with uncertainties, challenges, and risks. It requires faith and persistence, resilience, and hope. Yet it is also a journey toward a new vision of community and interconnectedness, toward an ecowomanist perspective that values all life, human and nonhuman alike, and sees in each a reflection of the divine.

In this postindustrial wilderness, we learn to resist the illusion of control that Pharaoh's empire promised. We learn to depend not on the excesses and extravagance of Egypt, but on the manna that God provides each day—a lesson in sustainability and sufficiency. As we decolonize our minds and hearts from the imperial logic of domination and extraction, we learn to honor the earth as our kin, to live in harmony with its rhythms and cycles, and to participate in its healing and renewal.

We learn that our liberation is bound up with the liberation of the earth. Just as Moses could not be free while his people were enslaved, we cannot be free while the earth is oppressed. Just as the liberation of the Israelites required the dismantling of Pharaoh's empire, our liberation requires the dismantling of the oppressive systems that exploit the earth and its vulnerable communities. This understanding moves us from an anthropocentric view of the world, where humans are the center, to an eco-centric view, where all life is interconnected and interdependent.

This journey requires faith—faith in a God who hears the cry of the oppressed, whether they are enslaved people or suffering ecosystems. It requires trust—trust in the promise of liberation, in the dream of the promised land. It requires hope—hope that a better world is possible, and that we have the power to bring it into being.

In the face of the overwhelming challenge of the climate crisis, the story of Exodus reminds us that we are not alone. God is with us, guiding us, strengthening us, and calling us to act for justice. The same God who led the Israelites out of Egypt and through the Red Sea is with us now, leading us toward a future where all life can flourish.

As we embark on this journey of liberation, let us draw inspiration from the strength and resilience of Black women who, throughout history, have faced the twin Pharaohs of racial and gender oppression with courage and determination. Their fight for justice, their resistance against domination, and their vision of a better world light our path.

In their struggles and victories, we see a reflection of our own journey from bondage to liberation. We are reminded that liberation is not just a destination but a process, not just an end but a journey. It is a journey that we undertake together, for our liberation is bound up with each other and with the Earth. And just as the Israelites sang a song of victory after crossing the Red Sea, we too shall sing a song of hope, of resilience, and of liberation. For the earth is the Lord's, and its fullness thereof.

In the words of the African American spiritual, "Go down, Moses, way down in Egypt's land, tell old Pharaoh, to let my people go!" Today, we are called to go down to the depths of our hearts, to confront the pharaohs within us and around us, and to set our earth, our communities, and ourselves free. The journey may be long, the wilderness may be vast, but the promise of liberation is sure. The promised land awaits us, not just a land flowing with milk and honey, but a world flourishing with justice, sustainability, and love.

Let us heed this call. Let us begin this journey. For the sake of our earth and for the sake of us all, let us escape Egypt and embrace the unknown, for the potential of the promised land beckons us forward.

ESCAPING EGYPT, LANDING IN WILDERNESS

Today, we find ourselves much like the Israelites: on the precipice of a vast and unfamiliar landscape. Our Egypt, our place of bondage, is a world held hostage by the chains of consumerism, the tyranny of fossil fuels, and the oppression of unchecked capitalism. We are escaping a land where corporations spew toxins into our atmosphere, where seas are acidified, and where our siblings of color bear the brunt of environmental exploitation. Our Egypt is a world that privileges the wealthy few over the impoverished many, a world where petrochemical plants poison low-income, majority-Black communities with carcinogenic toxins. Our journey, much like the Israelites', is one fraught with uncertainty and unease. We are leaving the known dangers of our Egypt for the vast, uncharted wilderness of climate change.

As we stand on this precipice, we might be filled with fear. Like the Israelites, we may even yearn for the familiar oppression of our Egypt. This nostalgia for our place of bondage, this longing for a past that was simpler, though unjust, is a powerful force that can stall our progress. Yet, we must resist this urge. For while the wilderness may be fraught with dangers, it is also filled with possibilities. The wilderness is a place of transformation, of revelation, and of liberation. It is a place where we can reimagine our relationship with the earth and with each other, where we can lay the groundwork for a world that is just, sustainable, and equitable.

The wilderness we face is one marked by rising temperatures and sea levels, by increasing frequency and intensity of floods, droughts, tornadoes, and heatwaves, by the loss of biodiversity and the degradation of ecosystems. It is not just a physical landscape but a social and political one as well. It is home to the bitter waters of climate denial and apathy, of policy inaction and corporate greed. It is a wilderness where those who contribute the least to climate change, such as the island nations that depend on the fish that are now being killed by acidified oceans, are the ones who suffer the most from its effects.

Yet, we must not let the daunting challenges of change deter us. For in this wilderness, we also find opportunities for radical transformation and healing. As we traverse this wilderness, we can strip away the shackles of our consumeristic and exploitative ways and embrace new paradigms of living that are in harmony with the earth and each other. We can leave behind the hierarchies and divisions that our Egypt fostered and build communities that are rooted in equity, inclusivity, and justice.

Here, we can learn from the wisdom of Black women, who have long been at the forefront of struggles for liberation and justice. Black women, like Sojourner Truth and Harriet Tubman, guided their people through the wilderness of slavery and segregation to the promise of freedom and equality. Today, Black women are leading the way in the fight against the climate crisis, advocating for intersectional solutions that address the complex and interconnected problems of racism, sexism, and environmental degradation.

These Black women-led social movements do not simply address one issue but recognize the interconnectedness of all our struggles. They understand that we cannot separate the fight for racial justice from the fight for climate justice, or the struggle for gender equality from the struggle for ecological sustainability. Movements like #MeToo, Say Her Name, and Black Lives Matter, guided by the principles of Womanism and Black queer feminism, center the voices and experiences of those most affected by the climate crisis while also challenging the colonial structures of power that perpetuate it.

We can learn from these movements how to cultivate resilience, adaptability, and a spirit of communal responsibility. We can learn how to draw on our spiritual resources, our traditions, and our collective wisdom to navigate the challenges of this wilderness.

PLACE MAKING IN UNCERTAIN TIMES: THE IMPACTS OF CLIMATE CHANGE ON PLACE

We are faced with the challenge of place-making in uncertain times. Throughout history, Earth's climate has changed, reflecting the complex interactions and dependencies of the cosmic, solar, oceanic, terrestrial, atmospheric, and living components that make up planet Earth's systems.

We are coming to terms with the impacts of climate change on the places we call home. From disappearing islands and coastal cities threatened by rising sea levels to communities ravaged by more frequent and severe wildfires, floods, heatwaves, tornadoes, snowstorms, and hurricanes, climate change is reshaping our landscapes and our lives. Yet, this challenge is not equally distributed. Just as the Israelites faced different challenges in the desert, so too do our communities face varying degrees of vulnerability to climate change.

One of the most significant challenges of our time is the disproportionate impact of climate change on historically marginalized communities, especially Black communities. These communities are often located in areas most vulnerable to the effects of climate change, such as low-lying coastal regions and urban heat islands. They are also the least equipped to cope with these impacts due to decades of systemic discrimination and disinvestment.

As we navigate the climate crisis, we must bear in mind that climate change is not just a scientific or technical issue, but a deeply social and political one. It is a manifestation of our failure to live in harmony with the earth and each other, of our failure to uphold the principles of justice and equality. It is a challenge that calls on us not only to reduce our greenhouse gas emissions, but also to dismantle the structures of power and privilege that perpetuate inequality and injustice.

Despite the hardships they faced, the Israelites were able to create a sense of place and community in the wilderness. They were able to forge a new identity and a new vision of the world, guided by their faith in God and their commitment to justice and equality.

Today, we are called to do the same. We are called to build communities that are resilient and adaptable, that are rooted in a deep respect for the earth and a deep commitment to justice and equality. We are called to create places that are not just physically safe and sustainable, but also socially just and spiritually fulfilling. We are called to make a home in this wilderness, not out of fear or desperation but out of hope and faith in a better world.

CLIMATE CHANGE AND BLACK COMMUNITIES

Now let's delve into the specific struggles and trials faced by our Black communities in the climate crisis, paralleling the plight of the Israelites as they faced their wilderness. We have seen that the impact of climate change is not evenly distributed, that it preys upon those who have been marginalized and disenfranchised by a system that has systematically devalued them. Just like the Israelites, our Black communities bear the weight of this struggle disproportionately.

Our tale begins with a storm, not unlike the storms that marked the beginning of the Israelites' journey. This storm, Hurricane Katrina, is etched into the memory of our nation as one of the most devastating natural disasters in recent history.

This deadly storm devastated New Orleans, but its impacts were felt most acutely in the city's majority-Black neighborhoods. These communities, situated in low-lying areas, were the hardest hit by the flooding. Their residents, many of whom lacked the resources to evacuate, were left stranded in their homes, cut off from emergency services and essential supplies. In the aftermath of the storm, these communities were also the last to receive aid and the slowest to recover.

Katrina is a stark reminder of the intersection of climate injustice and environmental injustice. It highlights how the effects of climate change are exacerbated by systemic racism and socioeconomic disparities. Yet, it also bears witness to the resilience and tenacity of Black communities in the face of adversity. In the aftermath of Katrina, it was the local community organizations, led by Black women, that were the most effective in providing immediate relief and driving the recovery effort.

The impact of climate change on Black communities extends beyond these extreme weather events. As we learn from the work of our Black feminist scholars, womanists, and activists, the climate crisis exacerbates existing social and economic inequalities. It is tied to systems of racism, sexism, and heterosexism, systems that have oppressed and marginalized Black women for centuries.

The gentrification of our cities, for instance, has pushed Black communities into low-income neighborhoods that are more prone to flooding, urban heat islands, and other environmental hazards. These communities lack the resources and infrastructure to cope with the effects of climate change, making them even more vulnerable to its impacts.

Simultaneously, we are seeing the effects of environmental racism, where hazardous waste sites, landfills, and polluting industries are disproportionately located in Black and Brown communities. The toxic pollution from these sites compounds the health risks posed by climate change, leading to higher rates of respiratory illnesses, cancer, and other health problems in these communities.

Yet, in the face of these adversities, Black communities have shown remarkable resilience and capacity for survival. Their survival is not just a testament to their strength, but a critique of the systems that have put them in this position. Their survival is a call to action, a call to dismantle the structures of power and privilege that perpetuate these injustices.

In this fight, they are not alone. They are joined by a diverse coalition of activists and organizations, many of them led by Black women, who are working tirelessly to combat climate change and environmental injustice. They are pushing for policies that prioritize the needs and rights of the most vulnerable, advocating for sustainable and equitable solutions to the climate crisis. Whether it's advocating for food security, pushing for clean energy solutions, or engaging in transformative conversations around climate justice, Black women are first responders for climate justice. Their work is a testament to the transformative power of faith, resilience, and community. Their work reminds us that the struggle against climate change is not just a fight for survival, but a fight for justice, for liberation, and for a better world.

Majora Carter, an urban revitalization strategist from the South Bronx, turned a waste dump into a waterfront park, providing her community not only with a much-needed green space, but a beacon of hope. Carter's story is one of countless examples of Black women turning oppressive structures into liberation spaces. Her work, rooted in the understanding of the interlocking systems of oppression, reshapes the physical and metaphorical landscapes of her community.

Similarly, consider the awe-inspiring work of Naomi Davis, founder of Blacks in Green (B.I.G), a Chicago-based organization that has championed energy efficiency, green jobs, and sustainability in Chicago's African American neighborhoods. In September 2021, the organization secured the historic preservation of the Emmett Till home and created the Mamie Till-Mobley Forgiveness Garden. Davis's relentless advocacy underscores the profound relationship between environmental justice and climate justice.

These women and countless others are the bearers of the promise of a better world. We are reminded that our fight against climate change is not merely a fight against rising temperatures and destructive weather events. It is a fight against systems of oppression, against structures of power that have long valued profit over people. It is a fight that requires us to question and dismantle these systems, to seek justice and liberation for all people and for our planet.

In the face of the climate crisis, Black communities are not merely surviving, they are leading the way toward a better world. For it is in this struggle, in this shared journey, that we find our way toward a promised land, a world of justice, liberation, and love for all.

RETHINKING THE PROMISED LAND AS PLACE: A REINTERPRETATION OF A TRADITIONAL AFRICAN AMERICAN INTERPRETATION OF EXODUS

Today, we find ourselves in a similar wilderness. We have been enslaved by a global system that prioritizes consumption that is driven by greed and the incessant need for growth. This system, much like Pharaoh's Egypt, has brought untold suffering upon our communities and our planet.

From Enslavement to Freedom

As we face the environmental crisis of our time, we are called upon to seek our own liberation. This is a liberation from the forces of capitalism and colonialism that have plundered our earth and exploited its resources. It is a liberation from the systems of power that prioritize profit over the well-being of our communities and our planet.

It is also a liberation from the mindset of overconsumption, from the belief that we are separate from our environment. As the Israelites discovered in the desert, our liberation comes not only from escaping physical bondage, but from freeing our minds from the structures of power that have shaped our worldviews.

This liberation, however, is not a solitary journey. As we navigate our way through the wilderness of the climate crisis, we must remember that our liberation is bound up with the liberation of all people. Our struggle for climate justice is also a struggle for racial justice, for economic justice, for gender justice. It is a struggle that calls upon us to challenge and dismantle the intersecting systems of oppression that shape our world.

Adapting to Life Away from Fossil Fuels, Overconsumption, and Disregard for Limited Resources

As we move away from a lifestyle marked by consumption and resource excess, we are called upon to reevaluate our relationship with our environment. Just as the Israelites had to learn to live sustainably in the desert, we must learn to live in harmony with our earth.

This means adapting to a lifestyle that respects the limits of our planet, that values sustainability and regeneration over exploitation and destruction. It means shifting from a mindset of scarcity, where resources are hoarded and exploited, to one of abundance, where resources are shared and revered.

The story of the manna in the wilderness provides a powerful illustration of this shift. The Israelites were instructed to gather only as much manna as they needed for each day and to trust in God's provision for their needs. In the same way, we are called upon to trust in the abundance of our earth, to take only what we need, and to ensure that resources are equitably shared among all people.

Surviving Loss: The Lamentations in the Desert

In the Exodus narrative, the loss and grief experienced by the Israelites as they wandered in the desert was profound. The story paints vivid images of desolation, thirst and hunger, and a deep yearning for a home that was no longer theirs. These scenes, as bleak as they may appear, echo the sentiments and lived realities of communities worldwide, particularly Black communities, as they bear the brunt of climate change.

In the twenty-first century, we are witnessing a slow, creeping exodus that is less marked by the sudden drama of a parting sea and more by the subtle, insidious effects of climate emergency. Global temperatures are escalating, precipitating disasters such as floods, hurricanes, and wildfires, whose cataclysmic impact dwarf those of the biblical plagues. According to climate scientists at the National Oceanic and Atmospheric Administration (N.O.A.A), the rate of warming over the past half-century is about double the rate over the past century, highlighting the rapidly deteriorating state of our planet. Moreover, warming is largely human-induced, stemming from the increased concentration of greenhouse gases in the atmosphere, such as carbon dioxide and methane, mainly resulting from fossil fuel burning for electricity, heat, and transportation.

The lamentations in our modern-day desert take on new forms. There is the weeping mother in Bangladesh, cradling her child as they are displaced by flooding—a natural disaster now intensified by rising sea levels and abnormal rainfall patterns. In the Lake Chad basin, the steady shrinking of the lake due to extended periods of drought, climate change, and extensive water withdrawal threatens nearly forty million people in Chad, Cameroon, Niger, and Nigeria. There is the desperate plea of the family in Florida, praying for mercy as they lose their home to a hurricane. These are the faces of climate grief—mourning their own personal exoduses triggered by our warming world.

As we revisit the Exodus narrative and its subsequent desert wanderings, we find a God who is deeply present in the midst of suffering, a God who grieves with God's people, and a God who acts in the face of injustice. The story of the Israelites' desert sojourn is not a story of abandonment; rather, it is a story of divine solidarity, of survival, and, ultimately, of liberation.

The call to survive loss in the face of climate change is a call to recognize the grief and lamentation that accompanies this crisis. We need to make space in our hearts and our communities to mourn the losses inflicted by the climate crisis. This mourning is both an act of remembrance and a call to action. It honors those who have suffered and continue to suffer from the impacts of climate change. It also disrupts our complacency, urging us to actively fight against the forces that perpetuate climate injustice.

In the Exodus narrative, the Israelites' lamentations were not expressions of hopeless despair; they were acts of defiant hope, testimonies of a people who refused to be silenced by their oppressors. Our climate grief can be transformative in a similar manner. It can stir us to cry out against the destructive systems that have led us into this climate crisis. It can inspire us to work toward a world that values all of creation, a world where the earth is not exploited for profit but nurtured for future generations.

As we grapple with the immense grief that the climate crisis brings, let us remember that survival is not a passive state of existence but a radical act of resistance. It is resistance against oppressive systems that exploit both people and the planet. It is resistance against narratives of doom that tell us the fight is lost. And it is resistance against the despair that threatens to engulf us.

The Exodus story shows us that surviving loss is more than merely getting through the desert; it is about transforming it. The desert, a place of desolation and death, becomes a site of revelation and rebirth. The Israelites, under God's guidance, learn to build community, to create life-sustaining systems in a place of death. They learn to see beyond their present reality, holding onto the hope of a promised land.

Surviving the loss wrought by climate change demands a similar transformative gaze. It is a gaze that refuses to accept the destruction of our planet as an inevitable outcome. It is a gaze that envisions a world where Black communities are no longer disproportionately affected by environmental disasters. It is a gaze that sees beyond the desert of the present, daring to dream of a sustainable and equitable future.

Our lamentations, like the Israelites', can be a source of strength. Our tears can water the seeds of a climate justice movement that seeks to dismantle systems of oppression and construct in their place systems of care that respect the earth and all its inhabitants.

Today, our common home, the earth, is being usurped by those who seek to profit from its resources without regard for the consequences. Our inheritance—the clean air, the diverse ecosystems, the bountiful seas—is being handed over to the relentless machinery of overconsumption and disregard for limited resources. Our lament, then, is not just for what we have lost, but also for what we stand to lose if we don't act urgently.

But, like the biblical lamentations, our cries are not devoid of hope. They bear witness to our resolve to fight for a just world. They fuel our pursuit for environmental justice, echoing through the halls of power and resonating in the hearts of those committed to change. Our laments, steeped in the spirit of the exodus, become rallying cries, inspiring action and demanding justice.

In the face of loss and devastation, let us remember that we are a people of the exodus. We are survivors, able to withstand the heat of the desert and the bitterness of loss. In this climate crisis, we must harness the power of our shared grief to ignite the spark of change. For it is in our collective lament that we find our collective strength. And it is in this strength that we find the hope and the means to traverse our warming world, making a way out of no way, until we reach a place of justice and peace—a truly promised land.

We are called to transform our lamentations into action, our despair into hope, our desert into a home. For in the midst of the climate crisis, we have the opportunity to imagine and create a new world, just like the Israelites imagined and eventually reached their promised land. Let our surviving of loss thus be an act of defiance and an affirmation of life in the face of climate change.

Making Promised Land Anew: Referencing How the Notion of Promised Land in African American Interpretations of the Exodus Story Has Changed Over Time

In the grand arc of our collective struggle, now we stand, gazing across the troubled waters of a heating planet into a future where we must envision a new promised land, one shaped by our collective will to ensure that all people, and the very Earth itself, can flourish.

The sacred text, so often echoed in our songs and sermons, speaks to the God-given right to a land of abundance, the promised inheritance that awaits at the end of a long journey. But in this critical moment, we must revisit and reinterpret this promise. Today, our promised land cannot be one seized from others, but one shared with all. It must be a place where the mighty hand of domination is replaced with the open palm of cooperation. It must be a place where the opulence of a few does not come at the cost of many, and where the earth is not a possession to be exploited, but a living entity to be respected.

In the African American interpretation of the Exodus story, the promised land represented a place of freedom, away from the shackles of slavery. After the Civil War, the promised land was depicted as a return to Africa or the move to northern cities during the Great Migration. During the civil rights movement, the promised land meant full inclusion and equality in American life and during the Black power movement, emancipation meant autonomy for Black communities, freedom from police brutality, equal access to housing and education, and full employment. In each movement, the vision of the promised land reflected the aspirations and struggles of the time.

But what does the promised land look like in the face of the current climate crisis? In a world where the very air we breathe and the water we drink is threatened by our own actions or indifference, where our children inherit a planet in peril, the vision of the promised land must be one of not just personal freedom but collective survival.

As we imagine this new promised land, let us draw wisdom from the ecowomanist perspective that merges environmental justice with the Black women's social and climate justice perspectives. In the merging of these three, we can find a pathway to a promised land where environmental justice is achieved, where systemic racism is dismantled, and where every human being, regardless of their race, gender, or economic status, has a chance at a healthy life.

A promised land must no longer signify a place, but an idea—a concept of justice and equity. It must be about equitable distribution of resources, about respecting the rights of Indigenous peoples and marginalized communities. It is about making room at the table for everyone and ensuring that all voices are heard, especially those that have been silenced or sidelined.

The pathways to reduce the severity of climate change are well understood, but they require political will, innovative thinking, and an acknowledgment of the historical and continuing contributions to the crisis. We need to shift from fossil fuels to renewable energy, we need to move away from a disposable culture, and we need to create a new system that values people and the planet over profit.

In our quest for this new promised land, we have the opportunity to redefine what freedom looks like. Instead of a freedom that promotes unlimited consumption, we can aspire to a freedom that promotes harmony with nature and respect for all forms of life. We can strive for a freedom that not only tolerates but celebrates diversity, that rejects discrimination and inequality, and that works toward the betterment of all communities.

The path to the promised land was never easy, and it won't be easy now. But as the Exodus story tells us, with faith, perseverance, and the guiding hand of the Divine, it is a path that can be traversed. As we stand in this pivotal moment, let us choose the path of justice, equity, and environmental stewardship. Let us reimagine the promised land, not as a place of material abundance, but as a paradigm of holistic well-being—for people, for creatures, for our shared planet.

As we collectively reshape this vision of our promised land, let us also redefine who leads us to it. If the traditional narrative centers on Moses, the charismatic, chosen liberator, the time now calls for a shift in focus. The world we live in and the crises we face require not one Moses, but many, and not just the charismatic figures at the front, but those unnamed and often overlooked individuals at the heart of our communities. From young climate activists on global platforms, to the local community leaders advocating for environmental justice; from the Indigenous women who safeguard biodiversity, to the Black mothers fighting for clean air and water for their children—these are the true leaders guiding us toward the promised land. These are the individuals embodying Zora Neale Hurston's vision of the collective building a world of freedom together, as presented in her book *Moses, Man of the Mountain*.

It is important that we recognize and appreciate these leaders. For they are the ones who, like the midwives Shiphrah and Puah, act not out of obligation to authority but from a sense of justice and respect for life. They remind us that leadership can be nurturing, can be communal, and most importantly, it can be shared.

The promised land we seek must be one that embraces these shared leadership models, where power is not hoarded but disseminated, and where the well-being of the collective triumphs over individual gain. This promised land must also recognize the earth as an equal stakeholder, as a living entity that sustains us, that nurtures us, that, too, demands respect, care, and a seat at the decision-making table.

And, in this quest for our new promised land, let us never forget that we are not alone. We walk this path guided by the wisdom of those who came before us, arm-in-arm with those who share our struggle now, and leaving footprints for those who will continue the journey after us. We walk in the footsteps of Sojourner Truth, Harriet Tubman, Fannie Lou Hamer, Ella Baker, Wangari Maathai, and many more. We walk with Leah Thomas, Vanessa Nakate, Greta Thunberg, and countless other young, brave activists.

We are held and guided by an enduring faith, a faith that carried our ancestors through the wilderness, a faith that lights our path through this climate crisis, and a faith that will sustain our children as they continue this journey.

This new promised land, therefore, cannot be reached by the few, but must be forged by the many. It is a promised land that expands its borders to include the marginalized, the silenced, the overlooked, and the earth itself. It is a promised land that needs us as much as we need it.

This is the vision, the blueprint of the new promised land. It will demand more of us than we may think we can give. But remember, as we stand on the brink of this heated world, we have been here before. We have stood at the edge of the Red Sea, the water before us and danger behind us. And what did we do? We moved forward. We crossed over. With faith, with determination, and with God's grace, we made it through.

And so, we will again. Together, we will create a promised land where the freedom of all people and the health of the earth are intrinsically linked. We will build a world where justice rolls down like water and righteousness like a mighty stream. Because the promised land is not just a place we reach; it is a reality we create. Together, let us move forward and create it.

EXODUS FROM DOMINATION LOGICS TO SPIRIT FILLED, EARTH-AFFIRMING LIVING

And so, we reach our final destination in this sermon. A call to move from a worldview entrenched in domination and exploitation to one of reverence and respect, of harmony and interconnection, of Spirit-filled, Earth-affirming living.

In her seminal book *Sisters of the Yam*, bell hooks explains the vital connection between liberation of Black life in the United States, environmental justice, and the creation of peace. She writes, "The sense of union and harmony with nature . . . is echoed in testimony by black people who found that even though life in the new world was 'harsh, harsh,' in relationship to the earth one could be at peace."[1] Her words ring true in the context of our current ecological and climate crisis.

---

1. Bell hooks, *Sisters of the Yam: Black Women and Self-Recovery*, 2nd ed. (Routledge, 2014).

There can be no true liberation for Black communities, for women, for any marginalized groups until we liberate the earth from our unending assault upon her.

In her work *Breaking the Fine Rain of Death*, womanist ethicist Emilie M. Townes calls for us to embrace an ethic of care, a culture of love that treats people and the planet with kindness, respect, and attention.[2] This is the heart of ecowomanism, a call for love that transcends boundaries and heals wounds.

Ecowomanism calls us to the truth that we are not separate from the earth; we are a part of it, woven into the fabric of life. In a world on fire, where hurricanes ravage our coastlines and droughts scorch our crops, where the temperature keeps climbing and wildlife keeps dying, we need to relearn this truth. And we need to live by it.

Our tradition teaches us that God did not give us dominion over the earth to exploit her, but to care for her, to till and keep her, to be good stewards of the gift that we have been given. Our liberation is deeply intertwined with the liberation of the earth. Our healing is bound up with her healing. In taking care of the earth, we are caring for ourselves and for each other.

Our exodus journey has taught us that survival is possible, even in the face of overwhelming odds. It has taught us that liberation is not a distant dream but a tangible reality, a promised land we can reach if we work together. It has taught us that hope is not naive but necessary, a guiding light in our darkest times. And now it is teaching us that a different way of living is not only possible but essential.

To move from a dominion-centered worldview to an Earth-centered one requires a radical reimagining of our relationship with the planet. It requires us to dismantle systems of oppression that exploit both people and the planet. It requires us to recognize the rights of nature and the rights of future generations. It requires us to replace our culture of consumption with a culture of care, and our ethos of extraction with an ethos of reciprocity.

Black women have long been the bearers of this wisdom. They have been the keepers of the earth, the healers of their communities, the visionaries charting a course toward a more just and sustainable world. They have taught us the power of resistance and resilience, the strength of community and connection. They have shown us what it means to love the earth and each other, and what it means to fight for justice.

The story of Black women's survival, resistance, and transformation is a testament to their Earth-centered, Spirit-filled way of living. The wisdom of these women calls us to an ethos of care and respect, to a practice of

---

2. Emilie Townes, *Breaking the Fine Rain of Death: African American Health Issues and a Womanist Ethic of Care* (Wipf and Stock, 2006).

sustainability and reciprocity. They embody the ethos of the earth, the ethos of the exodus. They are, in essence, earth futurists, visioning and working toward a world that honors the sacredness of all life.

As we face the realities of our warming world, let us be guided by the wisdom of these earth futurists. Let us relearn the ancient truth that we are a part of the earth, not apart from it. Let us heed the call of the exodus, not just to survive, but to thrive. To make the journey from a place of bondage to a place of freedom, from a land of oppression to a promised land of harmony, equity, and justice.

This earth-affirming living is not a dream but an imperative. The times we live in demand us to shift our values, our behaviors, our systems to be more in sync with the rhythms of nature, to treat all of creation with the respect and reverence it deserves. This requires a profound shift in consciousness, one that acknowledges that our fate and the earth are inseparably intertwined.

We must remember the teachings of our ancestors, the wisdom of those who lived in harmony with the earth, of those who understood that true power is not in domination, but in communion. They knew that our well-being is tied to the well-being of the land, the water, the air, the plants, and the animals. This wisdom must guide our actions moving forward, for the health of our communities and the survival of future generations.

The Exodus story serves as a powerful metaphor, a call to action in the face of climate change. Just as Moses led his people out of Egypt, out of a land of bondage, we too must lead our communities, our nations, our world, out of this era of climate extremes, environmental degradation, and social injustice. And like the Israelites, we must understand that this journey is not easy, it is fraught with challenges and uncertainty. But it is a journey we must undertake. We must choose the path of liberation, of life, of love for each other and our shared home, this beautiful blue-green planet.

We must also recognize that the promised land is not a distant place, but a new way of being in the world. It is a way of being that values the sacredness of all life, that sees the divine in every creature, in every tree, in every river. It is a way of being that recognizes our interconnectedness, our interdependence. It is a way of being that honors the earth, that works toward justice and equity, that promotes healing and reconciliation.

And in this journey, let us draw strength from the Spirit that moved over the waters at creation, that gave life to the dry bones in the valley, that descended upon Jesus at his baptism, that led the Israelites through the wilderness. This same Spirit is moving in our midst, calling us to a deeper relationship with the earth and each other, inspiring us to action.

Let this Spirit-filled, Earth-affirming living be our compass as we navigate the challenges of the climate crisis. Let it guide our steps as we work toward a just, sustainable, and inclusive future. Let it strengthen our resolve as we join hands with sisters and brothers around the world to build a movement for climate justice.

In closing, let us remember the words of June Jordan; Alice Walker uses the same words for the title of one of her recent books: "We are the ones we have been waiting for." We are the ones called to make the journey from bondage to freedom, from a culture of domination to a culture of care, from ecological devastation to environmental restoration. We are the ones called to embody the lessons of the exodus, to live out its promise in our time. We are the ones called to be stewards of the earth, to be bearers of hope, to be agents of change. And in this sacred work, may we find our liberation, our healing, our hope, our home.

Ashe and Amen.

3

Rocky, Earthy Dreams

KENNETH NGWA

Sermon Delivered at Chapel Service Drew Theological Seminary, January 2019

Good afternoon. It is good to see you, on this day, in this place, at this time. And speaking of time and place: it is now 12:20 here in Madison, New Jersey. But I want to invite you to participate in an exercise of mental time-travel: name a geographical location anywhere in the world and then tell us what time it is there, at this very moment!

- 5:20 p.m. in London, England
- 6:20 p.m. in Yaoundé, Cameroon
- 4:20 a.m. Saturday morning in Seoul, South Korea
- 8:20 p.m. in Nairobi, Kenya
- 5:20 p.m. in Monrovia, Liberia
- 1:20 p.m. in Caracas, Venezuela
- 12:20 p.m. in Kingston, Jamaica
- 9:20 a.m. in Los Angeles California

Thank you. This big beautiful blue earth is doing different things at different places. This imaginative "time-travel" through different parts of the world allows us to imaginatively see and hear and come to know some of the sounds and sights and rhythms that define this big beautiful blue earth. Perhaps we have memories associated with those places. Some of these memories may be pleasant; some may be difficult. Time, space, travel, and location come together for us as we try to imagine the rhythms of life in this world.

The passage we read, Genesis 28:10–18, is a remarkable passage; a narrative of a dream. It is only one of several such dream narratives in Genesis. Interpretations of this text generally explore it as a form of dream theophany. As dream theophany, the critical point of the story is the moment of revelation when Jacob—very much like Moses in the burning bush—realizes that "this place" (the unnamed place where he lay down) is divine space. Unlike Moses, however, Jacob will name the place Bethel. As part of understanding the history of human control over the earth, dream theophany triggers an urge in us to figure out which specific place this was. Interpreters and scholars engaged in form-critical analyses of the text continue to debate that issue. Does the text function as an etiology for Moriah or Jerusalem?

On the other hand, as dream symbolism, the passage is understood as highlighting a larger narrative pattern within the patriarchal and matriarchal stories; the pattern of exile and return. Here, focus is on the ascending and descending angels on the "stairway." The message is that those who go into exile will return, under the guidance of the divine being.

These are certainly credible and interesting ways of reading the text, and I will draw insights from those methods. But let me suggest that we connect insights from dream theophany and dream symbolism to the work of returning or repositioning ourselves to the earth, the *eretz*; and to the ground, the *adamah*.

And let me suggest something further—that this story can be read as a story of the earth's rocky, earthy dream. The dream is not Jacob's; it's the earth's dream, and Jacob is only a part of it. A major part of his role within the story is to transmit the earth's dream.

When the story begins, Jacob is on the move; he exits the land. But then he stops and lodges at a certain place. The writer tells us why Jacob's movement and activity changed: it is because of the sun's activity. In the Hebrew language of the text, the sun had "come" or "gone in." So while Jacob was exiting the land, the sun was coming (or entering). We find out that Jacob is not the only subject moving in the text; even more, that his movement and activity is in response to the movement and activity of the sun.

Now, before we think all this talk about the movement of the sun moving is nothing but pre-enlightenment beliefs about the sun, remember that even today we still talk of the sun rising in the east and setting in the west. But I digress. The point is that we are entering a dream world—and it is that of the earth. In this moment of revelation, when the earth is sleeping, Jacob also lodges and turns to the earth—or in the language of the Hebrew text, he turns to that place; an unnamed place. It is the dream space provided to him by the earth. And that is where we meet Jacob.

Now, the back story here is that Jacob is in the process of fleeing and separating himself from the life of the fields, represented by Esau, whose identity he stole and whose lifestyle he corrupted. Now, the sun's activity causes him to lodge. Jacob finds a stone from the place and uses it to support (Hebrew: raise) his head and sleep. The Hebrew word for head is the word used in the creation story—beginning. In the midst of separating himself from the earth, Jacob has been compelled by the sun to slow down, and then to hand over his beginning to an element of the earth—in this case, to the stone. The place and the stone function as new hosts for displaced Jacob. And then it happens. To quote the biblical writer: "he dreamed, and behold!"

What's the earth's dream? A stairwell, with angels moving up and down. The Lord stands at the top of the stairway, beside Jacob. God speaks about Jacob's descendants becoming as numerous as the dust of the earth. God promises blessings for Jacob's descendants and connects those blessings to the families of the ground, the *adamah*, spread out all over the earth, the *eretz*—to the west and to the east, to the north and to the south. The dream takes Jacob all over the earth. Jacob, it turns out, is not the dreamer here. When he laid his head on the stone in that place, it turns out, he linked in to the rhythms of the earth and to the creator of the earth.

But there is more. It is as if we are in the world of the movie *Inception*, in a dream within a dream. Jacob wakes up from his dream while the earth is still sleeping and dreaming (it is not the next morning yet). Upon waking in the dream, Jacob begins to transmit what the earth is saying; he begins to make major claims about radical hospitality: God is in this place and the nature of that divine presence is not limited to enlightenment epistemology.

In that newfound realization about the radical hospitality of the earth, Jacob continues his theological reflection: this place is holy. He calls the place Bethel, the house of God. But that new name is also a name change; the place used to be called Luz. (I will leave it to Hebrew Bible students to find out the etymology of that word. Hint: it has to do with movement and even deviant movement.) This is the gate of heaven; not the city gate, not the gates of the state or the empire, but the gate of heaven.

Jacob must be dreaming. Has he heard of colonial mapping and renaming of the earth? Has he heard of the recent partial government shutdown all because someone wants to build walls and construct national gates? Has Jacob heard of the burdens that global violence puts on migrant bodies and on the earth? Has Jacob heard of the prisons and prison-like spaces where children are separated from their families? Has Jacob heard of exhausted migrant workers who live in the shadows of state and imperial policies of extraction? Has the transitioning Jacob heard that many churches and theological institutions in this country and around the world are expelling fellow faithful members who dare to transition and embody the generosity of this earthy place?

In a text where almost everything is named and claimed, the story puts Jacob—and us—in contact with the earth; he stands in the unnamed place. As Jacob aligns himself and allies himself with the tired and sleeping earth, he begins to share in the earth's dreams. What did the earth show him? What was the earth dreaming about? Was the earth experiencing the trauma of colonialism? It turns out, the dream was not induced by the earth's natural sleep cycle; it is from trauma and stress. We are told that when Jacob wakes up—while the earth is still sleeping—he is afraid.

For the ancient Yehudite community reeling from the power and deep wounds of exile this story must have carried significant weight. After being subjected to the exploitations of empire, after witnessing its resources extracted, concentrated, and consolidated into the hands of a few "chosen," through the machineries of colonialism and patriarchy, the earth was tired and traumatized and closed its eyes, and started to dream and to communicate that trauma to its children. Part of the anguish of such devastation is trapped in the ground itself, as we read in the story of Cain and Abel, where the blood (*dam*) cries out from the ground (*adamah*). And so, when Jacob hears God's promise that the families of the *adamah* shall be blessed, in association with him, that promise must evoke memories of Esau (the progenitor of the Edomites) from whom he is violently separated and separating.

God's word to Jacob, when he wakes up, is a promise that God will bring Jacob back to this place. But what is this place? It is a place where the earth dreams, except the dream is quite real; a place where we wake up frightened because we have shared in the anguish of a distressed earth and its distressed people. It is also the place where, through our theological education and justice commitments, we resolve to gather around broken places, around unnamed places, the places of colonial and patriarchal erasure, to recognize its sacredness and affirm God's presence there. We resolve through the dreamlike work of our scholarship and administration and studies to build ladders and pillars and support systems for tired vulnerable migrants rather than build walls to keep them out, and to care for the earth rather than exploit it.

Yes, Jacob is dreaming. But his dream is a gift from the earth, which is itself dreaming. Dreaming of a new way to understand and name what holiness and hospitality mean, what church means, what theological education means in a world where truth and justice are under assault, and where the voice of innocent Abel joins other such voices in the United States and Syria and Cameroon and Venezuela and Israel and Palestine and Kenya and France and the Democratic Republic of Congo—all calling out from the *adamah*, the ground. Jacob is dreaming, but his dream is a gift from the earth about what faith means, what family and friendship mean, what residency and migration mean in a world that has largely stopped listening to the earth and her children, a world—even a theological world—that, in looking for God has forgotten to listen to the earth, the *eretz* and the *adamah*. But the rocky, earthy earth pulls Jacob into her dream and lets him see and experience her anguish but also her hospitality, her creativity, her blessings. Holiness is connected to this place, this unnamed place. Blessing is connected to the earth. Family is connected to the *adamah*.

The earth's dream is BIG, and, like Jacob, we are a part of it. The dream is sacred. It is earthy. It meets us in our moments of revelation and new theological insights—insights that connect our ancestral faith to new faith, the faith that we inherit and the faith that we create. It is the dream that meets and challenges us not just in the books and essays we read, but also in the migrants we meet and interact with, in the trees and rocks and earth and ground we repeatedly return to for nourishment and hospitality.

We know from the next chapters in Jacob's story that he will engage a stone again, this time in Haran, where he tries to access waters from a well. His journey is wrapped up in the story of the earth—including places violently ripped apart. So the question is this: What will we do when the earth wakes up the next morning and we are awake too?

What happens when we wake up but the nightmare is still ongoing? What does it mean to inhabit this rocky, dusty, earthy space-time? I am talking, for example, about the space-time of colonial and postcolonial necropolitics that Achille Mbembe theorizes in *On the Postcolony*, the space-time of postcolonial trauma that Emmanuel Katongole explores in *The Sacrifice of Africa*, and the space-time of enslavement and its "after lives" that Christina Sharpe excavates in *In the Wake*.[1] Once we wake up—like Jacob—in that space-time of environmental and historical violence and wreckage, do we "rise" as the poet Maya Angelou defiantly proclaimed? Rise in the form of dust, rise from the dusty wreckage? As Maya Angelou has taught us, we can indeed rise from the ground, like dust.[2] In this defiant dusty resistance against erasure, we hear the promise of the Lord in the dream: "your descendants will be like the dust of the earth" (NIV). It is in mimicking the earth's expansive generosity that we find hope and resilience.

The earth's dream also includes people going up and coming down, in the context of imperial and colonial violence and governance. In its dream—a dream from which Jacob wakes frightened—the earth sees bodies sinking to the bottom of the sea/ocean, offering down their blood to the saltiness of the oceans, and living on in that cycle. To quote Christina Sharpe: "The amount of time it takes for a substance to enter the ocean and then leave the ocean is called residence time. Human blood is salty, and sodium . . . has a residence time of 260 million years. And what happens to the energy that is produced in

---

1. Achille Mbembe, *On the Postcolony* (University of California Press, 2001); Emmanuel Katongole, *The Sacrifice of Africa: A Political Theology for Africa* (Eerdmans, 2011); Christina Sharpe, *In the Wake: On Blackness and Being* (Duke University Press, 2016).
2. Maya Angelou, *And Still I Rise* (Virago Press, 1978), 41.

the waters? It continues to cycle like atoms in residence time. We, Black people, exist in the residence time of the wake."[3]

When the children of the earth in the Black Atlantic watch the oceans, do we hear the ancestors whose blood joined the cycle of the oceans? Does one then hover over the watery face of the broken community (in the creation story, the divine hovers over the face of the water—Gen. 1:2), or go up and down like a pillar of cloud (Exod. 13:21), like the spiritual beings—the angels—in Jacob's dream? We no longer simply think about the waters; we think with the waters and with the ground and the earth (cf. Ps. 139:1–14).

Whether we rise or sink or fly in the face/wake of environmental and historical violence, the text says Jacob embraced his new self, attached himself to the place by giving it a name and still recognizing what it used to be called. What fertile ground for cross-cultural study! What fertile ground for understanding sacredness as a gift from the one we haven't fully understood; the one who comes to join us in this unnamed place! And, if I rework my Presbyterian theologies of predestination, what a way to understand transition as a return to the table of radical hospitality where our dreams meet the earth's dream (cf. Ps. 126:1). Rocks become receptacles for new beginnings. Unnamed places receive affirmation without distortion. Transition is honored.

For natural and traumatic reasons, our relationship as humans (the earthling, *adam*) to the earth (*adamah*) has been broken. That relationship stands a chance of being healed when we begin to reconnect to the *adamah* and the *eretz*, when we ask the earth to assist us in our survival and when we refrain from exploiting the earth. If God's promise to Jacob is true for us as well, then I think we can reposition ourselves—reengage the earth in modes of existence that are infused with healthy theologies of the earth's rocky, earthy dreams to survive and thrive, whether we find ourselves among farmers in rural communities or IT technicians in Silicon Valley or on the campus of a theological school in Madison, New Jersey.

Dream world stuff, only it is too real! Why, because God and the earth are both talking to us. Are we listening?

---

3. Sharpe, *In the Wake*, 41.

4

Transcendentalism and the Harrowed Black Earth

Sofía Betancourt

*Sermon Delivered at the Climate Justice Revival,
Unitarian Universalist Association, Fall 2024*

Environmental justice asks that we be mindful of life in motion. As Earth rotates on its axis, the pull of its gravitational field anchors existence as we know it. All beauty, all loss, all struggle, all survival is affixed in this lifetime to the good blackness of rich soil by our dancing, rotating home. This circling grounds me each time I sit before a simple spinning wheel, wool in hand and feet in motion.

If I am honest, the practice of handspinning—creating yarn from unspun fiber and manual labor—liberates my mind from the unhelpful stressors of the day and frees me to contemplative practice. There is joy in the return to a simple, spinning, wheel. The rhythm of feet on the treadles keeping the wheel in motion; the recurring pinch, pull, release of the fiber; the trust that the wheel will draw new spun yarn onto itself without breaking so long as balance remains—all these serve to reorient body and spirit to the intricate requirements that sustain us in our living. Equilibrium lies at the center of Earth wisdom.

Our Unitarian Universalist tradition holds the teachings of transcendentalism as a proud theological inheritance. Here too there is a desire for balance, and for new knowledge born of relationship with Earth. Some of the most beloved teachers of the Americanist environmental canon were transcendentalist thinkers whom we hold as religious ancestors of our liberal and liberating faith. They taught the unity of God and the possibility of human progress.

Over time through the writings of Margaret Fuller, Ralph Waldo Emerson, and Henry David Thoreau, among others, they centered the natural world in their quest for the elevation of human society and human living. Thoreau in particular developed the idea that our interconnection with wilderness in its purest form serves as a vital center to our moral development and our understanding of life. We claim Thoreau's story as one that grounds our shared values for interconnection, sustainability, repair of Earth, and the work of justice. Unitarian Universalists have a significant responsibility for Thoreau's legacy and how it is used to promote environmental justice or to silence the reality of environmental racism that weaves from the violence of our nation's founding through today. We have not always held this legacy well. Thoreau based his claim of wisdom born of relationship with Earth in part on his famous two-year retreat at Walden Pond, captured in his writings in *Walden*.[1] In his time of contemplation, Thoreau expanded his sense of neighborly love and community to include the specific birds, trees, and experiences of land that he witnessed at Walden. His is a philosophical experiment that remains up close and personally connected to a particular place and time, one that yearns to understand what life has to teach him.

Yet what we tell of Thoreau's analysis does not extend to the fullness of human expression. Thoreau's retreat was not limited to birdsong and the character of winter mornings. He set out inspired by the heroism and independence of those who were formerly enslaved and wanted to experiment with living independently as they did. He chronicled many aspects of the history of slavery in the area and the lives of his neighbors after emancipation.[2] By misunderstanding the harrowing of people and Earth as fundamental to what Thoreau witnessed during his time at Walden Pond, we delude ourselves into thinking that an unbalanced story centering white exceptionalism can hold the key to Earth's liberation. Would that we pay more attention to Thoreau's time with the handspinners among the trees.

Elise Lemire is a Professor of English and Global Literature at Purchase College in New York. She was raised two miles from Walden Pond and, like Thoreau, grew to love the land and its inherent wisdom. She writes of the privilege of polite white society in the Concord area and how the erasure of Black history and lived experiences in New England leads many to know almost nothing about the establishment of one of the most loved natural reservations in the country.

---

1. Henry David Thoreau, *Walden* (Beacon Press, 2012).
2. Elise Lemire, *Black Walden: Slavery and Its Aftermath in Concord, Massachusetts* (University of Pennsylvania Press, 2009), 1.

We are certainly not alone in this sanitizing of history. Lemire writes about never really reading *Walden* closely, as is true of many of us, and her surprise in finding an entire chapter dedicated to the "Former Inhabitants; and Winter Visitors," half of whom were formerly enslaved Africans and African Americans. Her book *Black Walden: Slavery and Its Aftermath in Concord, Massachusetts*[3] is an intentional continuation of the reclamation of history begun by Thoreau. It is an unearthing, and a more complete storying of home. For our purposes, it is an attempt to be accountable to Earth justice by repairing the mythologies of whiteness that have clouded the landscape of Walden today.

As I share with you Zilpah's story, and the story of Walden that precedes many of our tellings, know that I am drawing on Professor Lemire's good work, and that each of us has a role to play in laying the foundation for new knowledge. Guided by Earth and an honest reckoning with history, may we find our way to just-Earth futures.

Henry David Thoreau's retreat to Walden Pond was a separation from society via retreat into Black space. It was Black space because of the aridness and sterility of the soil. It was Black space because those who succeeded in threatening their enslavers politically and gaining their freedom were still not allowed to relocate to new communities. It was Black space because only the least desirable land, seen as unvaluable to the white ruling class because of the difficulty of farming, was free for formerly enslaved people to squat on and build new lives together. Lemire echoes Thoreau when she tells us that "the history of slavery and its aftermath reveals that at least some of our nation's cherished green spaces began as [B]lack spaces, with Walden Woods a particularly striking case in point."[4] This history of land left to the trees because of farming difficulties gets romantically and untruthfully retold as a preservation of wilderness left to inspire wisdom across the ages.

Instead, the story of Walden is one of Black erasure. Not only are our beloveds' lives, skills, triumphs, and losses redacted from shared memory, their very existence in Concord, Massachusetts, became a cycle of disappearance where enslavement led to living on depleted soil that necessarily resulted in inescapable poverty, death by malnutrition, or departure from the region. The pristine wilderness that lives in the commons of an American imagination challenges us to reckon with lived histories made possible by pretending our green spaces came into being through the protection of Earth rather than the devastation

---

3. Elise Lamire, *Black Walden: Slavery and Its Aftermath in Concord Massachusetts* (University of Pennsylvania Press, 2009). This book details the story of Zilpah White and the black community of Walden.

4. Lemire, *Black Walden*, 11–12.

of Black and Indigenous communities. In truth, both Black beloveds and Earth bear the scars of a predatory disvaluing of black bodies.

Yet Zilpah lasted forty years by spinning in Walden Woods.

Many women, after their release from slavery, would stay on as paid laborers in the same houses where they had been enslaved. Some looked for new families to serve, and others did their best to find work that promised them room and board. Zilpah, however, chose complete independence. She lived on a thin strip of depleted land at the edge of Walden Woods. Her one room cabin was similar to Thoreau's place of retreat, but born of necessity rather than experimentation. She was one of many women gifted with, or who liberated, a spinning wheel from a former enslaver in an attempt to guarantee her livelihood going forward. Unlike my own association of spinning yarn with contemplative thought, the endless work of spinning cotton, flax, wool, and more into yarn for woven cloth was taxing on both mind and body in her day. Zilpah lost much of her sight from spinning throughout her lifetime, yet she made her mark on Walden Woods, filling the air with her "loud and notable voice" as documented by Thoreau.[5] She lived in those woods for forty years, an unheard-of length of time and survival in her community.

Why does it matter that one formerly enslaved woman worked her fingers to the bone twisting fibers into yarn rather than recommit herself to the care of her enslavers for an inadequate wage? I find it telling that she did not try to force her will on the small tract of Earth where she lived to turn it into farmland. Spinning animal and plant fibers keeps us intimately aware of life outside of our own, their textures, smells, colors, density, beauty, and possibility all slipping through the fingers of both hands. The innate relationship such craft requires speaks to me of the womanist ethic of *making do*.[6] This priority of Black women as the holders and teachers of community values to elevate survival and thriving over an imagined liberation is central to the work of justice. What can Earth itself bear? What is sustainable and still allows for the thriving of all? How do we build life at the margins in ways that center our freedom? What can this one body we have been given do to hold us accountable to Earth, its rhythms, and our own knowing?

Beloveds, where and how are you called to live the re-storying of what you think you know about the community where you live, the work of this lifetime, and the place you call home? What do our inherited theologies ask of you as someone living your faith morning by morning, and day by day?

---

5. Lemire, 131–32.
6. To learn more about the womanist ethic of making do, consider the work of Karen Baker-Fletcher *Sisters of Dust, Sisters of Spirit: Womanist Wordings on God and Creation* (Fortress, 1998), and Monica A. Coleman, *Making a Way Out of No Way: A Womanist Theology* (Fortress, 2008).

I imagine a transcendentalist legacy that centers the lived experience of those most driven to the margins—including Black women writ large, and Earth itself. I imagine a transcendentalism whose wisdom is drawn from the healed scars of our human failings and that unflinchingly speaks to the sacrifices long overdue in the work of environmental justice. As our tradition reckons with crucial questions in the work of liberation—from the right to a fossil-free future to the reparations owed to Black, Indigenous, and People of Color, communities alongside Earth itself—what stories will you center to deepen your own knowing and keep you faithful to the work ahead?

This is the kind of reckoning and vision that calls us when the harrowing of Earth and our own Black beloveds are reintroduced into our historical knowing. For all of us, the resilience that we nurture in these times can be woven together, through a creative reimagining, into that which might heal us all. It does not require us to be superhuman. It does not ask us to measure up to a false understanding of perfect Unitarian Universalist practice that we might carry in our mind's eye. Instead, it invites us into the unknown. To respond with creativity in the face of climate devastation. To hold fast to the vision of a nation that cares for its people. For *all* of its people. To move faithfully into a future that celebrates all we have overcome.

A beloved colleague reminded me recently that "we can dwell in hardship and still stay together in community." In fact, we must. Hold fast to the power and possibility of our beloved community, and of our sacred Earth home. We are uniquely suited to this consideration as Unitarian Universalists because our tradition is built on a foundation of inquiry and an ability to sit with uncertainty. We live into the challenging questions of life and find a new hope together. Find practices that remind you of the larger whole when all seems bent on destruction, even something as simple as the spinning of a wheel. May it remind you of the power of liberation and of the equilibrium born of Earth's turning. Then go back out into the world and create justice anew.

Amen, Ashe, and Blessed Be.

5

Collapsing the Hierarchy

JOHN W. KINNEY

Beautiful Are the Feet Acceptance Speech,
Samuel DeWitt Proctor Conference, February 2018

Honoring the God who privileges us with this moment, and embracing the presence in the memory of ancestors whose fidelity and investment in life make it possible for us to claim this moment, I say good evening.

Giving honor to Mother Iva (Dr. Iva Carruthers), to all of the members of the Samuel DeWitt Proctor board, and to all of you gathered here, I am grateful for this moment because by the structures of logic I should not be standing here. I'm not from Memphis. I have no greeting from Memphis, but I stand here simply to say thank you to this body.

At the Samuel DeWitt Proctor Conference last year, Tina (Mrs. Kinney) and I were so richly blessed by an authentic and genuine expression of appreciation that is rare in this world today. We were touched deeply, and through an anonymous gift we were privileged to travel this summer on an amazing trip. I thank you for last year and I want to thank you for this year because we have been blessed by the workshops at the SDWC annual conference that we have attended.

I want to thank God for the Vanderbilt crew that sat at table today and shared their spirit and energy with me and blessed me. I want to thank the Duke Divinity students, with whom I had the pleasure of sharing covenant on the plane here. They blessed me as I shared with them through a teaching and learning opportunity we shared together in the fall.

I want to also acknowledge the gift of my colleagues at Virginia Union where Dr. Iva Carruthers instructs, Rev. Dr. Gina M. Stewart instructs, Dr.

Yvonne Delk instructs. I know Dr. Earl Bledsoe is here, Reverend Dr. Nathan Dell is here, Dr. Patricia Gould-Champ, and I've seen just a bushel of alums, and I thank you all for sharing. And are any other Virginia Union folks in the house? Just say so. Amen.

I want to thank you for the privilege of sharing your presence with me and teaching me. I am the product of the gifts of so many, and I am grateful. I must admit the privilege of going on this trip. My wife and I went to Alaska, and we didn't take the normal routes. We went in vehicles—by rail, bus, and sea and we didn't do the kind of normal things one might expect. We got off the beaten path to experience nature. It created some dissonance in my spirit because you cared for us so well and as we talk about justice; I was kind of conflicted about the privilege that was mine, so much so I couldn't even share it with my wife as my soul was so troubled.

But the more I looked through the sky on a clear night and saw the canopy etched by our Creator, the more I experienced clean air and clean water and witnessed the sturdy presence of the moose and the grace-filled movement of the reindeer, the more my soul ignited with energy climaxing with the privilege of seeing the sun shine at night and seeing the day dim with rays from the mighty sun prismatically refracting the moisture in the evening frost, giving a splendid brilliant display of all of the variegated hues of the chromatic spectrum, the more my soul settled. And God just simply spoke to me and said, "Be still, and know that I am God."

We were privileged to spend some time—and we thank you—to really have conversation with First Nation people. Listening to them talk about their entirely different lens of interpreting history, different than the one that we hear about; when they talk about gold they say, "You call it your discovery. We call it our disaster."

The news was telling us about the wildfires in Alaska, and how much money the government had to spend to put the fires out, and things like that; but when we visited a First Nation village they said, "You call it a wildfire, we call it a restoration event. Because, if the fire does not come, these trees are not consumed. And, if these trees are not consumed, these little trees do not grow. If these little trees do not grow, the moose does not eat. If the moose does not eat, we have no food on our table. What you call a wildfire is a restoration event, where the Creator is restoring the earth, and God will put the fire out, you won't have to do it. God will just keep on doing God's restoration, God's restoration *thing*."

I was deeply touched by that observation of a God who's in the restoration business, when you recognize the connectivity. But something else touched me. A Native elder said to me, "You must realize, the moose is as precious as my child, and the death of a moose grieves me as much as the death of my child would. That awareness comes to me when I have to kill the moose for my food. That is why you see me kneel next to the moose and thank the moose for giving life to me, and so it's my job to make sure that in life and beyond the moose is treated with respect, honor, and dignity. It is my job to make sure that the moose is well."

The belief in the interconnectedness of all beings is consonant with an African cosmology that does not understand anything in creation outside of God's being. E. Bọlaji Idowu, a Nigerian theo-philosopher, explains this in his book, *African Traditional Religion: A Definition*.[1] Here he describes the concept of diffused or implicit monotheism and explains that Western perspectives on religion *violate* African cosmology, because they call us, African peoples, polytheistic. The truth *is* that we honor a radical monotheism that is not marginal like those of white-colonial western perspectives. In essence, we cannot understand any aspect of being without being the presence of God, so I gotta talk to the God in the tree. I gotta talk to the God in the dirt. I gotta *talk* to *the God*.

I thank God for you all privileging us to reconnect with these values during our visit, the values of interconnectedness, the sacredness of earth, and the depth of God's love in all things. Because the cosmologies between African and Native peoples are so close, we got to visit the motherland through some First Nation peoples in Alaska. Experiencing freedom and understanding freedom from a variety of perspectives are important to me, and I am always seeking help from others who can help me understand freedom more deeply. This commitment to understanding freedom is one that I share with Tina. And this understanding of freedom provides insight. I hear people all the time talking about the first shall be last, and the last shall be first. But their understanding of that is the inversion of a hierarchy. In this mode of thinking, they position themselves, and often only a select few, at the top. These at the top have a particular view of privilege, such that they view liberation only from a hierarchical frame. In other words, the system is set up so that only a select few see through a lens of privilege and these folks see themselves as better. They say, "we're higher." If in fact your quest for justice only repositions people for participation in a privileged hierarchy, but does not interrupt the system of the hierarchy, then the next prophets will have to pull down the people you raised up. The struggle is not about altering positions in a hierarchy; it's about collapsing it. And in this way of justice, there *is* no last or first because we're all whole.

Because of you, Tina and I experienced wholeness between us, between Mother Earth, and the God we serve. And we remain committed to collapsing the hierarchy. Thank you. Amen.

1. Idowu, E. Bọlaji, *African Traditional Religion: A Definition* (Orbis, 1973).

6

By Any Greens Necessary

OTIS MOSS III

TheoEd Talk, Emory University, 2022

Arguably, one of the greatest cultural icons of the twentieth century is a gentleman by the name of el-Hajj Malik el-Shabazz, more popularly known as Malcolm X, previously known as Malcolm Little. His family revered a wonderful Black Jamaican liberationist Christian by the name of Marcus Garvey. He eventually fell under the teachings of a person by the name of the Honorable Elijah Muhammad. Malcom was a prophet. He was our prophet of Black self-esteem. Unfortunately and tragically, he was assassinated in 1965 in the Audubon Ballroom in Harlem, New York. But people today are still inspired by his words and his methodology.

Now, some may raise the question, why do I lift up a Muslim icon at this moment? I say to you that truth is not held solely in Christian vessels. The truth can be held because God is sovereign. The truth is not only held within a Christian vessel, but also can be held within a humanist framework, or even a Jewish Torah or Buddhist practice.

God is sovereign, and God can use whomever God determines to use. By any means God determines necessary. God can use Malcolm X, Nipsey Hussle, or Kendrick Lamar. You can be hustling all your days to sacrifice, or you can find out that, to paraphrase Brother Lamar, I'm messed up and you're messed up, "but if God got us, then we gon' to be alright."[1] It is Malcolm who stated

---

1. Kendrick Lamar, vocalist, "Alright," by Kendrick Duckworth, Pharrell Williams, and Mark Anthony Spears, on Kendrick Lamar, *To Pimp a Butterfly*, Top Dawg/ Aftermath/Interscope, released June 30, 2015.

that we must declare our right on this earth, to be a man, to be respected as a human being, to be treated as a human being, which we intend to bring about by any means necessary.

Malcolm gives an invitation to us all to let us know that the community will determine the methodology that it will use for transformation. He is talking about self-agency, self-determination, and that we must look within the community that has been marginalized to be the creative force that will design and create new ways of transformation.

I have found an ally of Malcolm. An ally within the Old Testament. They didn't know each other, but I believe they function with the same particular artistry and imagination. A person by the name of Nehemiah.

Nehemiah believed in doing things by any means God deems necessary. The walls were broken in Jerusalem. Nehemiah first did an evaluation, praying and evaluating, saying "what should we do about these walls?" And then he brought the community in and said, "you will be the contractors and the subcontractors to benefit from the rebuilding. We're not going to bring in someone from the outside to build the walls." And then they did something magnificent that really fascinated me. They decided that they would rebuild the walls, but *they* would rebuild the walls, with techniques that they had learned from their ancestors. The bricks would not be imported from somewhere else. They would design them. They would create the wall, fix the wall using green sustainable techniques. Malcolm X and Nehemiah both recognizing that we must do things by any means we determine necessary.

But I give a remix, and say that Nehemiah was really saying that we must do this *by any greens necessary*. Our greatest challenge in this world today is not that we lack the resources, not that we lack the funding; but we lack the imagination to imagine a new world. It is often said, "imagination is greater than genius."[2] Give me imagination, because the genius will always work in a box. But one who has imagination will continue to break out of the boxes that other people have created. Malcolm and Nehemiah give us an invitation around imagination.

An imagination is what we lack at this moment. An imagination is what we need if we're talking about community development. If we are to develop the community, those communities that have been marginalized, we must use imagination or what I like to call moral artistry.

The African American community historically has utilized moral artistry, moral imagination to look in the face of despair and say, "I refuse to take hold." It is from within the African American community that we brought forth into this

---

2. George Sylvester Viereck, "What Life Life Means to Einstein," *Saturday Evening Post*, October 26, 1929, https://www.saturdayeveningpost.com/wp-content/uploads/satevepost/what_life_means_to_einstein.pdf.

country a unique and new perspective in reference to faith. Many will say that they are Christian, but in the African American community, it is known as Black religiosity or Black spirituality. And it is older than Protestantism, and it reminds Western Christianity that it did not come from the West, but it has African roots.

Christian mystic Howard Thurman called it mystical activism, embodying themes of democracy and human rights and supporting the recognition that every human being has the mark of the sacred upon them, by any greens necessary.[3] How do we build a new community? In the face of great challenges, maybe within our own network in Chicago, we have a perspective that can assist us. We use the terms moral artistry, moral imagination, and say "by any greens necessary."

I serve at a church on the South Side of Chicago. Come by if you can. And there in that church, we made a decision that we were going to be a part of the rebuilding of our community, using a framework known as *by any greens necessary*. Let me share a story with you. Right down the street from our church, there is a library known as the Carter G. Woodson Library. It has the largest collection of African American literature in the Midwest. But this local library was falling apart. It had a scaffolding outside of it, because I guess the city of Chicago, when they got their contractor, well the contractor didn't do the job quite right. The city was afraid the bricks were going to fall on people's heads, so they put a scaffolding out there. The scaffolding had been out there for twenty years. It had been out there so long that people assumed that the scaffolding was a part of the architecture.

Our Community Development Corporation, along with several other organizations, got together and said that we want this library rebuilt, renovated. We met with the library commission, and they came to us and said this: "We appreciate you all so very much. We love the collection of this library, but we don't have the money to rebuild this library." Our community development corporation, just like Nehemiah, had already done the inspection and had done the research and pulled out a piece of paper at that meeting and said, "Well, according to your records, you built five libraries, but none of them were in Black communities. We want you to know that we are well aware that your spending priorities are not on the South Side." At this we exited the meeting, but not before I turned and said, "Oh, by the way, when is your next library commission meeting?" They said, "Next week." I said, "Thank you very much."

---

3. See Sameer Yadav, "Howard Thurman's Mystical Activism: Connection, Alienation, and Black Vitality," Yale Center for Faith and Culture, accessed January 30, 2025, https://faith.yale.edu/media/howard-thurmans-mystical-activism.

That Sunday I stood up in the pulpit. I said, "I have an announcement to make. For those of you who are available on Wednesday at 7:00 p.m., we want you to go to the library commission meeting." I did not go to the library commission meeting, but I kid you not, the library commission meeting was adjourned at 7:59. I got a call at 8:01 saying, "Could you please meet with us? We think we have a solution to the library."

You must understand, nobody goes to a library commission meeting unless you are a Dewey Decimal nerd. That's the only reason you go. Yet, several hundred people showed up with one single question, "Why is the Carter G. Woodson Library, which has the largest collection of African American literature, falling apart?" The library commission met with us and then they said to us, "We want you to know we found the money. We have a grant for $10 million to rebuild the library."

We stopped them right there. We said, "That's not enough. That's not enough because the people in this zip code have to rebuild the library. The people in this zip code have to benefit from the rebuilding. What you must do is find a contractor who looks like us. You must utilize green techniques, but also use people from the mass incarceration system so they can be trained." They looked at us and said, "We've never seen anything like that before." We said, "Well, we want to share with you that we did the same thing at our church when we renovated our church. We used these same principles in order to rebuild our church. We used green techniques. We employed people from the mass incarceration system so they could benefit from receiving skills and training. We also had people from our community fully engaged in the process." Long story short, the library was built with that three-prong strategy, but we did not stop there because we were committed to our community.

We also purchased homes that were delinquent, and tax delinquent properties, and we used that same framework to rebuild those homes. The homes that we purchased for about $30,000 after we were finished with the renovation, they were worth $150,000 to $199,000. But they were only sold for $110,000 because we wanted people to walk in with equity. We didn't stop there.

We purchased twenty-seven acres of land down the street, partnered with one of the largest health care providers in Illinois, Advocate Health, and a medical center was built, not a clinic. A medical center. Next to that medical center will be a healing garden. So instead of just prescribing pills because someone's in pain, maybe they can walk through nature to reduce their stress. And now we're working on housing and a hotel and creating space for what will be the largest urban farm in the city of Chicago.

We are using the same principles outlined above by our method, *by any greens necessary*. We are engaging moral artistry and moral imagination. Thus far, we have invested and facilitated the investment of $35 million already on the South Side of Chicago. By the time we are finished, we believe that $125 million will be reinvested in a community people said could not come back. When you have the imagination and turn that imagination over to God, anything is possible. It is through this idea of moral artistry, partnering with other people and communities, that transformation can take place. I like to borrow from the African American tradition the tradition of jazz, which is really not only a musical tradition but is also a spiritual tradition. Jazz taught America democracy before America even knew what democracy was all about.

It was those people from Haiti who made their way to New Orleans and a place called the Congo Square. In the Congo Square on Sundays, it was Africans who were able to spend time freely singing and dancing and reflecting upon their own experience. And in those spaces, they were able to hear the sounds of Indigenous people, Spanish and German and French. That is where jazz was created, out of that space.

Jazz gives us an ethic that I believe is transformative for our nation because jazz takes music, musicians, and instruments that are not supposed to play together, but they do. The saxophone is supposed to play for the marching band. The piano is to play that classical European style of music. The drum is not to play polyrhythms that come out of the African tradition, but simply a twelve-beat marching rhythm. If you play the bass, you are to play it with a bow, not with your fingers. But, in the jazz band, all of these elements come together and they begin to play. Just play. What is so beautiful about the jazz band is that the jazz band says that everybody has the right to solo.

Everybody has a right to express themselves uniquely from their own particular tradition. So you will never hear the saxophone trying to tell the piano "you have to sound like me." You would never hear the piano trying to tell the bass, "you have to sound just like me." You will never hear the drum telling everybody "you just got to sound like me." No. Everybody is given the right to solo. Jazz uses moral artistry and imagination. It recognizes that imagination is greater than genius. If we as a country choose to imagine, we might be able to do what a person by the name of W. E. B. Du Bois said, we might be able to become these "yet to be United States of America."

If we use an ethic of self-determination, self-agency, moral artistry; if we are willing to empower people in communities that have been marginalized; if we are willing to use green techniques, and reach out to sisters and brothers from the mass incarceration system, we might be able to see our community transformed.

A church on the South Side of Chicago did it. We're not a wealthy church. We're just working-class folks who live up south, on the South Side of Chicago; the city of Big Shoulders. We are functioning. We are changing our community day by day, *by any greens necessary*. Thank you.

release

by Melanie L. Harris

old lungs
release us
from breathing stale air
and
spinning broken sermons
help us
come into a new song
awake to sorrow
embrace grief
enough
so we may know
joy
let us
love different
find rest
be fully present to the moment
assured that grace
is more than abundance
and accompanies
struggle
unfold with us
hope
that earth is
breathing
new

PART II

Earth Heart, Earth Hope

Conversations on African American Environmental Justice and Ecowomanist Spirituality

Melanie L. Harris

Sharing mutually enhancing dialogue is a central aspect of ecowomanist thought. Evidence of this can be found in the process of the seven-step ecowomanist method, which, while described as a step-by-step process, actually works like a spiral, with insights and reflections weaving in and out of movement with each step. The sixth step is engaging in dialogue. Since the method moves like a spiral, dialogue can be witnessed, observed, and practiced in the midst of and throughout the engagement with any of the steps: (1) honoring experience and mining eco-memory, (2) critical reflection on experience and eco-memory, (3) conducting womanist intersectional analysis, (4) critically examining African and African American history and tradition, (5) engaging transformation, (6) sharing dialogue, and (7) taking action for earth justice.

As a method influenced by liberationist theological frames, primarily approaches from Black liberationist, womanist, and feminist theologies, the process of dialogue shapes the theory and practice of ecowomanism. That is, similar to Black feminist approaches that insist on a reflexive relationship between theory and practice (praxis influences theory, and theory influences praxis) the practice of dialogue in ecowomanism includes honoring Indigenous wisdom, deep listening, open hearted reflection, mindful speech sharing, and mindful contemplation to bring about new and fresh insights for being and for living (ethical guidelines) in earth community. Some of this practice is developed from the practice of learning, studying, and reading together shaped by interreligious dialogue.[1] The interreligious nature of ecowomanism is important because of the nature of Black women's wisdom that is highlighted by an ecowomanist lens. That is, as an approach that features the work, thought, scientific understanding, and spirituality of women of African descent, ecowomanism recognizes that the spiritual practices that are related and connected to these women's understanding of climate justice are varied.

In my book *Ecowomanism: African American Women and Earth-Honoring Faiths*, I devote an entire chapter to the interreligious nature of ecowomanism. Here I claim that the vastness and urgency of climate change demands that religious leaders, activists, and practitioners learn to speak, share dialogue, and understand how we need to live interreligiously and sometimes intrareligiously in order to hear what the planet really needs right now. In the same way that Alice Walker chides readers in the early days of the environmental movement to join the movement and protect the earth, saying that this is "no time to quibble about survival being 'a white issue,'"[2] I urge religious thinkers, scholars, and practitioners to stop allowing doctrinal differences and religious conflict to set them apart from one another. Rather, religious bodies, beings, and groups ought to come together using practices that unite us for climate justice and allow the particularities of our religious traditions to infuse and inspire one another for the sake of earth justice.

In my earlier work, I write about specific teachings, models, and strategies of doing this kind of interreligious work. In several articles featuring strategies used to facilitate Buddhist-Christian dialogue, I write about the communal reading practices that I have led and shaped with Buddhist scholar Dr. Charles Hallisey. Noting the great potential for scholars to learn from each other, we organized the gatherings in a way that communicated radical hospitality; modeled the values of kindness, humility, and respect; and were committed to practices of and deep listening during our interreligious gatherings. Deeply influenced by Buddhism myself and seeing the necessity for a mindful way of being to support Womanist, Buddhist, and African religious scholar gatherings at Harvard Divinity School featuring Buddhist texts, my articles describe the skillful means we used to cultivate a deep allowing of each heart and mind present. Instead of coming as experts and scholars, we invited each participant

---

1. For more on this, see Melanie L. Harris, *Ecowomanism: African American Women and Earth-Honoring Faiths* (Orbis, 2017).

2. Alice Walker, "Nuclear Madness," in *In Search of Our Mothers' Gardens: Womanist Prose* (Harcourt Brace Jovanovich, 1983), 345.

to come to the gathering with fresh eyes and embodying a spirit of openness to learn, receive, and share with one another. Nonviolent and committed to values of compassion, justice, and equality, the gatherings were built on a foundational practice of reading texts together in community inspired by the Jewish tradition *havruta*. *Havruta* originated as an Aramaic word and means friendship or companionship. The communal reading practice is inspired by the understanding that the meaning of sacred or religious texts can truly be revealed through shared dialogue and "struggling" or wrestling with the words.

This sense of struggling with or wrestling with is also common in the work of African American biblical hermeneutics and Black theology as one brings their life questions and inquiries of justice in dialogue with God in the work of theology. Rev. Dr. John Kinney, pastor of Ebenezer Baptist Church in Beaverdam, Virginia, and former Dean of Union Theological Seminary in Virginia, calls this kind of wrestling "fussing with God" for the purpose of understanding and wisdom seeing. In a sermon titled, "Frustrated Faith" Pastor Kinney explains fussing as a form of communication that validates a kind of maturity of relationship, featuring deep faith and trust. While some cultural perspectives shame fussing with God and see it as a forbidden practice because of the power differential between humans and God, Kinney describes the ability to fuss with God, or any other being, as a sign of spiritual formation and growth. For our purposes of modeling the interreligious nature of ecowomanist dialogue and providing multiple examples of religious inquiry and ways of approaching the sixth step of ecowomanist method—sharing dialogue—I include Kinney's explanation of "fussing" as faith formation and theological growth:

> When the relationship is not mature and committed, you have to be guarded in your conversation . . . because you recognize, "if I say this, it might damage or injure my relationship". . . [they are guarded] not because they have changed but because they are secure enough in the relationship to be honest about their feelings. If you always have to walk on eggshells and hide your feelings, it means you are in an insecure or threatened relationship and you are not allowed to speak truth because the truth will hurt what you have. But when you really know you've got a tight relationship, every now and then you are going to have a nice fuss.[3]

Contrary to a Christian hegemonic practice of evangelizing or use of a logic of control to try to "win" an argument, thus silencing the "opponent" by

---

3. John Kinney, "Frustrated Faith," sermon preached at Ebenezer Baptist Church, Beaverdam, VA, August 18, 2024, https://www.facebook.com/ebcbeaverdam/videos/806320061346767, accessed August 21, 2024.

not allowing others to speak, or by silencing others from the conversation, the practice of fussing, wrestling with words in community and engaging dialogue requires a deep allowing. This orientation guides participants away from ego and away from models of perfectionism based on hierarchical thinking and control and leans, rather, into the practice of sharing ideas and values foundational for interreligious dialogue. Here the point is to invite participants to listen deeply, notice, and release all mental formations that lead into blame, criticism, or competition in the process of sharing with one another.

While the practice of deep listening is associated with many traditions and social movements, I find it best to teach the practice through the model of Buddhist teacher and venerable monk Thich Nhat Hanh. In this Buddhist approach, conversationalists are invited to mindfully practice listening as a meditative practice in a way that allows them to honor and practice self-compassion and also honor and practice compassion for their conversation partners. Similar to the process of looking deeply for the purpose of understanding, the contemplative practice of deep listening as a part of engaging dialogue is not a Western or Eurocentric practice of being heard. The focus is not on the ego of the talking person but rather on the reshaping of their ear; the focus is on the practice of their heart toward awareness, respect, and love—and their capacity to truly respect another as they engage in hearing or deep listening.[4] Noting the temptation to attach the mind to a particular thought or idea, and aware of the ego's tendency to want to be right, deep listening rests on the practice of resting the mind and opening it to hold all ideas lightly and to perceive them simply as ideas. This mode of nonattachment can be achieved through contemplative mindfulness or meditative practice and helps one's mind to stay fully open and present as they allow others' voices to be heard, cherished, and understood.

A quick look at the mindful contemplation of deep listening is helpful in explaining how dialogue is understood as the sixth step of ecowomanist method. For this, I turn to the practice of deep listening taught by Thich Nhat Hanh in *Love Letters to the Earth* and *Teachings on Love*. He describes deep listening as a practice that invites true openness of mind and heart to have compassion on the self and others in a way that is nonviolent, loving, and promotes deep understanding and thus healthy connection. He writes,

---

4. For more on my insistence that white feminist and the wider guild open or reshape their ears to engage in thoughtful deep listening of Black women's and Indigenous voices, see Melanie L. Harris, "Reshaping the Ear: Honorable Listening and Study of Ecowomanist and Ecofeminist Scholarship for Feminist Discourse," *Journal of Feminist Studies in Religion* 33, no. 2 (2017): 158–62, https://doi.org/10.2979/jfemistudreli.33.2.16.

Suppose your partner says something unkind to you, and you feel hurt. If you reply right away, you risk making the situation worse. The best practice is to breathe in and out to calm yourself, and when you are calm enough, say, "Darling, what you just said hurt me. I would like to look deeply into it, and I would like you to look deeply into it, also." Then you can make an appointment for Friday evening to look at it together. One person looking at the roots of your suffering is good, two people looking at it is better, and two people looking together is best.... If you make an appointment, you will both have time to calm down and look deeply. This is the practice of meditation. Meditation is to calm ourselves and to look deeply into the nature of our suffering.[5]

In light of the first noble truth in Buddhism—suffering is a part of life—the practice of deeply looking into suffering allows us to recognize the wisdom of the second noble truth, that there are discernable causes for this suffering. It also invites us to engage the reality of a third noble truth: the causes of suffering can be transformed and terminated. As a mindfulness practice, the art of deep listening then can also be done through meditation, ritual, or peace/affirmation sharing or through contemplative practice in community and classroom.

For example, in the religious and theological classroom, Dr. Vincent Harding's pedagogy was influenced by this first step of honoring the self and others in conversation (and as colleagues) by first allowing each student or community member to introduce themselves by naming their full name, place of birth, life work, giving the full name of their maternal grandmother (or a similar nurturing figure), her place of birth, and her life work. As the members of the community name themselves and their own stories and mingle this with the stories of their ancestors or kinfolk, a sense of belonging and community emerges that honors the beingness and investment of every being in the circle or community. Through the engagement of this process, a foundation for trust is set for a deeper practice of respect for oneself and one another in the class.

The skillful means for deep listening, modeled in Harding's classroom, were influenced by community organizing and activist practices shaped by the civil rights movement and the work and practice of nonviolence.[6] The importance here is the connection between nonviolent action and healthy communication for the sake of community building. The Social Movements and Innovation

---

5. Thich Nhat Hanh, *Teachings on Love* (Parallax Press, 2007), 76.
6. For more on the work and practice of nonviolence in the civil rights movement, see the work of Vincent Harding. For more see, Dr. Vincent Harding, *There Is a River: The Black Struggle for Freedom in America* (Harvest Books, 1993); *Hope and History: Why We Must Share the Story of the Movement* (Orbis, 1997); and *Is America Possible: A Letter to My Young Companions on the Journey of Hope* (Fetzer Institute, 2007).

Lab defines deep listening as a tool of activism, suggesting that the practice unhooks both listener and speaker from unconscious bias even as feelings and emotions are shared in conversation. As a tool of deep listening, the truth of the ailment, injustice, or inequality and sometimes the solution emerges from the creation of space to allow for deep listening and holding of the perspective of persons impacted by an issue.

Through deep listening, social justice folks can strengthen their listening skills by observing the nonverbal cues and distinguishing between facts, feelings, and emotions of a conversation. Through deep listening practices, social justice folks focus less on their own perspectives and feelings and strive to learn something new.[7]

Inspired by ahimsa and emphasizing compassionate connection, the nonviolent approach of deep listening regards all beings as important. Ahimsa values all perspectives as important and worthy of being heard. These values are deeply embedded in the practice of contemplative pedagogy as witnessed in many Indigenous cultures, and these values lead to practices of deep listening and peacebuilding.[8]

Deep listening is especially effective for contemplative ecowomanist practices because it enhances reflection on eco-memory as instructed by the first methodological step. For ecowomanist approaches, how we listen to earth and for earth wisdom is central because it both guides us and teaches us how to do the work of environmental and climate justice. In part two of *Preaching Black Earth*, you will observe how deep listening is engaged by noting the flow of mindful speech that takes place in the interviews with the author.

Fresh spiritual insight flows from the passion ignited in the dialogue about ecowomanism between me and Rev. Dr. Frederick Douglass Haynes III. Pastor of the Friendship-West Baptist Church in Dallas, Texas, for more than three decades, former executive director of the Rainbow PUSH Coalition, and a powerful leader in social justice in the United States and across the world, Dr. Haynes's particular interests in environmental justice stems from his theological commitment to Black liberation theology and justice. Noting the spiritual values of community, solidarity, and freedom emerging from the traditions of African American religion and African indigenous belief systems that honor the earth as sacred, Dr. Haynes stresses the importance of activating community and movement building for the work of raising earth consciousness in Black communities in this age of climate change.

---

7. Social Movements and Innovation Lab, https://socialmovementsinnovation.org/tools/deep-listening/.
8. For more on this, see the conclusion of this book.

Part II: Earth Heart, Earth Hope 79

Deep listening between me and the next interviewee, Senior Pastor of Christ Missionary Baptist Church and former President of Lott Carey Ministries, Rev. Dr. Gina M. Stewart reveals the joy and liberation available to Black people especially in following the ecowomanist method and charting their eco-memory. Many peoples of African descent living in the south have deep roots to nature and the environment through memories of their parents, grandparents, and great grandparents. Connection with earth is webbed with connection to family for many peoples of African descent, making the process of engaging eco-memory not only a cultural memory process of engaging the terror of being descendants of enslaved persons but also engaging the triumph of being a part of families and communities who healed trauma and resisted slavery, Jim and Jane Crow, and other practices of white supremacy through cultivating a sacred connection with earth and honoring the earth as a partner in full liberation.

Following this is the shared dialogue featuring Dr. Larry Rasmussen. It is a testament to the depths of relationship and connection that is possible through engagement of deep listening through a practice of antiracist friendship established by the two of us. While a doctoral student at Union Theological Seminary in the City of New York, I studied with Dr. Rasmussen, then the Reinhold Niebuhr Professor of Social Ethics. Since retired, Dr. Rasmussen has continued to write and be an active voice in environmental ethics through the publications of *Earth-Honoring Faith: Religious Ethics in a New Key* (2012) and the *Planet You Inherit: Letters to My Grandchildren When Uncertainty's a Sure Thing* (2022) and through co-program direction of a ten-year teaching seminar and initiative with Ghost Ranch Education Conference Center in Abiquiu, New Mexico.

Reflective of the openness and inclusiveness of ecowomanism is my interview with scholars Rev. Dr. Heber Brown and Rev. Dr. Christopher Carter on their reflections as Black male scholars and activists in the environmental justice movement. Both Dr. Brown and Dr. Carter have served as pastors, movement leaders, teachers, and scholars; and as such their deep listening practices provide deep insight for the environmental justice movement as a whole. And more specifically they speak to the importance of shedding gender hierarchies and practices of patriarchy for the sake of honoring the sacred in women environmental leaders and for the sake of honoring the earth.

Finally, I engage in conversation with renowned environmental justice and ecowomanist scholars working in the movement. In this interview, led by Dr. Katie Common, with Dr. Frances Roberts-Gregory and me, you will witness the practice of deep listening through the ways that questions are formed, and responses given, that accent deep understanding, affirmation, and shared dialogue.

Sharing dialogue through an ecowomanist contemplative approach comes through cultivation of friendship, healthy connection, and earth community.

The inclusive nature of ecowomanism through its attention to interreligious dialogue and practice of trust and peacebuilding is central to the future of ecowomanist thought. Being self aware and mindfully connected to partners in the work of environmental justice undergirds the importance of all of the steps of the ecowomanist method, especially step six—sharing dialogue. As the interviews in the following section unfold, you are invited to participate in the practice of deep listening.

7

Ecowomanist Prophetic Voices

Black Liberation Theology and A Vision of Earth Resurrection

INTERVIEW WITH FREDERICK DOUGLASS HAYNES III

This interview is a snapshot of an ongoing conversation between Harris and Haynes that consistently uplifts and expands the contours of Black liberation theology and womanist thought, especially as these discourses expand the work of church ministry in environmental justice.[1]

Melanie L. Harris: Thank you so much, Dr. Haynes, for joining us in this work of *Preaching Black Earth*. This is an edited volume with a collection of sermons, meditations, earth poems, and spiritual reflections on environmental justice. Recognizing that so much of African American life and spirituality comes out of the preached word, I'm hoping that our conversation will enlighten people on not just how to preach about earth justice but how to do environmental justice.

I want to start, Dr. Haynes, first by asking a question about the food justice work that Friendship-West is connected to. And then, if you can just give us a little bit of information on what inspired you and what inspired Friendship-West to do environmental justice work. I know that so much of it was around the VIP program and its basic tenant of caring for and feeding the hungry.[2] But because you're in Dallas, so much environmental justice work has to be curtailed to the realities of that city.

---

1. This interview was recorded with permission on June 21, 2023.
2. The VIP, Very Important Persons ministry at Friendship West Baptist Church is a part of the social justice ministries at Friendship West Baptist Church dedicated to persons who are housing insecure or experiencing homelessness. This ministry is one of the most vital ministries of its kind in Dallas and feeds, clothes, and cares for the needs of those experiencing homelessness. For more information, see https://www.friendshipwest.org/social-justice.

Frederick Douglass Haynes III: Thank you so much for this opportunity to share with you. I thank you for the tremendous work that you are doing, informed by your brilliant mind. And thank you so much because you've inspired and helped to hold us accountable when it comes to the work of environmental justice. So I salute you, Dr. Melanie, for your amazing work.

When I read the Genesis account of, you know, God basically entrusting humanity with stewarding the earth, we have a responsibility to manage the creation that has been entrusted to us. And the more I lean into that and sit with that, it is incumbent upon us to do all we can to make sure that we are indeed trusted managers of the beautiful, phenomenal life-giving creation that the creator of the universe has so generously entrusted to us. So, I begin there.

I also must testify that this awareness of climate change—not just climate change, but our responsibility to be stewards of the earth— has caused me to be on a collision course, as it were, with environmental racism—the intentional practice and placement of environmental waste in communities of color. As keepers of environmental justice on the south side of town, our work helps to expose unjust environmental policies that allow children and adults to be poisoned in their communities. Over the years, because of where we are located and our practice of doing ministry that serves the people globally, nationally, but also exactly where we are, I have discovered that there are twenty-nine landfills south of downtown Dallas. We don't have that on the north side of town.

And then most recently, we were in a justice fight. One of our members, who lives, again, on the south side of Dallas, had placed literally next door to her some ten-stories high—several tons—of roof shingles. And it came to be known in a very disparaging fashion as Shingle Mountain. Imagine that. Ten stories of shingles from rooftops here in Texas. And you already know of the heat that we experience in Texas. And they literally placed it not just in her community, but next door to her. And, unfortunately, she's experienced health challenges, especially when it comes to respiratory issues, in light of Shingle Mountain. Because of racism in zoning and planning, it was allowed to be placed next door to this wonderful Black woman, who is a human being. Her humanity—her health—was totally disrespected and not taken into account when zoning persons allowed this in the name of capitalism.

Unfortunately, the greed of capitalism has fueled so much of the environmental injustice that pollutes certain areas and, at the same time, ensures that other areas are doing well. And then Dr. Melanie, as you well know, it's so sad. In Dallas where I am called to serve, we've discovered that you can live fifteen minutes from an area where the life expectancy is just totally different than the life expectancy you may be in.³

In one particular area, the life expectancy is some fifteen to twenty-five years longer than those who live in South Dallas. And we know who lives in South Dallas already. So speaking of Black, Brown, and poor people, the great Harvard scholar Dr. Williams talks about the fact that life expectancy is not determined by your genetic code but by your zip code. It's a reflection that we are in a nation where your life expectancy will be determined by the zip code you live in. And again, that has everything to do with the air we breathe, access to water, and access to fresh and healthy food or the lack thereof. And so, all of that has been motivation for me. And so now I am sandwiched between Jesus declaring, "I've come that you might have life and have it more abundantly,"⁴ and being contradicted by the environment that we find ourselves in simply because of the color of our skin, simply because of our economic status—all of these literally determine life expectancy.

And so, my prayer is, you know, that those who claim to be pro-life will take another look at abortion as something that takes place when my life expectancy is cut short simply because of the color of my skin, because of my economic status. I have discovered that the color of my skin and economic status in this nation may well be hazardous to my health. So that got me into this fight for environmental justice.

I've been to Flint, Michigan. I've been to Jackson, Mississippi. Environmental racism is not going to take place in the fanciest sections in Michigan or Mississippi, let alone here in Dallas, Texas. As my colleague Bishop William Barber says, sadly, there are too many people who have a lack of resources to buy unleaded gas, but they end up drinking leaded water. And that is sinful, especially when we claim to be one nation under God. And so, the bottom line is that public policy fueled by the greed of capitalism oftentimes creates what a Southen Methodist University study revealed last year.⁵ With infrastructure deserts and also environmental injustice, my life expectancy is cut short because of

---

3. For more on research in health equity and research regarding how life expectancy can now be connected to the zip code you reside in see, Robert Wood Johnson Foundation, "What Makes a Long Life?: Look to your ZIP Code," https://www.rwjf.org/en/insights/our-research/interactives/whereyouliveaffectshowlongyoulive.html.

4. Adaptation of John 10:10.

5. The research study links wastewater injection with recent blowouts in the Permian Basin (a top-producing oil field in the United States) and provides details about water recently spraying up from previously active water wells, negatively impacting the groundwater. Dylan Baddour and Carlos Nogueras Ramos, "Ranchers Reported Abandoned Oil Wells Spewing Wastewater. A New Study Blames Fracking," *The Texas Tribune*, https://www.texastribune.org/2024/08/07/texas-oil-fracking-wastewater-injection-blowouts-permian-basin/.

the side of town that I live on. That contradicts Jesus saying, "I've come, that you might have life and have it more abundantly."

Harris: Thank you. Thank you so much. There is an echo of Martin Luther King Jr. always in your voice and in your presence as a homiletician. And I'm reminded that it was he who really did open up our eyes in terms of the environmental health hazards that the sanitation workers were facing in Memphis, Tennessee. And so much of the ecological justice that you do in Dallas is indeed a continuation of King's struggle and the work of racial justice even at that time.

But you're talking to a different group of people now. You preach to different folks, and certainly post-COVID churches all over have changed dramatically in terms of who's coming to church, who's hearing the word. Can you talk a little bit about the reality of what we're facing as African Americans? As you know, so many African Americans are returning to the South. They're coming back to Dallas. They're coming back to North Carolina with the reality of what's going on in New York City, you know, from smog and wildfires in Canada to everything else. People are having to move, and people are being literally displaced because of climate change. So Black folks are finding their way back South. And the lynching tree is in the South and the stomping out of the agricultural genius of Black people is in the South. Can you reflect more with us about the significance of environmental justice preaching, especially in the South, noting that so many African Americans find themselves in the pew on Sunday morning, trying to figure out how to work and move toward climate justice by applying the gospel of Jesus Christ as a lens through which to understand the paradox of the existence of white supremacy with the reality of God's vision for abundance in Earth? How do you as a homiletician, how do you as a preacher and a social justice leader in our time, how do you help Black folk reconcile their relationship with Earth when our relationship with the planet is different? It is very different because of capitalism, as you name, because of white supremacy, and getting our hands back into the earth is not as easy as grabbing an iPhone.

Haynes: Right, right. No question. That's a phenomenal question. For me, it's been important for us to, on the one hand, create the kind of homiletical narrative whereby we connect stewardship of time, talent, treasures, which we often talk about, to a stewardship of the earth; and so on one level, it's very important for me to preach that—Dr. King said it so well—"injustice anywhere is a threat to justice everywhere." So, if there is environmental injustice in South Dallas, I've got to be concerned about it if I'm in Oak Cliff; because injustice in South Dallas, environmental injustice in South Dallas, will eventually be in Oak Cliff. But as you so again, brilliantly pointed out, the world is open.

COVID basically pushed the church into fulfilling or being positioned to fulfill the Great Commission for going into all the world.[6] And my challenge now as a pastor, trying to be responsible homiletically, is to make sure that I am addressing this concept of environmental justice globally and not just in South Dallas. I have a responsibility to speak to what our children are experiencing in the Congo as they dig out of the earth those metals that are placed in our phones, and at the same time, they're being exposed to chemicals and toxins that cut short their life expectancy. That injustice in the Congo is basically being funded by the greed of capitalistic countries.

And so, we have to connect the dots that, you know, we are on this planet together. And that's my prayer. I'm hoping that COVID has taught us that something can start in China and before you know it, the whole globe is shut down. And we are all on this planet together as stewards, and we have a responsibility to live accordingly. So my preaching, my ministry consciousness has to reflect that. And it's something I am trying to educate myself as much as possible on a continuous basis because this planet is on fire right now. We just have to be real. This planet is crying out. For those who believe in any kind of biblical authority, all you got to do is look at Romans 8. This earth is groaning right now.

We're moving into hurricane season. God, I'm praying, because the hurricanes are becoming more and more volatile. I'm in Texas, and the South has been hit in recent days by vicious tornadoes. The extremes that we are experiencing in weather. And it breaks my heart that it hits anyone. But I'm watching the news, you know, a few days ago and this Black community in Moss Point, Mississippi, is literally devastated by a tornado such as they've never seen before. The earth is on fire.[7] Paul is right. In Romans 8, creation is groaning and hoping for a resurrection. Faith and your leadership, Dr. Melanie, have been so vital to helping us raise that kind of consciousness that what's happening right now is not accidental.

And I want to say this gently and with sensitivity, but it's almost hypocritical for us to pray. You know, God, please bless those families who have been hurt by, you know, quote unquote, "natural disasters." And I say that in air quotes for a reason—I'll come back to that later. But we're not doing anything to cool the earth and preclude climate change and the environmental racism; that is going to always wreak havoc on who Jesus called the least of these. And so, Jesus today may well say, "I was hungry. You didn't feed me. I was thirsty. You contaminated water, with your toxins. I was a stranger. You did not welcome

---

6. Matthew 28:19.
7. For more see Tracie Sempier, "Moss Point Tornadoes Highlight Growing Threat in Southeast,"Mississippi-Alabama Sea Grant Consortium, https://masgc.org/article/moss-point-tornadoes-highlight-growing-threat-in-southeast.

me. I was in prison. You did not visit me. My life expectancy was cut short by environmental injustice."[8] And the country will say, "Well, Jesus, when did we do this?" And his response would be, "In as much as you did it to the least of these my sisters and brothers, you have also done it unto me." And so this is biblical.

If we believe that God is the creator and sustainer of life, we have a responsibility to do all we can to make sure that we're doing our part to cool the earth, to be good managers and stewards of the earth. And so again, my preaching has had to change because now when I say, "The earth is the LORD's, and the fullness thereof; the world, and they that dwell therein," it really means a whole lot.[9] It means it's bigger than the United States. And so, there's a global consciousness that I am doing my best to grow into, to embrace, and to make sure that it comes out as we raise the consciousness of a people who too many times are so caught up in the experiences of just trying to make it. They may not have the opportunity to connect the dots between why my mother is dying of lung cancer at an early age and praying that God will heal her. I'm down with that; at the same time, we're asking God to clean up what has been messed up. And we're not doing our part to partner with God in answering that prayer so Mama does not inhale those toxins and drink that water that will cut short her life expectancy. So now it's about connecting all the dots because it's hard to pray for healing when you're living in a sick world.

Harris: Hallelujah. You talked about a resurrection faith in the last question and about what that means, particularly for African American peoples and Black peoples who, as you've challenged us to think globally, should not just think about Compton but think also about the Congo, not just think about Accra but also think about our own places where we are. What does that resurrection faith look like, particularly for Black people? Because connecting the dots means recognizing, as Fannie Lou Hamer did, that there were so many Black children, so many Black families who were literally dying of poverty. As you remember, she, in the last years of her life, really did lead a lot of environmental justice work and aligned this with the civil rights movement. It was Hamer who helps us to open a conversation about communal self-sufficiency. Through the freedom farms she started to feed people, to create farms, to create abundance right where they were. But she fed white people too. She saw the reality of how as an African American woman, not only her people, but white people were poor people also. So there's a kind of transformation that we can witness in her, that can be linked to a shift in her worldview and a deepening of her theology that resulted in a

---

8. See Matthew 25:31–46.
9. Psalms 24:1 (KJV).

practice of radical love and antiracism. In this light, we celebrate Fannie Lou Hamer because she existed, she survived, and found a way to thrive, and we celebrate her work because she produced some of the very foundations of social and human transformation work that ground our practices of faith inspired social justice today.

How does that model of Hamer speak to us in terms of a resurrected faith? As an African American woman living and actively protesting injustice in the Jim and Jane Crow South, she suffered extraordinary racial trauma. In many of her recorded speeches and in interviews with her, she talks about the abuses to her body, her mind, her psyche, and attempts to snuff out her spirit; but she survived. Hamer's testimony of surviving this brutal trauma is somehow linked to her ability to see God in earth, to recognize beauty in nature as a healing balm. It was her faith in God, evidenced through her relationship with earth that allowed her to acknowledge the impact of the trauma, yet also be grateful for the beauty of earth. She recognized, through her faith, that Psalms 24:1 says, the "earth is the LORD's and the fullness thereof," and this gave her hope. And that hope gave her a clarity of vision to see the truth about the systemic nature of food and economic injustice that resulted in pervasive poverty throughout the South at that time. She recognized that maintenance of an unfair, unjust economic system cost everybody, regardless of race. As such, Hamer is an important model of faith as well as a model of environmental justice activism because she stood up and said, I want to take care of my Black community and Black families and make sure that we have food and abundance, even if it means going off the grid. But there's a Jesus call for me to recognize that the practice of creating an economic system that traps everyone into poverty isn't right. Hamer helps us think about an ecowomanist ethic that creates racial justice, but also builds upon the wider work of environmental justice that eradicates poverty and in essence is antiracist, antioppressive, and insists on equality and liberation.

Haynes: Exactly. And I think that, you know, we began this conversation remembering Martin King. And to marry the legacy of King with the legacy of Hamer, I think is quite fitting and appropriate as we look at the concept of resurrection faith and the healing of the earth, which I think we are called to and whatever else.

Again, I go back to the lesson COVID taught. You know, COVID taught, and again, I quote my brother, William Barber, that viruses always expose the fissures in the structure of society that allow infections to thrive. And so when you look at the structures that allowed for a Black community that was being tested least but dying most, and then before you knew it, that virus was not missing any socioeconomic status. It was a fresh reminder that we are all on this planet together. What infects me directly may well be contagious and infect someone else indirectly and vice versa. What infects my white brother?

Sister? However they self-identify, it may infect me directly or indirectly. The bottom line is the infection has spread.

Our responsibility, if we are about that justice life, is to make sure that the infection not only does not spread, but no one gets infected. It's getting on the front end to make sure that there is a healthy whole earth, and a healthy whole earth means I've got to look out for everybody because I'm looking out for the whole earth. We cannot afford for any part of this planet to be sick because sickness spreads. This is important to note, as this kind of ethic of care is imperative if we are to live out the life of the Christian faith. In other words, abiding by a planetary care ethic helps us to live out our resurrection faith in our everyday lives.

I'm really proud of the fact that a number of churches have joined this healthy food movement. We have our own garden here at Friendship-West where we are producing on the regular fresh produce. One of the sicknesses in our society is the fact that there are those grocery stores that determine whether or not they're going to be in a community based on the educational socioeconomic status of those who live there. And so there are certain stores that are not on our side of town. And what we've done is decide, okay, store owners, you may not want to come here. (Parenthetically, that's a sickness because you're missing out on the interconnectedness of the whole of humanity. And if we're sick over here, eventually you're going to get sick over there.) What we've decided to do is fight for just policies that will bring about, you know, those kinds of stores on this side of town, like Whole Foods, Sprouts, and Central Market that refuse to come over here.

In the meantime, we have a responsibility. We have a biblical mandate to take care of this earth. As African people, we've always been connected to the earth. We've grown our food, we've grown our produce, and we've always seen God in nature. It's real difficult to be following African values and violate nature completely. We have that spirit of Sankofa, and we go back to where we've come from in order for us to move forward. A part of our resurrection faith is going to involve doing everything we can to retrieve that Africanity. And upon retrieving that Africanity, there's a love for the earth and a commitment to cultivating the earth, partnering with the earth for life.

The beautiful thing about reconnecting with our Africanity is that one of the values of being African is hospitality. That means we're not out to hurt anyone else. We're not just going to greedily take over all the good of the earth, but instead, we welcome all to join us in reconnecting with the earth that we might experience the resurrection of this planet. And in the resurrection of this planet, I believe God will not only honor it, but God will . . . I'm a preacher, I can say this and refer to the scripture, 2 Chronicles 7:14 . . . "if my people called by my name, humble themselves and pray, seek my face, turn from their wicked ways, then will I hear from heaven? And heal the land." I think that's what we're called to in these days.

Harris: Reverend Dr. Frederick Douglass Haynes III, Senior Pastor of Friendship-West Baptist Church in Dallas, Texas, global justice keeper, and worker and leader for us all. Thank you so much for your wisdom, for your prophetic word and witness, and for your gifts of grace in this time.

Haynes: Well, God bless you. Thank you for your amazing leadership, for your scholarship, and for wedding scholarship with Spirit, because you are, without question, a woman of remarkable faith and prayer. And you love the Lord your God with all your heart, with all your mind, soul, and strength, and your neighbor as yourself. Thank you for embodying that. So brilliant.

Harris: Thank you. Thank you. Bless you.

8

Ecowomanist Spirituality

Earth Home and Homiletics

Interview with Gina M. Stewart

This interview gives an inside view into ongoing womanist conversations between Harris and Stewart that engage themes of academic and ministerial leadership, womanist theology and ethics, African American preaching, and ecowomanism.[1]

Melanie L. Harris: Thank you so much and welcome to Reverend Dr. Gina M. Stewart. I am so grateful for your presence for this special interview for *Preaching Black Earth*, featuring themes connecting environmental justice, ecowomanism, and African American homiletics together! Thank you again for sharing your wisdom with us and welcome.

Gina M. Stewart: Thank you, Dr. Harris, for the invitation to participate in such a worthy project. I'm honored to be included in this volume. Thank you.

Harris: One of the gifts of being in conversation with you is the opportunity to reflect on the incredible worship that many of us experience Sunday to Sunday as you lead worship as senior pastor of Christ Missionary Baptist Church. In person or online we are able to hear the prophetic word come to life every week through your wonderful preaching and extraordinary leadership. You embody so powerfully a womanist identity as pastor, leader, and social justice keeper. One of the specific ways in which womanism shows up in your ministry is through your leadership as an environmental justice leader in food justice in the church. This work can be understood as an example of ecowomanist practice.

---

1. This interview was recorded with permission on July 6, 2023.

Ecowomanism, of course, helps us to see connections between earth justice and all social justice issues. The seven step method of ecowomanism begins with an awareness of the intersections between environmental justice and all justice issues. The first step invites us to reflect on our own experience. So, Dr. Stewart, let's begin our conversation with a question about your own experience with the earth, with nature, and particularly how it weaves into your theology and your practice of Black spirituality. I know that you have traveled globally and especially to Africa many times. If you wouldn't mind, please share some about your experience with nature in Africa and reflect with us how these experiences deepened your own commitment to earth justice.

Stewart: Thank you for the question. I'm happy to answer that and would like to begin by backing up just a little. As you were asking your question, I was reminded that although I've spent all my life in the city, my paternal grandfather was actually a farmer. And as I reflect, I am aware that my parents also had strong connections to nature in their rural context and upbringing. It was not uncommon for us as children to travel to what my father called "out home," which was his home of origin and where his father still lived.

My grandfather was very active as a farmer for many years up until his health started to fail. I think he died in his, I'm not sure whether it was in his 70s or 80s, but he actually farmed until he became ill with leukemia. Even when he was sick, he went to the fields every day. So often when we would go to visit, he would still be in the fields well into the late afternoon or evening and we would be at the house. He would arrive, you know, basically just in time for dinner. It is interesting because your question evoked in me some strong memories associated with that, with family. Of course, as children, we had no concept of eco-justice, ecowomanism, or how you should care for the environment as a part of justice work. We just knew that our grandparents had lots of land; it was almost like a park really. They did not have a large house, but lots of land.

There was a field where they grew corn on part of the land, and then there was just this open space with lots of trees. As children we played volleyball, we played kickball, we played hide-and-go-seek, and all of those things. I realize now, in retrospect, what a gift that was to my life.

Now at age sixty-three, I'm just realizing, because it was really a no brainer, that access to land and beauty and space was just a given for me and my siblings. It was a part of our practice in terms of how our family navigated life. They always gathered there. But as I think back over that, what a gift that was to be a Black man in the South who owned land. Dr. Floyd Flake often says, "God is not making any more land." So the fact that my grandfather owned land and that that land is still in the possession of my father's siblings is really amazing. Our family still owns that land. As I think about that now,

I didn't realize how significant it was, our Black family-owned land. We were just going out to Papa's house. That's all we knew. That was probably my first introduction to some type of appreciation for the earth.

I've never been what you call an outdoor person. I like air conditioning, and I don't like bugs. But I do remember the joy and the freedom that we would often experience as children because there were plenty of trees and lots of grass. It was our playing space. Although we had no concept of stewardship as children, we just knew that this was our grandparents' land, and it was accessible to us. And so I wouldn't say that I had any deep, signature experiences of earth stewardship growing up. It is only in retrospect that I'm really recognizing what a gift the land was to us.

When I started traveling internationally, one of my most signature experiences occurred in South Africa. I've gone to South Africa several times: a couple of times to preach, once with my church as a cultural and missional immersion experience, and as team leader for the Lott Carey Baptist Convention Pastoral Excellence Program. I later became the first woman to lead Lott Carey as president.

One of my most significant memories was the trip to Victoria Falls, in Zimbabwe, which is known as one of the Seven Natural Wonders of the world. I discovered in doing some research the name is actually a colonized name and that the actual African name is Mosi-oa-Tunya from the Sotho language, which means "the smoke that thunders." It's the largest curtain of falling water in the world or the largest natural waterfall in the world. It's breathtaking to behold. And we didn't even go when the water was at its peak! Just to witness and to see it created this deep connection in me. It invoked this deep connection in me with the God of the universe.

One cannot look at the wonders of nature and the wonders of creation without somehow saying to themselves, "somebody much bigger than me or you had to do all of this." And not only did they do it, but they are such an artist. It is the artistry and the creativity of God. When I look at nature, it just makes me want to break out into singing "How Great Thou Art." And of course, we know that God is a creative. God created lands, God created oceans, vegetation, all before creating us. One of the things that I began to think about when I was in those various contexts—Victoria Falls, Cape Point, and Table Mountain in South Africa—is how God created the earth with such creativity, beauty, and variety.

When I visited Table Mountain in South Africa (which is at a high altitude), we rode up to the table of the mountain in a cable car. One of the first things I noticed were flowers growing at such a high altitude. Now, you know that only God could do something like that, where flowers can thrive at a high altitude where they would not be expected to survive. And I'm not talking about just vegetation. These were colorful beautiful flowers and all kinds of varieties. That experience gave me a deeper appreciation not only for the creativity of God, but the way that God demonstrates diversity, and how everything is so different, and everything has its own traits and characteristics. To see all of that on a mountain where flowers and vegetation are not supposed to thrive, at high altitudes, was certainly breathtaking. I would call this a signature experience in my eco-memory.

A final example of an eco-memory occurred at Cape Point. My friend and I traveled to South Africa and decided to travel to the mountain Cape Point, on the Cape of Good Hope Peninsula in South Africa. Visitors are invited to climb the steep incline to the lighthouse at the top of Cape Point. There were so many steps to the top of the mountain that it appeared to be a "staircase to heaven." Legend says Cape Point is where the Atlantic Ocean and the Pacific Ocean meet.

As we were walking up the steps, my friend noticed that there was an older woman climbing the steps alone. She had her little jacket over her arm and a cane. My friend noticed that tourists were whisking past this woman, and she suggested that we ask her if she needed help. When we inquired about assisting her, she responded, "I'm just trying to get up to that place where the oceans meet." And we told her, "We'll walk up with you." The trek up the steps seemed to take forever, but it was worth it. And I tell you, Dr. Harris, what a powerful moment that was when we finally reached the landing and looked out across the ocean, a rainbow appeared in the sky.

Harris: Wow.

Stewart: It was so powerful because it seemed as if God was smiling on the experience. And our older friend was just grinning and smiling. So, to be up at that altitude, to have taken the time to help her up the steps, then to get up the steps ourselves, and to witness such amazing natural beauty was breathtaking. In retrospect, this was a signature eco-memory (although I didn't have the language to describe it at that time). Witnessing the beauty from that specific landing place, because as far as the eye could see there was nothing but ocean and water.

The sight of earth's beauty and witnessing the joy in our older friend's face made that an unforgettable moment. And so, once again, you look at all of this and you say, how can anybody not believe that there's a God? How can anyone see all of this and not echo the words of the psalmist—"the heavens declare the glory of God." All those experiences, just take me back to the book of Genesis and remind me of the creative genius of God. God is a creative who has created all of this for the blessing of all creation. Because I was raised in the city, I don't think I was attuned to that.

When we traveled to Grand Junction, as a child, I remember looking out on the vastness of land and sensing the vastness of God. For the children in our families, the land and all of nature existed for our purposes to play and to run and have freedom. But now I see what a blessing that was for a Black child, for Black children, to have that kind of access and freedom in the 1960s. To be in that space that was not inhibited by fear of racial harm; to know that this was our land and that it was fully owned by a Black family. It is in retrospect that I appreciate the connections between land, Black freedom, and farming. This is important because we must make the connection between environmental injustice and its impact on Black farmers. But everything depends on farming. I mean, we don't eat without farmers. Those are my signature experiences or eco-memories.

I will share one last eco-memory. When I look out of the window when I'm on a plane (I often like to take pictures of the clouds when we fly up above, when we reach those high altitudes), I witness the majesty of God. And, you know, I just feel myself wanting to burst out singing because I believe that is the appropriate response when beholding that kind of beauty: to break out in praise to God.

Harris: Amen. Thank you, Pastor Stewart. As always, you weave so much beauty and brilliance into such deep reflection, and we are so grateful for your response. The final eco-memory that you shared with us of being on a plane and experiencing your spirit being so full, ready to praise God, is a wonderful contemplative moment. What I heard in what you shared was a true spirit of worship emerging from the experience of being in nature and "feeling" God in earth.

I also appreciated what you shared around freedom. This is so important, especially for Black people. Communing with nature as divine and also experiencing this kind of freedom as a part of one's communion with earth, these are tenets of ecowomanism. In terms of the justice work of creating equal accessibility, your example shows the impact of Black people having full access, and what can happen when Black people feel fully free to be connected to the earth community—as you name so powerfully— apart from racism, apart from the threat of being racialized. This is a right and a miracle—to be free to experience the fullness of the beauty of earth community.

Your reflection was so deep because it does lead us to think about that kind of freedom for Black people particularly, and how we recover this, in the same way that you were doing in your memory. Reclaiming the space, reclaiming the memory so as to be able to cultivate the spirit; to be able to come to this place of freedom in mind, in spirit and body. To be able to be open to the clouds, be able to be open to God's spirit, be open to the rainbow and really receiving that moment as a worship moment. A kind of communion with God.

The reality is, as you mentioned, many of us African American folk have actually been kind of trained to ignore or disdain the land, the earth, farming. In part because there are so many generations just ahead of us who were trying to protect us from the historical reality of the trauma and bondages of slavery and the kind of traumatic memory that this has left, right? The kind of paradox of being owned as property and working the property. So being earth ourselves as property, but then also working the earth. Right now this is a part of the crisis, really, and particularly in BIPOC and African American communities. How do we heal our relationship with the Earth? And what you have just articulated is such a beautiful kind of teaching really, of how to come back into contemplative practice and connection with the earth to be able to notice it, right?

And the artistry of God, as you named, weaves so beautifully into what Alice Walker talked about in the womanist definition. I mean, really looking at the different colors of all the flowers in the mother's garden. Can you talk a little bit about how you would preach that? How would you teach that? What would be the approach?

You talked about the magnificence of God and Genesis. There are a lot of folks right now who do lose hope in the existence of God. And it's almost as if a part of the movement of ecowomanism and a part of the ecojustice movement are to just help people get outside so they can see God and commune that way. Not just that, but, you know, also all of the other work, the food justice work of feeding the community and being fed in just ways as well as creating moments of communion. Through this justice work, people can experience the kind of salvific moments they need to reclaim the gifts of nature as gifts from God. Do you mind reflecting a little bit on that? How would you preach that?

Stewart: I'm happy to share, and I'd like to add an addendum to my reflection about my grandparents' land. They owned it, and we lived from it. It was a source of provision for our lives because my grandparents grew food, vegetables, and owned cattle. They owned cows, chickens, and pigs. I remember making the connection about the generosity of the earth, and the generous way that my grandparents gave food to neighbors and family. The cows provided beef, the chickens provided meat and eggs, the pigs provided sausage and ribs.

And as I'm talking to you about this, I'm thinking back over how we (my sister and I) didn't reflect a lot on the level of privilege we had, having immediate access to food, shelter, family, and resources that the earth provided. We took for granted what we had because it was always available. Because my grandparents were farmers, this provided a means of self-sufficiency and independence. As a farmer, my grandfather specifically did not have to be subject to the dehumanization of his era. Owning his own land gave him independence and therefore nurtured a deep sense of freedom for me and my entire family.

In reflecting on these signature moments and experiences with nature, these eco-memories can evoke a kind of worshipful response to God. This sense of ecological spirituality is something I am still learning about but sharing these eco-memories with you helps to remind me and all of us that we owe our existence to the creator. As a woman of faith, I understand the creator as God. From this perspective I recognize myself as a creature in coexistence and in relationship with all of God's creation. This earth consciousness shifts my perspective from a domination framework to a more relational framework.

I remember an experience with one of my mentors. We were in the park, and while we were walking she was dropping wisdom nuggets. As she was talking, I distinctly remember stepping on a bug. My mentor immediately reprimanded me. She asked, "Why did you kill that bug? That bug was not bothering you." I mean, she just gave me this tongue lashing, and I'm thinking to myself, "It's just a bug?" In hindsight, I understand now that she embodied a kind of earth consciousness, an awareness of a web-of-life connection that we (humans) share with all beings on earth. Even though she didn't explain it explicitly as earth consciousness, or name it as an ecowomanist framework, I can now appreciate the sense of respect and honor for the earth that she had; and I admit I didn't have this at the time. I was just starting seminary and had not yet been exposed to relational frameworks that are non-hierarchical. Even though I experienced a kind of gender equity in my church context, I was still in the process of learning about how vital nonhierarchical, nonoppressive frameworks are for ministry, justice work. My mentor's awareness in that moment helped to deepen my own understanding of sharing life on earth with nonhumans. I was convicted by that conversation.

I think that there's probably some parallel here between our care or lack of care for the earth and what we have experienced as women in particular. Ecowomanism helps us to see the parallel negative treatment that nature and women have experienced. Women, and especially women of color, have often been dominated and intimidated. My behavior toward the bug mirrored this practice. I was bigger than the bug, so I felt that I could do what I wanted to do. My mentor challenged this hierarchical mindset and pushed me to embrace a more relational way of being and thinking.

When I think about that experience and your question about how I would teach about our connection with the earth, I would go back again to Genesis and address the problem of language in Genesis 1:27–28. The use of "dominion" language can be problematic because it creates hierarchy. This word, "dominion," can be interpreted as dominance, which can also be misused to justify oppressive practices or be understood as a license for hierarchy rather than stewardship, responsibility, and care. I heard Reverend Dr. Neichelle Guidry say that nothing destroys a community like hierarchy. In teaching this, I would invite students to interrogate the definition of dominion, examine the translation of the word, and begin a conversation about how we can create a more expansive definition of "dominion." I would encourage students to consider what can happen when power is concentrated at the top. When dominion is understood as hierarchical, "others" may experience their agency being diminished. As was the case with the bug. King described this dynamic as commodifying or objectifying a human being and explained that this was done as a practice of white supremacist abuse to devalue and debase Black folk with a mean spirit so as to hurt, harm, or crush their self-worth and self-esteem. Often this move to commodify or objectify a person was done to make the person lose all sense of self and power, thus leaving them vulnerable to being controlled or possessed. The commodification or objectification of a being follows a pattern of abuse and can also be called the "thingamazation" of another human being. When we commodify one another and dismiss the sacred value and instinctual worth of "the other," we can perpetuate a logic of domination that can lead to cruelty, injustice, and indifference. This is why liberative and womanist theologies are so important as corrective lenses. They help to transform our understanding of being in relationship *with*, rather than being in relationship *over*. They give us a new vision of what's possible in our relationships, in our relationship with the earth and other human beings. Dr. John Kinney's teachings are also helpful here, in that they point out the danger of the desire for hierarchy. He calls it "snakeology" and explains that forms of oppression that are built into the structure of a theology can often be damaging and detrimental. They can distort the character of God and destroy healthy relationships.

This understanding of dominion has been at the root of colonization, slavery, systemic racism and gender inequity, and other injustices. Uprooting these forms of injustice begins with challenging our interpretation of "dominion" found in Scripture. Rather than dominion, stewardship would be a better word and translation of the biblical text in Genesis because it encourages us to take responsibility and care for, rather than control, exploit, and oppress the earth that God has created. The call is not to have dominion over but rather to be in relationship with the earth.

Harris: Absolutely. Thank you. Thank you. Wow. Pastor Stewart, thank you so much for your time. This has been so nourishing, so powerful. There's so much more that we could ask. For example, it would be wonderful to hear more about the food justice ministry and justice work you lead as Senior Pastor of Christ Missionary Church.

Stewart: You did ask me about that. I can answer that if you'd like.

Harris: Please.

Stewart: Our commitment to food justice work really dates back to my predecessor, Rev. Eddie L. Currie. Our commitment to food justice is woven into the mission of our church but is a part of my own ministerial philosophy. Theological education helped me to reflect on what it means to respond to food insecurity and food injustice. This practice is informed by Dr. J. Deotis Roberts's book *The Prophethood of Black Believers*.[2] He describes the body of Christ as an extension of the incarnation; that God was most concretely and supremely revealed in Jesus Christ and Jesus's ministry is public, priestly, and prophetic. My theology and ministerial leadership are shaped by that perspective. I believe that there's a public, priestly, and prophetic aspect to ministry.

If the church is indeed the body of Christ as metaphor and reality, and if it is indeed an extension of the incarnation, then our ministry should translate into a public, priestly, and prophetic kind of ministry, which means we should be concerned about the things that Jesus was concerned about. Food insecurity is a major problem in America, and doing food justice work is our response to Jesus's ministerial vision. This is one of the ways that our church has chosen to respond to the disparities throughout the world and in communities that we serve. Jesus said, in Matthew 25:35, "I was hungry and you fed me." I call that the pop quiz of Jesus; an unexpected test of our faithfulness that reveals the condition of our hearts. Here in the text, Jesus is teaching a parable that serving others is synonymous with serving Jesus.

Harris: Wow. Thank you, Rev. Dr. Gina M. Stewart, Pastor of Christ Missionary Baptist Church, for your powerful sharing and insights on environmental justice and ecowomanism.

Stewart: Thank you, Dr. Harris.

---

2. J. Deotis Roberts, *The Prophethood of Black Believers: An African American Political Theology for Ministry* (Westminster John Knox Press, 1994).

9

Ecowomanist Community

Antiracism, Love, and Justice

INTERVIEW WITH LARRY RASMUSSEN

This is a special interview for *Preaching Black Earth* about the importance of engaging antiracism as a primary frame for environmental justice.[1]

Melanie L. Harris: Thank you so much for your presence, Dr. Rasmussen. To start, would you mind sharing a little bit about your academic journey, maybe even starting with your college life and moving forward, so that we can get a sense of the atmospheres that helped shape your intellectual journey and spirit.

Larry Rasmussen: I grew up in southwest Minnesota, and I went to college in south central Minnesota. I was a history major at Saint Olaf College, which is a good church-related liberal arts college. As I look back on it now, I was grateful for my education at that time. But what stands out in retrospect is that my entire class was lily-white. I thought nothing about that because my entire high school class was the same way, and the community in which I grew up likewise. It did not really enter into critical thinking, even though I was a college philosophy minor. I took courses that encouraged critical thinking, but they never tracked on matters of race, gender, or class. Those were absent on the horizon of what was at that time deemed a good education. It wasn't until I went to Luther Seminary that I was introduced to critical thinking about race, class, and gender. It's amazing to look back and see what one didn't think twice about at the time. There was, for example, not one woman in my Luther Seminary class, and that was more typical than not.

---

1. This interview was recorded with permission on June 16, 2022.

In fact, it was, if you will, "normal." And so it wasn't until I went for a PhD at Union in New York that social issues became a vital part of my desire to learn and think differently.

Now, these were the 1960s, and my life was shaped by the social movements of those years. Specifically, it was the latter half of the 1960s at Union. Considering your question, "What were some of the persons or events that shaped my work in environmental ethics?" I can tell you that taking a class on race with Roger Shinn (White) and Larry Jones[2] (African American) was an epiphany event for me, and I can point to a slender book: It was James Baldwin's *The Fire Next Time*. I went back to it during the COVID years, as well as to other Baldwin texts, and they deeply influenced the letters I've written these last few years to our grandsons in my book, *The Planet You Inherit: Letters to My Grandchildren When Uncertainty's a Sure Thing* as well as essays I've written for publication in academic journals. So that time, the 1960s, that course with Professors Shinn and Jones, and then spending time with Dr. Martin Luther King Jr., influenced me and my thinking very deeply. One of those times was at the Riverside Church in New York City when Dr. King gave his famous address, "A Time to Break Silence." He linked poverty and the war in Vietnam with race issues. I will add that after hearing him, I remember many of us trying to weave and hold these connections together and shape our approaches to integration accordingly. King was already doing it, this kind of intersectional thinking; and you know it was from Dr. Vincent G. Harding, a drafter of that speech.[3] There were also other times when I joined Union students marching with Dr. King for justice, even that same weekend to the United Nations. All these events, and others of the 1960s, inspired me to become an activist myself.

2. Dr. Roger Shinn was the Reinhold Niebuhr Professor of Social Ethics at Union and author of many works, among them *Forced Options: Social Decisions for the 21st Century* (Harper and Row, 1982). Dr. Lawrence Jones was the Dean of Students at Union Theological Seminary.

3. Dr. Vincent Harding was a speech writer and drafter for many of Dr. Martin Luther King Jr.'s speeches. He was a religious historian, scholar, and leading nonviolent activist in the civil rights movement. Author of many books, including *There Is A River: The Black Struggle for Freedom in America* (A Harvest Book, 1993) and *Hope and History: Why We Must Share the Story of the Movement* (Orbis Books, 2008), Harding taught at many colleges and universities, including Spelman College, Temple University, and Iliff School of Theology. He is mentioned here by Dr. Rasmussen as an important thinker who paved the way for many theologians and theological social ethicists, especially white social ethicists, to take seriously the intersectional realities of oppression that many black people, and especially black women, faced historically in the United States of America. It is worth noting here that Harding's thinking was deeply shaped by the activism, movement work thinking, and strategizing of Fannie Lou Hamer, a black woman leader in the civil rights movement. While she experienced much suffering from the patriarchal practices and sexism upheld within the civil rights movement by black male leaders in the church, her witness, words, and work to expose the violence of white supremacy, gender oppression, and economic injustice created a path for both theory and praxis in all social justice movements since. Harding's legacy left a huge imprint on King, and King's imprint on Rasmussen and many other social ethicists trained at Union shape much of the progressive and liberal movements in social justice today.

Here's one turn our activism took. A group of us Union students started an antiapartheid movement. We took our money out of the Chemical Bank at 111th and Broadway, New York, and put it in the newly formed Freedom National Bank in Harlem, a creation of the civil rights struggles. Ours was a protest against Chemical Bank's lending to the apartheid government of South Africa. We were idealistic students so, like all idealistic students on a mission, we didn't know what we couldn't do, so we just did it! Never mind that our family bank account, Nyla's and mine, never had three numbers left of the decimal point; it wasn't a huge threat to Chemical Bank, much less the South African government. Yet something started happening. We started talking with people at the Church Center. (Folks called it "the God Box" because the headquarters of a lot of national and international church organizations were there.) And to our delight the women's division of the United Methodist Church got on board. Next we hit a home run when Union's Board of Directors took the seminary's funds and put them in Freedom National. But the big breakthrough came when, after this antiapartheid movement got some legs across the country, the pension fund of the teacher's union in California joined. It was huge and brought others in its wake.

A moment of button-popping pride came when Nelson Mandela, not all that long after he was released from prison but before he was elected President of South Africa, came to the United States and made one of his first stops at a packed Riverside Church. He was there for one reason: to thank churches in the US for their part in the antiapartheid movement. Of course, it was the South Africans, especially the unions and church leadership, who were the real shakers and movers. But Mandela knew that the international dimensions of the antiapartheid movement were important as well.

As noted, the 1960s were also times of antiwar activity. Dr. King helped a lot with that and was heavily criticized for it. But his leadership was a catalyst for making people consciously aware of the environmental and human cost of war and poverty. These, linked to race, gender, and class, were the big issues for me then. The outcome was the realization that I wanted to teach social ethics as a vocation and career.

Interestingly enough, we read and talked at great length about theology during these years. Consequently, I never saw a divide between theology and ethics. Later when I joined the Theological Field at Union, I joined people who continued in much the same vein. We always talked about teaching both theological ethics and social ethics as a common enterprise.

In short, all this was a consequence of leaving my lily-white college class and seminary and going to Union Theological Seminary. It wasn't my doing. It was what was done to me by a changed context and pressing issues. Union shaped me. My experiences, the people in my life, were other than they had been. Whom we are with matters. The company we keep makes us who we are. Paying close attention to whom we're paying attention goes deep.

Harris: Beautifully said. Thank you so much for sharing. My goodness, it is incredible to be able to talk with you about from whence you have come. When I reflect on my own time at Union Theological Seminary, I resonate deeply with the wisdom you are speaking about the context and how it shapes us. My first year at Union was 2001, and within my first few weeks of being in New York City, as a student at Union, the Twin Towers came down.

Rasmussen: Yes.

Harris: September 11th. So this wisdom you are sharing is a beautiful reminder about the kind of protests roots that emerge out of Union, in part because, as you said, of the thinkers that were there, the students that were there, the kind of consistent revival of resistance that lives in theological education in that particular space, not to mention the energy of New York City—just powerful. There's no other city like it. Everyone is there in some sense, every culture, every people is there. And so, the justice issues become magnified because so many different people with so many different backgrounds are there.

Now, I'm so excited to hear you talk a little bit about your encounter with Dr. King and how he influenced your thinking. Dr. King's work and much of his writings, especially his "I've Been to the Mountaintop" speech, have influenced me and the shaping of ecowomanism. This last speech by King was given in 1968 in Memphis, Tennessee, as he was fighting on behalf of environmental health rights of sanitation workers. Dr. King's speech makes particular connections between racial justice, environmental justice, and economic justice. These connections are key for the development of environmental justice and environmental policy.

Can you share more about how you use this same kind of intersectional frame in your work and how you got involved with environmental ethics?

Rasmussen: Just a footnote about Dr. King and Memphis, and then from there I'll go to my own education that led to environmental justice. You recall the placards that the protesters had said simply, "I Am a Man"[4]—they helped expose the denigration of their personhood and race and pointed out the economic plight they were in as those who held jobs regarded as menial. This all elicited something profoundly human. Namely, all of us know something about dignity. And if it isn't there because someone else says it isn't there, it doesn't mean we don't rebel against that absence and against that accusation. So, "I Am a Man" or "Black Lives Matter" or "Me Too" all speak

---

4. Colette Coleman, "The 1968 Sanitation Workers' Strike That Drew MLK to Memphis," History.com, July 21, 2020 (updated March 6, 2025), https://www.history.com/news/sanitation-workers-strike-memphis.

to something profoundly human in all of us, something that inspires a kind of resistance which will not accept denigration and depreciation of who we are. King understood that in siding with the sanitation workers he was spreading the message of their dignity and worth.

I recall talking with Delores S. Williams when we were colleagues at Union.[5] She was the Paul Tillich Professor. I was curious what she was after in a seminar one semester and asked her about it. "It's a search for the human."[6] And then she said, amidst all of this difference and amidst especially the kind of tribalisms that show up—with "we/they" thinking, and "they" is never on the same level as the "we," and the "we" always sets the norms also for the "they" and judging them—amidst all of that, we've got to discover the common humanity that is always trying to get through. My translation is this: Whether it's "I Am a Man" or some other such slogan, the message of dignity, or shared oneness, is felt by everybody. This oneness and connection between all beings is expressed in the work of environmental justice.

Regarding my own path, before Union I was teaching in Washington, DC, at Wesley Theological Seminary. I never expected to teach in seminary in my life. I mean, life is kind of what happens when you're making other plans! About all I've ever done is be a seminary professor, and it was never on my screen of future plans. In fact, I initially went to Washington because Nyla and I had such a good time in New York we knew we wanted to return when the chance came to move to a metropolitan area of diverse human beings and cultures. And Northfield, Minnesota, where we both taught college briefly, was lovely, but it wasn't New York! So when we were in Washington as our next-best-to-New-York choice, when OPEC was organized and everybody was at the gas stations, and President Carter talked about the energy crisis, I thought I best be thinking about energy and ethics. I don't remember exactly the year—probably 1979—but I did turn to energy issues, and they led me to research earth issues more widely. Energy at that time meant fossil fuels, although there was also some attention to alternatives. President Carter put solar panels on the White House, which Ronald Reagan immediately removed when he became president. By the time I returned to Union as faculty, I was interested in doing something in ecology and ethics. The thinking then—the mid-1980s—about ecology and ethics circled around two strategies, preservation and conservation. But it was the preservation of wild lands and conservation of wild lands. There was some attention to pollution, but even there the focus

---

5. Delores Williams was a pioneer in womanist thought. See "The Legacy of Dr. Delores S. Williams," Union Theological Seminary in the City of New York, accessed November 13, 2024, https://utsnyc.edu/blog/2023/02/23/the-legacy-of-dr-delores-s-williams/.

6. Delores S. Williams. For more on Williams's theological work reflecting humanity, see *Sisters in the Wilderness: The Challenge of Womanist God Talk* (New York: Orbis, 1993).

was on remedial work so that polluted land or polluted air could be conserved and preserved, thereby maintaining the base arguments of the two primary strategies.

Nobody was paying any attention to ecology and urban issues, at least that I knew about. Now there was lots of activity, but I didn't know about that until I started developing an urban ecology course that invited students to different neighborhoods in New York City to find out what the issues were for them. I read a piece about Van Jones in the *New York Times*, in which he just talked about what a funny scene it would be if he went knocking on doors in the South Bronx and Harlem and said, "Would you sign the petition for saving polar bears?"[7] Those weren't the environmental issues for New York City dwellers. So, I set up a course in which we went through different neighborhoods at different times and talked to the people about their community's issues. Right down the hill from Union, in Harlem was a grade school with a large playground, and the playground was like a parking lot. I mean, it was just tarmac. That's where the kids were playing. And just across the street from them was a huge facility for city buses. And I mean huge. I think there were only a few in the whole city, maybe five in all five boroughs. That's where buses started their routes and ended their routes. The buses were coming out of the bus stations, onto the street, across from the playground. We wondered how much these school graders were exposed to the large amounts of diesel exhaust from the buses going in and out day after day. So we started talking with parents and teachers about, as I called them, "environmental issues." That wasn't the right name. The parents and teachers weren't thinking about "the environment," at least in the way environmental activity was being cast—recycle, reuse, renew; or preservation and conservation. Here, it was a serious public health issue. And once I learned that these were the public health issues that the community bore, I recognized that these were also ecological issues. Then, when you examine the situation and peel back the top layer, you get to the race, class, gender issues in this case. In this case, it intersects age issues; it's about youth and their health, and the ethical issues about what long-term life effects this kind of exposure to pollutants would have on them, even into their own old age. What I was seeing, what we were all seeing, made me shift my thinking about how to approach the issue as an ethicist. I had to change my vocabulary because the approach necessary depended on the location. The ethical lens here saw environmental issues connected to issues of public health. Here, and in other places, the constructive approach needed strategies outlined in good community organizing. If you're going to address urban ecological issues, the issues have to be addressed as they're lived in microcosm, not only in macrocosm. I realize that's a rather obvious, even

---

7. "The Green-Collar Solution," *New York Times*, October 17, 2007, https://www.nytimes.com/2007/10/17/opinion/17friedman.html.

simplistic, answer to the question of how I entered ecology and urban issues. But a fuller account wouldn't change the difference it made in the way to do this from the ground up, so to speak.

Here's another instance. In the course of moving the class into city neighborhoods, I got acquainted with WE ACT for Environmental Action, headed by Peggy Shepard. That group objected when the city, without consulting the neighborhoods involved, decided to put a sewage treatment plant in the Hudson River off West Harlem. WE ACT said no and started protesting by shutting down the West Side highway with people spread across traffic lanes during rush hour. The protest raised visibility about the issue but did not reach its goal of canceling the sewage treatment plant in that location. Instead what it got was the only state park in Manhattan, literally on top of the sewage treatment plant. That brought most everybody on the west side on board, including a lot of white folk with nice homes up and down Riverside Drive. Of course, they wanted no sewage treatment odors in their neighborhood, but the park itself was the only green space around, and it was well located providing residents nearby with beautiful views of the Hudson River. The city had to work a long time to get the anti-odor technology right. But they did, and this became a relationship between city officials and the neighborhood folks that worked and lasted.

In retirement I returned to Union as a guest professor in the spring of 2018 and taught two courses, one in climate ethics and the other in community resilience. I had the students affiliate with an organization on the ground for that semester. Much of their individual study emerged from their community experience. I spent a day a week visiting the environmental justice projects and kept in touch with Peggy Shepard. I also stayed connected with two of the students affiliated with WE ACT and was a part of that group's community efforts for a Climate Action Plan for Northern Manhattan.

The discovery here was that all the issues I thought I was being avant-garde about in my theorizing were already taken up in these community organizations. Why? For an utterly obvious reason: Those were their issues on the ground. They already felt the impact of climate change, and they were starting to work out the plan to combat it not just for themselves but for whole neighborhoods. I shouldn't have been surprised, just as I shouldn't have been surprised to learn that one of the serious communities engaged in environmental justice in the United States is that of Hispanic Catholics living in the border regions, whereas one of the least active groups are white Catholics living elsewhere. This means that issues show up where people can't be buffered from them. So people there are already taking action. If you ask me what's happening out there on climate ethics today, I won't say, "Well, I've been looking at what academics, especially scientists, have been writing about." I will check in there, but first I'll try to find out who's directly impacted and how they are responding.

Harris: That's so helpful. Thank you. That kind of racial consciousness comes to many white people very late or only because of some kind of crisis. I am aware of how deeply racially conscious you are, and you've talked a little bit about the institutional climate at Union that shaped your own interest. But I wonder, Larry, if you could also reflect more on your racial consciousness and how that has grown in the way that you just talked about it. There's a sense in which your own ability to name your social location as a white male has developed over time. Most white folks have to be taught to name their own social location and align their values with an antiracist way of being. Whiteness is so normative, and the assumptions about white culture can be pervasive, especially in the United States. To be able to extract yourself from normative whiteness, even partially, is difficult and a deep, even moral challenge. But this work of developing one's racial consciousness as a white person also signals that a kind of courage is developed to extract yourself from the norm and overcome blindness so that you can actually see the truth. The truth that you have just named here is that Black and Brown people have been doing environmental justice work for a long time—forever. Acknowledging this hasn't always been easy for white male academics. Entire fields of study within the environmental movement are still learning how to recognize this properly. Regrettably, while many white scholars are late to the game, they are usually first to name themselves as the original thinkers, and maybe, just maybe footnote others. You do your work so much differently. So I just wondered, what motivates you to continue the path of staying racially conscious, and what deepens your commitment to be self-aware? This is unique and rare among white antiracist in so many ways.

Even among really powerful scholars in the environmental movement, and there are many new, younger generations of white scholars, particularly in environmental justice, who work with more interdisciplinary and intersectional approaches to environmental ethics. That's great. But I believe partly because of antiracist models of people like you that these and many other scholars take the work of developing their own racial consciousness more seriously and think more carefully about how their lenses and social locations impact their work. To be critical of whiteness is a risk. I wondered if you might share a little bit about your journey of racial consciousness. How did you get to a place where you could see yourself and then also make some decisions about how you were going to live in solidarity with peoples of color, particularly around environmental justice concerns?

Rasmussen: Yes. Glad to. It'll take all the time that we have. So, if you need to call time, do so. It's a long story. And I'm not extracted and never will be. I'll tell you why. I mean, you're a mother of a little one and you probably already know this, but I'm more and more convinced that the imprinting of our childhood goes very deep.

Let me explain. A child's way of taking in the world is key to shaping their sense of belonging. It's about their space (where the child is) and identity (who the child is). Their reality and their sense of reality is embedded there. No child grows up knowing critical thinking from birth. What is "natural" is what is experienced day to day. And I grew up in a community where neither African Americans nor Native Americans were seen. That doesn't mean we didn't learn racist ditties, however. We sang them, some with the N-word. "Eeny, meeny, miny, moe, catch a n . . . ." And it doesn't mean we didn't play endless rounds of cowboys and Indians. In the game, cowboys never took a casualty and Indians never won. Nor were they ever on the side that "should" win. In my dad's filling station I heard, now and again, "The only good Indian is a dead Indian." The paradox, of course, is that I grew up in a totally white community in a state that has thousands of Indian names for counties, towns, and lakes. The state's name itself, Minnesota, is Dakota for where the water is so clear it reflects the sky.

So, everything was white. I mean, everybody I saw, everything I knew, all my aunts and uncles, my grandparents, all the neighbors' kids and all the kids in schools, all the TV programs, all the magazines, all the ads, all the history was white. I remember my dad and his best friend, Lauren, at an annual talent show at our grade school. There was a stage there for the annual talent show. Dad and Lauren did their best at minstrel even though I doubt the Al Jolson songs and a little jig and their efforts at Black speech were very convincing. That mock-up act was about the only thing I remember that "deviated" from the fact that everything was white. And that was white, too. I've sometimes said that one of evil's charming guises is innocence, and that this innocence is the crime here. I was "innocent," too, in this sense. The little village of about fifty people was called Petersburg. But Petersburg's whiteness was no different than Petersburg's air. We didn't think about the air we breathe. And we didn't think about race either, except in this slanted way of denigrating mentions.

How deep does this cultural ethos go? We Petersburg pupils studied Minnesota history all year long in sixth grade. And if there was anything in our text about Minnesota as a state where there were Native Americans living, or their lives were part of our history, I have no recollection of it. I was fifty years old, had a PhD in social ethics, and was a history major from a Minnesota college when I learned for the very first time that the largest public lynching in all of US history took place ninety miles from my house in Mankato, Minnesota. Thirty-eight Lakota men were lynched on the same platform at the same time on the second day of Christmas, 1862. I had heard about the Sioux Wars and the massacres carried out by Sioux "savages," but that only reinforced, rather than broke through, the whiteness narrative of my childhood.

I now cringe when I hear the phrase "people of color" and white people aren't included. It means that "white" is a kind of neutral norm used to view and to judge everyone who is non-white. In this normative way of thinking about race in our culture, white isn't a color and whiteness and white privilege aren't critically examined. Now never mind that white is the most popular color of paint used anywhere; the white gaze doesn't include whites among the peoples of color. But until it is, the white gaze will be the normative, and norming gaze. I don't know what your response is to that, but that's just how I think about how deeply whiteness goes. And it isn't something I've thought my way out of. I didn't extract myself, and I'll never be fully extracted.

I've a good friend here who has worked for years with First Nations People of Canada and thereafter with the Pueblo People in northern New Mexico. His wife is Diné/ Navajo, and their kids identify as Diné. He's Anglo, and he's a psychologist. Joe says that whenever something comes up about an Indigenous way of seeing something or responding to it and Joe thinks about it, he's almost always wrong about what the Indigenous response would be. This after decades—and even with a marriage—is what happens. The default position is so entrenched. As white folks who take their own position as normative, this is going to be the case. I'm not just "normal," I'm "normative," not just "the way it is" but "the way it should be." In short, I don't trust my initial reactions. They always have to be checked by those for whom racism (or misogyny or a different economic location) is a firsthand experience, and not a secondhand experience, as it is for me.

On this, Union Seminary truly was transformative. Any extraction from the white gaze, even partial, happened only by being with and being in relationship with people who were very different than me. It was only by being in community with the people I was with and hearing about how they experienced and understood what was going on that I had a chance of recognizing how my white privilege protected me from experiencing the world much differently than they did. One memory is my dissertation defense. When I walked into that defense in February of 1970, there was a fourth person I'd not met before on the examining team. That's because at that time there was a fourth examiner who was considered "the outside reader" and who came to the dissertation afresh. I didn't know who this young man with a huge Afro was but learned that his name was James Cone and that he had just joined the faculty. I did not know, either, that he was the author of *Black Theology and Black Power*. I hadn't seen it, and I hadn't read it even though it was published the summer before. I had been so busy finishing my dissertation and doing all those preps that you have to do in your first year of teaching that I had paid no attention to any literature that didn't have to do with Dietrich Bonhoeffer, or even Dietrich Bonhoeffer's reflections on Black life and the important part that Harlem played in Bonhoeffer's life. So I didn't know this young professor. But that began a relationship. I went and got *Black Theology and Black Power,* and it, too, like Baldwin's *The Fire Next Time,* was another epiphany for me. I'm only saying that what matters is who you're with and what's happening and what they're saying about what's happening. So, who's on your left, and who's on your right? Who's in front of you, and who's in back? You pay attention to that because that will be who you are in this community and who you become in and for this community.

In the late eighties into the nineties, Union was one emerging liberation theology after another. It was Black liberation theology. It was Latin American liberation theology. It was feminist and womanist liberation theology. Except for a guest professor like George "Tink" Tinker, there wasn't much in the way of Native American liberation theology, however. (There were some important Native students, Robert Warrior among them).[8] And then came queer theology and ecological theology. It was proliferating liberation theologies that was formative for this white guy, someone who came without any liberation theology whatsoever. I had to pick it up from others. But it soon became very clear that the white, and especially white male voice, had no credibility any longer as a (presumed) universal voice. Other bells of truth had been struck, and bells struck, can't be unstruck. And when you have different optics, like seeing the world through Black theology, Black womanist theology, then the optics are set for seeing something else. Any claim to a universal voice actually denies that our human perspectives are always both our strengths and our limits. We can't see everything. We can only see as far as our horizons. We can turn and change our horizons, of course. But we can't see all horizons at once, much less can we peer over all horizons at once.

Harris: Brilliant. Thank you. One of the things that I am hearing you talk about is the power of relationships and your commitment to be in solidarity with other people in order to correct your own vision. And as you mentioned "I do not trust my own reactions. I have to be in collaboration with others. I have to be in conversation with others to be able to see more clearly." One of the great gifts that you have given to us is your book *Earth Honoring Faith.* And so much is really not just seeing from the variety of different peoples and their perspectives, but also seeing from the perspectives of a variety of different parts of earth, water, air, and energy. And this is, as you know, a very Indigenous cosmological way of being in communion with earth.

---

8. Robert Warrior, *The People and the Word: Reading Native Nonfiction* (University of Minnesota Press, 2006). "Robert Warrior," Harvard Divinity School, accessed October 31, 2024, https://hds.harvard.edu/people/robert-warrior.

I wonder if you would speak a little bit, Larry, about how your commitment to antiracism shows up in your work in classical theology, such as in your significant contributions to theological ethics on Bonhoeffer, and your own rereading of Bonhoeffer as a result of expanding your analysis of the impact of his experiences in Harlem. This seems to me to be a good bridge between Bonhoeffer studies, so to speak, and Black liberation theology that opens us to a conversation about race. As a thinker, how have you been able to track your thought or what are the intellectual leaps that you make to carry you from one space in classical theology and interrogating Whiteness to move into engaging an antiracist conversation with Black liberation theology and about race, all while developing and engaging a deeply antiracist and intersectional way of thinking about environmental ethics.

Rasmussen: First a couple preliminary footnotes and then to your question. It's another indication of not being fully extracted that I never picked up on Bonhoeffer and his experiences in Harlem as formative for his own thinking until Reggie Williams came out with the book *Bonhoeffer's Black Jesus*. That was yet another epiphany! I knew Bonhoeffer up close, yet I had never seen how formative that experience was for him. That's in keeping with what I was sharing with you earlier in the interview.

But there are blind spots in Bonhoeffer, too. There is a story told in the book *Black Jesus* retelling a moment when Bonhoeffer took all the records he could back to Germany and played the spirituals for the (German) seminarians at the illegal seminary of the Confessing Church in Finkenwalde. Granted he was a white male, German theologian who unlike most German theologians of the day, knew he had something to learn theologically from African Americans and members of Abyssinian Baptist Church, but there was a kind of romanticism about the Black experience that Bonhoeffer brought with him from Union. It is important to recognize this because it helps us see the blind spot, the embeddedness in his own culture and social location that limited his ability to see the full truth of Black life, and the struggles of systemic oppression that were expressed through the beauty and deep resonance, sound and tone of the spirituals. Yes, Bonhoeffer had an openness to learning from Black peoples that his family nurtured that most German theologians didn't have. Nonetheless it is just as important to see that he romanticizes Black life, even in his use and sharing of the spirituals among his seminarians.

Now, regarding the intellectual leaps that I was able to make in part because of my commitment to antiracism and environmental ethics, it's worth noting that I moved disciplinarily from social ethics into ecosocial ethics. This was in one sense a new dimension for me and in another sense the logical path. It was logical, as we've already touched on, because my teaching located the event of education in communities doing the work of environmental justice in an intersectional way. Witnessing, observing, and studying how environmental justice issues were addressed in those communities opened a path for me to develop a research trajectory into ecosocial ethics. And I remember someone writing that "social justice is earth justice." That was Dr. Melanie Harris, and that was the experience in these communities. So that part of getting in touch with the earth came easy. It started with witnessing, connecting, and learning from communities. I learned a great deal, for example, from the Youth Ministries for Peace and Justice in the South Bronx, with whom I've been in touch since they started and most recently in 2018. What they did as racially diverse, interfaith youth was clean up the polluted South Bronx River, create some green spaces, and start some gardens along the river, grow native plants there and do education at every stage on dimensions of race, class, gender, and nature. In the approach that they were taking it, the intersections among environmental health, race, class, gender, and nature were clear. Witnessing environmental activism like this made it easy for me to make the transition from a study in classical theology (Bonhoeffer) to a focus in ecosocial ethics using an intersectional lens.

The difficulty was the gap in my education. Now I had to read a lot of science, especially the ecological sciences and evolution. The book that came out in November 2022, *The Planet You Inherit: Letters to My Grandchildren When Uncertainty's a Sure Thing* has a lot in it that tracks how we got to where we are. In one of the letters, I address my grandchild, young Martín, who is the same age as your John Asante. I recall when Martín turned two. In the letter, I ask him, "How old are you, really?" And for the answer I go through the story of evolution. I go back to cosmic evolution's beginnings because you can't have a child, any child, without the universe preparing the way with the natural elements that exploding stars blasted into space. We are stardust, then earthdust, then eventually creatures. Considering this timeline, he's 13.8 billion years old at age two! We are all that old. Granted, *Homo sapiens* didn't show up until the last two hundred thousand to three hundred thousand years. We weren't on the scene before that, and Earth got along well enough without us. But we wouldn't be here at all apart from nature's much longer history. So I've needed to learn a lot of prehuman history in order to make the shift from a classically trained theologian to an environmental ethicist. I've had to read earth sciences that were never part of my education but are necessary to ecological ethics.

I must note that my doctoral advisor, Roger Shinn, was one of the first people on the scene in theological education to pay attention to Earth issues. *The Limits to Growth*, written by Donella Meadows and colleagues, and published in 1972, opened the discourse and basically argued you can't have infinite growth on a finite planet. I remember Roger waving that book around most everywhere he went, telling those of us who were or had been then in his classes, "You got to read this and get with the program." Roger also worked with a group of scientists who explored the limits to growth, and he joined Paul Abrecht of Church and Society at the World Council of Churches in this endeavor. Here was a glimpse and an impulse of what would become my focus in environmental ethics.

By the 1990s, I was cochairing a Unit of the World Council of Churches, the Justice Peace Creation Unit. The World Council of Churches, for whatever reasons, was way ahead of its member churches in putting justice, peace, and creation together and understanding the importance of what the later papal encyclical *Laudato Si'* calls "integral ecology."[9] As cochair, I was meeting with people from many different places with different issues around the question of how justice, peace, and creation go together. It was clear in every conversation we shared that the work of integrating ecology into justice and peace work was key. And as a cochair, I was often given the task of writing a preparatory document for our discussions when a Unit Commission met. Or I was given the task of drafting summaries of our meetings, or, sometimes drafting a position statement for the World Council as a whole.[10]

Harris: Let me ask, Larry, as we start to conclude the interview, how did you find courage to give yourself a new education? You created a whole pathway, several different pathways among students and in the field. And I think it's very common for us to read scholars like you and to assume that they actually had command of all this knowledge when they began their intellectual journey. But there is something about your journey as a scholar that suggests you gave yourself permission to evolve as a thinker and as a scholar over time. How did you find the courage? Who told you that this was okay? Who said to you, "go find a discipline, and if you don't know enough about that discipline, just keep reading and transform it so that your new question is addressed"?

Rasmussen: Well, this was not difficult, and I'll try to say why. Yet again it starts with Union Seminary. And I've mentioned to you that one of the things I most appreciated about Union was teachers who encouraged us to find our own voice even if we didn't yet know exactly what it was or would become. In short, we weren't there to become acolytes to the person we went to study with.

---

9. Pope Francis, Laudato Si': *On Care for Our Common Home (Encyclical)*, 2015, https://www.vatican.va/content/francesco/en/encyclicals/documents/20200524-laudato-si.html.
10. "Commission on the Churches on International Affairs," World Council of Churches, accessed November 13, 2024, https://www.oikoumene.org/programme-activity/ccia.

Here's an example. When I went to Union as faculty, Bev Harrison was the senior Christian Ethics professor.[11] Bev was really the founder of Christian feminist social ethics, and she did so by finding her own feminist voice and taking it to her teaching. Emilie M. Townes came when Bev retired.[12] I remember Emilie was adamant that her students, especially those whom she advised as PhD students, find their own voices. And she would let them know what hers was—as a force for Christian womanist social ethics. But she never asked them to imitate her. I learned from that model of permission and encouragement and wanted to do the same with the students with whom I worked.

You asked about courage. I never felt I needed courage because I was tenured at an institution that I didn't want to leave and nobody was pressing me to leave. No one was going to stand in the way or say, why are you doing that? Or how dare you? Yes, I got occasional negative feedback about some things. I remember, for example, a group of us writing a letter at the behest of the National Council of Churches [NCC], a letter trying to wake up the churches to multiple environmental crises. The NCC got lots of negative feedback in response to that letter. One of those responses was from the US Secretary of the Interior in the Ronald Reagan administration. He wrote a nasty letter that Bill Moyers responded to in a gracious but candid way. So, there were times when I was a part of a group that got negative responses. (Signing a full-page ad on a woman's right to choose abortion was another instance.) But my secure position meant that I never needed to find courage. That would be very different for you as a woman of color and for lots of other people. I was white, male, educated, and well established. I could use my privilege to take what was minimal risk.

Harris: Thank you. It is helpful to hear the stories of how you intentionally used your privilege to create change. I am so grateful that you have, over the course of your entire career, been willing to share your privilege and been willing to find ways to create paths of opening access for so many other voices. That is remarkable. Your character is incredible. The goodness of your heart and the goodness of who you are. The faith, path, and journey that you've invited so many of us into as a Christian, as someone who believes in and as the one who sings the songs of the freedom protest tradition. That, too, I think, is a part of the reason why I experience you, and so many of us, as a kind of

---

11. Beverly W. Harrison, *Justice in the Making: Feminist Social Ethics* (Westminster John Knox, 2004) and *Making the Connections: Essays in Feminist Social Ethics* (Beacon, 1986). For more information see, "In Memory of Beverly Wildung Harrison," Feminist Studies in Religion, December 20, 2012, https://www.fsrinc.org/memory-beverly-wildung-harrison%C2%A0/.

12. Emilie M. Townes, *Womanist Ethics and the Cultural Production of Evil* (Palgrave Macmillan, 2007), and *In a Blaze of Glory: Womanist Spirituality as Social Witness* (Abingdon, 1995). For more information, see "Emilie M. Townes," Boston University School of Theology, accessed November 13, 2024, https://www.bu.edu/sth/profile/emilie-m-townes/.

deep mentor who points us all to our own divine anchor, courage. This is the work of a great teacher. And you certainly are a prophet in our time, not just in the area of climate change, but your wisdom about the basics of how to care for one another is vital.

As we turn to the end of our time, Larry, would you reflect a bit about what gives you hope. Having named so much about the context, people, movements, and schools of thought that shaped you, what is it from those elements of your life that breathes hope for you now? How can we have a goodness of heart and access a deep, deep wisdom that allows us to deeply acknowledge each other as sacred, and also honor the earth as sacred? What kind of hope is required to do this? Is it the songs from the church? Is it good service? What are the ingredients that create the kind of hope that sustains you?

Rasmussen: I think back on my parents and the community in which I lived. It was a shock to me to discover how this community of really good people was also deeply racist, a community of good people who never thought twice about helping each other out whatever the need was. When my dad and granddad got the bricks together to build our house, it was a community project that none of the participants were paid anything for because they knew that the same folks would be at their place to do whatever needed to be done there. The farmers—my uncles, aunts, and grandparents on my mom's side were all farmers—purchased their big machinery together and all went from farm to farm at harvest time. I grew up, then, with a sense that we're all obligated to one another to address what is needed. I'm grateful for that part of my sense of community.

Now what does that have to do with gaining and sustaining hope? The forms will be different from community to community, but I think that hope comes with being human. I believe communities that don't find some way to remain hopeful or to resurrect hope when things turn hopeless, as they sometimes do, suffer. This probably happens because we learn we're the kind of creature that actually lives life as if suspended across a big gap. On one side is the way things are. On the other side is what could be and ought to be. We live our lives suspended across this gap, and we'll probably not give up hope as long as we're creatures that have imaginations and are discontent with the way things are when we know they could be better. Hope seems to generate itself out of restless human nature.

Now, if people ask me now what makes me hopeful in the face of the planetary eco-crisis? What sustains my hope there? It comes from reading the long story of evolution. There life never gives up. Evolution never gives up on life, even when extinctions happen. Earth has gone through terrible times, including those mass extinctions. (We're probably in another one right now.) In short, life is just irrepressible and somehow or another has made it to the other side. So, when people ask why are you hopeful, I say something a little weird, like "just follow the science." Granted that isn't a convincing "pastoral" answer to anyone feeling hopeless in the moment, but it is an answer on a grander scale if you read the long story of evolution. It might mean that God never gives up on hope.

Harris: Larry, thank you so much for your wisdom and your sharing today. This is such a gift. I'm so grateful to you for being who you are.

Rasmussen: Likewise to you. This, too, has been a gift of community, people loving one another and learning from one another.

10

Ecowomanist Leadership

Black Women, Freedom, and Environmental Justice

INTERVIEW WITH CHRISTOPHER CARTER AND HEBER BROWN III

Collaborators in the work of environmental justice, Rev. Dr. Melanie L. Harris, Rev. Dr. Heber Brown III, and Rev. Dr. Christopher Carter joined together in the summer of 2022 for an in-depth conversation about the importance of ecowomanist thought for leaders in environmental justice and about the unique gift the leadership and legacy of Fannie Lou Hamer has been for intersectional earth justice and freedom movements.[1]

Melanie L. Harris: Welcome. We are here to have a conversation with two extraordinary minds and activists in the environmental justice movement, Dr. Heber Brown and Dr. Chris Carter. Thank you both.

We'll begin by asking you both to share a reflection about your own eco-memory. This question models the first step of the ecowomanist method and invites reflection on your own earth story or experience. Specifically, how did you all come into the environmental justice movement? Both of you represent extraordinary interdisciplinary interfaith and intra-racial groups, most primarily work with African Americans and the environmental justice movement. To me, it is amazing to see all that you both have written, all the work you have been able to do, and to witness how you have helped activate Black people in terms of their own healing with the earth. And so I wondered if you could give us a snapshot, each of you, about how you came into the movement in the first place.

Christopher Carter: Yes. So, you know, I did not grow up necessarily thinking about environmental justice. It wasn't the kind of language that we used

---

1. This interview was recorded with permission on June 17, 2022.

in my family. Interestingly, I think one of the challenges that the academy has in terms of translation is that quandary of language and meaning making. The language, word use and meaning of words used in the academy, is not the language my grandfather, who was a migrant picker (farmhand and fieldworker) in what I would call a small-scale homestead farm, used. He uses the language of stewardship: stewardship and care. And I know that word conjures up different things for particular Euro-American folk. But I think there's a way in which this word needs to be decolonized or can be decolonized. And there's a way to really recognize how their epistemological assumptions—like the places they're getting their knowledge from when they're talking about and thinking about it and framing language—can be rooted in their own colonial worldview and not necessarily taking seriously the ways in which people of color can use terms and use words that have a different meaning or different kind of significance to their own particular kind of communities.

For me, we were called to be stewards of the resources that we had because we didn't have a lot of resources. And so it's like, "Hey, man, you got to take good care of what you got because we ain't got a lot." We grew up, my grandfather grew up in Brookhaven, Mississippi, a tiny town. He grew up extremely poor.

He, through force, had to leave and ended up in Michigan for lots of reasons. That is really his story. But I'll just say that he needed to leave and migrate to Michigan for his own safety. And eventually he was able to send for his wife, and he got a job in a factory. And that's how he really moved my family out of generational poverty. And he was the first one to buy a house and own a little bit of a plot of land in the back.

I grew up spending summers with my grandfather in Three Rivers, Michigan, helping in the garden, usually unwillingly. It wasn't like something I was wanting to do; it was something I was forced to do. And just being outside, being outside in nature. And so in a sense, I would say that my love for the environment started there, my love for being outside and being in nature started there. I didn't know any different. And so I honestly can say I didn't realize it was something that I missed or that I loved until I moved to California, just outside of Los Angeles, and I'm in a super-urban space. And I realized, "Oh, wow, I actually miss nature."

And so for me, what got me activated to environmental justice was being able to connect those experiences of growing up, being able to spend the summers in the country and with the stories of my grandfather, and his particular kind of exploitation—environmental exploitation and ecological exploitation, from being a farmworker. In the ways in which he was treated with injustices, I saw taking place, particularly in California, Southern California, Central Coast, California, and the farmworkers there who are now mostly Latinx.

So, I happened to be in Southern California. One of my wife's good friends is Mexican. Her family or these people who are just immigrating there, basically they have the same story as my grandfather. And so I'm making these connections: I'm seeing the spaces in which they're exploited and learning about Cesar Chavez. And I'm realizing that these stories are so deeply interconnected. Again, to my own particular experience as a Black person, as a person whose ancestry can be traced to the South. And for me, this becomes a theological issue. It becomes a moral issue. Right? If I'm going to be concerned about the preservation and promotion of community, if I'm going to be concerned about what it means to be liberated from oppression and structures of evil, if I'm going to take seriously the call, I have to love my neighbor as I love myself. The environments within which we find ourselves, particularly people of color, have been disproportionately harmful for us. And so, it became more of a moral imperative to me over time.

But, you know, I had to grow to see these connections. These connections weren't made explicit to me; but as I got older, I was able to understand how and why Black people lived in certain neighborhoods. Like when they talked about the other side of the tracks. Why are we on the other side of the tracks? Oh, this is because of the history of segregation and redlining. Like, you know, why are Black people living near these factories? Why are we working in these fields? Like you start seeing the throughline of racism and then you see how religion has been at play.

Given the consequences of global climate change and the way things are changing, I felt like this is the only direction I can take my work if I want to make the biggest impact in the world. And that's the way I felt like God was calling me to. And so that's what I did. It's been an interesting road. I've enjoyed parts of it, and other parts I did were more difficult than others. It's been great to develop relationships with both of y'all, you know, but it definitely has its challenges. But if we are going to survive not only as a species, but as a people, as Black folk, this is where we need to focus our energy for the next fifty years, because we are really kind of at that threshold moment.

Harris: Thank you so much.

Heber Brown: Thank you, Dr. Carter. You make me push rewind on my own journey. And thank you, Dr. Harris, for this question, because it gives me a chance to memorialize my great-grandmother, Geraldine Castor, who we called Mama Geraldine. Mama Geraldine lived in a town called Kilmarnock, Virginia. Kilmarnock is a little dot on the map in eastern Virginia on the water. And I'm remembering now going down the country, as we would say, when school let out. Before the advent of amusement parks everywhere or all-inclusive vacations around the world (we were not in that income bracket as a family), our vacations were going down to the country to Mama Geraldine's house. And

Mama Geraldine's house was like an adventure. It was a space where there were surprises around every corner. She had all these little figurines on the table. It was like the classic Black grandmother's house and so, yeah, we enjoyed going to her house. She had one of those long driveways where the house is like a mile back from the main road and all you see is a cloud of dust until you get to the front porch. She always had snacks for her great grandchildren. There was always something to eat. And she had mason jars, shelves and shelves of mason jars of things that she had grown and preserved.

Of course, there was a garden right outside the kitchen window. My great grandmother could walk the field and identify plants by sight. If we got a scratch or a bump or something, she would pull a plant up from the ground, mash it up either in her mouth or in her hands, and rub it on our skin; we'd be fine in a few minutes.

Mama Geraldine had quilts all over that house that she had made. And even though there were holes all through these quilts, they were the warmest. If you wanted to keep warm in the country night, you'd roll up in those quilts and you'd be alright.

And so that's my Mama Geraldine. She raised her ten children in that setting with those same kinds of agrarian impulses. Even when they moved north and west (my grandmother, her oldest child, moved north to Baltimore), her children continued with those same agrarian impulses, an earthiness of how to just manage day to day. And so when we left "down the country" and came back to Baltimore to my grandmother's house, Solone Henrietta Crockett, she would take us into the backyard to snap string beans. And I would imagine being kids, we probably were doing more to get in the way of her work than actually helping her. But it was something that was important to her: to have us close to her as she was getting the food literally from her yard and getting it ready for the meal. And so I just want to lift up my grandmother's name. I could share my grandfather's as well.

My grandfather, Franklin Crockett, was born and raised not far from Kilmarnock, Virginia. In another little dot on the map called Sunnybank, Virginia. And for Grandpa, he was a crabber. He was more on the water. He spent a lot of time in the Little Wicomico River, in this place where First Nations peoples were first encountered by Europeans. And the language of the river and the lands there still stand as a version of a monument to the fact that there were Native people here in this space. My grandfather worked that land and also spent a lot of time in those waters crabbing and fishing as well. And so, my maternal grandparents come from that experience. Interestingly enough, I did not fully connect my own upbringing to that kind of context until some years after when I began in this work with the Black Church Food Security Network. As the connections came later for me, it was one of the members of our church who really showed me the potential of a garden's impact in the life of a church.

It was Maxine Nicholas from Roanoke Rapids, North Carolina, who helped her young pastor (me) and said, "That young man don't know nothing about no gardening. Let me help him." She heard the vision, and she was the one that really put flesh and bone to my words in the pulpit, "I think we need to start growing our own food." Over time, I was able to make the connection and see that the profile of Sister Maxine Nicholas—and her eight brothers and sisters—in rural North Carolina was similar to the profile of my grandmother and my great grandmother. And I will hold or pause here. [pause]

But the light bulb moment for me with respect to launching the Black Church Food Security Network was to remember my own story and realize that my great grandmother or a profile of a person just like her was in every Black church that I ever encountered. There was at least one, or most times a committee, of this profile of my great-grandmother all around me. Recognizing the gift of that genius and presence in every Black church and seeing the institutional possibilities of the Black church as a system, I realized that the way, the mode, the method toward food justice was right under our noses, y'all. We have the people and the stuff that, if organized and aligned in a deeply spiritual and thoughtful way, could help transform the material and spiritual conditions of our people. And the Black Church Food Security Network came into being.

Harris: Thank you. Brilliant. Thank you so much. If you don't mind, we will go back to that holding space or the pause moment that you created later in the interview, Dr. Brown. What is helpful as we continue is a focus on a term I've heard you use before; alignment, as well as the theological frame you mentioned that is necessary to do this kind of environmental justice work. You named this work as a kind of spiritual route or path. Can you share more, Dr. Brown? And then we'll ask Dr. Carter the same question. Can you share more about the theological frame and spiritual route, so to speak, not just of the Black Church Food Security Network but also of ecological justice for Black people?

Brown: So I appreciate the question, and I will admit that sometimes it can be difficult for me to point out and lift up the theology of the work. Which is why I'm so appreciative of your work and Dr. Carter's work. I say it's difficult for me because sometimes it feels like asking a fish to explain water. That kind of question invites me to consider myself more deeply and to be more theologically reflective of the whys behind the things that we do. So, I will put that forward as a disclaimer.

But I was reared to understand God as a being of abundance. I grew up in Black Baptist churches where ministers would stand in the pulpit and talk about God having cattle on a thousand hills. Not fully understanding this as a child (and maybe still even processing it as an adult), what I did understand is that God is a creative and creating God who owns and has everything. Looking back, my theological foundations were also set by my experience in children's choir. I would go to children's choir, and there Miss Janet Haskins, our choir director, would teach us a song, "God's Got the Whole World in God's Hands." As I reflect now, what comes up is the impact my mother had on my spiritual and theological formation. My mama would take us around to churches and even to the malls where me and my brother Anthony Brown would sing that same song all throughout the community. And so, this idea of God being a God of abundance is very foundational for me and helps to shape my theology and the questions that give rise to it.

If God is a being of abundance, then all that flows comes from God—including me and you—all are invited into this abundance. And so, it helped me to embrace a particular kind of birthright. My birthright is abundance and not abundance in the Western capitalist framing of the perversion of abundance and prosperity and the like, but an abundance that understands that deep wells of love and joy and somebody-ness and connectedness. That all is a part of this divine abundance, and that as creator, God is making available this depth of abundance: a reflection of the very nature of Gods' divine being. When I see systems in societies and messaging from institutions that feed on an idea of scarcity or forward this idea of scarcity, I have to pause. These ways of thinking invite greed and selfishness that lead people to sink into a mindset of careless disregard for the abundant and ignore the beautiful gifts of this planet. These scarcity models rub me in a way that feels deeply uncomfortable. And so, in a deep sense, the Black Church Food Security Network is fueled by a theology that in a spirit of resistance confronts these models of scarcity and stands firm to a theology of a God of abundance. It exposes the selfish and oppressive nature that can flow out of a scarcity mindset and says this is in direct conflict to a God of abundance. Part of our work and ministry is to invite a reclamation of a spiritual, earth-based biblical abundance and point a way forward—to draw closer to that and to get back to that kind of not only intellectual embrace, but the practice of recognizing and celebrating abundance in our day-to-day lives. So that's one of the things that comes up for me when you ask me about the theology that undergirds my understanding and the work of our organization: that God is a being of abundance and that there is enough. There is enough.

Harris: Thank you.

Carter: Yeah, I think that was such a great answer. The first thing that came to my mind in thinking about the question is the Bible. While I'm ordained as a United Methodist clergyperson now, I grew up, as probably the vast majority of Black folks, Baptist. And I say that to say, we Methodist aren't mostly known for our memorization of Scripture; but if you grew up Baptist, you know the Bible. I always tell my students that if I am quoting Scripture and it comes out of my mouth as a quote from the King James version, that means it's something I learned before I was twelve. Because this is the version of the Bible that I was raised learning, I can date when I learned a passage based on the way in which I say it. Even in writing my book *The Spirit of Soul Food* and kind of thinking through some of this theology, the Bible is such a foundational starting point for me. It has been for me, and I think it is that way for a lot of Black folks.

The Bible has to have some influence on the ways we construct our theology, what we do and how we do it. I bring this up because I've encountered some resistance to this position, not only broadly but also in the publishing world. People are like, "Well, you're not a biblical scholar, so why are you talking about it?" Or the idea that maybe the Bible is not as influential in motivating people to take environmental justice seriously or ecotheology seriously? And I just have always said that if you want to inspire Black folks, especially Black Protestants, to do this work, it has to come from this place that takes the Bible seriously and is rooted in the text. And so, for me, you know, it starts with my reading of Genesis. When I read these creation narratives, I read them as an invitation to be in community, an invitation to care. I think this in part because of the way in which I was raised and how we read those passages in Genesis 1:26–27 with an acceptance of us being created in God's image and a hermeneutic of suspicion, especially regarding the language of "dominion."

And you "have dominion," which is the language that is in the King James Version. According to our hermeneutics, we didn't read that with respect to the environment; that is to think that we controlled it or that we owned it, or that we could do whatever we pleased with it. That latter interpretation was just totally foreign to me, like it was just 100 percent foreign to me. Now, I'm not trying to say that there weren't some problematic hermeneutics taking place in the Black church. I want to be clear. I'm not saying we were reading it perfectly. I am saying with respect to ecology, we had a very good understanding that this means we have responsibilities, so stewardship comes right back up as a value according to a Black hermeneutic of the Bible. The interpretation is saying, "This earth is God's and we have responsibilities to care for this planet."

And then you read the second creation story (Genesis 2:4–25). According to a Black biblical hermeneutic it was always clear that if you don't care for the earth, there are consequences. And that's pretty consistent with what the biblical commentaries say. The stories are a divine poem. Reading it this way helps us understand some of the ways that the writers were trying to convey the consequences of not taking care of the earth. Right? If we consider this, questions emerge, including, What does this mean, to not be stewards? What happens if we don't take care of the planet? What does it mean for us if we actually go down this path? And how might we cultivate a relationship with the land? Reflection on these questions, and especially on the passages in Genesis 2, opens up a theological understanding of humans' connection with the earth and God to be deeply relational.

My theology comes out of this place of taking those narratives seriously. It recognizes that we have responsibilities rather than dominion over. For me, I'm always trying to think how can I translate "dominion" in the text to make sense to the hearer? How do I help point the hearer and reader to the actual emphasis on stewardship? The word "mastery" is another way you might translate the words in the Genesis text meaning that we are to develop an excellence in the practice of caring for the earth. This emphasis is on practice. Almost in the way we might envision a "master chess player" or a basketball star player such as Steph Curry, who "mastered" basketball shooting. This interpretation of mastery should not be misunderstood as having a power over or having ownership of something. Rather, this interpretation of the Genesis passage—using the word "mastery"—would be better understood as an ever-deepening practice of caring for the earth that, because it is so consistent, ends up shaping our very way of being and doing for the planet in ways that shape our ethics, virtues, and values. We have to practice.

Stewardship and caring for the earth is something we learn, a skill. We are always practicing doing this better, learning, listening to what nature is telling us, and responding accordingly. And so that's how I was raised to think about my relationship with the land and with the environment in light of the biblical text. And it was very clear to me that we didn't own the land but that we had responsibilities to it. If we tended to it, it would take care of us. And again, this understanding, this hermeneutic comes from family. Just as Dr. Brown talked about, in my family too, we just didn't have a lot, so we had to take care of the things that we had and do well with them.

I also want to address one of the points that Dr. Brown so brilliantly made about a theology based on abundance. I think as I got older, and in some of the pieces I have written more recently, I remember coming to grips with the connections between a theology of creation and a theological claim of abundance. Dr. Brown's sharing as well as biblical commentaries that will suggest the Genesis passages be read as a divine poem, signal to me the importance of including sources from the Black intellectual tradition to also be used as sources through which we understand stewardship and a theology of creation. The poem that immediately comes to mind is "The Creation" by James Weldon Johnson, from his book *God's Trombones*. In this poem God looks out upon God's creation and says it's good and very good. It's VERY good right now. From a theological perspective, this means to me that a very important interpretation of the biblical creation stories is that God created earth as good, God created us as good and that as humans, we actually have an opportunity to honor the good that God has created, to notice the good that's right in front of us. The passage reads like an invitation not only to care for but take seriously the beauty and goodness of all that's here.

The biblical understanding of the Genesis passages not only speak to the goodness of earth but the goodness of us as Black people, and this is extremely important in a society that is too often shaped by white supremacist ideas. A rereading of these passages through this kind of Black biblical hermeneutic suggests something liberating about earth and our connection to earth as good, yes, but also something powerfully transformative for seeing ourselves as Black people as created good and very good.

If we might manage earth better, learn about how to actually relate to earth, what can we actually do regarding justice? With respect to Black bodies, what does it mean to create an image of God and view ourselves as good and very good? Because this is what it is, right? Unrooted, a part from a Black biblical hermeneutic, there is a way in which the lens of a traditional European-American-centered environmentalist can read these same passages so as to create a kind of performative act toward environmentalism, but not necessarily justice. That is, it models a kind of nineteenth-century European-American-centered environmentalist viewpoint, which is, you know, for the preservation of lands and is much more leisure based.[2] It's not taking seriously the ways we have to work with the land or work on the land. Since we've been in America, the people who've had to work the land, that've grown the food, have been people of color; with the elimination of Indigenous folks and the importation of Black people, then Chinese people, and now Latino/a folks to grow the food. And so this European-American notion of environmentalism can be easily disconnected from work because they haven't had to do it. But it's not realistic, and it's not practical, and it's not, I would argue, biblical. So, for me, this idea of coming to see ourselves as created in an image of God and accepting that we too are good is crucial as an anti-oppressive and empowering and liberation move toward racial and environmental justice. That we are modeled in this image of God; that we are created in the image and likeness of God; that we too are good and that bears an important witness to the fullness of creation that we are a part of and underscores that we belong to the whole earth community.

2. For more on the difference between the viewpoints of nineteenth-century White male environmentalist perspectives and those of Black and Brown peoples, see the work of Dorceta E. Taylor, *The Rise of the American Conservation Movement: Power, Privilege, and Environmental Protection* (Duke University Press, 2016).

We are also accountable to earth community, so then, our responses would be that we have to do as Jesus calls us to do. I would say that this is loving our neighbor. This more inclusive perspective comes from seeing from the perspective of those who have suffered oppression and marginalization.

In 2010 or 2011, for the first time, I drove from LA to San Francisco on Interstate 5, which is basically a highway that goes right through central California. And I saw the people working in the fields in 100-degree heat. They had two bathrooms at the edge. Signs had skulls and crossbones down there about hazardous chemicals in the area. While driving, my mind immediately recalls the times my family would drive from Michigan to Brookhaven, Mississippi, for family reunions. And my grandpa would say, "I done work in that field. We did all this." He took us to the fields that he worked. And so, when I was driving in California, I'm like, "I can't believe this is still happening." I knew it was happening, but seeing it gave me a whole different perspective.

And so again, this became a moral problem for me. The greatest commandment is to love God and to love our neighbors as we love ourselves. Once we get to the point in which we actually love ourselves again, and see ourselves as created in an image of God, see ourselves having more worth and value, then we should care for ourselves. How does that translate to how I see others? How does it translate to being in solidarity with others? This moral dilemma was a huge motivation for me to dig deeper into the theological perspectives that inform work in environmental justice. Generally, the traditional environmental movement has constructed an ecology that's built on exploitation, that's built on oppression, and that is inconsistent with the vision and practicing of Christianity. And so those for me are some of the theological motivations that are reflective in my work: stewardship, care, and this idea of loving our neighbor. And I think wrestling with the moral dilemma of the absence of environmental justice throughout people of color's history and the attempt to align this with Christian practice. This as much as anything keeps me in the work.

Harris: Thank you for the gift of story that you raised for us, Dr. Carter, and your attention not just to the hermeneutics of suspicion that many of us carry into the practice of reading the biblical text but also use in the actual reading of the text to glean the significance of the text and apply it to our everyday lives. This is something that I want to explore as we weave in the voice of Fannie Lou Hamer into our conversation. As you mentioned, Black liberationist, womanist ethical, and ecowomanist perspectives use the Bible as a source for the development of ecotheologies. As such, the two passages in Genesis are important and so too is the poetry of many African American eco-literary writers, including James Weldon Johnson. And there are also other sources for ecotheology, such as the profiles of grandmothers and great-grandmothers, as you have talked about, Dr. Brown. These voices are central for us to include in our ecotheologizing, and they are the voices of women.

For many of us in Christianity, the ancestral presence of these women in the work of environmental justice shows up powerfully as a source of inspiration and encouragement. Sewn throughout both of you-all's work is the gift of honoring Fannie Lou Hamer. I wondered if you would just speak briefly about her influence on both of you-all's work and scholarship. You might even share with us how you see your own work as an extension of her vision.

Carter: I want to say something quickly, and then I want to ask Dr. Brown to speak to this. First, I want to acknowledge for the record that it was you, Dr. Brown, who really connected me to the depth of Fannie Lou Hamer's work, and particularly to the work of Monica M. White. I don't know if you remember this. We were having a conversation in a car driving to dinner, I think leaving Methodist Theological Seminary of Ohio during a conference, and you were talking about this. You mentioned Monica M. White's book, *Freedom Farmers: Agricultural Resistance and the Black Freedom Movement*, and I had not read her book. And you were like, "No, you got to get this book." And I went home and got the book. Dr. Brown, I want to thank you because you have had such an influence on me with respect to this organizing work. You're doing and looking at White's work and her study of Fannie Lou Hamer and then saying, "Okay, what does that mean for the church today?" So I just want to let you know that you definitely played an important role in my life, helping me to see the connection between Hamer's work and what I am doing in my own work.

Brown: Wow. Thank you for that. Now, your recalling that memory of the two of us talking about White's book brings me right back to our deep conversation night in the car on the way to dinner. And I appreciate your expression of appreciation too, because I share gratitude for you, for both of you. I see myself as occasionally visiting the world of academia from time to time, and I'm grateful that I have siblings in those spaces to invite a brother over every now and then. But if I had my druthers, if I had my choice, I would stay right in the community and right in the gardens, gardens and farms, because that's where I feel more at home. That's where I feel like my skill set is sharpest. I appreciate being in a relationship with the both of you, who have helped to stretch me, to think, and sit in very deep ways with the whys behind the work that I do.

I also have deep gratitude for Mrs. Fannie Lou Hamer and think often about the deep influence she has had on my life and work. She helps to encourage and validate how I show up in this world and in this work, as she was a practical theologian. And I just got a book on Fannie Lou Hamer as a revolutionary practical theologian, *Fannie Lou Hamer's Revolutionary Practical Theology: Racial and Environmental Justice Concerns* by Karen D. Crozier, published by Brill, that I'm excited to dig into. But Dr. Carter, you say it right. I have to lift up Dr. Monica M. White and her book *Freedom Farmers,* and Jessica Gordon Nembhard and her book *Collective Courage* as important models of the work in environmental justice.

Before reading their books, I, like many others, had boiled Mrs. Fannie Lou Hamer's life down to nine words, "I'm sick and tired of being sick and tired." It's almost like she came down from the cosmos, said those nine words, and then flew off into the sunset. Then it seemed like the discourse opened up to share a little bit more about her: Mississippi Freedom Democratic Party and her work organizing for voting rights for Black folks. Finally the discourse of movement work and leadership, especially the work of women's leadership in the civil rights movement, became more and more apparent. I was amazed at the work of Ella Baker, Victoria Jackson Gray Adams, Fannie Lou Hamer, and others and the ways that they organized in Ruleville, Sunflower County, Mississippi. But it was not until I was introduced to the work and scholarship of Jessica Gordon Nembhard and Monica M. White that I understood more of Mrs. Hamer's journey. And I'm sure there's so much more I'm going to learn in the days, weeks, months, and years to come. But her influence, good Lord, have mercy, on our work. In one of those texts I read a description of the latter half of Mrs. Hamer's activist life, and I was astounded. The author was describing Hamer as the Malcolm X of the South. Or, if we flip it, that Malcolm X was the Fannie Lou Hamer of the North. The ways the author was describing the organizing work that she was doing around Black food and land sovereignty ignited my political imagination. I mean, it put kerosene to it.

When I went to visit Ruleville and I walked the sacred grounds where she lived, where she farmed, and where her earthly remains are buried, it took me to a whole other level, to the point where she is one of the ancestors on the ancestral altar in my mind. I see in her vision a way forward and, through her life with Freedom Farms Cooperative and the work that she was doing to teach people how to grow food and then the ways that she studied Heifer International's work, a great model. The way that Hamer adapted this model and brought it to a grassroots level with her idea of the pig bank and her idea to provide and teach families how to use that pig to care for themselves. I'm like, listen, if this dynamic woman and her community could figure out how to do this in Ruleville, at that particular place in time, what can we figure out as well in our time? And so you cannot overstate the influence of Mrs. Fannie Lou Hamer's life, her witness, her work on me personally, and with the Black Church Food Network. And I will admit quite proudly that so much of what we're doing is shaped by how she organized in her community. So much of how I show up—she would go on speaking circuits and raise money and then take the monies from the speaking engagements and devote it to her work—I do this because I read that Mrs. Fannie Lou Hamer did that. I want to thank you all for every invitation you give me to come speak at your events, because that honorarium gets poured into this work so that we might grow in furtherance or pay for needed supplies or whatever in our community.

And so I got from Mrs. Fannie Lou Hamer, and I'll end here, her fire, I mean, prophetic fire. She was willing to stand up and speak up to whomever, wherever, and her work, including her stance on the war in Vietnam, was revolutionary. She was active in the antiwar movement. And I'm a Baptist preacher, so I'll say as I go to my seat for one last time, the way that she spoke of love . . . and I'm thinking in this particular moment about the love that she had for Perry Hamer, her husband, Pop Hamer as he was called. Her love for Mr. Hamer is admirable. I keep saying Mrs. Fannie Lou Hamer because, as I read in Dr. Monica M. White's work and the work of others, the love that Mrs. Fannie Lou Hamer had for her husband was inspiring. From that, I got the picture of them walking together in the field, and that love is evident in their smile and in their glide together in this picture. And so I see the combination of love, prophetic fire, organizing, asset-based community development, all that together having a deep influence on me in so many powerful ways. I'm excited about how I will continue to blossom as this great ancestor continues to visit and whisper words in our ears as we make our way, trying to find our way on our own journey.

Harris: Thank you, Dr. Brown, for that deep reflection. Dr. Carter, if you would, please also reflect upon that question about Fannie Lou Hamer's influence on your life. Following that perhaps we can share more conversation about the theme and model of love in Hamer's life that you mentioned, Dr. Brown. One of the aspects of what you've reminded us by painting the picture of this image of Black love between she and Mr. Hamer is that all of us are connected and interwoven into this beautiful practice of love. You two, especially, are sons of that love as evident in your work and honor of Fannie Lou Hamer, and also in your love of earth, love of planet, love of people, love of God. And I wonder if it is that base of love, that understanding of love that allows you all to connect as brothers and as activists. Dr. Carter, if you'll take us to the mountaintop so to speak, as we finish up our last few minutes here together. Share with us a little bit about the influence of Fannie Lou Hamer on you. But also, if you don't mind, speak a little bit to the kind of kinship and connection that's possible but also radically necessary to be scholars and activists in this work of love together.

Carter: What is most influential for me about Hamer's work, and I think Dr. Brown said it best, are the ways she was a practical theologian. One of the challenges I think we have, especially those of us who are firmly planted in the academy, is understanding how we actually apply the principles of what we're talking about on a very practical, tangible level. And I think one of the things I've tried to do in everything I write is answer the question, What does it mean for us to live this out on a practical level and give people guidance? I think that's in part because I've always worked at a church in addition to being an academic. And for me, it's not always the easiest thing, but it's been necessary for me because they both fuel and inform the way in which I construct theologies and how I identify myself at my heart as a practical theologian. Hamer's work helps me paint a vision for my congregations and my communities about what environmental spiritual activism actually looks like and how it is deeply theologically motivated. A lot of folk are afraid of doing the wrong thing, or they are afraid that it's not going to work or that the work of environmental justice is not directly tied to building God's kingdom, which for many means getting more people in a church. I believe Hamer's work guides us to not lean into these fears, but rather do something different.

Carter: When some congregants say that building God's kingdom is more about building up our space—as opposed to doing the work of justice, the love work, the work we're called to do—or when they say that building larger buildings and expanding the church is about bringing life to Jesus's prayer, "thy kingdom come, thy will be done," I push back. I'm like maybe your version of kingdom building is a little bit incorrect. And, so, through my own study of Hamer, and one of the reasons I am so appreciative of her work, is that I was able to talk about Hamer's work and ministry as a corrective point of view. Because as you correctly stated, Dr. Brown, people know about her political activism. Because of her model, as a pastor and community organizer, I am also able to point to Hamer as a model and say, here is Fannie Lou Hamer who was a Christian, and also did the work of the gospel through her environmental spiritual activism, which is directly tied to Black liberation.

Mrs. Hamer fought for farmers and sharecroppers who were being removed from their lands if they tried to vote. She created the Freedom Farms co-op as a matter of survival, because the layers of oppression that were happening to these farmers and sharecroppers was obvious. It was like the community, through the awareness and teaching that came through Fannie Lou Hamer was realizing the connections of oppression and saying, "They are starving us because we are trying to exercise our rights and our freedoms." And the people who were starving them were Christian. They went to church, and they believed they're theologically justified to dehumanize folks like this. And so, Hamer constructs this counternarrative about what it means to actually care for our neighbors by creating this co-op, allowing white folks in, many of whom also lost their jobs because of the injustices of sharecropping and the cost of being in solidarity with Hamer and her Black community. What is interesting to note is the impact Hamer's organizing had on other white folks, those who were practicing deep white supremacist and exploitative values and who were not in solidarity with the poor. By allowing white folks into the co-op, Hamer takes an antiracist turn, based on her Christian practice and theology of love. Her embodiment of loving your neighbor presents for us a truly radical, radical love. Contrary to the rules of racial segregation and the practices of separation, Hamer allowed white people to participate in the Freedom Farms co-op because she actually cared about people. She did love her neighbor. She actually took that Christian value seriously, therefore exposing the absence of Christian love in the exploitative practices of the white landowners who were oppressing both white and Black sharecroppers. And so for me, Mrs. Hamer is an inspiration, and her work is one of the most important community organizing models out there to show people what can be accomplished when people work together, have a collective vision, and recognize the connection and the importance of food justice and food sovereignty for collective flourishing and community flourishing.

What I've been able to do when I speak at different churches is to point to Mrs. Hamer as the primary example that I lean on. And then, secondarily, I lean on the work you all are doing at the Black Church Food Security Network. I'm like, if you can't grow food—because some people can't if they're in urban places, one of the models that is presented by the Black Church Food Security Network is the model of becoming a hub. To me, the Black Church Food Security Network is an excellent model of what many local farmers are doing. Inviting connection with local farmers, particularly Black and Brown farmers, to become a hub of commerce and operate outside of the framework of destructive capitalism that extracts resources from communities of color especially, but particularly farm workers of all colors, is living out the revolutionary vision that Hamer gave us. The hub works in a way where farmers actually benefit and can make the most amount of money for the food they're growing. Honoring their calling, and understanding their livelihood is the work of justice for the church, I believe. Farmers organizing in this way do this because they feel as though they are contributing to the well-being of the world. Like if you actually talk to farmers, you know. That's how I see the benefit of Mrs. Hamer's work and the work that the Black Church Food Security Network is doing.

This conversation with you both, Dr. Brown and Dr. Harris, has helped me think through and discover even more about the influence Mrs. Hamer has on environmental justice workers. What's been most helpful for me from her work is that Hamer's organizing gives me not only a framework of what can be done but the inspiration that folks need because they want to believe in love, in community, in hope. They need to believe in order to have hope. Right? They need to have hope. People need to have hope that this work of environmental justice can work. It's going to require some deep changes in our theological thinking, and it's also going to change what it means to do the missional work in the church. I believe this is the work we are called to do as people of faith, and Mrs. Hamer's practical theology of love is what it looks like.

Her work presents a model so that people can see that this kind of environmentally just community organizing can be effective, that it can be sustainable, and that it can transform communities and transform individuals. And so for me, being able to develop a relationship with you all in this conversation and beyond and learn more about your work and read more about your work and find ourselves running in the same circles has been a privilege because there just aren't a lot of us in this Venn diagram of food activists who are Black, who are also religious, and who take their religion and religious practice seriously.

Now, I must say there are folks who do food justice, but what I've observed is that many have been wounded by religion. They have been wounded by that kind of Christianity that the colonizers had that said, "it's okay for me to theologically dehumanize you." And so, most people are like, "I don't want to have anything to do with it." And then we have other folks that have adopted that kind of Christianity that have an anti-ecological worldview that is focused on eschatological blessings that happen at another time or just maybe are so focused on race they don't understand how ecology—how it's all—interconnected. I see the work that we are doing as bridging this gap. To find people to be in community with is crucial for our ability to serve, for us to survive in this work and to not get burnt out and to have spaces of retreat and people who we can talk to and be in conversation with who can live this out. We need to be lifted up and encouraged so that we can be a healing presence to others. That's crucial for me. Otherwise, I don't know that I could have the confidence that this is something I could continue to do. Having the relationships with people doing the work is vital for maintaining courage to do the work of environmental justice. Without relationships the work just feels too overwhelming. Those are some of the reasons our relationship with each other has been the most fruitful for me, and I am excited about the future of the work, and our work and visioning together that honors Fannie Lou Hamer and so many others.

My hope, my vision, is to have a Black church with greater network hubs out on the West Coast. And now that I'm tenured, I have time to do a little bit of what I want to do. We'll see because family balance remains important to me. But my next step is to apply as much of what I've been writing and thinking about practically in communities and help folks be able to do that as a form of justice work. People are motivated to do this. And so I feel this is what we're going to be working on in the next few years, and we'll see what happens. But I have good feelings about where things are headed.

Harris: Powerful, powerful. Thank you for naming that. And definitely an affirmation of that work moving forward. I am so grateful for each of you for your extraordinary sharing. Thank you especially for the mutuality and the solidarity that we practice together. And thank you, Dr. Carter, for naming the importance of this for the work. It is significant to know that we are working together. I am also grateful to you, Dr. Brown. We could continue the conversation but we will end it here with deep thanks and gratitude. I thank you both so much.

Brown: Thank you.

11

"Loves . . . Roundness" Ecowomanist Shape, Theory, and Method

A CONVERSATION WITH KATE COMMON, MELANIE L. HARRIS,
AND FRANCES ROBERTS-GREGORY

This panel conversation with public and practical theologian Kate Common, ecowomanist scholar Melanie L. Harris, and ecowomanist scholar and environmental scientist Frances Roberts-Gregory was hosted by the Science and Religion Digital Dialogue Series of Methodist Theological Seminary of Ohio on March 28, 2022.[1]

Kate Common: Welcome, folks. We're here today with an exciting panel on ecowomanism with Dr. Melanie Harris and Dr. Frances Roberts-Gregory. And I'm Dr. Kate Common. I am assistant professor of public and practical theology at Methodist Theological School of Ohio. This panel is in connection with my seminary course Justice and Practices of Ministry with a special focus on ecology, which will circulate around ideas of justice, ecology, science, and ministry and will dovetail great for our talk specifically about ecowomanism.

With us today is Dr. Melanie L. Harris, a leading scholar in ecowomanism, poet, professor, and mother. A graduate of Spelman College, Union Theological Seminary in New York City, and Harvard University, Harris weaves her academic work with her artistry as a singer, researcher, and writer. Ordained in the African Methodist Episcopal Church, Harris cultivates practices of compassion through interfaith dialogue and interreligious practice featuring Buddhist meditation, Christian mysticism, and ecowomanist thought. Dr. Harris is the author

---

1. This series was made possible through grant funds from the Science for Seminaries Project with the American Association for the Advancement of Science Dialogue on Science, Ethics, and Religion Program, and in consultation with the Association of Theological Schools.

137

of multiple books, including *Gifts of Virtue, Alice Walker and Womanist Ethics* and *Ecowomanism: African American Women and Earth-Honoring Faiths* and dozens of scholarly articles. She is the executive director of The Ecowomanist Circle, a nonprofit 501(c)(3) organization dedicated to celebrating the life work and writings of ecowomanist and environmental writers.

Melanie Harris: Thank you; good to be here.

Common: Also with us is Dr. Roberts-Gregory. Frances Roberts-Gregory received her PhD in Society and Environment at University of California, Berkeley, with a focus on environmental science, policy, and management. She is a cofounding member of the feminist agenda for a Green New Deal, a Future Faculty Fellow at Northeastern University, and an Environmental Fellow with the Harvard University Center for the Environment. Her feminist activist research explores the experiences of women and youth of color advocating for environmental energy and climate justice, with a specific focus on women and youth on the Gulf Coast of Louisiana. Welcome, Frances.

So, just a little bit more about myself: I am, as I said, assistant professor of public and practical theology. I recently finished my PhD at Boston University which focuses on feminist theology, queer theology, biblical studies, ecclesiology, with a focus on reimagining church. I have come to divinity school via graphic design. So, I use graphic design and design thinking praxis as an intersectional lens in all my work. Part of that is looking at wicked problems or deeply intersectional problems, which I'm sure we're going to touch on today.

Both of you have such impressive biographies, and I know there's probably a lot that you each could talk about with your work. But to start, I'm wondering if each of you could talk about the work you're doing these days that you are particularly passionate about as a way for us to get to know you.

Harris: I always like to honor the newest mind in cutting-edge scholarship. So, please, go right ahead, Frances.

Frances Roberts-Gregory: Okay, I will. Awesome! I will be smiling. I love Dr. Harris so much. She's inspired me *so* much. I attended Spelman College for undergrad. I believe Dr. Harris did as well, and this connection to Spelman is important. I conducted my graduate research at UC Berkeley, and right now in addition to healing from the violence of the pandemic, I think, which goes without saying, I'm really excited about my work with the feminist agenda for a Green New Deal and most recently joining the steering committee for the Hive Fund for Climate and Gender Justice. My work, which is now moving more into national and international policy realms, science policy realms, climate policy realms, is inspired by my doctoral research, and also, I would say, my activism as an undergraduate and graduate student.

And so the feminist agenda for a Green New Deal is a transnational ecofeminist coalition. We're thinking critically about how do we integrate environmental justice, human rights, and Indigenous rights into Green New Deal policies, and how do we ensure that everyone's basic needs are met by focusing on care economies. The Hive Fund for Climate and Gender Justice is a regranting organization, which is focusing on supporting women of color, folk who engage a feminist analysis, folk who are focused on gender, and their fights around extractive industries, petrochemicals, and the fossil fuel industry. I'm really excited to be on the steering committee for that particular organization, which is funding a lot of the folk that I'm inspired by on the daily.

Harris: Thank you. That's phenomenal, Frances. I am excited to hear about all you are doing. I am also happy to share a little bit about the research that I'm doing right now.

I'm working on a book called *Mama May Have*, and it's looking at an ethics of self-sufficiency that comes to us through the work of Fannie Lou Hamer as an ecological activist—and not just during her day but certainly as a model for our time. A lot of my research focuses on womanist ethics in conversation with environmental ethics, which are the two ground spaces or discourses from which ecowomanism comes. What we're still doing, which is exciting, in ecowomanism as a field is tilling the ground theoretically and examining the methods applied by so many extraordinary thinkers. Some of the theory in feminist thought and also in womanist thought has been really helpful in community organizing, and these theories are used by activists in practical ways in environmental justice work. Ecowomanism also opens the door for us to think about the scholarship and ideas that have emerged from peoples of color, particularly Indigenous women and women of African descent.

As Frances mentioned, the wisdom, knowledge, and truths that come from these women and their perspectives about the environment are central for addressing the time of climate change we are living in now. A part of the work of ecowomanism is to uproot the logics of domination, such as the logic of white supremacy. One way to do that is by raising consciousness around the environment, the interconnections of ecosystems and exploring new ways of building ethical ways of being that honor the sacredness of all beings and the earth community. *Mama May Have* features a careful look at the environmental justice work of Fannie Lou Hamer and models of other proto-ecowomanists such as Rosemarie Harding and Dr. Iva Carruthers with the Samuel DeWitt Proctor Conference, whose work has been key to raising the consciousness of African American churches and churches throughout the African diaspora about the importance of environmental and climate justice.

Common: Great, thank you so much. Fascinating work that you're both doing. I meant to mention, Dr. Harris, that we'll be reading your book *Ecowomanism: African American Women and Earth-Honoring Faiths* as one of our course textbooks. So, the students will have your introduction to ecowomanism and the different theoretical streams that feed into the method and theory. So, it's great to hear from you.

Harris: That's great! Thank you for using the book.

Common: It's a very helpful resource. So, I'm wondering if each of you could talk about how you came to use ecowomanist methods and practices in your work. Maybe a little bit about your history with the theory and methods, and then more specifically, how ecowomanism informs your work.

Roberts-Gregory: I am deeply inspired by Rev. Dr. Melanie Harris. I read her book *Ecowomanism*. I identify as an ecowomanist and also an ecofeminist. For me, sometimes they're interchangeable. And I also would say ecofeminism from the perspective of one of my former mentors Dr. Carolyn Merchant at UC Berkeley, who's known as a proponent—you could say—*architect* of ecofeminism from an environmental history perspective. At Spelman College, I was engaged in student activism. I was president of the Environmental Task Force. I later was involved in food justice activism. I started a slow food chapter at Spelman.[2] As I shared, I came to this work inspired by Dr. Rev. Melanie Harris, but also from an ecofeminist perspective and from an environmental justice perspective.

While in undergrad, I was able to present at the HBCU Climate Change Conference hosted by the Deep South Center for Environmental Justice, and Dr. Beverly Wright, the center founder, of course, is another one of my mentors. And then in graduate school, I was able to participate in the Environmental Fellows Program that was designed by Dr. Dorceta E. Taylor. Also in graduate school, I was mentored by Dr. Carolyn Finney, who wrote the book *Black Faces, White Spaces* about African Americans in the great outdoors. I surrounded myself with all these brilliant Black women who were thinking critically about this intersection of environmental science, environmental justice, and, later, climate and energy justice with folk like Shalanda Baker.

I would also say that as an undergraduate and graduate student, I was able to conduct research at the National Center for Atmospheric Research in Louisiana and work with Indigenous communities. So, I started to learn that Indigenous fights around pipelines were deeply inspired by the Indigenous women in Louisiana and also folk in the Dakotas. So, I know you had a lot

---

2. Slow food is a global movement that emerged in the 1980s to protest the fast-food industry and unsustainable food systems. Abiding by values of food justice, promoting support for local farmers and food providers and for slow, traditional ways of cooking, the movement emphasizes the importance of good (fresh), clean (sustainable), and fair (equitable) food practices. For more, see https://www.slowfood.com/.

of questions, but that's a bit of my background and how I came to be an ecowomanist scholar-activist.

Harris: Thank you for your work. Frances is absolutely right. We both hail from the *same* college, Spelman College, and Spelman women *are* achievers in many different ways. We do help to transform the world. Spelman women throughout the world are great models of excellence in leadership, ingenuity, wisdom, and innovation who share deep commitments to equity and justice. Especially, in the work of climate justice, the model of sisterhood and working collaboratively is central for the work of climate justice. I am really grateful to share this identity and Spelman sisterhood with Frances.

My own introduction into ecowomanism began by following *another* Spelman woman, Alice Walker. Alice Walker is the Pulitzer Prize-winning author of *The Color Purple*. In doing my own dissertation work, I really started looking at African American humanism. Alice Walker's name kept coming up in part because of her essay "The Only Reason You Want to Go to Heaven Is That You've Been Driven Out of Your Mind (Off Your Land and Out of Your Lover's Arms)."[3] It opens up a kind of ecowomanist spirituality and invites the development of an intersectional and critical lens featuring Black women's engagement with religion and theology. The essay takes a critical view on the impact of colonial frames on the lives of Black women and helps readers to interrogate particular Christian norms that too often silence and devalue women. Walker's essay also prompts us to think critically about theological, religious, and cultural norms across a variety of different religious traditions in a way that dissolves the idea of separateness. Instead her essay suggests that we, as humans and as earth beings (beings on the earth) are deeply connected with the planet, and so too each other. Rather than see ourselves as only different and distinct from each other, Walker's essay prompts us to see and relish our connections and connectivity to planet Earth. In that essay, Walker names herself as a pagan, meaning earth dweller. She literally uses a particular definition of that word and talks about her own lineage as a girl child, being raised in Georgia, being very deeply connected to trees and being very deeply connected to nature.

Throughout the book *Anything We Love Can Be Saved* and that essay, and also throughout a lot of her nonfiction work, Walker writes about the earth consciousness of the women in her family, including her mother as well as many other members of her family and the sense of love that flowed in and from the Black community of her youth. That signaled to me something of interest in part because I recognize the same passion for the earth inside my

---

3. Alice Walker, "The Only Reason You Want to Go to Heaven Is That You Have Been Driven Out of Your Mind (Off Your Land, and Out of Your Lover's Arms): Clear Seeing, Inherited Religion, and Reclaiming the Pagan Self," in *Anything We Love Can Be Saved: A Writer's Activism* (A Ballantine Book, 1997), 3–27.

own self and inside my mother and inside my grandmother, and that earth consciousness was deeply embedded in Black women and webbed into their own spirituality and way of being. This way of living out their religion was of deep interest to me. And so I shifted gears in my dissertation project to work with different sources, different scholars, and to reframe the way that the discipline of womanist theology at that time examined Alice Walker's work. I included a focus on her nonfiction work in order to create a space, make a space for her own theoretical voice to be taken more seriously among womanist religious scholars and theologians. In the dissertation I made the argument that Walker had articulated an earth consciousness throughout her own spiritual and life journey, and this was deeply reflected in her life as a writer and activist.

I met Alice Walker for the first time while writing my dissertation thanks to a mutual connection we shared to Dr. Vincent Harding, a renowned African American religious historian, civil rights activist, and writer. Dr. Harding was a cherished friend and colleague of Walker's, and he was my primary graduate studies mentor and advisor at Iliff School of Theology. Dr. Harding was also a dear friend of my father's, John A. Harris Sr., and our families are still very close. Our mutual connection to Dr. Harding sparked an amazing relationship and this deepened my own research and real passion for developing ecowomanism. Our relationship has really kept me going in a lot of ways not just to uncover new questions but also to recognize the intersection of justice issues that deeply impact women of color around the planet, particularly Black women. So, I started by honoring my own intellectual womb space, and I started by honoring the intellectual womb spaces of the women in my life. And as Walker writes, in search of my mother's gardens, I found my own.

Common: Wow, thank you both so much. That's really beautiful and also the mentorship or relationship you had with Alice Walker. It's just poignant to then hear that you've really influenced Frances's work, and then to have you both here—that's really moving.

There are so many threads here to pick up on, but where I would like to go next is to bring in science, particularly environmental science. And I know, Frances, as a scientist you may have wrestled with some of these questions. But I hope that Dr. Harris will have something to say on them. But we're wondering, how does environmental science inform your ecowomanist praxis? Does it?

Roberts-Gregory: Definitely! At Spelman College, I was an environmental science major for four years and then eventually I added anthropology and sociology to my course curriculum. I was always interdisciplinary; it was just hard to figure out how to go about it within the constraints of the academy. And so I served as an intern for many different national labs, like I mentioned earlier, the National Center for Atmospheric Research. I also worked for the Department of Energy and the Department of the Interior. And so I've always identified as a scientist. Before Spelman, I was in a mentorship program for women in science, technology, engineering, and math called WiSTEM, so I've always identified as a scientist. However, I think it got a little tricky once I decided I was also an anthropologist, and also I was a feminist scientist inspired by feminist philosophy of science. Dr. Harris mentioned the importance of ecowomanist spirituality, and I see the connection between ecowomanism and environmental science really relates to praxis. As an environmental scientist, I'm a methodologist: theory and action inform my work.

However, I have to critique environmental science, and I would say STEM in general, for its exclusions of particular types of knowledges, exclusions of particular bodies, and exclusions of spirituality. And so ecowomanism, as developed by Dr. Harris, informs the way I approach my science from a feminist perspective and how I incorporate spirituality and engage embodied knowledge, because there's different ways of knowing.

And so, yeah, very broadly speaking, I am a scientist; environmental science is very important. Environmental scientists, anthropologists, and sociologists have been very useful when we talk about the anti-toxics movements, the environmental justice movement, and even public health.[4] But at the same time, I think it's important to have a critical perspective of science and the methods and theories we use, because historically many of these disciplines excluded Black-Brown women and queer folk. Our knowledges and our theories weren't included in science or considered real science.

Harris: Thank you. This is where I've learned from you, Frances, so much. I am not trained as an environmental scientist. I was trained at Spelman as an English major and a writer and journalist. My entrée into eco-literature really is through that lens of the literary kind of genius that we have in Alice Walker and so many others. I am inspired deeply by Dorceta E. Taylor, and she's actually the scholar who opened the door for me in terms of thinking about science differently and helping me recognize that there are abolitionist figures, such as Harriet Tubman, who were also environmental scientists.

As you mentioned, Frances, there is a deep connection between science and spirituality, and for ecowomanism, African cosmology is an important base from which to think about interconnectedness. That is, rather than using Western binaries or normative Christian theological dualisms that separate

---

4. Anti-toxics movements refer to protests movements of the 1970s and 1980s in the USA that globally raised awareness of the risks of the use of toxic pollutants, such as agent orange, herbicide defoliant, or others. These campaigns frame their protests around health risk, corporate indifference, and ethical responsibility. For more, see Liam Leonard, "The Anti-toxics Movement," in *The Environmental Movement in Ireland* (Springer, 2008), 119–29.

heaven and earth, ecowomanism values the connections between the earth/nature realm, the spirit realm, and the human realm. In this sense the elements of wind/air, fire/energy, earth, and water are important to pay attention to, for it is often through these elements of earth that we feel most deeply connected to our most sacred selves, to ancestral and sacred spirits. Another way of framing this theologically is that we can find rest and peace in God through nature, and this union, this connection can remind us of who we are, and awaken our devotion to care for the earth. This devotion points to a spiritual life with earth, with nature that not only guides (human) life and decision making but also provides a moral map of how to honor and engage all beings in the earth community. It's a kind of ecowomanist spirituality that embodies ethics and an ethical way of living in, with, and as a part of earth. It also guides our relationships with all beings. So, the synergy between science and spirituality becomes key and normative if we're thinking about African cosmology in this way. In this spirit, ecowomanism is deeply indebted also to the wisdom of Indigenous religious traditions, and for me, this refers to my own heritage and Native American ancestry. Like many families of African descent in North America, my family, too, embodies Native and Indigenous roots. My family is a part Cherokee and Blackfoot and so much of my ecowomanist spirituality is interwoven with many of the Indigenous peacebuilding rituals, traditions, and cultural and cosmological understandings of this Indigenous heritage. The embodied science that I know comes from these wisdom traditions. Many who understand ecowomanist spirituality to be linked to their Indigenous culture and spiritual roots, understand ecowomanist spirituality as a way of living and being with and in communion with earth community. So, I would say that ecowomanism is growing, in light of what Frances shared in terms of her remarkable work as an environmental scientist, but then also still connected to these roots of spirituality and religion.

Common: I appreciate you bringing forward that sort of synergy between cosmology and different African and Indigenous worldviews and how they have more of a platform in science than some of the Western ones.

Harris: That's a key place for us to continue the conversation. What I've found even in the academy, but also in some of our organizations, is that the split between science and religion is oftentimes where the conversation starts and stops. And that split does not function in the same way in conversations about ecofeminism and ecowomanism because the cosmologies are often so different and the worldviews about the planet are so different. The logics of domination that operate very normatively in Western understandings presents a rift between science and religion. But this logic is interrogated in ecowomanist thought. That is not to say that it does not exist, but there is a concentrated effort to highlight any dualistic thinking in order to examine it for any remnants of colonial frames so as to uproot logics of domination from the start. And so it's important to lift that up as well.

Roberts-Gregory: You said it so beautifully, Dr. Harris. Coming from an environmental justice perspective, the environmental justice movement was started by Black-Brown indigenous folk. It was started also by church women, like Black church women who were protesting a PCB (polychlorinated biphenyls) landfill in Warren County, North Carolina, and faith-based communities who are engaged in environmental justice activism in the area known as cancer or death alley.[5] So, there's always been this connection to spirituality and faith-based communities, but it goes by different names, you know.

Common: That's really relevant in terms of thinking about this grant and the science and seminaries project sponsoring this discussion. The project is trying to bridge the gap that is often so pronounced in Western cosmology. So, along these lines, and this may be a more practical question, how does ecowomanism incorporate environmental science into its approaches toward climate justice or food justice activism? How do these things connect? Or do you see them connecting?

Roberts-Gregory: For me as an ecowomanist, environmental science is already incorporated. But that's just because of my positionality and just how I come to the work. I think that it's important for folk from all different disciplines and different backgrounds to learn to collaborate because we have these wicked environmental issues, and they require different partial perspectives, different methodologies, and different approaches. So, I think that's a really great place for folk who identify as ecowomanists and folk who identify as scientists, planners, and engineers to come together because we need all of our perspectives to address these issues. And when I think of climate justice, it's really an extension of the environmental justice movement, which is an extension of the civil rights movement and the women's movement; I think of it as a place where we can imagine these more just futures. Climate energy and environmental justice approaches are all about imagining fossil-fuel-free or fossil-fuel-free*ish* futures. And I think that themes of spirituality and pleasure and joy and healing are all really important.

Sometimes, in the science spaces or even planning spaces, we forget about the importance of healing and how there are traditions of healing and rituals of healing. And I think it's really exciting to think about how we can bring ecowomanist principles into our imaginings of climate just futures.

5. *Cancer alley* is a term that refers to a regional area along the Mississippi River between Baton Rouge and New Orleans and the River Parishes of Louisiana where over two hundred petrochemical plants and refineries exist.

Harris: Thank you. I do think that we're in a time of imagining and reimaginings. I appreciate your use of that language, Frances. I think one of the spaces that ecowomanism shines the most is its way of being inclusive. This opens the door for us to think through multidisciplinary and interdisciplinary approaches to see what would need to shift in order to be inclusive of all beings, human and nonhuman. And so, generally, ecowomanism invites a number of different theories, a number of different approaches, and a number of different disciplines. And so it's appropriate—and I think that what you've just named is so true—that climate justice, that the environmental justice movement, has deep roots in the civil rights movement, in the women's rights movement, and in a lot of different social movements; but it also has deep roots in the lineage of various Indigenous religions, including Christianity, African spirituality, Indigenous religious practice, Buddhism, Black Buddhism, and Buddhist ecology. One of the reasons ecowomanism is inherently interfaith and interreligious is because it taps into a deeper wisdom that we need access from the perspective of multiple religious traditions in order to bring about climate justice. I agree with you, and I think a basic invitation for students, who are still learning all the vocabulary, is to learn how to think interdisciplinarily. This is going to be key, particularly coming out of the pandemic. The world of the mind, the world of the academy, has a tendency after surviving a crisis moment like this to return to its cement-like, stoic-like disciplinary lines and boundaries.

We—as academics, thinkers, scholars, and activists—are going to have to be really careful as we regather and reenter into community not to reinscribe a tradition in a way that hinders us from moving forward and dreaming and reimagining what community needs to be. Another way of saying that is as we reenter into community following the pandemic even in institutional school settings this fall, there'll be a tendency to go back to community as if it was "normal," in quotations. And I think particularly with religious communities and faith communities, that would be a mistake. To ignore the racial injustice that has gripped our entire country here in the United States, to ignore the deaths of so many women like Sandra Bland, to ignore the deaths of so many men like George Floyd, to ignore the deaths and the reality of white supremacy in our country, the insurrection on January 6th—to ignore that and to pretend that we can come back to a normal where this is all silenced would be a mistake.

We have to come into an interdisciplinary way of being. That includes interfaith, interreligious, and *intrareligious* perspectives, and a number of different other fluid kinds of being and thinking together to really effect change. And in my understanding, I think we're going to have to learn again how to be together. Ecowomanism, in this sense, offers a door, an opening, a window into how to be together differently in this particular time.

Common: Thank you so much. I love the warning about not going back to sort of this concretized vision of how things were. And I think this is really going to be relevant for the folks in my class. Many of them are already in ministry settings and are dealing with some sort of the reopening, the going back and figuring out; what is that going to look like? Also, the piece about imagining, Frances; thanks for bringing that in and, Dr. Harris, for expounding on it a little bit. That seems key right now.

Like if we can't dream it, how are we going to get there? And it does feel like we're at this interdisciplinary moment. It's going to take all of us coming from our different perspectives to dream that new vision. And ecowomanism, I think, is one of those places that could lead us.

Harris: Yeah, I think that the prophetic is a part of ecowomanism. In some instances it's a warning. But in other ways it's prophetic in the way of prompting a kind of inner knowing, and it reminds us to listen to wisdom, Indigenous wisdom and wisdom from within. It invites contemplative practice to be able to enhance this ability to listen to wisdom from the planet and cultivate the wisdom of the earth every day. What is the earth saying right now? This is one of the questions that ecowomanism asks. Ecowomanism also links deeply to self-care and planetary care. Self-care is especially important for students and really anyone working in a ministerial context. It is also important for activists who have been working overtime during the pandemic against white supremacy. When we disconnect ourselves from the planet we risk disconnecting ourselves from ourselves and the wisdom within us. Oftentimes taking care of the planet is an opportunity for us to recognize that the planet deserves care and so do we. So, self-care and the prophetic vision are what we might consider less visible principles of ecowomanism; they're central to the actual embodiment and the working and practice of ecowomanist thought.

Common: Amen to that. So, along that line, I want to ask a question about self-care. Cynthia Moe-Lobeda in her book *Resisting Structural Evil*, another text we're reading, talks about a sort of moral oblivion. She describes it as when people are looking out and seeing all of these intersectional issues—climate justice, racial justice, you know, problems of economics—it just seems so massive, and individuals in communities can just be faced with this apathy of moral oblivion asking, "What can I do?" But then it's also a paradox: like, yeah, one person doing one thing isn't going to solve the problem, but if nobody does anything, it's not going to be solved; so, everybody has to do one thing. So, part of that is overcoming the moral oblivion or the hopelessness in the face of these wicked problems.

I'm wondering if each of you could speak to how you deal with the moral oblivion at times, if you do ever come up against that hopelessness, and what keeps you going. And then, also, if you don't mind sharing, what are some of your self-care practices that keep you doing the good work even when sometimes it can be difficult facing challenges—white supremacy, patriarchy, and capitalist institutions— that are just death-dealing against our being?

Roberts-Gregory: That's an excellent question. I've been focused on self- and community care for a few years partly to just get through a doctoral program; it's very rough. And then as an environmental scientist, as an environmental educator, as a feminist, I talk about violence all day, different types of violence, and I use different language when I'm talking about violence. And then as a woman of color, I am experiencing that violence on the daily, and my communities are experiencing the violence. And, so, guarding my sanity and fortifying my nerves are extremely important.

I would say that my self-care practices have changed over time. For example, I joined an environmental educator's collective that was focused on climate grief and eco-anxiety. They ask how do educators prepare students to deal with these different emotions, and how do we promote emotional resiliency and posttraumatic growth. And, so, through my pedagogy I include different activities to assist students to cope with these different emotions. Also, I was inspired by Dr. Harris's ecowomanist pedological strategy to ask students to create ecowomanist manifestos and also environmental histories, or what I call ecowomanist autoethnographies, to help connect the personal to the political. So that's been very useful in addressing this, what you, I think, term "moral oblivion."

During the pandemic I returned back to the basics. I lost a few family members to COVID, so I created a pandemic sidewalk garden because I don't have a front yard or backyard unfortunately; but I was able to plant flowers and herbs and vegetables in memory of some of my family members who passed away. I also joined GirlTrek, which is a national walking boot camp to encourage Black women in their families to get into the outdoors and is part of this long history of Black woman's health movement. So, I joined GirlTrek, and I started walking because I was inside my house during the pandemic. Other spaces of joy are dancing —like I'm a dancer, so dancing, social dancing—roller skating, and a lot of physical activity. There's so many different strategies I used, even therapy at times; it just depends on the season. But I love that Dr. Harris focuses on earth care, and self-care. That's been very liberatory for me and also enabled me to release fear. I realized that freedom and liberation, in order to achieve them, sometimes we have to release fear and also require sacrifice. So, I've been focused on freedom as my self-care praxis.

Harris: That's beautiful. Thank you. Wow, those are terrific. It's a gift to hear how we take care of ourselves and our own souls in the midst. . . . I too really recommend therapy or other professional assistance for full mental health. I think that taking care of one's mental health right now, particularly for people of color, particularly for Black people, is key and really important. I have been a part of a lot of different conversations with church groups, leading spiritual direction, for example, leading different forms of group therapy, but also recognizing the importance of spiritual care. And that can be particularly important for those of us who are from communities of color. As you mentioned, Frances, there are many of us who have lost family members, so I'm thinking of you in that moment and care and in love and holding you in light too. That form of care and community can be central, and also getting outside can be really central. I love the idea of planting a garden in honor of those whom we've lost because it helps us to recognize their ancestral presence, which is still with us, and deeply, deeply present to us, and can be experienced through the earth. And so that the earth avails herself as a vehicle or a vessel to hold the love or the connection, the energy or the ashe between an ancestor and a being who's still living is really a gift of the earth for many of us who believe and operate in that cosmology.

I say that a lot of my spiritual practices are aligned with contemplative and self-care practices. I am one who believes very strongly and deeply in spiritual baths, which is an African traditional religious tradition whereby one essentially creates a space to wash oneself, wash oneself in its entirety with water and also with particular herbs. I come from a family that is deeply embedded in both native and southern cultures, and also with connections to West Africa, particularly Ghanaian peoples, and so ginger as a root is a really important self-care tool for me in my home. I usually boil ginger in the morning, particularly when I'm not feeling well, either physically or mentally or emotionally or spiritually just to clear the space in the same way that one might use sage to clear the space in a ritualistic kind of way.

As a self-care practice, I sleep. I really enjoy sleep and giving myself permission to rest. Resting has been in so many people's minds. I'm thinking of a nap ministry and a beautiful sister who's engaged that work, Tricia Hersey.[6] Rest is actually a work of resistance. It's an ability to continue to recenter ourselves, particularly those of us who are facing racial trauma of violence, repeatedly every day. So, I do try to rest as much as possible. Walking and getting outside are really important. So, getting in the sun as much as possible is also a really major self-care practice.

---

6. Tricia Hersey, *Rest Is Resistance: A Manifesto* (Little, Brown Spark, 2022).

And I'm a meditator. This is the gift of religion and particularly interfaith work. An ordained Christian minister, I have often been invited to experience different religious traditions, rites, and rituals. One of those that I was introduced to pretty early in my journey was the gift of meditation, both Christian meditation and also Buddhist meditation. And so, as a practitioner of meditation, I strongly believe in the power of contemplative practice. And it's important here at least to mention the intellectual and spiritual roots of this for me. I'm thinking of Howard Thurman here, whose work, I believe, contemplatively combines a variety of soul-keeping practices; and I am thinking about Rosemarie Harding, who combined Eastern traditions and Western traditions as a Mennonite, mother, writer, scholar, activist, and African American woman inspired by Black southern spirituality. The contemplative practices that these and others inspire are very good for everyday ways of being. These practices are particularly instructive for Christian seminary students. It's not just this idea of devotion, like reading a Scripture with a particular prayer and a particular saying every day, but attending to the word within and however that word may come from the earth. It may not come from the Bible. A word from the earth and a word of sacred song and a word of life may not come from a particular text; it may come from the tree, it may come from the rain, it may come in a different way. Even as a seminary student, you can actually be open to hearing from the divine in new and different ways that can be life-affirming.

Common: Thank you both so much. You've just given us all a broad list, a deep list of things. And I love the idea of the word coming from the earth. When you were mentioning earlier, Dr. Harris, about Alice Walker describing herself as an earth dweller, just that image of ourselves in that way opens up another relationality to the earth, to the divine, and to our practices of care. So, thank you both for that.

Many of the students in my course are going to be future ministers or organizational leaders. So these self-care practices will be vital. I'm wondering if you have any advice for folks who are and will be leading communities. Many of these communities are going to have a heart for ecojustice or climate justice, but, you know, as justice work goes, sometimes we can get in our own way and maybe perpetuate more harm than good. I'm wondering, from an ecowomanist perspective, or just from your own personal perspectives as activists and people who have been in this work, theoretically and on the ground, what advice you might have for future folks who will go out to lead communities or who are currently leading communities, and connected to communities who want to do climate justice. What advice do you have for those leaders?

Roberts-Gregory: That's an excellent question. I have some training in community-based research. For me, it's really important not to come in with this idea that you know better than the community, or that you're there to save people or even help people. You're going there to facilitate conversations and to facilitate community transformation, and to perhaps bring in resources or networks that other folk might not have access to. So, I think that's really important when you're engaging with communities that you're a part of, or that you're not a part of, because sometimes it's a mixed bag; you can be both an insider and an outsider.

I think it's also important to lift up community voices through multiple mediums of communication. Sometimes, you can do great work, but nobody knows. It's really important to have a communication strategy that engages local audiences, regional audiences, but also national and even international audiences. And the work is long-term, and so it's important to have self-care and community-care strategies. Also, it is important to take breaks periodically, because as Dr. Harris mentioned, rest is resistance. Sometimes, the work can become overwhelming, so you need to take periodic breaks to make the work sustainable.

Lastly, I would say it's important to engage folk and create spaces of intergenerational learning. Because sometimes in our movement spaces, there may be just the elders or just college students, and so hopefully you can create spaces of community engagement where you have youth, elders, and working professionals. That means having accessible entry points, because not everyone can come to every meeting, not everyone can come to every protest, or not everyone might feel safe. It might not actually be a safe space to be on the frontlines in that way. So just having different entry points for folk to plug in will create a stronger movement. Also, be in solidarity with other movements. Sometimes we think it's so tough, but there might be another community focused on a similar issue. By networking you can learn from each other, and also you don't feel so alone; that's part of the community-care work.

Harris: Thank you. I agree. There are deep ways in which community organizing and knowing some of the approaches and strategies around community organizing can help anyone in any context be able to bring people together in inclusive ways.

I would simply add that inclusiveness is really important. What we are after here, especially for the development of intellectual and intersectional communities, is the capacity to build spaces that are radically inclusive. Yes, that means interdisciplinary, but what I am envisioning goes even beyond that and reaches into the work of justice and equity. For those of us in environmental justice work, we want to bring as many voices to the table and into the space in a spirit of equity as much as possible, but this also means paying attention to racial equity. It means paying attention to all forms of equity.

I would add that there are lots of different ways in which we can bring communities together by looking at the truth of who we are. I have found in my work that antiracist framing and antiracist work have been central to doing the work of environmental justice, because there are so many white churches and white students and white people who have not had an opportunity to examine their own white privilege and how that white privilege is complicit in environmental and racial harm. While some people are able to look at the environment and climate change from a perspective of the earth being a resource and always beautiful and always kind, the reality of the fact is, most people of color in the United States of America have had many experiences with environmental violence wherein the earth has been used against us as Black peoples as a tool of white supremacy. We have not always had the same relationship to land as many white people. Therefore, the descendants of all those people working together to open a community garden or a church garden and the history of those peoples need to be examined and brought forth. And so, antiracist pedagogy and antiracist framing are often ways that allow people to come together as human beings to examine their own relationship with the earth. In that sense, ecowomanism is an approach that offers a methodological first step, to honor experience that invites us to think carefully about how we might engage antiracist strategies of doing justice and solidify spaces of solidarity.

Common: Wow, thank you both. That's really solid advice for folks. And a lot of our students are going out to different types of churches with different demographics, so this is going to be helpful. We have a few more minutes here. Frances, ecowomanist scholar Elonda Clay and I were reading on your website where you describe yourself as a STEMinist. We were wondering if you could describe or define STEMinist. We hadn't heard that term before, but we both loved it.

Roberts-Gregory: A STEMinist is a feminist in science. And that means that I'm definitely concerned about the underrepresentation of folk who are traditionally othered in conventional scientific fields but also the underrepresentation of folk who look like me. Also, I'm concerned about this transition to a climate just future. So, when we talk about renewable sectors, for example, energy sectors, women and people of color are underrepresented. However, as Dr. Harris was mentioning earlier, we've always been scientists; we've always been interdisciplinary systems thinkers. And so, for me, a STEMinist is really about taking an intersectional lens to othering and promoting. When I was in Berkeley, I facilitated two workshops at the annual Women of Color Empowerment Conference. And that was really exciting and also a little sad. There were so many folk there who graduated with STEM degrees, and we asked if they identify as scientists. Most folk did not raise their hands. So you have a degree in biology, physics, chemistry, but you don't identify in science because there's this narrow conception of who is a scientist and who's a researcher. So yeah, for me, that's what it means to be a STEMinist.

I'm a product of the mentorship of Dr. Harris, directly and indirectly, and other brilliant BIPOC thinkers. I want to pass the baton forward and increase the representation of women and queer folk and communities of color in climate science, climate policy, and environmental decision making broadly speaking.

Common: Thank you. I appreciate hearing that. We have time for one more question. Since my class is going to read Dr. Harris's book and will engage with a couple of ecowomanist ideas, methods, practices, I'm wondering whether both of you could identify one key concept or key theme from ecowomanism or from your engagement with the methods and praxis that you think the students should focus on, pay attention to, or take away after their engagement with the topic. It could be cool to hear from each of you what you might think that is. It doesn't have to be one, but just key take aways.

Roberts-Gregory: Dr. Harris, I'll let you go first.

Harris: I would say that it's the method. It's not actually just one idea, but it's the seven steps of the method. I think that the method of ecowomanism is such a practical tool to invite anyone into the process of thinking about how to raise their own environmental consciousness and also how to raise their quality of life, their energy, and also their ability to see other beings and—literally to see them in the way that we talk about in the Black Lives Matters movement—to see people with darker skin and to recognize that those beings too are earth beings and deserve to live fully. So, I would say definitely it's the method.

We've talked a lot about self-care and planetary care. And I think in this moment of reentry from the pandemic, if there's any wisdom that ecowomanism can offer, I think that is to take care of oneself and that you have a right to take care of yourself. You have a right to take care of your health and the planet wants you to take care of yourself, while also living mindfully in earth community. In this particular time, I think we'll just be in a season where mental health is key. It won't always be named as something really important or valued, but it will be key to people's survival and how they continue to live through the rest of the pandemics (poly-crises) that we're also in the middle of.

Roberts-Gregory: Yes, I agree completely. In my personal and professional life, I have shifted. As an ecowomanist, I have shifted or pivoted my attention to healing justice. That's important to me, especially when we have layers and layers of violence and interconnected systems of domination to attend to, as Dr. Harris pointed out.

I love Dr. Harris's point that we need to focus on methodology. I consider myself a methodologist. And so, her spiral methodology, the seven steps for our methodology, inspires my own autoethnographic work. And so, I would just echo what Dr. Harris said about the importance of the prophetic visioning, which identifies the Afrofuture. I'm always imagining what the future will look like and what can I not tolerate in the status quo in the present day. I want to ensure, as a lot of Indigenous folks say, seven generations.

I think it's about connecting the personal to the political as mentioned earlier, and also about healing at a very, very, very deep, profound level. For me that also means a focus on health and well-being, and as I mentioned earlier, freedom. I'm trying to free myself. I'm trying to free my community. I'm trying to free the earth. So, this is about resistance. This is about freedom struggles, this is about abolition, and how do we create abolition ecologies when we have so many sacrifice zones and toxic geography. Let's focus on abolition.

Common: Thank you both so much. Those are powerful words to end on. I'm just so grateful for both of you sharing your wisdom here with us for an hour.

Harris: Thank you very much for the honor. Thank you, Dr. Roberts-Gregory. Thank you so much, Dr. Common. And special thanks to ecowomanist scholar Elonda Clay for organizing this gathering for us to be together.

Roberts-Gregory: Yes, thank you for doing this. This has been such an honor.

You Can't Shift the Stars

by Liv Parsons

In her childhood dreams
she holds onto the earth,
stops the bleeding
with her own two hands,
a little girl sits on her bedroom floor
head tilted towards the stars,
and imagines she could shift them,
reform the heavens into perfection,
reshape the sky till it reflects a prettier world,
maybe everyone is a god at seven years old.

To the little girl dreaming of change from her bedroom floor
writing novels in your head,
between darkness and sleep
because
little girls' minds run wild
and the world is so vast
and you are so small
and who will be there to save it
when it all burns down

because it is burning isn't it?
the tv said it is
and mama can't explain
how they're going to fix it,
and you thought mama could mend anything?

You believed in perfection
and infinity.

It all seemed so clear from your bedroom floor:
just tell the leaders
to get down from their podiums
crawl on the floor till they remember their childhood
play in the dirt
pick the flowers
swing from the trees,
remind them what they're losing,
remind them what they're burning,
after all who could look the earth in her eyes and tell her goodbye.
But you watch the tv
and the leaders are stuck at their podiums
and they have forgotten what it feels like
to be a child,
and you can never play god
and you will never shift the heavens.

But I hope you know
I carry your dreams in my lungs,
I breathe in deeply,
your hope makes a home
in my stomach
it hugs the tired parts of me
till they sprout new dandelions,

did you know
you are a garden?

You have watered yourself since childhood
painstakingly
with love and laughter
even on the days,
especially on the days,
when hope feels impossible.

There is a garden within you,
there is a world within you,
there is a galaxy within you,
but it is up to you to find it.

Take out your pen
take out your paint brush
take out your camera
take out your megaphone,

and you will discover that the littlest things
can be a revolution.

You can't stop the bleeding
you can't shift the stars
but you will discover love is powerful
our voices are powerful
our stories are powerful
we are powerful
a little girl on her own can't reshape the universe
but a movement sure can.

earth speaks

by Melanie L. Harris

earth speaks
we listen
in fear
knowing the harm
we've caused

confessing
begging
god
and the ancestors
for grace

to fall
easy
like mist
showering every heart
with home

earth speaks
we listen
trembling in hope
knowing the striving
for green
peace
is not ours alone

we call community into being
praying, acting, moving
always

earth speaks

for love
for peace
for justice
for earth
for fierce compassion

honoring
body

blessing us all
to be
still

and receive courage,
humbling us to learn new direction
on how
to breathe
with her

Conclusion

Engaging Contemplative Thought, Ethics, and Practice

MELANIE L. HARRIS

PREACHING BLACK EARTH AS SACRED OFFERING

A deep sense of the sacred is felt through every page of *Preaching Black Earth*. This artful, creative, collaborative, and contemplative way of approaching environmental justice is by design. The collection of eco-poems, meditations, sermons, and interviews from religious leaders and political activists, scholars, preachers, and poets in the environmental justice movement connects the legacy of African American writing and eco-literature with voices of women of African descent in environmental science, climate change analysis and climate justice work, and the prophetic tradition of Black preaching.[1] This interdisciplinary discourse invites the best of the Black preaching tradition to move environmental justice forward, as it acknowledges the power of words, to live and promote justice both on and off the page. Through a contemplative process of learning, the ecowomanist reflections, sermons, eco-poems, and interviews in this volume inspire us to share in the creation of prophetic wisdom. This wisdom can transform the way we live in earth community.[2]

The prophetic wisdom that emerges from *Preaching Black Earth* does so, in part, as an outcome of the contemplative approaches and practices embedded

---

1. For more on the tradition of black preaching see the work of Henry and Ella Mitchell, and the contemplative preaching and spoken word practice of Howard Thurman, *Meditations of the Heart* (Beacon Press, 1999), and healing paths in pedagogy modeled by Rosemarie Harding in *Remnants: A Memoir of Spirit, Activism, and Mothering* (Duke University Press, 2015) by Rachel Harding.
2. For more on the prophetic voice and nature of ecowomanism, see Melanie L. Harris, *Ecowomanism: African American Women and Earth-Honoring Faiths* (Orbis, 2017).

in the sermons, poems, meditations, and interviews. Contemplative practices can be found in each of the selected sermons, spoken words, poetry, and shared dialogue of the interviews. As such they are additional resources of living earth wisdom that flows from the pages. These words are not just those crafted by the pen of one writer to the hearer or reader, but rather from earth beings who are listening to earth to other earth beings who, in service to earth justice, are invited to hear, read, listen, and act upon the earth wisdom they have heard. In each sermon, every poem, and throughout the interviews found in this text, reference to, or examples of, earth-honoring practices can be found that can help the reader develop their own earth-honoring faith practice.

Preaching Black Earth is not a preaching book. That is, it is not a study guide in homiletics, nor does it dictate a particular style of preaching or spoken word. *Preaching Black Earth* is an offering. On and through the pages of carefully constructed sermons that raise consciousness about environmental justice, felt through the poetry voices of ecowomanism, and experienced through the mutually enhancing interviews featuring scholars, artists, and activists, *Preaching Black Earth* offers models of effective earth-honoring practice through spoken work, dialogue, poetry, and practice. The book offers us the invitation to experience several contemplative practices including deep listening of earth and each other, communing with nature, and acting in earth-honoring ways committed to environmental justice; it is an invitation into sacred presence that honors earth and helps us honor ourselves.

The contemplative aspect of ecowomanism is key to understanding the experiential learning that takes place when we engage environmental justice from an approach that honors the voices, beliefs, and earth-honoring spiritualities of Black women. Noting the ways that reception, cultivation, and production of knowledge is formed by Black women and how Black women's epistemologies are honored (or not) in society, the contemplative aspect of ecowomanism honors the fact that knowledge and wisdom come through more than words. That is, it is Black women's practice with earth, their own spiritual connections, and sacred worldviews that make up their approaches to analysis and shape their solutions to climate injustice.

To understand more about the contemplative aspects of ecowomanism, it is helpful first to review a definition of contemplative thought. It can be defined as mindful practice engaging "head and heart," intellect and spirit in the work of social action, including the work of climate justice. It is a primary way, or mode of being, in ecowomanism, because the scope of analysis pays special attention to the life and spiritual practices of women of African descent whose spiritual practice is woven into their understanding of honoring earth. For example, consider the Black church women in North Carolina in the 1970s, whose faith led them to act in nonviolent protest against the state of

Conclusion   163

North Carolina's designation that a landfill be placed in Warren County. The landfill was designed to dispose of polychlorinated biphenyls (PCBs), a group of toxic chemicals. As documented in the United Church of Christ landmark 1987 report *Toxic Waste and Race in the United States* and books, including *Toxic Communities: Environmental Racism, Industrial Pollution, and Residential Mobility* and *To Love the Wind and the Rain: African Americans and Environmental History*, it was the theological understanding of humans' responsibility to be proper stewards and partners with the earth that led these activists to take a faith stance.³ Taking their faith to the streets, they protested in order to protect the earth community. Laying their bodies down in front of dump trucks carrying PCB contaminated soil while crying out for justice, these demonstrators linked their own faith and religious beliefs to the work of environmental justice.

ECOWOMANIST CONTEMPLATIVE PEDAGOGY

Spiritual activism for environmental justice is a strong foundation for ecowomanism, so attention to the ways that spiritual activism is taught and nurtured is important to explore. We do so through an analysis of ecowomanist contemplative pedagogy. Ecowomanist contemplative pedagogy and teaching styles are used to approach the ways we invite learners into conversation about intersections among religion, race, gender, ecology, and, more broadly, environmental justice. Contemplative pedagogies are teaching methods designed to cultivate awareness, deep concentration, and insight. Rather than centering deposit-only forms of knowing, contemplative teaching or pedagogy fosters Indigenous ways of knowing and multiple intelligences that challenge colonial methods of education.

Examples of these wisdom ways of knowing include a focus of the heart and mind connection, acknowledgment of non-dual awareness and presence of spiritual insight that may not be accessed through the intellect as valid sources for religious and spiritual reflection on moral and social action. Cultivating relational wisdom and recognizing the challenges and gifts of social location, especially diversity and difference, are the outcomes of effective contemplative pedagogy. Along with these outcomes is the soft dissolve of mental formations that lean toward social constructions. Recognizing this latter movement of the mind is important to the work of racial justice and environmental justice in that it signals the importance of paying attention to specific categories of

---

3. Dorceta E. Taylor, *Toxic Communities: Environmental Racism, Industrial Pollution, and Residential Mobility* (New York University Press, 2014). Dianne D. Glave and Mark Stoll, *To Love the Wind and the Rain: African Americans and Environmental History* (University of Pittsburgh Press, 2005).

race, class, and gender to form and shape the lenses through which we conduct analysis; it also identifies the way concrete structures of these same categories disallow or limit our capacity to realize our own connection to earth and to each other. This very important contemplative thought can serve as the window or practice through which deeper awareness, knowledge about connecting with earth, and earth community comes. Practices such as meditation, contemplative reading in community, and mindful speech and conversation can help release the mind from concrete ideas and mental patterns that result in the development of attitudes about certain groups of people or species. Unfortunately, this movement of mind to "other" or separate one group from another, instead of seeing all as "inter-being" can form unhelpful and unhealthy stereotypes. These stereotypes, whether through practices of white supremacy or through attachment to logics of domination, can lead to terror: terrorizing the earth and earth beings in such ways that Delores S. Williams writes about in her essay "Sin, Nature, and Black Women's Bodies."[4] Moving toward an imperative of inclusion and justice, contemplative pedagogies can be seen as modes of teaching that nurture understanding and connection with self, others, and earth, thus opening the door to build trust anchored in spiritual wisdom and deep contemplative practice.

For example, Kenneth Ngwa's sermon invites us to pose the question to ourselves, "What time is it" on the face of the planet in light of climate change? Posing this question, honestly in contemplative reflection or through journal writing, might encourage us to focus more deeply on creating life-affirming and sustaining relationships and let go of more trivial concerns based on competition and maintaining power in hierarchal relationships. Rather than allowing "foolishness of the fools" to continue to take place in institutional contexts that negatively impact the lives of marginalized beings, we can focus on reflection on the time we have left to undo the impact of anthropocentric systems that are killing the planet would be wiser.

Another example of contemplative practice that can be gleaned from reflection on the eco-poetry in *Preaching Black Earth* is through a learning or pedological practice that invites readers to share the poems in the book with friends, colleagues, and classmates. For example, as a contemplative pedagogy practice, consider inviting students to rewrite the words of the eco-poem at the beginning of the book. Upon studying and even reciting the poem three times by individuals in small groups of three, students can be invited to write their own eco-poems, share them, and add them to the voices recorded here.

---

4. Delores S. Williams, "Sin, Nature and Black Women's Bodies," in *Ecofeminism and the Sacred*, ed. by Carol J. Adams (Continuum, 1993), 24–29.

Through contemplative thought, ecowomanism invites us to slow down and reflect on earth and with earth in a contemplative way that allows us to take root in the very practices we need to save ourselves, our earthliness, and our earth-honoring faith communities. Reading this book contemplatively changes and transforms the very spaces of our lives. The space in between each line creates space for hope and has the power to reshape our everyday ethical life and way of living with and in earth.

PREACHING BLACK EARTH AS ETHICS AND PRACTICE

This section focuses on two ethical values that can be gleaned from contemplative reflection on *Preaching Black Earth*: sacredness of earth and interconnectedness. In *Gifts of Virtue, Alice Walker, and Womanist Ethics*, I developed a womanist virtue ethic approach to inform the study of Black women's voices in literature for the sake of ethical inquiry that simultaneously sheds light on how to develop an ethical way of living for Black women.[5] *Gifts of Virtue* studies the nonfiction work and writings by Walker and explores the virtues and values embedded in her life, most notably those that inform her spiritual activism for social and environmental justice. To do this work of uncovering, I developed a womanist virtue ethical approach that foregrounds three steps used to mine or glean values for the shaping of an ethical path of living or names guidelines to follow when facing a crisis. Informed by the model and method of the Black womanist ethic of Katie G. Cannon, the womanist virtue ethic method helps to glean womanist values that shape the moral lives and enhance the quality of life of Black women and the earth community.

On the path toward recognizing a list of virtues toward the building of a larger ethic, the first step begins with highlighting experiential themes recorded in an analysis of a specific life, writings, or life work. The second step in the method is to glean ethical implications and sift values from these themes. The third step is naming and explicating each of the virtues gleaned and framing a list of values. The summary of these values can provide the blueprint for a constructive ethic. Since the scope of this book is primarily to showcase the sermons, meditations, eco-poems, and interviews therein, this section will not go through the analysis of every contribution in *Preaching Black Earth* for the sake of analyzing themes, gleaning ethical implications, and sifting values for the building of an ethic. However, to illustrate the common threads that weave through each of the sermons, meditations, eco-poems, and interviews, it will explicate two primary values: sacredness of earth and interconnectedness.

5. Melanie L. Harris, *Gifts of Virtue, Alice Walker, and Womanist Ethics* (Palgrave Macmillan, 2010).

Sacredness of Earth

The sacredness of earth is best understood as a belief that the true nature of all beings carries a divine light or spirit that is shared with the whole earth community. Expanding upon the traditional Judeo-Christian theological concept of *imago Dei*—that human beings are uniquely created in the image of God—the sacredness of earth claims that all of earth carries a sacred beauty, innate worth, and value. Honoring this value is the focus of ecotheologies that expand theological perspectives about human relationship to and with the earth and interrogate and shape religious understandings about rites and rituals that celebrate the earth and honor the perspective of earth as a part of a connected cosmology. Similar to the intersectional analysis used in environmental justice theory, many ecotheologies apply intersectional analysis, including sociopolitical, spiritual-cultural critical, and liberative theological lenses, to interrogate language and worldviews that are steeped in colonial frames, dualisms, and hierarchies. For example, S. Lili Mendoza and George Zachariah define decolonizing ecotheology as "a spiritual and political vocation for all those who are committed to restoring Earth's and earthling's—flourishing."[6] Noting that ecotheologies are attempts to transform religions into "public-oriented religions" or empower "spiritual activism," the work of decolonizing ecologies helps to reset theological foundations for "engaging creation-care and initiate programs for the restoration of creation."[7] Decolonial ecotheologies also help point out some critical misalignments in theological perspectives that separate earth justice from social justice and use colonial frameworks that allow anthropocentric hierarchies to exist. Ecowomanism can then be considered a decolonial ecotheology or perspective.

A review of the meaning of the term "ecowomanism" is helpful here.[8] Ecowomanism is an approach to environmental justice that centers the voices and environmental scientific methods and perspectives of women of African descent as it conducts intersectional, decolonial analysis that is helpful in dismantling the logics of domination that still permeate environmental studies. Like Womanist theory and praxis, it insists on an ethical principle of justice. Therefore, ecowomanism is deconstructive and uses intersectional analysis and decolonial frames to point out the correlation between environmental injustice and the maintenance of unjust systems that devalue the worth of all earthlings or "defile" the sanctity of earth, and the innate dignity of earthlings, including

---

6. S. Lily Mendoza and George Zachariah, eds., *Decolonizing Ecotheology: Indigenous and Subaltern Challenges* (Pickwick Publications, 2022).
7. Harris, *Gifts of Virtue*. Layli Maparyan, *The Womanist Idea* (Routledge, 2011), 114–44.
8. Harris, *Ecowomanism*.

Conclusion 167

Black women.[9] Ecowomanism critically examines the logics of domination used to silence earth and devalue—even destroy—the voices of women of African descent and nonhuman beings being sacrificed in an age of global capitalism. Noting the similarities between the logic of domination that has historically silenced Black women and the logics of domination that has limited the flourishing of earth, the ecowomanist seven-step method consists of (1) contemplation on individual and collective eco-memory to raise consciousness about our beliefs, values, and connection with the earth; (2) reflection on these eco-memories to examine the parallel nature of sufferings experienced by Black and Indigenous women and the earth; (3) analysis of these eco-memories using an intersectional lens to reveal points of harm that take place against the bodies of women and the bodies of earth (nonhuman beings); (4) a call out of dualistic frames and hierarchal thinking woven into "traditional" forms of theology, philosophy, and Western thinking that actually perpetuate violence against women and the earth; (5) the engagement of transformative decolonial discourse that untangles women's agency and earth-honoring ethics from unjust structures and systems in order to (6) share in dialogue (often interfaith dialogue) that can construct new ethics and ways of being that shed dualistic frames and include (rather than exclude) the epistemologies of Indigenous and Black women and communities of color so that (7) action can be taken for earth justice. Calling for action that supports ecological reparations, ecowomanism offers a constructive approach and a more inclusive lens to work in environmental justice.[10] The sacredness of earth is explored as a value in various ecowomanist perspectives, and the common and shared understanding of this principle often serves as a crucial entry point for interfaith and interreligious dialogue within ecowomanist circles globally.[11]

Interconnectedness

A second religious and spiritual principle of environmental justice that can be gleaned from contemplative thought on the sermons, eco-poetry, and interviews in *Preaching Black Earth* is interconnectedness. This refers to the interconnection of all beings, and an intimate relationship between the divine, earth, and human realms. Aligning with worldviews often held in Native Indigenous, African,

---

9. Williams, "Sin, Nature, and Black Women's Bodies," 24–29.
10. Harris, *Ecowomanism*.
11. While, accepted by many theistic religious perspectives, the sacredness of earth is also shared by dark green religious and deep ecology perspectives, which can include nontheistic perspectives such as naturalistic animism. See Louisa Johanna (Hannelie) du Toit, "A Dark Green Religious Analysis of the Life and Work of Wangari Maathai (1940–2011)," *African Journal of Gender and Religion*, 27, no. 1: (July 2021).

Caribbean, African American and Latinx diasporic spiritual traditions, interconnectedness of all beings is reflective of non-dualistic cosmologies wherein the earth/nature realm is interconnected with the human and divine realms in a kind of mutually enhancing framework or harmonious web of life.[12] In African cosmology, for example, the earth/nature realm is even understood to embody certain ancestral spirits (i.e., orishas, divine entities, spirits). When these ancestors or ancestral energies are honored, the harmony of balance can be witnessed through care of earth and justice in human community.[13] When an imbalance occurs or when discord such as overuse of land, pollution of air and water, oppressive divisions among humans, or climate violence happens, then the entire cosmos is out of alignment.

The imbalance can create disconnection between the realms, and environmental degradation and climate violence can become normative. In African cosmology, as all three realms of life are interconnected, harmony, honor, and reciprocity are key for wellness in the entire earth community. A norm and ethical mandate to take care of the earth can be gleaned from this understanding held in many Indigenous spiritual traditions, including Yoruba, Candomblé, Santeria, and many Afro-Latinx liberation spiritualities. The theme of interconnectedness is also evident in the first of seventeen principles listed by the National People of Color Environmental Leadership Summit in 1991. It states, "Environmental justice affirms the sacredness of Mother Earth, ecological unity and the interdependence of all species, and the right to be free from ecological destruction."[14] The Black Church Food Security Network and many other nonprofit organizations in the food justice movement are evidence of this principle.[15]

In her essay *Touching the Earth*, scholar and activist bell hooks explains an important nuance to interconnectedness in the work of ecological and racial reparations. Noting the history of farming and agricultural knowledge among many communities of color globally and how colonialism and practices of white supremacy separated many peoples of African descent from connection with the land, reestablishing the connection as a form of self, communal, and planetary care becomes a strategy of ecological reparations:

---

12. See Melanie L. Harris, "An Ecowomanist Vision," in *Ethics That Matters: African, Caribbean, and African American Sources*, ed. Marcia Y. Riggs and James Samuel Logan (Fortress, 2012), 189–94.
13. Harris, "An Ecowomanist Vision."
14. "17 Principles of Environmental Justice," Center for Biological Diversity, accessed April 18, 2024, https://www.biologicaldiversity.org/about/17-principles-of-environmental justice.html?gad_source=1&gclid=Cj0KCQjwiYOxBhC5ARIsAIvdH50lMa2IKsHJ2 x9aSC wLyIrezIO4tBs8bZJAwaf8MDybQzH4JNvEVhwaAj4jEALw_wcB.
15. For information on the Black Church Food Security Network, see their website: https://blackchurchfoodsecurity.net/.

Living in modern society, without a sense of history, it has been easy for folks to forget that black people were first and foremost a people of the land, farmers . . . that at the first part of the 20th century, the vast majority of black folks in the United States lived in the agrarian south. . . . There is also a tendency to see no correlation between the struggle for collective black self-recovery and ecological movements that seek to restore balance to the planet by changing our relationship to nature and to natural resources. . . . Recalling the legacy of our ancestors who knew that the way we regard land and nature will determine the level of our self-regard, black people must reclaim a spiritual legacy where we connect our well-being to the well-being of the earth. This is a necessary dimension of healing.[16]

Here, planetary care is also understood as an important step in reparations, self-care, and empowerment for Black peoples and peoples of color globally. This move to expand the prescription for doing ecological reparations invites approaches in the wider environmental movement to honor Black lives, cherish the environmental history of people of color, and include their legacies in discourse about the environmental movement.[17] Echoing a Christian understanding of the Golden Rule, or honoring the neighbor as the self (Matt. 7:12), which is central to many religions, ecological reparations uproot an individualistic paradigm and insist on a principle of interconnectedness wherein all are wrapped in an "inescapable network of mutuality."[18]

Aligned with narratives in many Judeo-Christian traditions, as well as in Islam and in Eastern traditions such as Buddhism and Hinduism, the normative ethic to care for the earth can be gleaned from many religious stories and traditions that understand earth's origin story as deeply connected to an earth ethic for human communities.[19] As Alice Walker reminds readers in her essay, "This Was Not An Area of Large Plantations: Suffering Too Insignificant for the Majority to See" inviting religion and spiritual tradition into dialogue with the work of environmental justice can help humans reconnect to the environment, and this is central to creating a life of happiness for all beings.[20] Answering the question

---

16. Bell hooks, "Touching the Earth," in *Sisters of the Yam: Black Women and Self-Recovery* (South End Press, 2017), 136–40.

17. Taylor, *Toxic Communities*, and Dorceta E. Taylor, "Race, Class, Gender, and American Environmentalism" United States Department of Agriculture (USDA) Forest Service, accessed April 12, 2024, https://www.fs.usda.gov/research/treesearch/3259.

18. Martin Luther King Jr. "Letter from Birmingham City Jail," in *A Testament of Hope: The Essential Writings and Speeches of Dr. Martin Luther King, Jr.*, ed. James Melvin Washington (HarperSanFrancisco, 1986), 289–302.

19. See, e.g., Gen. 1:1–2:4.

20. Alice Walker, "This Was Not an Area of Large Plantations: Suffering Too Insignificant for the Majority to See," in *We Are the Ones We Have Been Waiting For: Inner Light in a Time of Darkness* (The New Press, 2006), 99.

of how religion and spirituality move us toward environmental justice, Walker retells the story of the Buddha's enlightenment. The essay recalls the moment the Buddha confronts Mara, king of delusion, and points to the fact that this is the same moment of the highest enlightenment. The "Buddha clearly placed himself in the lap of the Earth Mother and affirmed Her Wisdom and Her support" Walker writes; and by doing so, Walker suggests, for the sake of environmental justice, that humans use religious, sacred, and spiritual teachings such as the eightfold path to direct humankind away from suffering and toward finding joy in each moment and happiness in everyday life with earth.[21]

While not the specific subject of a sermon, poem, or interview in *Preaching Black Earth*, the themes of the Green Belt Movement and the work of Wangari Maathai align with the themes of sacredness of earth, and interconnectedness and Maathai's work serves as an illustration of the importance of these values. In her book *Replenishing the Earth: Spiritual Values for Healing Ourselves and the World*, Wangari Maathai, founder of the Green Belt Movement, reflects on decades of activism in the Green Belt Movement (GBM). Noting the importance of the scientific data collected and discoveries made, what seemed to most surprise her was the empowerment that women received from the GBM as well as the significant inner transformation, decolonialization, and healing that many communities experienced as their spiritual roots in Indigenous ways of knowing and being in community were acknowledged, valued, and embraced as a part of the movement designed to uplift women's sense of agency, help eradicate poverty, and change entire societies to be less autocratic and patriarchal to being more woman-centered, affirming, and democratic.

Maathai names four core values of the Green Belt Movement that essentially serve as an ethical guide and frame for the movement: namely, (1) love for the environment, (2) gratitude and respect for Earth's resources, (3) self-empowerment and self-betterment, and (4) the spirit of service and volunteerism. While these core values are partially influenced by the traditional practices of the African Kikuyu indigenous community to which she belonged, the traditional worldview of this community acknowledged the earth as sacred in such a way that "is generally representative of many native and indigenous communities."[22] Naming the harsh realities of Christian colonial practice throughout Africa, which destroyed many traditional African communities and values, Maathai explains that while Christianity was not a faith that she grew up with, often in order to work with Kenyans and others around the world who did practice Christianity, the Green Belt Movement drew from stories in the Old and New Testaments of the Bible

---

21. Walker, 99.
22. Wangari Maathai, *Replenishing the Earth: Spiritual Values for Healing Ourselves and the World* (Doubleday, 2010), 21.

to draw out aspects of the faith that honored and respected the natural world. Shaping what some scholars might call a decolonial theological approach, GBM workers helped people and especially women in their communities to rebuild religious worldviews that built on faith perspectives that honored the earth, and deepen values embedded in their Indigenous traditions. According to Maathai, this move helped build the movement and restore communities' relationships with the earth through the practice of planting trees. While not an expressively religious person for most of her life as a researcher and scientist, Maathai writes that the deep levels of life transformation that she witnessed was more than an exact combination of earth science, climate research, and liberal ideology about women:

> After a few years I came to recognize that our efforts weren't only about planting trees but were also about sowing seeds of a different sort—the ones necessary to heal the wounds inflicted on communities that robbed them of their self-confidence and self-knowledge. What became clear was that individuals within these communities had to rediscover their authentic voice and speak out on behalf of their rights (human, environmental, civic, and political). Our task also became to expand democratic space in which ordinary citizens could make decisions on their own behalf to benefit themselves, their community, their country, and the environment that sustains them.[23]

The Nobel Peace Laureate's approach in Kenya and throughout the world highlights ways that environmental justice is linked to issues of social justice, especially in the lives of women.[24] Maathai's work with the GBM illustrates how interconnectedness and the values of the sacredness of earth move the work of environmental justice forward.

As we see in *Preaching Black Earth*, the lens of ecowomanism invites readers to embrace a fresh imperative for environmental justice through the power of spoken and preached word, eco-poetry, and shared wisdom through interviews. In this way, the book offers new models and insights about how communities of color, and especially African American and antiracist allies can shape, empower, and lift environmental justice from the pulpit, to the pew, to the garden. If read contemplatively, the book is an invitation to deepen our connection with the divine through strengthening our connection with earth.

Foundational to ecowomanism is an African cosmological worldview that sees all things are interconnected and thus interwoven with earth community. This perspective shapes our way of being in community that leads to a more ethical and environmentally just way of life. As we move from a discussion

---

23. Maathai, *Replenishing the Earth*, 14.
24. Layli Maparyan, "Spiritual Activism," in *A Womanist Idea* (Routledge, 2011).

of ethics and return to practice, it is important to note how close an African cosmological worldview is to a Native Indigenous worldview wherein humans are connected to the earth as two-legged members of the earth community.

PREACHING BLACK EARTH AS PRACTICE

Deep Listening and Peace Circles: How Ecowomanism Honors Indigenous Wisdom and Environmental Justice

In a 2022 teaching presentation for the Elders Talking Circle recorded on Facebook Live, Cheryl Demmert Fairbanks (Tlingit-Tsimshian) explains the role Native cosmology and spirituality play in the practice and development of peace circles. There are many different kinds of peace circles. Some are devoted to healing, others to empowering children, individual, and communal voices, and still others are peacebuilding circles that address adversarial conflicts in advance of or in lieu of moving in a more formal litigious way. In this sense, Demmert Fairbanks states that peace circles are spaces "where people can talk it out together to resolve conflict. It is a community-based consensus process that addresses the concerns of all interested parties."[25]

The process of building a peace circle begins by engaging deep listening to earth, ancestors, cultural values, and tradition. The presence of wisdom and spirituality evokes a synergy toward building resolution. This first step in many Native and Indigenous communities begins with an earth-honoring practice and a reminder of cultural and spiritual values such as respect, community, and reaffirming the sacredness of all beings. In a peace circle devoted to environmental justice and strengthening ecowomanist wisdom, this first step could be an invitation for all involved to engage a shift from western way of logical thinking, based on capitalist systems and Eurocentric logics of domination, to a healing circle, native, earth-centered, and spiritual way of opening the mind and living in a way that recognizes all beings as valued and connected.

These shifts of mind, as Demmert Fairbanks explains, are key to creating an atmosphere of peace, unity, and deep presence in peace circles. She explicates these movements of mind by using the acronym S-H-I-F-T. The first letter, *S*, stands for *sacred/spiritual*. She explains that a part of the shift or change in thinking (thus reshaping a mental formation, to use Buddhist language) that

---

25. https://alaska-native-news.com/elders-talking-circle-with-cheryl-demmert-fairbanks-topic-peacemaking-circles/63578/.

must happen in each participant is a shift into sacred and spiritual awareness. This helps to set the stage for safe, inner, social and communal transformation. In Buddhism, we might call this an invitation into a meditative state of awareness, or a recognition of equanimity and inclusiveness, where everyone is valued and "has a chance to speak and silence is ok."[26] A note about silence is important in that in many indigenous practices, silence allows for or creates a pause through which earth, the divine realm, and ancestors can speak to the heart, body, and spirit. This mode of contemplation, honoring silence, is also reflected in Buddhist meditation or Christian centering prayer, whereby the art of silence is cultivated to leave room for the movement and speaking of the Holy Spirit.[27] Pulitzer-prize winning author Alice Walker writes about the "power of the pause" in her essay "All Praise to the Pause."[28] Noting her own spiritual practice and the wisdom of Indigenous peoples, she recognizes the power of the pause as a valuable lesson, especially to those celebrating the end of a major accomplishment. Instead of charging forward into the next thing, Walker suggests pausing to listen for the wisdom necessary for the next part of one's life journey or path.

The second letter, *H,* in Demmert Fairbanks' acronym stands for *health* and *holistic*. They signal a way of being and thinking that uplifts holistic ways of connecting and being in community as well as promotes healing for individuals and earth community. Recognizing healing as vital for the entire community, this focus on health not only serves individuals but also the earth community as a whole.

The third letter, *I,* stands for *issue*. It reminds the participant to engage the root causes of the dispute, invoking self-compassion and compassion for others in the peace circle. This is especially important in the case that participants feel led to share stories and lessons from their experience that highlight or trigger memories of complex trauma, including historical and racial trauma. Since peace circles generally are understood to be healing spaces for all involved, most Native Indigenous peace circle facilitators believe that a greater, deeper power of healing is present. That is, similar to traditions such as Buddhism or Christian mysticism, there is an understanding that a sacred healing spiritual power (i.e., Holy Spirit, Buddha nature, Ancestors, God) permeates and holds the entire process of the peace circle.[29]

---

26. https://www.facebook.com/watch/live/?ref=watch_permalink&v=7991846578964361.
27. For more on centering prayer, see Cynthia Bourgealt, *Centering Prayer and Inner Awakening* (Cowley Productions, 2024).
28. Alice Walker, "All Praises to the Pause," in *We Are the Ones We've Been Waiting For* (New Press, 2006).
29. https://www.facebook.com/watch/live/?ref=watch_permalink&v=799184657896436.

The practice of building peace circles should be trauma informed. This means recognizing that in addition to the sacred unity of healing presence, it is also important to pay attention to the trauma that individuals might carry. Acknowledging the individual, historical, and communal harm that might be present in a peace circle helps trauma survivors move toward healing. One way to weave trauma informed practices into a peace circle is to recognize and name resources, practices, and spaces of emotional, psychological, spiritual, and bodily safety or refuge that each participant has access to in the moment or beyond the circle that might help them through a triggering moment. In an interview with Cheryl Demmert Fairbanks, recorded on August 22, 2024, she even encourages peace circle facilitators to consider inviting trauma-informed specialists such as therapists, mental health providers, spiritual advisors, coaches, or counselors to join a peace circle process to offer assistance.[30]

The letter I in the acronym also stands for *Indigenous* and is a reminder for all participants to lean into traditional wisdom, language, and Indigenous worldview. Here, Demmert Fairbanks refers to the image of the butterfly to explain a Native way of understanding humans as two-legged beings deeply woven into the earth community and the value of inclusiveness. The symbol of the butterfly is intended to invite all perspectives, especially opposite or opposing perspectives, into the larger holding of the conversation. Acknowledging the opposite view helps to build a sustaining solution. Particularly when a peace circle is hosting conflict or adversarial perspectives, this larger holding by the community can be central to creating ease and well-being for all those present.

The fourth letter, *F*, stands for *facilitated discussion* and invites all to be open to a focused conversation supporting the best for the individual, family, and community. This kind of facilitation is very important for peace circles designed to heal and transform conflict. In the case of healing peace circles, the facilitation is understood to be a fundamentally fair procedure that the peacemaker uses to honor all voices in the circle in a spirit of equity.

The final letter, *T*, stands for *transition to change*, transformation that is hoped for in every individual and the circle community at large. It invites participants to understand that collaborative and cooperative approaches align with native and Indigenous wisdom and consensus, thus affirming healthy expressions of tradition, culture, and peace.

---

30. Interview with Cheryl Demmert Fairbanks with author, "Building Peace Circles" August 22, 2024, via Zoom and phone.

Conclusion 175

PEACE CIRCLE PROCESS

Once an atmosphere of peace has been created, both in the individual and in the community, the process of a peace circle can begin. This starts with establishing appropriate values and guidelines for the peace circle and naming the purpose of the circle. Moreover, a peace circle that is designed to be healing is particularly shaped to attend to participants who would benefit from a sense of confidence that their voice will be heard. This can be achieved through prayer, song, poem, or moment of silence to hold the sacredness and spirituality of the space. This is a crucial moment in a healing circle, as it sets both an individual and communal space of open heartedness and refuge. Cheryl Demmert Fairbanks comes from two tribes, Tlingit and Tsimishian. Both carry a worldview that centers the importance of honoring one's own sacred self. This process can be understood as an inner circle of integrity wherein one holds themselves accountable to acting in a way that embodies their best self, honors their ancestors, and honors the spiritual realm. In this sense, one's own sacred circle reflects core cultural values and is guided by a sense of ethics that is shaped by a spiritual awareness of oneness and equity with all beings.

A similar understanding of interconnectedness is found in Buddhist spirituality, wherein one understands their practice of mindfulness to be a gateway or opening to a greater awareness of interbeing. Interbeing is a word defined by Thich Nhat Hanh that generally means that all is connected; that whatever exists in you, also exists in another being. An example that Thich Nhat Hanh gave, throughout his lifetime of teaching, was to invite learners to reflect on the element of water. Noting its fluid nature and presence in all living things, including the embodied self, allows one to recognize the insight of interbeing. We are all water, air, earth, and energy, as we are all made up of these elements of earth. How we recognize and honor these parts of ourselves, and in each other, is crucial in shaping a relational way of being that allows us to be nonviolent toward each other. When acts of violence take place that take us out of our own sacred circle, the practice of building a peace circle can invite us more deeply into introspection and help us realign ourselves to our own sacred circle and sense of integrity.[31]

Reflection on our own personal relationship with ourselves, our ancestors, and our own values is key in the work of building community with others. For this reason, the practice of sharing compassion with self and community is highly valued as a guideline for peace making. Another guideline is to offer respect to self, facilitators, elders, and all participants. Every participant in a

---

31. For more on inter-being, see Thich Nhat Hanh, *Living Buddha, Living Christ* (Penguin Group, 1995).

peace circle is asked to use mindful speech, whereby each person is invited and expected to speak with care and respect. In peace circles, this means that only one person speaks at a time. There is no interrupting. A talking stick, basket, or other meaningful item is used as a sacred element to help determine who has the right to speak. Whoever holds the basket or talking stick is the one who is invited to speak at that time.

Peace circles operate with a consensus model with attention to fact-finding and the development and understanding of the issues. Rather than a western analytical approach such as deconstructing, a spirit of consensus is encouraged to understand each other's deep-rooted issues and help participants build off of each other's solutions and recommendations. Rather than challenging others' ideas in an unexamined way, a mode of consensus invites all participants to collectively think together and tap into wisdom that best serves the individual and community. This practice of consensus is important because it helps to affirm every participant's voice. It promotes open and honest dialogue and cultivates the values of humility, apology, forgiveness, and compassion. Sharing guidelines in advance of the peace circle and building consensus is important in the process as the participants develop and accept the agreement.

Another aspect of the agreements of a peace circle is comfortability with silence and the practice of deep listening. In peace circles, silence is honorably held when it comes and understood as a welcome part of the circle process. Every participant has the right to pass and not speak. Deep listening accompanies the guidelines and invites participants to honor words, silence in between words, and an embodied sense of communication. Observing hand gestures and other forms of nonverbal communication are also considered part of the process of deep listening. For many Indigenous and Native peoples, listening is more important than talking, and it is a skill that must be learned. Communing with the ancestors in one's own sacred circle through breathing meditation, centering prayer, or other rituals helps to enhance the skill of deep listening because one is listening for the voice of earth, the ancestors, or the voice of one's heart and best self. Quiet contemplation is key for this kind of connection.

PEACE CIRCLE AS ECOWOMANIST PRACTICE

The peace circle process can be a form of healing from an ecowomanist perspective and be especially helpful as a trauma-informed contemplative practice. As a contemplative practice, the peace circle process holds special significance for those engaged in ecowomanist and environmental justice. On one hand, the peace circle creates a community of accountability that can serve as a space for individuals to be held accountable for their relationship with the earth and with each other. On another hand, building a peace circle can assist participants by providing emotional support for those who may have eco-memories that uncover environmental or historical trauma. For example, for people of African descent in the US whose eco-memory is tied to both images of terror such as lynching and triumph such as the freedom of the spirit engaged through earth's beauty, the contemplative practice of building a peace circle can provide much needed trauma-informed support. Having a healing peace circle and community with whom to process environmental and racial violence is key for ecowomanism. True to the tenets of healing and justice woven within ecowomanism, an ecowomanist healing peace circle can create a form of justice by attending to the environmental trauma many people of African descent have survived.

The first step of the ecowomanist method asks participants to reflect on an eco-memory in order to evoke an insight they may have about their own relationship with earth. Often in sharing this eco-memory or earth story with themselves and others, one can identify deeply held beliefs about their own eco-theology or theological belief about the earth. By reflecting on an eco-memory, by using the first step of the method thinkers, activists and scholars often uncover a set of values that guide their belief and actions toward environmental justice.

In order to create the peace circle process as trauma informed, it is recommended that the facilitator provide an orientation of the concept of eco-memory as outlined in the book *Ecowomanism: Earth Honoring Faiths* and present one of the challenges and opportunities of this engagement to inter and intracultural groups. Noting the different historical realities of non-native (white people) and many communities of color regarding our connection, cosmology and understandings of environmental justice, the ecowomanist methodological step of honoring experience and opening to eco-memory invites deeper reflection on challenges and insights to move into racial justice conversations and engage anti-racist paradigms in service to environmental justice. Skillful means that help one deal with difficult emotions such as white guilt, and shame, and other tensions surrounding racial and environmental injustice can be woven into the peace circle process. Here is where the assistance of therapists, counselors, or additional facilitators might be called upon to assist. Also, the use of a recess for the entire circle is another part that can be engaged at any point in the circle to invite pause and allow the participants to recenter.

The second step of the ecowomanist method of a healing peace circle is to invite participants in a first round of speaking to reflect individually or in pairs on an eco-memory from their childhood that carries deep meaning for them. As discussed by Cheryl Demmert Fairbanks, a peace circle traditionally has several rounds whereby participants are invited to speak when they have the talking stick, and deeply listen to each other as the community takes shape. Another prompt question that might spark reflection is, What story or memory comes to mind from your childhood to bring back the feeling of earth on your skin, the freedom of fresh air moving through your body, or feels like warm water embracing your being in a comfortable and safe way? What of this memory feels sacred to you? What of this memory feels hard?

During the first round of the peace circle participants can share in pairs or with the larger circle. Once a recess is taken, as a chance to rest, renew, and recenter (this is also a time to invite participants to check in about their sense of safety and mental health), round two of the peace circle can begin with a prompt for all participants to consider a theme from the eco-memory shared in the previous round that allows one to deepen in their awareness of the environment and environmental justice. A third round of the peace circle can start with participants reflecting on the prompt: How do we make sure children in the next seven generations have the chance to feel the safety, love and nurturing that perhaps we experienced in our childhood? What resources do we need to find and name solutions for earth justice? At the conclusion of this round, the peace circle approaches an end. Each participant is invited to stand or move in a way that is comfortable and empowering for them so that they can recognize their own sacredness and magnificence. For this part of the circle, Cheryl Demmert Fairbanks invites participants to affirm themselves audibly in front of the group. She invites participants to stand and say "Now, great one, dear heart, stand in your own magnificence. Can you feel it?" Inviting each individual into their own sacred self, this part of the practice is designed to help participants experience their own sovereignty. Participants are then invited to share their sacred worth and presence with one another through prayer, greeting, handshake, hug, or embrace. Here, the contemplative practice of presence as a way of honoring the interbeing between self and other is engaged as the circle unfolds.

Before ending, each participant is invited to speak into the circle a wisdom that they now have, that can offer the peace circle greater wisdom for the sake of environmental justice. Or, in other words, each participant is invited to name and share a medicine that they have received during the peace circle that can move them forward on their healing journey with each other and earth. Closing the peace circle with sacred prayer and communion is central to the work. Naming peace, kindness, and sharing blessing is one way a peace circle remains connected in spirit and shared.

As a way of communing with earth, peace circles can be seen as ecowomanist contemplative practices that invite all sacred beings, and especially humans connected to environmental justice, together for healing, meeting, and organizing. Drawing upon this Indigenous practice and weaving ecowomanist wisdom into the shaping of peace circles is one way to begin to cultivate mindful ways of living and being with earth community.

Shaping our contemplative practices around ethical values inspired by ecowomanism helps us to establish new ways of being that we can be with earth in life sustaining and affirming ways. As a testament to the power of these kinds of practices *Preaching Black Earth* is an offering and some might say a spiritual toolkit. Sermons, meditations, spoken word, eco-poetry, and earth prayers weave justice through the two parts of the book. By design the spoken word, poetry, and interviews are shaped to inspire you, the reader, into climate change action and contemplation. As contemplative practice, ecowomanist thought and tradition is influenced by both theory and practice, and also by a rich and deep spirituality that influences the work of African and African American women in the work of climate justice. Whether through their work as scientists, such as the work and model of Wangari Maathai, or through their work and activism as writers, such as through the work of Alice Walker, ecowomanist scholarship helps point the way to engaging earth justice and environmental justice with other forms of social justice. Since for ecowomanism earth justice is social justice, and social justice is earth justice, reading this book is one step you, the reader, have just taken toward environmental justice. A next step is acting, through the practices modeled here on the justice you now know.

Ready? *Let us begin.*

Contributors

Stacey Abrams is an author, politician, lawyer, and voter rights activist who served in the Georgia House of Representatives from 2007 to 2017 and as minority leader from 2011 to 2017. In 2018 Abrams became the first African American woman major-party gubernatorial nominee (Democrat) in the United States. She is a fiction and nonfiction writer and *New York Times* best-selling author. A passionate advocate for education and social and environmental justice, Abrams also writes children's books. She is a graduate of Spelman College (BA), the LBJ School of Public Affairs at the University of Texas at Austin (MPAff) and Yale University (JD).

Sofía Betancourt is the tenth president of the Unitarian Universalist Association (UUA). The first woman to lead the UUA, she has an established career as a minister, scholar, professor, environmental justice activist, ecowomanist, and public theologian. Betancourt has taught at various institutions in higher education, including Yale Divinity School, Starr King School for the Ministry, and Drew University Theological School. She holds PhD, MA, and MPhil degrees from Yale University in religious ethics and African American studies as well as an MDiv from Starr King School for the Ministry and a BS from Cornell University. Rev. Dr. Betancourt is the author of numerous scholarly articles and books, including *Ecowomanism at the Panamá Canal: Black Women, Labor, and Environmental Ethics* (2022).

Heber Brown III is a cocreator of the Black Church Food Security Network, which advances food security and food sovereignty by creating food ecosystems anchored by nearly 250 Black congregations in partnership with Black farmers and other food justice stakeholders. An author, minister, environmental justice activist, and former pastor, Rev. Dr. Brown earned his BS degree in psychology from Morgan State University, an MDiv from Virginia Union University, and a DMin from Wesley Theological Seminary in Washington, DC.

Contributors

Christopher Carter is Associate Professor of Theology, Ecology, and Race at the Methodist Theological School in Ohio. A leader whose scholarship features research at the intersections of environmental justice and race, Rev. Dr. Carter also serves as a leader on a number of organizations and boards, including Farm Forward, an antifactory-farming nonprofit. An ordained minister in the United Methodist Church, Rev. Dr. Carter is also the lead Pastor of The Loft at Westwood United Methodist Church. He is the author of numerous scholarly articles and books, including *The Spirit of Soul Food: Race, Faith, and Food Justice* (2021).

Elonda Clay is Director of the Library at the Methodist Theological School in Ohio. A scholar, researcher, administrator, and ecowomanist activist, her scholarship features the intersections between technology, womanism, ecology, and religion in North America. At MTSO she served as principal administrator and co-lead of a 2021–2022 AAAS/DoSer Science for Seminaries grant, "Questioning Science with Good Faith," funded by the John Templeton Foundation. She holds an MLIS degree from the University of Missouri-Columbia, a BS from Kansas State University, an MTS from the Lutheran School of Theology at Chicago, and an MDiv from the Interdenominational Theological Center.

Kate Common is Assistant Professor of Public and Practical Theology at Methodist Theological School in Ohio. A scholar, activist, and theological educator, her scholarship examines the intersections among practical theology, feminist theology, biblical studies, and design thinking. A leader in transformative pedagogy, her work highlights the importance of interdisciplinary research methods for the work of liberation. She holds a PhD from Boston University School of Theology, an MA in theological research from Andover Newton Theological School, and a BFA in visual communication design from Kent State University.

Melanie L. Harris is a leading scholar in ecowomanism, a poet, professor, and mother. A graduate of Spelman College, Union Theological Seminary in the City of New York, and Harvard University, Harris weaves her academic work with her artistry as a singer, researcher, and writer. Ordained in the African Methodist Episcopal Church, Harris cultivates practices of compassion through interfaith dialogue and interreligious practice featuring Buddhist meditation, Christian mysticism, and ecowomanist thought. Dr. Harris is the author of dozens of scholarly articles and multiple books, including *Gifts of Virtue, Alice Walker, and Womanist Ethics*, and *Ecowomanism: African American Women and Earth-Honoring Faiths*.

She is Executive Director of the Ecowomanist Center in Research, Climate Justice, Leadership, and the Environment, a 501(c)(3) nonprofit dedicated to the life work and writing of ecowomanist and environmentalist writers.

Frederick Douglass Haynes III is Senior Pastor of Friendship-West Baptist Church in Dallas, Texas. Cofounder of the Samuel DeWitt Proctor Conference and former Executive Director of the Rainbow P.U.S.H (People United to Save Humanity) Coalition, Dr. Hayes is a leading voice in global movements for civil, human, and political rights. Author of several books and numerous scholarly articles, Dr. Haynes's prophetic writing, teaching, and preaching transforms individual lives and uplifts entire communities. His scholarship expands Black and liberation theology and womanist thought by engaging social justice, ethics, political theory, environmental justice, African American homiletics, religion, history, and cultures. He is a graduate of Bishop College in Dallas, Texas, earned an MDiv from Southwestern Baptist Theological Seminary and a DMin from Graduate Theological Foundation in collaboration with University of Oxford. Dr. Haynes is currently completing doctoral studies at the Christian Theology Seminary in Indianapolis in African American preaching and sacred rhetoric.

John W. Kinney is a leading voice in theological education, church leadership, and social justice and has served as Senior Pastor of Ebenezer Baptist Church in Beaverdam, Virginia, for over thirty-five years. A cherished pastor, award-winning writer, leader, and scholar, Rev. Dr. Kinney's career in education spans over forty years, including service as Dean of the Samuel DeWitt Proctor School of Theology at Virginia Union University and Senior Vice President of the University. Dr. Kinney's work weaves together social and environmental justice and Black liberation theology. Rev. Dr. Kinney earned his doctoral degree from Columbia University and Union Theological Seminary in the City of New York, an MPhil from Columbia, and an MDiv from the School of Theology at Virginia Union University.

Otis Moss III is the Senior Pastor of Trinity United Church of Christ in the City of Chicago and a leading voice in Black liberation theology and environmental and social justice. A preacher, poet, activist, filmmaker, and author, Rev. Dr. Moss's scholarship engages the intersections among history, African American religion, faith, and justice. He attended Iliff School of Theology and the University of Denver and is a graduate of Morehouse College (BA) and Yale University (MDiv). Dr. Moss completed his doctorate in ministry (DMin) from Chicago Theological Seminary.

Kenneth Ngwa is Donald J. Casper Professor of Hebrew Bible and African Biblical Hermeneutics and Director of the Religion and Global Health Forum at Garrett-Evangelical Theological Seminary. A leading voice in biblical studies, Rev. Dr. Ngwa's work and scholarship bridges global perspectives on social justice with African American hermeneutics, shedding fresh light on the exodus story and themes of liberation. He is a graduate of Princeton Theological Seminary (PhD and ThM) and Maitrise en Theologie, Faculty of Protestant Theology, Cameroon.

Liv Parsons is an environmental justice activist and award-winning poet. Weaving the themes of youth, social activism, and environmental justice, Parsons's work highlights the voices of emerging generations of scholar-activists working for climate justice. In 2023 Parsons was the New York City Youth Poet Laureate Ambassador and a finalist for the New York City Teen Poetry Slam.

Larry Rasmussen is a leading voice in Christian environmental ethics and has mentored three generations of Christian scholars and students in ecotheology. A graduate of Union Theological Seminary in the City of New York, where he also served as a professor and faculty person, Rasmussen's award-winning books *Earth Community Earth Ethics* (1998), *Earth-Honoring Faith* (2015), and *The Planet You Inherit: Letters to My Grandchildren when Uncertainty's a Sure Thing* (2022) have shaped the field of environmental ethics. Currently retired, Dr. Rasmussen lives in Santa Fe, New Mexico, where he continues the work of environmental justice through education and building up faith communities to become more earth-honoring congregations.

Frances Roberts-Gregory is a feminist political ecologist, environmental anthropologist, and ecowomanist scholar whose research connects the role of US Afrodiasporic communities and women of color in global climate negotiations and feminist climate policy. She earned her degrees from Spelman College (BA) and the University of California, Berkeley (PhD in environmental science, policy, and management). An innovator of feminist interdisciplinary method, her work transforms traditional environmental studies by expanding their praxis-oriented frames. A former fellow with the Harvard University Center for the Environment, Dr. Roberts-Gregory is a leading voice in ecowomanist scholarship and activism.

Gina M. Stewart is Senior Pastor of Christ Missionary Baptist Church in Memphis, Tennessee, as well as a scholar, professor, and community builder. The first woman to lead Christ Missionary Baptist Church, Rev. Dr. Stewart's womanist-style leadership has revolutionized global church culture in the

Baptist tradition and created a path for multiple generations of women clergy and faith leaders around the world. A graduate of the University of Memphis (BA), Dr. Stewart also earned an MEd in administration and supervision from Trevecca Nazarene College in Nashville, Tennessee, and an MDiv from Memphis Theological Seminary. Rev. Dr. Stewart is a graduate of the Harvard Divinity School Summer Leadership Institute and earned a DMin from the Interdenominational Theological Center. She is currently completing her doctoral education at the Christian Theology Seminary in Indianapolis in African American preaching and sacred rhetoric.

Index

Abrams, Stacey, 23–31
abundance, 12, 84, 123–24, 126–27.
   See also scarcity
activism
   in the 1960s, 102–3
   by Black women (see under Black women: justice efforts by)
   deep listening and, 78 (see also deep listening)
   by faith-based communities, 26–27, 87–88, 134, 145, 162–63, 169–71
   leadership of, 45–46
   self-care and, 147
   spiritual, 132, 163, 165–66
   by youth, 113
African Americans. See Black population
African cosmology, 8, 65, 143–44, 168
African Indigenous religion, 4, 11, 65, 69, 149
African Traditional Religion: A Definition (Idowu), 65
ahimsa, 78
"All Praise to the Pause" (Walker), 173
alternative spaces, 10–11
ancestors
   belonging and, 77, 144
   communing with, 173, 176
   as enslaved Africans, 8–10, 24, 79, 96
   faith of, 46, 55
   spirit realm and, 8, 168, 175
   wisdom of, 48
angels, in dream of Jacob, 52–53
antiapartheid movement, 103
antiracism
   framing of, 152

Hamer and, 133
   Rasmussen's path to, 102, 102n3, 103, 105, 107–17
   whites' development of, 108
   See also racism; racism, environmental
antiwar movement, 103, 131
any greens necessary method, 68–71
Anything We Love Can Be Saved (Walker), 141
apartheid, 103
artistry, moral, 68–71

balance, 168
Baldwin, James, 102
Barber, William, 83, 87
baths, spiritual, 149
beauty, 93–94
Betancourt, Sofía, 57–61
Bethel, 52–53
Bible
   creation stories and, 7, 27, 82, 97, 124–27, 169
   Exodus story (see Exodus metaphor)
   Jacob's dream story in, 51–56
   on stewardship, environmental, 24–25, 82
   theology construction and, 125–26
B.I.G. (Blacks in Green), 40
Black Church Food Security Network, 122–23, 133, 168
Black liberation theology, 6–7, 11, 81–89, 112. See also liberation
Black population
   African American religion, 4, 11, 65, 69, 149

communities of (*see* communities, Black and marginalized)
displacement of by climate change, 84
earth connectedness and, 8, 11, 19, 24, 60–61, 88, 92–96, 127 (*see also* interconnectedness)
eco-memories and (*see* eco-memories)
erasure of, 58–60
farming and (*see* farms/farmworkers)
goodness of, 127
green spaces and, 59–60
health and wellness of, 11, 29, 39, 70, 82–83, 88, 106, 143 (*see also* racism, environmental; self-care)
homiletics, 13
language of, 120
liberation and (*see* liberation)
nature, access to, 92–93, 95
women (*see* Black women)
Blacks in Green (B.I.G), 40
Black space, *Walden* as, 59
Black Theology and Black Power (Cone), 110–11
Black Walden: Slavery and Its Aftermath in Concord, Massachusetts (Lemire), 59
Black women
domination and, 167 (*see also* domination, logic of)
and earth connection, 60–61 (*see also* interconnectedness)
earth consciousness and, 141–42
as earth keepers, 47–48
ethical living of, 165
justice efforts by, 37, 39–40, 86–87, 140, 145, 162–63, 170–71 (*see also* Hamer, Fannie Lou)
religion and, 141–42
resilience of, 35, 47
values, teachers of, 60
wisdom of, 37, 44, 46–48, 74, 162 (*see also* wisdom)
See also ecowomanism; women
Bonhoeffer, Dietrich, 112
Bonhoeffer's Black Jesus (Williams, R.), 112
Breaking in the Fine Rain of Death (Townes), 47
"breathing earth" (Harris), 18
Brown, Heber, 79, 119–35

Buddhism, 7, 74–77, 150, 170, 175
by any greens necessary method, 68–71

cancer alley, 145, 145n5
Cannon, Katie G., 165
Cape Point (South Africa), 94
capitalism, 25, 34, 40–41, 82–83, 85, 133
Carter, Christopher, 79, 119–35
Carter, Majora, 39–40
Carter G. Woodson Library, 69–70
censuses, 30
Chicago neighborhoods, restoration of, 67–71
childhood
eco-memories and, 177–78
impact of, 109
Christianity/Christians
African Indigenous religious traditions and, 11 (*see also* African Indigenous religion)
colonization and, 134 (*see also* colonialism)
feminist social ethics, 115
interfaith experiences and, 67, 74 (*see also under* religion: inter experiences/dialogues)
justice in, 7
justice work by (*see under* environmental justice: faith-based communities and)
in Kenya, 170–71
oppression by, 132–34, 141, 170
planetary care by, 88 (*see also* dominionism, by humans of earth; stewardship, environmental)
roots of modern, 69
See also Bible
church demographics, post-COVID, 84–85
civil rights movement, 44, 86, 102–3, 130, 146. *See also* King, Martin Luther Jr.
Clay, Elonda, 33–49
climate change/climate crisis
collaboration and, 145
Exodus as metaphor for (*see* Exodus metaphor)
grief and, 41–43

Index

lack of action toward, 85–86
liberation from, 33–34
marginalized communities,
  disproportionate impact on, 37–40, 84
natural disasters and, 26–27, 36–39, 85
service to others in, 27
wealth gap and, 36
climate injustice. *See* climate change/climate crisis
Collective Courage (Gordon), 130
colonialism
  African, 170–71
  dominionism and, 98
  as earth's trauma, 54–55
  ecological reparations and, 168–69
  ecotheology and, 166
  frameworks of, 141, 144–45, 166
  history subjugated by, 20
  iniquities of, 25
  language and, 120
  liberation from, 40
commodification, human, 98
Common, Kate, 79, 137–54
communities, Black and marginalized
  care work of, 150–52
  climate change's impact on, 37–40
  environmental racism and (*see* racism, environmental)
  erasure of, 58–60
  hope and, 116
  Hurricane Katrina and, 38–39 (*see also* Hurricane Katrina)
  organizing of, 150–52 (*see also* Hamer, Fannie Lou)
  promised land and, 44–46
  rebuilding of, community member engagement in, 67–71
  resilience of (*see* resilience)
  social justice led by, 13–14, 67–71, 107
communities, white, 101, 109
compassion, 28, 76–78
Cone, James H., 7, 110
Congo, Democratic Republic of the, 85
consensus, in peace circles, 176
consumerism/consumption, 34, 40–41. *See also* capitalism
contemplative practice
  about, 5–6

  deep listening as, 76–78
  dialogue as, 79–80
  ecowomanism and, 161–65
  handspinning as, 57
  peace circles as, 176–79 (*see also* peace circles)
  spiritual practices and, 149–50
corporate greed. *See* capitalism
cosmology
  African, 8, 65, 143–44, 168
  Native, 172
  Western, 144–45
courses, use of this book in, 16–17
COVID-19, 28, 84–85, 87–88, 146–48, 153
"Creation, The" (Johnson), 126
creation stories, 7, 27, 82, 97, 124–27, 169
creativity, 60–61, 93–94
Crozier, Karen D., 130

Dallas, environmental racism in, 82–84
Davis, Naomi, 40
deep listening
  about, 76–78
  examples of, 101–17, 137–54
  peace circles and, 172–76
Democratic Republic of the Congo, 85
dialogue process
  deep listening and, 76–78
  ecowomanism and, 73–74
  with God, 75–76
  interreligious, 74–76
  mindful speech and, 76
dignity, human, 104–5
diversity, God's demonstration of, in nature, 94
domination, logic of, 8–9, 34–35, 144–45, 164, 166–67
dominionism, by humans of earth, 47–48, 97–98, 125–26. *See also* planetary care; stewardship, environmental
dream story, of Jacob/earth, 51–56

earth-affirmed living, 46–49
earth consciousness, 97, 141–42
earth futurists, 48
Earth Honoring Faith (Rasmussen), 111
earth justice

definition of, 2
social justice and, 2–3, 9, 166
in *Walden*, 59
See also environmental justice
earth/nature
  access to, by Blacks, 92–93, 95
  communing in, importance of, 64, 70, 87, 92–97, 120, 148–49
  dreams of, by Jacob/earth, 51–56
  eco-memories of (*see* eco-memories)
  God connection in, 93–95
  goodness of, 127
  human connection with, 19, 46–49, 56, 58–61, 141 (*see also* interconnectedness)
  Indigenous viewpoint of, 64
  sacredness of, as value, 166–67
  spiritual realms and, 143–44, 168
  stewardship of (*see* dominionism, by humans of earth; stewardship, environmental)
  as temple, 24–25
  trauma of, 54–56
  women's experience and, 97
"earth speaks" (Harris), 158–59
ecofeminism, 139–40, 144
ecological reparations, 1–2, 7–9, 20, 167–69
eco-memories
  of Brown, 121–23
  of Carter, 119–21
  deep listening and, 78
  of enslaved descendants, 8–10, 24, 79
  honoring experience through, 19
  liberation and, 95
  of lynching scenes, 10
  peace circles and, 177–78
  travel experiences and, 94–95
economic injustice
  climate crisis and, 34, 36, 39
  of enslaved, 59
  Hamer's justice work toward, 86–87
  Healthcare and, 29
  systemic, 83, 87–88
eco-poetry. *See* poetry
ecosocialism, 112–14. *See also under* interconnectedness: environmental and social justices
ecotheologies

construction of, 125–26, 128–29
decolonization of, 166
sources for, 128–29
ecowomanism
  about, 1–4, 9, 166–67
  African American religion connection and, 4–6
  Black liberation theology and, 6–7 (*see also* Black liberation theology)
  contemplative approach of, 161–63
  dialogue process and (*see* dialogue process)
  earth and human connection and, 47 (*see also* interconnectedness)
  environmental science and, 142–44
  Harris on, 139
  Harris's introduction to, 141–42
  homiletics, African American and, 13
  interdisciplinary of, 146–47
  King and, 13
  method, 19, 73, 75–76, 92, 119, 153–54, 167, 177
  peace circles and, 176–79
Ecowomanism: African American Women and Earth-Honoring Faiths (Harris), 74
education
  racial ignorance and, 109–10
  self, 113–14
  theological and ecosocial ethics, 112–14
energy issues, 105
enslavement/enslaved
  descendants of, 8–10, 24, 96
  eco-memories of, 8–10, 24, 79
  environmental justice's purpose for, 20
  Exodus metaphor and, 40–41, 44
  independence of former, 58–60
environmental justice
  about, 2
  by Black women (*see under* Black women: justice efforts by)
  call to, 25, 27–31, 35–36, 38–39, 41–42, 46–49
  collaboration for, 145
  faith-based communities and, 26–27, 87–88, 132–34, 145, 162–63, 169–71
  farmworkers and (*see* farms/farmworkers)
  as global, 84–85

Index 191

hopelessness feeling and, 147–48
King and, 13
mindfulness in, 57–61
path to, 102–3, 102n3, 105, 107–17
practical application of, 131–32
relationships in, 134
sacredness of the earth and, 170–71
social justice connection, 2–4, 7, 20, 37, 112–14, 121, 146, 171 (*see also* interconnectedness)
spirituality and, 4–6
systemic issues, actions on, 29
theological framework of, 123–27
trauma and, 8–10
environmental justice paradigm. *See* environmental justice
environmental racism. *See* racism, environmental
environmental science, 142–44
erasure, Black, 58–60
ethics
 environmental, 104–7, 112–14, 144 (*see also* environmental justice)
 womanist virtue method and, 165
evolution, 116–17
exile and return pattern, in Jacob's dream, 52
Exodus metaphor
 about, 33–36
 abundance and, 41
 as call to action, 48–49
 lamentations of, 41–43
 liberation and, 36–37, 40–41
 promised land and, 44–46

Fairbanks, Cheryl Demmert, 172, 174–75, 177–78
faith, 25–26, 35, 46, 55, 86–88. *See also* religion
faith-based communities, activism by, 13–14, 26–27, 87–88, 134, 145, 162–63, 169–71
Fannie Lou Hamer's Revolutionary Practical Theology: Racial and Environmental Justice Concerns (Crozier), 130
farms/farmworkers
 Black history of, 168–69
 Black-owned, 92–93, 95–97

exploitation of, 120–21, 127–29
hub model of, 133
voting rights of, 132–33
Fire Next Time, The (Baldwin), 102
First Nation people, 64. *See also* Indigenous populations
food
 healthy, access to, 88
 justice, 99, 122–23, 130, 132–34, 140, 140n2, 168
forgiveness, justice pursuit and, 26
framing, antiracist, 152
freedom
 of enslaved post emancipation, 58–60
 Exodus metaphor and, 44–46
 understanding of, 65
 See also liberation
Freedom Farmers: Agricultural Resistance and the Black Freedom Movement (White), 129–30
Freedom Farms co-op, 132–33
fussing, 75–76

gardens/gardening, 24, 26, 40, 70, 88, 113, 120, 122–23, 148–49, 152
gentrification, 39
Gifts of Virtue, Alice Walker, and Womanist Ethics (Harris), 165
GirlTrek, 148
global warming, 41–42
God
 abundance from, 123–24
 in all things, 7
 connection with in nature, 93–95
 as creative, 93–94
 dialogue with, 75–76
 hope and, 117
 image of, 7, 127, 166
 love of, 12
 presence of, 35, 46, 52–56
 promise of to Jacob, 53–54
 as provider, 41
 restoration by, 64
 as sovereign, 67
 suffering and, 42
Golden Rule. *See* neighbors, love of
goodness, 127
Gordon, Jessica Nembhard, 130

grandparents, 24, 92–93, 96, 120–23, 142
greed, corporate. *See* capitalism
Green Belt Movement, 170–71
Green New Deal, 138–39
greens, by any necessary method, 67–71
green spaces, 59–60, 113
grief, climate, 41–43
growth, limits to, 113–14

Hallisey, Charles, 74
Hamer, Fannie Lou
  literature on, 129–30, 139
  love and, 131, 133–34
  as model, 87
  practical theology of, 131–32
  trauma of, 87, 102n3
  work of, 86, 130–33
handspinning, 57, 60
Harding, Rachel E., 10, 12
Harding, Rosemarie, 12, 150
Harding, Vincent, 77, 102, 102n3, 142
Harris, Melanie
  on ecowomanism, 139, 141–42
  interview with, 137–54
  poetry of, 18, 72, 158–59
Harrison, Bev, 115
havruta, 75
Haynes, Frederick Douglass III, 78, 81–89
healing, 145, 154. *See also* peace circles
Heifer International, 130
hierarchy
  dominionism and, 97–98
  inversion of, 65
Hive Fund for Climate and Gender Justice, 139
holiness, of place, 51–56
homiletics, African American, 13
hooks, bell, 10, 19, 46, 168
hope, 42–43, 116, 133–34
hospitality, radical, 53–56
hub model, farming, 133
hunting, 64–65
Hurricane Katrina, 26–27, 36–39
Hurston, Zora Neale, 45

"I Am a Man" protests, 104–5
Idowu, E. Bọlaji, 65

imagination, moral, 68–71
imago Dei, 7, 127, 166
incarcerated, 70
inclusivity, 146, 151
Indigenous populations
  African Indigenous religion, 4, 11, 65, 69, 149
  colonialism and (*see* colonialism)
  eco-memories and, 167 (*see also* eco-memories)
  ignorance on, 109–10
  interconnectedness and, 64–65, 167–68
  land of, Indigenous vs white thought on, 64
  peacefulness and, 78 (*see also* peace circles)
  pipeline issues and, 140
  promised land and, 44–45
  wisdom and, 144, 147, 170, 174
interbeing, 175
interconnectedness
  in African thought, 4, 8, 65
  Blacks and earth, 8, 11, 19, 24, 60–61, 88, 92–96, 127
  Black women and earth, 60–61
  earth/nature, spirit, and human realms, 143–44, 168
  environmental and social justices, 2–4, 7, 20, 37, 112–14, 121, 146, 171
  environmental justice and Black liberation, 13, 34–35
  human, 105, 141
  human and earth, 19, 46–49, 56, 58–61, 97, 141
  King on, 104
  in peace circles, 175
  value of, 167–72
interdisciplinary, 146–47
interreligious dialogue, 2–3, 7, 74–76, 113, 146–47, 150, 167
intersectional analysis, 9
interviews
  with Haynes, 81–89
  with Rasmussen, 101–17
  with Roberts-Gregory, Harris, and Common, 137–54
  with Stewart, 91–99

Index

Jacob's dream story, 51–56
jazz metaphor, 71
Jesus Christ, 84–86, 99, 128
Judaism, 7, 75
justice, environmental. *See* environmental justice

Katrina, Hurricane, 26–27, 36–39
King, Martin Luther Jr., 13, 84, 98, 102, 102n3, 103–4
Kinney, John, 63–65, 75, 98

lamentations, 41–43
landfills, 25, 29, 39, 82, 145, 162–63
language, as colonized, 120
leadership, 45
Lemire, Elise, 58–59
liberation
   Black theology of, 6–7, 11, 81–89, 112
   from climate crisis, 33–34
   eco-memories and, 95
   enslavement and, 8–10
   Exodus metaphor and, 36–37, 40–41 (*see also* Exodus metaphor)
   interconnectedness and, 13, 34–35
   justice and, 46–47
   self-care and, 10
   spirituality and, 11–13
   theologies, 111
   transcendentalism and, 61
life expectancy discrepancies, 83
Limits to Growth, The (Meadows), 113
love
   Hamer and, 131, 133–34
   of neighbors, 128, 132–33, 169
Love Letters to the Earth (Thich Nhat Hanh), 76
Luz, 53
lynchings, 9–10, 109

Maathai, Wangari, 170–71
making do, womanist ethic of, 60
Malcom X, 67–68
Mama May Have (Harris), 139
Mamie Till-Mobley Forgiveness Garden, 40
Mandela, Nelson, 103
manna, 41

Meadows, Donella, 113
meditations, 76–77, 150
   on by any greens necessary, 67–71
   on collapsing the hierarchy, 63–65
   See also mindfulness
Mendoza, S. Lili, 166
mental health, 11, 149
migrant farmworkers, 120–21. *See also* farms/farmworkers
mindfulness, 57–61, 175. *See also* meditations
mindful speech, 76, 176
Mississippi Freedom Democratic Party, 130
Moe-Lobeda, Cynthia, 147
moral artistry, 68–71
moral oblivion, 147–48
Moses (prophet), 45, 52
Moses, Man of the Mountain (Hurston), 45
Moss, Otis III, 67–71
mystical activism, 69

National People of Color Environmental Leadership Summit, 168
Native Americans, 109–10, 172. *See also* Indigenous populations
natural disasters, 26–27, 36–39, 85
nature. *See* earth/nature
Nehemiah (Jewish leader), 68–69
neighbors, love of, 128, 132–33, 169
Ngwa, Kenneth, 51–56, 164
Nhat Hanh, Thich, 76–77, 175
Nicholas, Maxine, 123
1960s, social justice during, 102–3. *See also* civil rights movement; King, Martin Luther Jr.
nonhuman creatures, value of, 2, 34, 48, 97, 146
nonviolence, 75–78, 175

objectification, human, 98
"Only Reason You Want to Go to Heaven Is That You've Been Driven Out of Your Mind (Off Your Land and Out of Your Lover's Arms), The" (Walker), 141
oppression
   by Christians, 134

ecowomanism and, 3
hierarchies and, 98
of land workers, 120–21, 127–29, 132–33
liberation from, 8–13 (*see also* liberation)
of nonhuman creatures, 2, 97 (*see also* nonhuman creatures, value of)
See also oppression, environmental
oppression, environmental
capitalism as source of, 33–34
dismantling of systems of, 34–35, 47
impact of, on marginalized communities, 37–40
liberation from, 33, 39–41
models for transformation journey, 37
survival of, 41–43
See also oppression; racism, environmental

paganism, 141
pandemics. *See* COVID-19
Parsons, Liv, 155–57
PCBs (polychlorinated biphenyls) disposal, 145, 162–63
peace circles
ecowomanism and, 176–79
process of, 175–76
shifts of mind through, 172–75
See also nonviolence
people of color, term of, 110
pig banks, 130
pipelines, 140
place
as divine, 52
making, 37–38
planetary care
ecological reparations and, 168–69
ethic of, 88
self-care and, 5, 10–11, 147, 153
See also dominionism, by humans of earth; stewardship, environmental
Planet You Inherit, The: Letters to My Grandchildren When Uncertainty's a Sure Thing (Rasmussen), 102, 113
poetry
"breathing earth" (Harris), 18
contemplative practice of, 164

"earth speaks" (Harris), 158–59
"release" (Harris), 72
"You Can't Shift the Stars" (Parsons), 155–57
pollution, toxic, 39–40, 82, 106, 143n4, 145, 162–63
polychlorinated biphenyls (PCBs) disposal, 145, 162–63
postcolonialism, 55
poverty, 86
practical theology, 130–32, 134, 137
prayers, 30–31, 85–86
preaching. *See* sermons
prisoned, 70
promised land, 35, 44–46. *See also* Exodus metaphor
Prophethood of Black Believers, The (Roberts), 99
prophetic, ecowomanism as, 81–89, 147, 161–62
public health concerns, 106–7. *See also under* Black population: health and wellness of; racism, environmental

racial consciousness, 21, 108–11. *See also under* antiracism: Rasmussen's journey to
racism
blind spot of, 109–10, 112
implicit, 109
post-pandemic, 146–47
religion and, 121
See also antiracism; racism, environmental
racism, environmental
capitalism and, 34, 36–40, 82–83 (*see also* capitalism)
climate change and, 37–38 (*see also* climate change/climate crisis)
colonization and, 25 (*see also* colonialism)
community care and, 152
environmental justice and, 2 (*see also* environmental justice)
farmworkers and, 120–21 (*see also* farms/farmworkers)
peace circles and, 177
polychlorinated biphenyls and, 145, 162–63

privilege and, 36
systemic issues of, 29
toxic pollution and, 25, 29, 39–40, 82, 106, 143n4, 145, 162–63
urban issues and, 106–7
Rasmussen, Larry, 79, 101–17
reading, communal, 74–75
redemption, 27–29. *See also* reparations, ecological
religion
   activism and, 26–27, 87–88, 134, 145, 162–63, 169–71
   African Indigenous, 4, 11, 65, 69, 149
   Black women living out, 141–42
   Buddhism, 7, 74–77, 150, 170, 175
   Christianity (*see* Christianity/Christians)
   inter experiences/dialogues, 2–3, 7, 74–76, 113, 146–47, 150, 167
   Islam, 47
   Judaism, 7, 75
   planetary care and, 47–48, 97–98, 125–26 (*see also* planetary care; stewardship, environmental)
   racism and, 121
   science and, 144–45
   transcendentalism and, 57
   See also cosmology
Remnants (R. E. Harding), 12
reparations, ecological, 1–2, 7–9, 20, 167–69
Replenishing the Earth: Spiritual Values for Healing Ourselves and the World (Maathai), 170
residence time, 55–56
resilience, 35, 39, 47, 61, 148
Resisting Structural Evil (Moe-Lobeda), 147
rest, importance of, 149
resurrection faith, 86–88
reversal doctrine, 65
Roberts, J. Deotis, 99
Roberts-Gregory, Frances, 79, 137–54
Root Church, 10–11
Ruffin, Kimberly E., 8

sacredness of earth, as value, 166–67, 170–71
scarcity, 124. *See also* abundance
schools, environmental racism and, 106

science, 142–45
self-care, 5, 10–11, 147–50, 153
self-expression, 114–15
sermons
   on dreams of Jacob/earth, 51–56
   environmental, significance of, 84–85
   on the Exodus story as a climate change metaphor, 33–49
   King's, 13
   on stewardship, service, and redemption, 23–31
   on transcendentalism and environmentalism, 57–61
service to others, obligation of, 25–26
sewage treatment plants, 107
sharecroppers, 132–33. *See also* farms/farmworkers
Sharpe, Christina, 55–56
Shepard, Peggy, 107
Shields, A.W., 11
S-H-I-F-T acronym, 172–74
Shingle Mountain, 82
Shinn, Roger, 113–14
silence, 173, 176
"Sin, Nature, and Black Women's Bodies" (Williams, D.), 164
sins, eco, 23, 26, 30
Sisters of the Yam: Black Women and Self Recovery (hooks), 19, 46
sleep, importance of, 149
sleeping, earth as, 52–53
slow food, 140, 140n2
social justice
   in the 1960s, 102–3
   civil rights movement, 44, 86, 102–3, 130, 146
   community-led, 67–71, 107
   deep listening and, 78
   environmental justice connection, 2–4, 7, 20, 37, 112–14, 121, 146, 171
social locations, 108, 112, 163
South Africa, beauty of, 93–94
spaces, sacred, 10–11
Spelman College (GA), 140–41
Spirit of Soul and Food, The (Carter), 125
spiritual activism, 132, 163, 165–66
spiritual baths, 149
spiritual care, 149

spirituality
  Black, 69, 81, 142
  environment justice and, 4–6, 170
  nature and, 92–95, 97
  peace circles and, 172 (*see also* peace circles)
  science and, 143–44
STEMinist, 152
stewardship, environmental
  Bible on, 125–26
  vs dominionism, 98
  eco-memories of, 120 (*see also* eco-memories)
  obligation of, 23–25, 82, 86, 88
  See also dominionism, by humans of earth; planetary care
Stewart, Gina M., 79, 91–99
suffering, 42, 77
sun, activity of, 52
survival, 42–43
systemic injustice
  environmental, 29, 38
  white privilege, 10, 36, 38–39, 65

Table Mountain (South Africa), 93–94
Taylor, Dorceta E., 2, 143
Teachings on Love (Thich Nhat Hanh), 76
temple, earth as, 24–25
theological construction, 125–26
theological education, ecosocial ethics and, 112–14
theophany, dream, 52
Thich Nhat Hanh, 76–77, 175
"This Was Not an Area of Large Plantations: Suffering Too Insignificant for the Majority to See" (Walker), 169
Thoreau, Henry David, 58–60
Thurman, Howard, 69, 150
time, residence, 55–56
Touching the Earth (hooks), 168
Townes, Emilie M., 47, 115
toxic pollution, 39–40, 82, 106, 143n4, 145, 162–63
transcendentalism, 57–61
trauma
  African American and earth, 8, 96
  contemplative practices and, 6
  earth's, 54
  of Hamer, 87
  liberation from, 79, 148
  peace circles and, 173–74, 177
  postcolonial, 55
  racial, 10, 149
tree planting, 171
truth, as interfaith, 67
Truth, Sojourner, 37
Tubman, Harriet, 3n4, 4–5, 37, 143

Union Theological Seminary (NY), 102–4, 107, 110–11, 114–15
uniqueness, right of, 71
Unitarian Universalist tradition, 57–61
urban issues, environmental, 106–7

values, womanist, 165
Victoria Falls (Zimbabwe), 93
violence, historical environmental, 55–56. *See also* racism, environmental
voting
  importance of, 28, 30
  rights, 28, 30, 130, 132–33

Walden (Thoreau), 58–61
Walker, Alice, 5, 10, 49, 74, 96, 141–42, 169–70, 173
warming, global, 41–42
water quality, 83n5
WE ACT for Environmental Action, 107
wealth, 36, 96–97. *See also* capitalism; white privilege
White, Monica M., 129–30
white exceptionalism, 58. *See also* white privilege; white supremacy
whiteness
  enslavers' descendants, 9–10
  "people of color" and, 110
  racial consciousness and, 21, 108–11
  small town, 109
  theology and, 112–14
white privilege
  environmental harm from, 152
  protection from, 110
  systemic, 10, 36, 38–39, 65
  used for good, 115

in *Walden*, 58–59
white supremacy
   Black identity and, 11–12
   commodification of humans and, 98
   ecological reparations and, 8–9, 168–69
   environmental violence and, 152
   Hamer and, 102n3, 133, 139
   post-pandemic, 146–47
"Whose Earth Is It Anyway?" (Cone), 7
Williams, Delores S., 105, 164
Williams, Reggie, 112
wisdom
   of ancestors, 48
   of Black women, 37, 44, 46–48, 74, 162
   Buddhism and, 77
   earth, 57, 78, 162
   examples of, 163
   of Indigenous population, 144, 147, 170, 174

listening to, 147, 173, 176
multi-religious, 146
peace circles and, 172, 178–79
in *Walden*, 58–59
womanist ethic method, 165
women
   activists (*see under* Black women: justice efforts by; Hamer, Fannie Lou)
   Black (*see* Black women)
   earth/nature experience and, 97
   empowerment of, 170
   worship, nature and, 92–95, 97

"You Can't Shift the Stars" (Parsons), 155–57
youth, 107, 113
Youth Ministries for Peace and Justice, 113

Zachariah, George, 166
Zilpah (*Walden* former enslaved woman), 60

www.ingramcontent.com/pod-product-compliance
Lightning Source LLC
Chambersburg PA
CBHW022056290426
44109CB00014B/1116